D0856198

The University and the City

THE UNIVERSITY AND THE CITY

From *Medieval Origins* to the *Present*

Edited by

Thomas Bender

New York   Oxford
OXFORD UNIVERSITY PRESS
1988

Oxford University Press

Oxford   New York   Toronto
Delhi   Bombay   Calcutta   Madras   Karachi
Petaling Jaya   Singapore   Hong Kong   Tokyo
Nairobi   Dar es Salaam   Cape Town
Melbourne   Auckland

and associated companies in
Berlin   Ibadan

Copyright © 1988 by Oxford University Press, Inc.

Published by Oxford University Press, Inc.,
200 Madison Avenue, New York, New York 10016

Oxford is a registered trademark of Oxford University Press

Library of Congress Cataloging-in-Publication Data

The University and the city : from medieval origins to the present /
edited by Thomas Bender
p.   cm.
Essays presented at a conference on the occasion of the centennial
of the Graduate School of Arts and Sciences at New York University
in 1986–1987.
Includes bibliographical references and index.
ISBN 0–19–505273–0
1. Urban universities and colleges—History—Congresses.   2. City
and town life—History—Congresses.   I. Bender, Thomas.   II. New
York University. Graduate School of Arts and Sciences.
LB2328.4.U55   1988
378'.009—dc 19   88–1411
CIP

9 8 7 6 5 4 3 2 1

Printed in the United States of America
on acid-free paper

Preface

The centennial of the Graduate School of Arts and Sciences at New York University in 1986–87 provided the occasion for the conference upon which this volume is based. C. Duncan Rice, dean of the Faculty of Arts and Sciences at NYU, summoned me to his office to discuss the centennial in the fall of 1985. Fully aware of the ceremonial and self-congratulatory events that customarily attend such university milestones, he indicated that he wanted at least one component of the celebration to be of scholarly significance. What, he asked, would I think of an international conference focused on the theme of the university and the city historically considered? Would I be willing to organize it? What a remarkable opportunity! Of course, I would be delighted to do it.

Dean Rice had his own institutional purposes, of course. In a country where the academic ideal has been profoundly suburbanized, where a rural setting is part of the definition of academic excellence, it was to the advantage of New York University, situated in the heart of the cultural and economic capital of the world, to draw attention to its own tradition. Although NYU's urban location and engagement with the city—its "campus," which dissolves into the texture of Greenwich Village—makes it atypical of great American universities, it nonetheless falls rather comfortably within a European tradition that extends back to the founding of the first universities in medieval Paris and Bologna.

But if there were sound institutional purposes behind the dean's generosity—historian that he is (and graduate of one of the great urban universities in Edinburgh)—he had also formulated a theme of considerable general cultural as well as historiographical importance. Universities and cities as we know them, both creations of medieval Europe, have long been associated with the nurturing and advancement of culture. Yet they represent rather different principles of intellectual life. Down through the centuries they have been variously symbiotic and contending. At a time when it is commonly said that in the United States art and intellect are being suburbanized into a national system of universities, it is worth trying to understand the past and present relationship of universities to cities.

This topic also fits nicely into recent historiographical developments. Although there has been a good deal of writing about the university and society, very little attention has been given to one of the key nodes of interaction: the city. Most work on the interaction of the university and society, moreover, has been within the field of social history. Social history is not excluded here, but I consciously sought to invite contributions from cultural historians interested in both higher learning and cities. The intellectual work of universities, more than the pattern of social recruitment evidenced in their student bodies, is highlighted in these essays.[1] In this respect, the essays mirror a broader shift within the profession from social history—especially of the quantitative sort—to cultural or intellectual history, which is now attentive to the findings and concerns of a remarkably prolific generation of social historians.

It was rather easy to identify the scholars I would invite to contribute essays. In each instance the association of city and historian came readily to mind. In one case, however, I specifically asked a contributor to do what must have come as a surprise. Because of the occasion of the conference, I thought it fitting as well as potentially illuminating to have a scholar widely knowledgeable in the history of American intellectual life to assess the broader meanings of the conference sponsored by New York University in 1932 to commemorate the centennial of the university's founding. David Hollinger, whose various works dealing with intellectual history have done so much to establish a framework within which to understand intellectual currents in twentieth-century American society, agreed to write the essay; the result amply justifies the assumption that there was "something" there.

Many people contributed to the success of the conference and to the making of this book. Besides Dean Rice, let me also thank Ann M. Burton, dean of Arts and Sciences Administration, who was consistently supportive and often wise. I am indebted as well to Carl E. Schorske for an early and typically fruitful discussion on the theme of the conference. The single most important person in every aspect of the project was Andie Tucher, my graduate assistant. Without her attention to detail as well as her substantive contribution to the conference, I seriously doubt whether the conference or the book that grew out of it would ever have been realized. Another graduate student, Marc Aronson, was sufficiently stimulated by the conference to write an essay seeking to embrace its themes. I thank him for sharing his thoughts with me, for his essay stimulated my own thinking as I wrote the introduction to this volume. All of the following individuals were unfailingly and generously helpful: Liz Robinson, John Yadrick, and Robert Korchak of the dean's office; Lynn Anderson, administrative assistant in the history department; and Marilynne Johnson, a graduate assistant in the history department. More generally, I must thank the president of the university, John Brademas; the chancellor of the university, L. Jay Oliva; and the dean of the Graduate School of Arts and Sciences, Benjamin R. Bederson, for their support of the project. The National Endowment for the Humanities partially funded this conference. I thank this vital institution for the resources it made available to us. In particular, the encouragement of Crale Hopkins at the NEH, especially his immediate appreciation of the significance of the conference and the book, was important as well. Finally, Nancy Lane of Oxford University Press responded enthusiastically to the idea for a book based on the conference from the moment I broached the subject, and she supplied clever and useful advice along the way.

We were also fortunate in the course of our conference to have the opportunity to shift from the succession of publicly presented formal papers to two small and informal discussions. Sir Steven Runciman oriented us to our topic at the outset by speaking about the transit of learning from East to West in the time of the Crusades; François Furet, who had just stepped down as president of the Ecole des Hautes Etudes en Sciences Sociales, spoke about the differences between university culture in Paris and France, on the one hand, and New York and the United States, on the other. Both talks impressed upon all of us the elasticity of our topic.

I must conclude these prefatory remarks on a sadder note. J. K. Hyde, a participant at our conference, died soon after returning to England. It came as a shock to his friends and to those who had met Kenneth Hyde for the first time at the conference. He had promised to send me a polished version of his paper on Italian cities and their universities when he returned to England. He never had the chance to do that. However, we did tape his oral presentation. It is not what it would have been had he lived to transform it from a spoken text to a written one, but it opens this book nicely, as it opened our conference. I have adapted it for publication with the assistance of my colleague David R. Hicks. I hope Kenneth would approve of our publishing his not quite polished essay. It is, in fact, a fine contribution in its present form; in publishing it we not only add weight to this volume but also honor the memory of a distinguished medievalist.

New York T. B.
January 1988

NOTE

1. For different approaches, see the pioneering and influential work by Lawrence Stone, ed., *The University in Society*, 2 vols. (Princeton, N.J., 1974); and the more recent work by Konrad H. Jarausch, ed., *The Transformation of Higher Learning, 1860–1930* (Chicago, 1983).

Contents

Part IV
The Modern University and the Modern City

The University and the City

1

Introduction

Thomas Bender

We in the United States have been so captured by the tradition of Anglo-American academic pastoralism that we forget how much more common has been the tradition that associates universities with great cities. The revival of cities and the revival of learning under the aegis of the university in medieval Europe were coincident, and since then the city and the university have shared more of a common history than we usually recognize. Although some of America's greatest universities are closely identified with great cities—two of them, the University of Chicago and New York University, taking their names from their host cities—our inclination is to idealize the rural campus. (Indeed, the word *campus* in its modern meaning was first used in the eighteenth century to describe the greensward surrounding the newly built Nassau Hall at Princeton.)[1]

Yet the Anglo-American tradition, based on the model of Oxford and Cambridge and nourished by an Anglo-American tradition of antiurbanism, is a major deviation from the central theme of the history of universities. Since their inception they have been identified with cities, sometimes second-order cities but often those great cities that dominate the political, economic, and cultural life of nations.

The topic of this volume is as capacious as it is important. It is moreover a topic rather difficult to define, once one gets beyond the immediately compelling rubric of "the university and the city." The variety of orientations to the topic represented by the essays brought together here provides enough range, I think, to probe the boundaries of even so vast and amorphous topic as we have before us. Collectively these essays give quite significant shape to the topic, as well as urging upon us a number of illuminating and even provocative themes that help define the relationship between the university and the city since their mutual medieval origins.

One has only to read the newspaper today to realize that the university—whether in its urban or pastoral version—is searching for its proper place in modern intellectual and social life. The historical essays in this volume free us from much of the overheated rhetoric of crisis that currently surrounds

3

us, but the historical perspectives offered by our cast of distinguished historians and social scientists may contribute usefully to our search for academic identity and purpose.

Living in New York City, one is always aware of how fragile is the civility that makes urban life and academic life possible. To me, then, it was encouraging rather than otherwise to realize that the great subtheme of this book is the persistent, if fortunately constrained, swing in the life of the city and the university between coherence and fragility. At times the university in crisis has been rescued by the urban dynamic surrounding it, though at other times urban developments have threatened to undermine the stability of the academy. Conversely, the university has at times successfully provided a focus and a principle of coherence for the cultural life of a city, though at others it has withdrawn from the city and undermined urban culture.

The origin and persistence of the university, Professor J. K. Hyde reminds us, is a remarkable fact. Within a decade of the year 1200, universities were created, apparently independently, at Bologna, Paris, and Oxford. There have been important changes in the subsequent eight centuries of the European university's history, most notably the incorporation of the research ideal and the adoption of a bureaucratic style. Yet no one can mistake the institutional continuity. No institution in the West, save the Roman Catholic church, has persisted longer. From small medieval beginnings this institution has become diffused throughout the world, assuming everywhere principal responsibility for advanced teaching and, more often than not, research.

The terms of the university's connection to society, particularly the way in which the city has formed a nexus for that connection, have, of course, changed. But the continuity is striking; there is a persistent, if limited, homology that associates the university at its best with the city at its best.[2] One does not have to accept all the rhetoric of Henri Pirenne's paean to the medieval city to appreciate his insight that the revival of cities ventilated medieval society and represented a new order of freedom.[3] Similarly, the university was a far more open and diverse scholarly institution than the monastery, the institution that preceded it as the principal sponsor of learning in the West.

Professor's Hyde's examination of the emergence of the university at Bologna, which places the city within a broadly comparative perspective, recaptures the novelty as well as the significance of what happened. Emphasizing that the guild or corporate form distinguished the university from the earlier schools, Hyde also reminds us that this form was shared with merchants and shoemakers. In its origins and in its subsequent history, the university has valued security most highly, more so than the shoemakers and merchants who would in time embrace the market, favoring enterprise over security. It has been its corporate form that has enabled the university to persist through the centuries, surviving long eras of mediocrity, as local academies, for example, did not. The university, Hyde observes, has excelled at the "long, steady slog," needing, as late essays will reveal, occasional prods from the more dynamic (and mercurial) economy and culture of the city to revitalize itself.

Most of the early universities were, like Bologna, located in medium-sized (though prosperous) cities, often, at least in Italy, dominated by a more powerful neighboring city. The university of Paris was different. Paris was not a city-state, nor was it a provincial city. It was a very large city in the process of becoming the capital of what would emerge as one of the first and most powerful European nation-states.

There is a way in which the University of Paris was both in and not of the city *and* in and of the city. Evidence supporting the former interpretation includes the limited ties to the city and the constant threats, once realized, of dispersion. The faculty and students clearly thought of their university as being portable. Yet it is equally clear that they defined the necessary conditions for university life in urban, not court or monastic, terms. It is evident, moreover, that their active interest in the government and commerce of the city was assimilated into the moral theology and canon law developed by Parisian scholars, particularly regarding such matters as usury, the conduct of war, and the morality of capital punishment. Stephen Ferruolo points out further that "it was in the city, by living and working independently and in close quarters with merchants and artisans, that scholars for the first time came to think of teaching as a business (*negotium*), as a way to make a living." Then as now, it was difficult to balance the ideals of disinterested pursuit of ideas with the material facts of life surrounding academics in cities. There is a constant danger of corruption, of succumbing to the lures of power and wealth. But mostly it has been a creative tension.

At Florence intellectual and cultural activity flourished without a university—or at least without a significant one. In Renaissance Florence, but perhaps in the early modern period generally, cities were becoming more vital as crucibles of culture than their universities. One cannot but wonder whether universities between, say, 1400 and 1700 may have come very close to extinction.

If the case of Florence poses such a question, it does not supply an easy answer. If any answer is suggested, it is that even in Florence university learning could not be jettisoned, even if it was marginalized. Florence, of course, had the luxury of access to universities in neighboring cities. But there is a more important point to be made: the city on the Arno provides an example of a rich humanistic culture flourishing outside of the university, a culture that could nourish the likes of Leonardo da Vinci. One also sees in Florence—as elsewhere in early modern European culture—the powerful influence of the law and lawyers. Although the law was not entirely independent of the university, Gene Brucker points out that except for initial training, lawyers did not seem to require a local university to pursue scholarly and professional interests at the center of Florentine culture and politics. Much the same, he further observes, can be said of the medical profession. It was in fact the pluralism of intellectual cultures (scholastic and humanistic), with their diverse social bases, that accounted for Renaissance Florence's achievement in thought and scholarship. Yet all of these forms of higher learning relied on the intellectual tradition nourished and preserved by the university as an institution.

With this specific service of the university in mind, one's reflections on the survival of the university acquire an important specificity. One realizes that it was as an intellectual tradition, even if nearly moribund from time to time, that was at risk. The many and various training functions of the university could have been managed—and often were—by alternative institutions, but the intellectual core would have been lost.

The university was rescued when that tradition was engaged and transformed by contact with dynamic early modern cities. The confrontation of tradition and modernity that was evident in the remarkable invigoration of university learning at Leiden, Geneva, and Edinburgh in the seventeenth and eighteenth centuries represents the potential (not always realized) of a vital city contending with, transforming, even incorporating university tradition. The revival of university learning and influence in these three early modern cities—the embrace of new science and, especially in the case of Edinburgh, polite culture—is interesting in part because these universities were civic, even literally municipal, in ways that we do not usually associate with major moments of intellectual innovation in the history of the university. Precisely when it was most weakened and vulnerable, the university was saved, I think we must say, by the strength and stimulation it received from city life.

The essays on each of these three cities make this point, either directly or indirectly. But each emphasizes a different aspect of the process and uses a different window into the process. In the case of Anthony Grafton's study of Leiden, the emphasis is on the way two of its most distinguished classical scholars lived their personal and professional lives within and between the university and the city. This biographical approach allows us to see with considerable precision the dimensions of the social and intellectual interaction. If for Grafton the contest among different civic groups to influence appointments and the curriculum is a background theme, Michael Heyd makes it the focus of his study of the transformation of learning at Geneva. Here we see how ambitious urban interests pressed the university to redefine itself in ways that associated it with the new learning and a cultural cosmopolitanism. The movement at Geneva from a Protestant academy to a civic university reveals quite pointedly how certain translocal cultures can be provincial, while cosmopolitanism is often rooted in the local culture of a city.

While Professors Grafton and Heyd illuminate the interaction of professors and city, in one case, and the university and the city, in the other, Nicholas Phillipson evokes for us a university at Edinburgh so indeterminate in its structure and reach that university and city are nearly assimilated into each other. Motivated by a spirit of improvement, civic leadership of the "Athens of the North" committed itself to politeness as a cultural and political construct that would define public life. In the interest of developing this ideal of politeness as a civic virtue, these leaders elaborated an array of educational institutions, all difficult to distinguish from the city itself. Yet out of the world of the city's taverns, salons, and university there emerged, in a way so entangled that one cannot separate out the division of responsibility, a "concern with the cultivation of taste and judgment that was of crucial importance to shaping the social and civic culture of contemporary Britain and indeed of the Western world at large." At Edinburgh the association of university and city probably went farthest, essentially dissolving any notion of the autonomy (in either the medieval or the modern sense) of the university. It was, quite specifically, the town's college, though in time the hegemonic authority of its definition of culture made the town, in a real sense, the possession of the university.

What strikes me most about the cases of Leiden, Geneva, and Edinburgh is the very complex way in which the tradition of university learning was at once preserved, transformed, and even secured in its independence as a result of the incorporation of the university into the cosmopolitan and contemporary civic cultures of these aggressively moderate cities of the Enlightenment.

There is a direct line that runs from the universities of Leiden, Geneva, and Edinburgh to the founding of London University and New York University. The founders of these self-consciously metropolitan nineteenth-century universities looked back to the civic practice and the curriculum of the early modern civic universities. If Edinburgh was always conscious of its predecessor institutions (and competitors) at Leiden and Geneva, it was very much with the Edinburgh ideal in mind that Lord Brougham and his associates (including Jeremy Bentham) founded London University. The founding of London University in turn prompted civic leaders in New York to establish New York University, originally known as the University of the City of New York. And to complete the circle, the first president of the university's Governing Council was Albert Gallatin. The scion of a Genevan patrician family, Gallatin had come to America in the 1780s, soon thereafter entering politics, eventually distinguishing himself as a statesman (secretary of the Treasury under Jefferson and Madison), bank president (National Bank of New York), and scholar (founder of the American Ethnological Society). After he retired from public life, the founding of a new and specifically urban and modern university captured his imagination briefly but intensely.

Both London University and New York University were established on utilitarian principles, though each, in different ways, quickly compromised the dreams of its founders. If they failed the ambitions of Jeremy Bentham and Albert Gallatin, however, they never escaped or transcended them either. (Indeed, the mummified corpse of Bentham still "resides" at London University.)

Each institution assumed its character in a significant degree from the distinctive qualities of London and New York. Each, as Louise Stevenson shows in the case of New York and Sheldon Rothblatt implies in the case of London, tried to prepare its graduates as participants in the public life of the metropolis. Neither fully succeeded. London was and is a "unique city," to use Steen Rasmussen's famous phrase.[4] It lacks the concentrated, spatially defined public culture of a Paris or an Amsterdam. It is, rather, an agglomeration of suburbs, with a more suburban quality to its cultural life. New York, by contrast, had such a raucous public life that the educated gradually withdrew from it. Neither institution, therefore, came to constitute the culture of the city, an aim both had.

Yet each, in itself and in its graduates, did represent the peculiar metropolitan character of its city. London served as a degree-granting institution for aspirants to education in the English provinces and in the British Empire; NYU, gradually recovering one of its founding ideals, provided educational opportunity for the many migrants to the world's most dynamically growing metropolis, young men and women from the American hinterland as well as immigrants from Europe.

When one gets to the modern city and the modern university, it becomes harder to define the city, the university, or the relationship between the two. But the essays in Part IV of this volume give us several revealing perspectives. The essays by Charles McClelland and Carl E. Schorske, each wonderfully insightful on its own, are even more compelling when brought together. The comparison between Berlin and Basel shows how complicated—even, in a sense, contested—the process of defining scholarship (*Wissenschaft*) was. McClelland portrays a university at Berlin rooted more firmly in the world of the court than in the larger city. And the scientific ideal it would come to represent, especially for Americans, strove toward a denial of place.[5] The ideal of an international discipline and academic profession (community without propinquity) seemed to sever intellect from locality, from cities.

At Basel, by contrast, the local texture of culture and politics importantly defined the vocation of intellect for Jacob Burckhardt and Johann Jacob Bachofen. The more or less industrialized research ideal of the Prussian universities was viewed with distaste in Basel, where the higher learning was a form of adult education, not for the workers as charity but for the local patriciate. By considering Basel and Berlin together, one begins to be able to specify the nature of the tension in modern times between the emerging academic ideal and the historic tradition of civic humanism.

Martin Jay's deft essay on the Institute for Social Research recovers the urban milieu (new and substantial wealth, Jewish cultural patronage, secular and experimental modernist culture) of the emergence of the phenomenon that has come to be remembered as the Frankfurt School. Yet he makes a more important point: there was a certain distance from the city (except perhaps in the cases of Walter Benjamin and Siegfried Kracauer, themselves marginal "members" of the school), but also from the academy and, for that matter, from leftist politics. As Jay puts it, the Institute "was never merely a direct product of its urban or academic origins, nor of any organized political movement. Rather, it emerged as the dynamic nodal point of all three, suspended in the middle of a sociocultural force field without gravitating to any of its poles." Once the Frankfurt group emigrated to America (after 1934), these urban, academic, and political associations were all weakened. A seminal intellectual movement named (though only retrospectively) by a place lost its connection, never to be recovered, to any place.

From the very beginning the University of Chicago has been associated with its city. One of the most remarkable achievements of scholars at Chicago was their ability to treat Chicago as if it were the whole world—and to get most of the world to concur. The interplay between international disciplinary communities and local living communities revealed itself at its most creative at Chicago.

New York provides a startling contrast. At neither New York University nor Columbia University was any tradition of urban social inquiry established. NYU, at its worst, simply missed the fact of the modern city and modern life. This was not the whole story, however, as David Hollinger observes. But even at its best, particularly at its downtown Washington Square campus, NYU set its sights too low, serving its local populations, whether through applied research or as a teaching institution, but without reaching for international theoretical significance. Columbia, by contrast, largely dismissed the city in two ways. First, it adopted admissions policies that limited immigrant access to the institution. Second, Columbia sought to associate itself with national affairs and the training of national leadership.

Yet, as Nathan Glazer shows, since World War II both institutions (and the City University of New York as well) have been deeply dependent on the city for both their opportunities and their problems. Perhaps never in the history of the university has the future of such important institutions of higher learning (two of the largest private universities in the nation and one of the largest public systems) been so dependent on the fortunes—social, economic, political—of their host city, perhaps the world's most powerful and vulnerable.

NOTES

1. Paul Venable Turner, *Campus: An American Planning Tradition* (Cambridge, Mass., 1984), p. 21.
2. See my afterword in this volume for a discussion of the problem with an homological approach to the city and the university.
3. Henri Pirenne, *Medieval Cities* (Princeton, N.J., 1925).
4. Steen Eiler Rasmussen, *London: The Unique City*, rev. ed (Cambridge, Mass., 1982).
5. On Americans and the German research ideal, see Abraham Flexner, *Universities: American, English, German* (London, 1930); Lenore O'Boyle, "Learning for Its Own Sake: The German University as Nineteenth Century Model," *Comparative Studies in Society and History* 25 (1983): 3–25; Walter Metzger, *Academic Freedom in the Age of the University* (New York, 1955); Richard J.

Storr, *The Beginnings of Graduate Education in America* (Chicago, 1953); Laurence Veysey, *The Emergence of the American University* (Chicago, 1965); Fritz K. Ringer, "The German Academic Community," in Alexandra Oleson and John Voss, eds., *The Organization of Knowledge in America, 1860–1920* (Baltimore, Md., 1979), pp. 409–29.

I
MEDIEVAL ORIGINS

2

Universities and Cities in Medieval Italy

J. K. Hyde

I want to ask a number of rather fundamental questions, for we are at a point where such questions are necessary in order to proceed. One still begins one's reflections by going back to the great work of Hastings Rashdall, the dean of Carlisle, first published, I think, in 1895 but usually consulted in its second edition, edited by my predecessor at Manchester. Since little new documentation has been unearthed, it is by attending to the background that we are most likely to achieve new insight.

We now understand the kind of society in which the early universities flourished rather better than was possible in the nineteenth century. The institutions of medieval Italy were so untidy and so violent in so many cases that much late-nineteenth-century work is tinged with a nationalist standard of institutional neatness that recoiled from this kind of chaos. Nineteenth-century historians were blinded also by their sense of hierarchy. The medieval universities were not very hierarchical in Italy; they were rather anarchical.

But I want to begin by phrasing a very extraordinary state of affairs: the university as we know it today spread to all the continents in the modern world in which the great majority of research and teaching in the higher faculties still continues. They all go back to three prototypes: Oxford, Paris, and Bologna. And they go back to a particular moment in the West, within a decade or so on either side of the year 1200. This is a remarkable circumstance, and I want to try to shed some light on it.

The statement that all universities are descended either directly or by migration or are descended by imitation from those three prototypes depends, of course, on one's definition of a university. And I must define a university very strictly here. A university is something more than a center of higher education and study. One must reserve the term *university* for—and I'm quoting Rashdall here—"a scholastic guild, whether of masters or students engaged in higher education and study," which was later defined, after the

13

emergence of the universities, as *studium generale*. A *studium generale* was general not because many different subjects were studied (that was not always the case) but because it drew students from a very wide geographical area and was open to all. It was essentially urban and public.

Now, why should this institution emerge in Europe around the year 1200? The time seems to be far more important than the places. Oxford might well have been at North Hampton or Lincoln; Paris, had it jelled a little earlier, might have been at Chartres. Bologna, maybe, could have been elsewhere. I don't find reasons why it wasn't at Salerno; it might have been at Padua, or it might have been in Milan. Milan is perhaps the best possibility. But the time is terribly precise—ten years on either side of the year 1200, both in France and in Italy, quite independently and spontaneously.

This would have been inconceivable had there not been the great growth of towns and cities in Europe, beginning at the end of the tenth century, gathering pace gradually through the eleventh, and becoming a breakaway rise in the twelfth and thirteenth. To quote Professor Gina Fasoli, "The university is a precisely urban institution," and not merely because no one ever thought of placing a university in a rural village or a mountain fortress. This is obvious enough under the conditions of a preindustrial society where the concentration of population involved in a university of any size including the logistic support it required in terms of food, accommodation, recreation (mainly taverns and brothels), specific services such as book production and retail, and, last but not least, student loans—would have created a town if one had not existed already. The spontaneous universities of Italy were formed in large, growing cities, distinguished, I think, by fat agricultural regions, with a food surplus which meant that relatively cheap living was possible for an idle student population.

Bologna, *la grassa,* long famous for its excellent cuisine, and Padua, both situated in the most fertile part of the North Italian plain, were early university towns. The attempt to migrate and transplant universities to smaller cities—such as Vicenza, Vercelli, or Reggio—never succeeded. The universities didn't take root there, although they staggered along. This was in the free economy of Italy, where university cities were in a state of competition. If a university was artificially protected by a prince or a king of a sizable territorial state, then it was possible to establish a university in a comparatively small urban center. At Cambridge, for example, and at the later German princely foundations such as Erfurt, Heidelberg, Wurzburg, and some of the Spanish ones, there was something like a balance between the burgher and student populations. But that was the result of princely intervention, concentrating study in a particular place. I do not think that it would ever have happened in the anarchical situation of Italy.

The geography of Italian universities is very interesting and curious. There were eighteen medieval universities in Italy—some of which only lasted for a relatively short time. The last university to be founded purely through migration was Verchelli in 1228, which didn't succeed. The first to be deliberately founded was Frederick II's first foundation in Naples in 1224. The places where universities succeeded were cities of the middle rank, the sort of city which, around 1300, had a population of about twenty to forty thousand. Cities of that size—such as Siena, Perugia, and Ferrara—were the places that were successful.

The place where universities either are not founded or do not succeed is in the super-cities—the very great cities of Milan, Genoa, Venice. Florence is the exception which proves the rule, and we shall learn more of that from Gene Brucker in another chapter, so I won't anticipate. It is curious that second-order cities are the homes of the Italian universities. One even finds in the fifteenth century a deliberate policy pursued by the Italian territorial state to place the university in the second city, so that the state of Milan favored the university of Pavia. Florence eventually transferred its university to Pisa. Venice took over the existing university of Padua. London, of course, did not acquire a medieval university. And that leaves Paris sticking out as unique on several accounts, as a capital city and also as a super-city.

A great deal has been written about the relations between town and gown, between the *popolo* and the student body, and between the professors and the statesmen. Regulation was necessary because of the openness of the university, the fact that very large numbers of students of different backgrounds, different nationalities, and different jurisdictions flowed together. This circumstance points to a deeper relationship between city and university. It's perhaps an obvious point, but I think it needs stating at the beginning of this symposium. The cities that grew up in the Western world, through the tenth, eleventh, and twelfth centuries, had to break from the mold of the territorial state and institute their own legal freedoms to cope with city life.

A city is not just simply a concentration of population. Monasteries very often built up considerable concentrations of population. Palaces, a royal court, in the ancient and early medieval world could create something the size of a small town or city. But the essence of the city is a permanent population, plus a marketplace, and a shift from human relations based on status to those based on free contract. Courts were needed; a legal structure was required for mercantile exchanges. The new institutions of learning were very much a marketplace of learning. That openness is what distinguishes them from monasteries (which have achieved great intellectual distinction at various times in the West). Access to a monastery was not, however, determined on simply academic criteria. The objective of a monastic community was not simply intellectual excellence or teaching, although they sometimes achieved greatness in both.

The essence of the new type of institution—the university—was relative openness of access to all people of all places, all social classes. This access was governed only by ability to subsist and pay fees, and this was helped quite considerably by patrons and charitable institutions. There was a strong tradition that poor scholars should be taught, if not free of charge, at very much reduced fees. This theme has been effectively explored by Gains Post, who explained the belief that if science were a gift of God it could not be sold. This view is still influential to this day and accounts for the feeling that education should not be sold as a straight market proposition. While the teacher should be rewarded for his labor, one cannot extort the highest price possible.

Movement was an essential feature of the new urban life, as against the rural world where movement was very much more restricted. Freedom of movement was shared by universities not only for individuals to come to the university, or to come to the schools, or to move from teacher to teacher, but also for the schools themselves to move about. We must recognize that the early schools and universities were potentially mobile and indeed did move. This was their ultimate threat against the cities who were their hosts—that they would get up and go. It happened several times in early-thirteenth-century Italy and accounts for the formation of universities such as Padua. It's fair to say that even the University of Paris in the early thirteenth century threatened at least on one occasion to move somewhere else in order to get better terms.

The other essential feature that links the city and the university is a concern for the fair and objective assessment of achievement. Although it may seem a fairly obvious feature of an educational system, there was not in the monastic schools or the palace schools any system of graduation and examination. The whole idea would have seemed rather unacceptable to proponents of a type of learning that was much more detached from the marketplace, much more concerned with the palace or with the closed community of a monastery.

What the towns of the twelfth century created was not in one step the universities, it was first the schools. There was a century of schools before the universities emerged. These schools, which were cathedral schools in northern Europe and lay schools in Italy, represent a pure application of the market mentality to the question of learning. Those seem to have been very ephemeral organizations. It was a case of individual teachers attracting as many students as they could, living from the fees that they extracted from the students. They gathered in certain places, but there was in fact a great deal of movement. To obtain the highest education in the twelfth century, it was necessary to move around from place to place to follow the great teachers.

Why did this not continue? Why was it that this phase of a free-for-all among the schools in Italy came to an end? Why was it necessary for the guild to arise to modify this freedom? The answer must lie in the particular situation in Bologna, because it was there that it happened. When we examine Bologna we see a city that epitomizes the extreme vitality of twelfth- and early-thirteenth-century European society—a rapid rate of demographic and economic growth coupled with considerable political dislocation and disorganization. Bologna, for example, seems to have had typical institutions of mixed Roman and Lombard traditions. Ravenna had a very much stronger Byzantine influence, and it was therefore much more neatly organized. Conditions were similar in Pavia. As the former capital of the Lombard kingdom, it had a proper organization of Byzantine guilds.

It was not in those places that the university grew. It grew on new ground in Bologna, where the last relic of the old system of government was destroyed in 1115, just as the schools were in the first generation of their flourishing. The royal palace was destroyed by the citizens in an uprising in 1115, and Bologna found itself in the eye of the storm of conflicts between pope and emperor. Bologna's position right in the center of the Lombard plain meant that it was pushed backward and forward. In the later twelfth century particularly, a conflict between Emperor Frederick Barbarossa and the papacy caused Bologna to be tossed from one side to another. There was a pro-imperial regime from 1158 to 1161, then in 1162 the emperor Frederick moved in personally. Then there was a reversion toward a free commune, which joined the Lombard league in 1167 against the emperor. By 1192 there was an imperious bishop, Gerardo, opposed by the magnates and favored by the guildsmen class. The 1190s were marked by intense social conflict, with rapid changes of regime.

To give just one example, the *podesta* in power, the chief magistrate in 1195, was deposed by the magnates for corruption, and he had all his teeth pulled out, we're told. This story is a late tradition, but I think it gives you the spirit of the place. These changes from imperial to papal and back again must have had an effect on the student body, which was mainly concerned with studying law in its two branches, canon (the law of the church) and civil (the law of the emperor). I'm not being so crude as to suggest that all the canon lawyers were pro-papal or that all the civil lawyers were pro-imperial. There was a great deal more to it than that. But confusion among the students, some of whom were Italians and laymen, the other half of whom were northern Europeans and clerics, must have been very considerable, though we have very little record of it. We have then the intervention of external bodies, the papacy intervening in 1199 to suppress the abuse of teachers leasing lodgings to students and the commune itself intervening in the same year (1199) to extract an oath from the professors—the foreign professors, not the Bolognese citizens—who were tied to the political authority of the state anyway. The oath imposed on the foreigners forbade them from leaving the city or teaching anywhere else. This oath was regarded as a violation of academic freedom.

Internal competition was also becoming extremely intense, if we can judge from the accounts of the rhetorician Boncompagno, who in his works includes a number of anecdotes about teachers bribing students to attend their lectures and to boycott the lectures of others. Another teacher claimed he was going to fly in order to attract a large crowd of students. What I think this boils down to—and one always has to take Boncampagno with a pinch of salt—is that the competition was becoming extremely uncomfortable, both for the students and for the teachers. Unbridled competition was really beginning to have adverse effects. Even without the external threats, there was a strong pressure on both the teachers and the students to form some kind of an organization—for their protection, for their mutual support, and also for the general regulation of the schools. This response fit in with the great wave of guild formation that was going on all over Europe, not simply in Italy but very forcefully in Italy, throughout the twelfth century and on into the thirteenth.

For example, we know that there was a guild of shoemakers that had property in Bologna. That's the earliest guild we know of—in 1144. There was a group of Societates, a guild in 1177 who elected seven consuls to run the city. There was from 1166 to 1177 a body called the *universitas populi Bononiae,* "the guild of the people of Bologna," which was the name for the city government. In 1178 it called itself the Populus of Bologna, Great and Small. These people in the late twelfth century created societies, institutions, and corporations rather like children blowing bubbles. They changed their form, their shape, and their color in a baffling way; any group of people could get together, form themselves into an institution or society, and people would listen to them. They were taken seriously.

The strict definition of a corporation was only beginning to take shape. The civil lawyers were working on it, and eventually it would make the spontaneous creation of such societies more and more difficult. But in the late twelfth century a group could create almost anything. The organization of students and of doctors and teachers arose during this fertile movement. They were later than the shoemakers, organizing themselves at about the same time as the long-distance merchants. There was in 1194, on the eve of the first positive evidence of the university, a trade agreement negotiated with the city of Ferrara. The terms of the export were to be interpreted by the consul, the official of the merchants, and the rector of the societies of the guilds' organization. In 1200, when the university was probably in existence, we have positive mention of the consul of merchants and the consul of the moneychangers, who was responsible for the organization of the mint. One must wait until the 1220s before the real artisan guilds—the shoemakers, the cobblers, and so on—reemerge. So the university students formed themselves into guilds for very much the same reasons as the merchants and the artisans—to protect their interests, to bury their members when they died, to look after their widows. In all cases groups who felt vulnerable organized to reduce that vulnerability.

Bolognese law did not give quite the same protection to a foreign student, a foreign layman, as it did to its own citizens. The first university of students was therefore constituted of the foreign students. Bolognese students were not allowed to belong to the university, because that would have put them under a different jurisdiction, the jurisdiction of the rectors. The doctors, on the other hand, got together in part to try to protect themselves against the oath that bound them to stay in Bologna. But they also got together to regulate examinations and graduations. Out of these different student and faculty problems, as two organizations, the University of Bologna began to develop. It was formed in that flexible period between 1190 and 1211, when the commune passed a law against the formation of more sworn associations that were not approved by the civic authorities. That really presents *a terminus ad quem.* After 1211 groups could not create this kind of thing without authorization from somebody else.

Some historians have been persnickety about the idea that universities originated in the same kind of organization that commended itself to money-changers or even shoemakers. I do not see any reason to be ashamed of this at all. What the university did as a guild was to create a series of legal privileges. As a legal entity, the university gained more than the means of property holding, though that was important, as was the capacity to receive and hold endowments of one kind or another. More happened, however; the creation of the university produced cooperation between students among themselves and doctors among themselves.

Academics are not naturally the most cooperative of people—particularly in a situation, such as the schools presented, in which they were in competition for student fees and for the limelight. The guild promised to counter these tendencies. The structure of the guild enforced cooperation, a consciousness of common interest. Of course, there were celebrated disputes, and indeed there still are, but the university did create a corporate organization.

Interestingly enough, it seems to have nourished extremely effective cooperation with another corporation that was forming at the same time, the corporation of *popolo,* the not-so-wealthy citizens who were coming into power during the twelfth century. Some of them were guildsmen; others were middling landowners or rentiers. It's very striking that in cities other than Bologna, such as Padua or Siena, the *popolo,* this middling group of citizens, and the student universities found a modus vivendi whereby the students were given the privileges but not the burdens of citizenship.

I puzzled over this for some time. Why should this be true? Why should it work? I realized then that the university student guild was very unusual. It was a guild of consumers. They were consumers of a product, which was teaching and learning. They regulated the product that they were receiving. That is, as we all know, they bound the teachers to maintain their lectures and, indeed, get through them in an approved time. And they fined the professors who failed to do so. The *popolo* was also overwhelmingly a consumers' organization. These two consumer organizations had a good way of reaching a harmonious way of living. After the upheavals of the early thirteenth century, relations between the university and the city settled down to a remarkable pattern of mutual support. The cities were immensely proud of their universities. They would take over the payment of salaries, they provided loans, they regulated the book trade, the lodgings, all the various services the students required. Why? Because the students brought in money, and they gave renown to the city.

This formation of an institutional shell around the business of learning was unique to Europe. This pattern did not exist in the Asiatic world, nor had it existed in Byzantium or in the Arabic world, where institutions of higher education depended on a prince or an emperor. The least successful of the medieval Italian universities were those closely dependent on a sovereign. The University of Naples was never very distinguished; the University of the Roman Couria was worst of all, because it was too close to the pope.

To understand the virtues of this situation, one has to look briefly at what happened next, the troubles that broke out in Europe around the middle of the fourteenth century. The Black Death and economic recession had a profoundly disrupting effect on the great institutions of medieval society. The German empire was more or less shattered by it, and even the kingdom of France was severely shaken in the fourteenth century and only recovered in the latter part of the fifteenth. The secular power was severely disturbed. The church was also affected, particularly if you look at the monastic institutions. The roots of the decline of the medieval monastic system, and many of the problems of the later medieval church, stem from this great recession to which the church had great difficulty in adapting. The *studium,* or the intellectual world, emerged from these upheavals remarkably successfully.

It's easy to criticize the late-medieval universities as being less adventurous, more cautious, more restricted in the social range from which they drew their students. Nevertheless one has to say that higher education went on expanding; the number of institutions went on expanding dramatically in these otherwise bad centuries. To restrict myself simply to Italy, the University of Florence, which had no great success, was founded in 1349, the year after the plague; Pisa was founded just before in 1343; and Pavia was founded in 1361. Pisa and Pavia had, in the end, long-term success.

When the economy began to recover in the fifteenth century, there was another wave of foundations of universities: in Turin (1405) and in Catania (1404), as well as revivals in Arezzo (1464), Pisa (1472), and Pavia (1412). In Germany this is even more striking. The spread of universities in the fourteenth and fifteenth centuries stands in striking contrast to the profound difficulties the secular states were experiencing.

It seems to be most unlikely that the *studia* would have come through had they not had this corporate existence. It made them part of the established institutions of their respective cities, so that it required a positive effort to wind them up. Herein lay the peculiar strength of the universities. If one examines the Renaissance period, with its academies, one sees that it was possible for relatively small, private institutions to achieve short spurts of immense brilliance—if they had a good patron and they chose their members carefully. But in the long run it was the ability of the universities to support mediocrity that we must appreciate. It was the long, steady slog in which the universities excelled, and they did so because of their corporate structure.

The record of the late-medieval universities is, in fact, not as bad as one might think. They invested very heavily, of course, in scholasticism, and they found it difficult to adapt to the new waves of humanism. But the contribution of the University of Paris to the question of the Great Schism was not unrespectable, and the University of Prague at the time of the Hussites did take a lead in the reform of the church in the appearance of a kind of nationalism. It is, then, this long, steady slog of the universities, established as a part of the urban scene, that explains why they have prevailed and why all of the institutions of higher education that we have in the world today, with negligible exceptions, go back to these medieval prototypes of the humble model of the merchant or artisan guild—very humble but very durable, and long may it flourish.

3

Parisius-Paradisus: The City, Its Schools, and the Origins of the University of Paris

Stephen C. Ferruolo

The city of Paris and its university grew up together. It was exactly in the same era—from the early years of the twelfth century through the first decades of the thirteenth—that Paris became the greatest city in northern Europe, the capital of an increasingly powerful French kingdom, a major commercial center, and the site of what was arguably the first and—certainly for a long time remained—the preeminent university. The connections among these three aspects of the city's development (political, economic, and educational) suggested by this temporal coincidence have not been explored as closely as one might think. Partly this has been a matter of the degree of specialization among historians, who have become less and less willing to cross the boundaries of their subspecialties. Historians of universities, and in particular those who work on medieval universities, have tended to write constitutional or intellectual history, focusing on the internal development of their institutions, rather than social history, which would require that they look more broadly at the relationship between the university and society.

In the specific case of Paris, geography has also played its part in separating the three aspects of the city's development. One tends to think of the three constituent parts of the city each with its distinct focus of activity: the Ile-de-la-Cité, with the palace at one end and the cathedral at the other, as the center of politics and administration; the Right Bank, with its ports and markets (Les Halles), as the commercial quarter; and the Left Bank, with its schools, as the educational quarter—each developing separately with its own internal dynamic.[1] But, as we shall see, the city's two ancient bridges, the Grand and Petit Pont, and its new walls were not the only things that bound these activities together.

Finally, there is the nature of the university itself—that is, its tendency not to think of itself as a local institution—and this is no less true of the medieval than the modern university. Even well before the university was formed, Paris drew its scholars from throughout western Europe. It was, in the terminology of the day, a *studium generale*, not a *studium particulare*.[2] Not only were most of its students from outside Paris and the Ile-de-France, but most of its masters were also not natives of the immediate area (Paris, in this respect, was significantly different from Bologna). These "foreign" scholars and masters had no particular attachment to the city. They enjoyed its amenities while they were in Paris but expected that their careers would sooner or later take them elsewhere, to a well-paying job, even if in a less pleasant city. For some it did matter that the French monarchy was making Paris their capital; the king was a major source of patronage, though, as we shall see, not as generous to university graduates in fact as he was in reputation. But for most scholars another city, Rome, and its ruler, the pope, mattered more. It was, moreover, to Rome and to the pope, not to their bishop or to the French king, that the Paris masters and scholars turned at critical points in the university's development to protect their liberty or to gain recognition of their privileges. And they were even prepared to leave the amenities of Paris behind and move to other cities when they felt that the liberty and privileges they rightly deserved and had once enjoyed were at risk.

In the Middle Ages, when scholarly privileges mattered much more than academic buildings, university migrations were a frequent occurrence. There were major migrations of scholars from Oxford to Cambridge (1209) and from Bologna to Vicenza (1204), to Arezzo (1215), and to Padua (1222), and then from Padua to Vercelli (1228).[3] In the case of Bologna, the migrations continued despite the repeated efforts of the commune to secure its *studium* by passing statutes penalizing masters who left or conspired to leave and prohibiting citizens from aiding or following those who did.[4] Later the commune even went so far as to prescribe the death penalty for anyone who conspired to remove the *studium* or for any master over age fifty who left to teach elsewhere.[5] (A law those deans confronted with increasing raids on their senior faculty might wish to bring back!) More effective in binding the university to the city was the action finally taken by the commune after the last major migration of Bolognese masters to Siena in 1321. The commune got the masters back (in 1322) by building, at its own expense, a chapel exclusively for the city's scholars; it was the university's first building.[6]

To return to Paris, a significant group of masters and scholars left the city during the university's dispute with the bishop and chancellor in 1218–19.[7] But far more important in the university's history was the organized migration of 1229, commonly called the Great Dispersion, when Paris masters left the city en masse and took up teaching in the French cities of Angers, Orléans, and Toulouse, where now *studia* were developing, as well as, at the invitation of King Henry III, at Oxford and Cambridge.[8] This migration from Paris, like those from Oxford, Bologna, and Padua, came about as a result of town-gown conflict. That there could be tensions and conflicts with a city serious enough to disperse—and almost destroy—a distinguished university reveals something of the fragile nature of this new institution. This is all the more remarkable when one realizes that it began with a dispute over the cost of some wine between some students and a tavern keeper in one of the city's smaller suburbs during carnival time. This, as anyone who has read about the history of the medieval university knows, is hardly exceptional. Medieval masters were quick to rally to the defense of their scholarly privileges, even when it was a matter of protecting rowdy students who got into trouble with local magistrates.[9]

This brings us back to the particular way that the university saw and defined itself in relation to the city. These masters and scholars did not conceive of themselves as the university *of* Paris but as the university of masters and scholars *in* Paris. The difference is significant, and I ask you to keep it in mind. Collectively, the Paris masters and scholars of this period did not yet identify themselves with the city, but they did live and teach or study in it, and they were directly affected and influenced by other aspects of the city's development.

What I propose to do here is examine the relations between the city and the university of Paris in what was the formative period of both. Though it will be necessary for me in tracing the city's political, economic, and educational development to begin back around 1100, most of my attention will be focused on the half-century or so before the Great Dispersion of 1229–31, when the university was forming, seeking to gain recognition for its rights and privileges, and involved in a number of disputes with the city. Though I have argued elsewhere against the tendency of historians of medieval universities to overemphasize the role of conflict,[10] I would defend this approach here on the grounds that our concern is not so much to explain the institutional development of the university as to explore the complex relationship between universities and cities. What drove Paris masters and scholars to leave the city in 1229 and then what it took to get them to return two years later are key questions in understanding the history of the relationship between Paris and its university, and it is for this reason that I have made the Great Dispersion the primary focus of the narrative part of my essay.

Before proceeding I think it is necessary to make one more preliminary point regarding terminology. So far, I have used both the word *university* and the Latin term *studium* without explicitly defining or distinguishing them. A university (Latin *universitas*) in the relevant medieval sense is a legal term, meaning a guild or a corporation, a group of men engaged in a common activity of any sort and having a collective status, that is legally recognized to be self-governing and to exercise control over its own membership.[11] In the strict sense of the term, there was no university in Paris until the masters and scholars in the city had formed their own corporation and had been formally recognized to have legal standing. This happened no earlier than between 1208 and 1215.[12] A *studium*, on the other hand, is a place of study, a city where there are several schools, that is, masters offering instruction. If the *studium* draws its students only locally, it is a *studium particulare;* if it draws its students from a wider geographical area, it is a *studium generale.*[13] (This term has other meanings later in the Middle Ages, but this was the original one, and it remained in use through the period I will be treating.) Paris was a *studium generale* for more than a century before it had a university. And when the masters and scholars dispersed in 1229, the *studium* ceased (temporarily) to function in Paris, but the university of (former) Paris masters and scholars still had legal standing though some of them were teaching at *studia* elsewhere.

This has significance for some of the broader themes of this conference. The medieval concept of the *universitas* was not tied to a specific place in the way the *studium* was; nor was the university intrinsically defined by function, again in contrast to the *studium*. Perhaps, then, implicit in the very fact that the term *universitas,* and not *studium,* came to be the standard name for this new institution is the sort of placelessness and abstraction that has been so often typical in its history and that seems all the more pronounced today.

But let's now go back to Paris and look at the city and its schools some seven centuries ago, at the very beginning of their great period of growth. In 1100 Paris was a small city, probably with well under ten thousand inhabitants, recovering from the devastating effects of the Norman invasions of the ninth century, and especially from the almost disastrous siege of 885–86. Most of these inhabitants still lived on the Ile-de-la-Cité in the middle of the Seine, but others were to be found in widely scattered settlements or *bourgs* near the great monasteries and churches on both sides of the river, settlements usually of several hundred, perhaps at times a thousand or more (including the religious community and its dependents), separated from one another by large fields and vineyards. (The wines of the Paris region were already highly valued.) Even a population of this size, of course, required trade and commerce—the import of grains, salt, and other necessities which they could not produce themselves. And this activity was bolstered by the agricultural surpluses again being produced by the vast estates of ancient monasteries located in the city (such as St.-Germain-des-Prés), as well as by the fact that the Seine was the major highway for east-west trade in northern Europe and Paris was one of the few places where the river was bridged. By this time the ancient port of de Grève, or the Gravia (presently the site on the Right Bank of the Hôtel de Ville), had probably already surpassed the ports on the Ile as the city's dominant area of trade, but though the potential was there, Paris did not yet show any signs of becoming a major center of commerce.[14]

Paris was, however, already a capital, and it was a center of education. Both parts of this statement need qualification. In 1100 Paris was not a capital in the modern sense of the term. It was not until Abbot Suger of St. Denis's regency, while Louis VII was away on the Second Crusade (1147–49), that departments of the royal administration began to be permanently based in Paris, and it was not until the reign of Philip the Fair (1285–1314) that the city became the fixed residence of the king.[15] The earlier Capetians, as feudal kings, were customarily itinerant; they traveled around their personal domains, which spanned the Seine and the Loire rivers, collecting their produce and revenues, enjoying the right of the hospitality of their vassals (the *gite*), and staying for varying lengths of time at each of their dispersed residences, castles, or palaces. In our period, Senlis, Poissy, Etampes, and Orléans, as well as Paris, were normally part of their itinerary.[16] But as far back as the reign of the first member of the Capetian dynasty, Hugh Capet (987–96), Paris had replaced Orléans as the favorite resting place of the French king. From the reign of his grandson, Henry I (1031–60), who completed the restoration of the palace on the Ile-de-la-Cité, more royal acts were dated from Paris than from anywhere else.[17] It was convenience rather than any specific amenities that seems to account for the political ascendancy of the city. Paris was ideally located, a center of communications, right at the heart of Capetians' personal domains.[18] And beginning with Henry's son, Philip I (1060–1108), the Capetians began to take a serious interest in clarifying and extending their rights of lordship within Paris itself in order to make the city a more secure base for their territorial ambitions.[19]

How the Capetians extended their lordship within the city is a complicated story which I shall touch upon several times in this essay. For now, just two points need to be made. First, as their power and prestige as monarchs grew in the twelfth and early thirteenth centuries, the Capetians came to exercise greater authority and control within the city of Paris. Second, the king's major rivals within Paris were ecclesiastical lords, the heads of the city's monasteries and churches, and above all the bishop and the chapter of the cathedral, who possessed temporal lordship over extensive parts of the Right and Left Banks, as well as of the Ile, and thus had legal jurisdiction over a large proportion of the population of the city.[20]

The bishop and the chapter also exercised direct authority over what was the city's one significant school, which was attached to the cathedral; over the master (or masters) who taught there, who were customarily also members of the chapter; and over their students, who, at the beginning of the twelfth century, were still mostly young men from the diocese training for the priesthood. The cathedral school in Paris (which dates back to the Carolingian education reforms of the ninth century) first begins to emerge from obscurity just before 1100, when the rhetorician-dialectician William of Champeaux became master there and an exceptionally bright young Breton called Peter Abelard became his student. Until then the records tell us more about other cathedral schools in northern France, of Reims, Loan, Chartres, and Orléans. It was the masters at these schools who had been able, at times, to attract students from outside the diocese to fill their classrooms and add to their fame.[21] But after 1100 Paris rapidly and decisively overtook them. By no later than 1140, and perhaps as early as 1120, Paris was not just *a* center of education but *the* center of education, drawing its students and masters in ever increasing numbers from throughout northern France and western Europe.[22]

Medieval scholars, like their kings, tended to be itinerant. They often traveled great distances and wandered from city to city in search of the latest teaching and the greatest masters. Paris enjoyed several advantages over the other cathedral cities of northern France in attracting these wandering scholars. Most obvious, again, is the city's location: Paris was centrally placed, within easy reach of most of the other well-known schools.[23] But far more important was the fact that, from soon after the arrival of Abelard, the prototype of the wandering scholar, Paris itself had several schools. In addition to the cathedral school, there was the school at the abbey of St. Victor, founded by William of Champeaux when he retired from teaching at the cathedral in 1108; a school on Mont Ste. Geneviève, first established when William prevented Abelard from replacing him at the cathedral school; and, before long, other independent or private schools on the Left Bank and the Petit Pont, catering to the students who had thronged to Paris to hear the disputes between these two famous masters.

This not only meant that Paris offered students an unusual choice of schools but also that the masters who ran these schools enjoyed a freedom not found in other cities. This was partly because the bishop and the chancellor of Paris were never able to exercise an effective monopoly over teaching in the city. From the time of Abelard, the abbey of Ste. Geneviève, which claimed an ancient exemption from episcopal jurisdiction,[24] was more than willing to accommodate masters who were prohibited from teaching elsewhere in the city. But we should not make too much of this divided jurisdiction, which may have been more important to the university in the thirteenth century than it was to the masters of independent schools in the twelfth. As long as the chancellor could charge a fee for issuing the *licentia docendi,* there was money to be made from allowing these masters to teach.[25] After all, schools could be a profitable business, and most masters seemed willing to pay, as long as the chancellor's fees were not too high and he did not otherwise restrict their activities.[26]

No less interested in the profit which could be made from encouraging the expansion of the schools were the chancellor's colleagues, the canons of the cathedral, who were quick to see the advantage of renting space in their houses in the cathedral cloister (or close) for classrooms and lodgings. This arrangement was first restricted in 1127 by Bishop Stephen of Senlis, who provided alternative space for classrooms by building a hall near the episcopal court.[27] Two later bishops tried to stop the practice altogether by getting the chapter to pass a statute strictly prohibiing canons from renting their houses to scholars or from accommodating them in any other way.[28] But, judging from the repeated legislation, it was a practice that died hard. The canons, like the chancellor, took advantage of the opportunity to profit financially from the expanding schools for as long as they could.

In letting their houses to scholars, the canons were meeting a critical need. As we know from both the complaints of students and the concerns expressed by theologians, lodging and classroom space were scarce and expensive. (It is true that academics have always talked about real estate!) When John of Salisbury returned to Paris in 1164, where he had been a student sixteen years earlier, he found the city's landlords were now demanding yearlong leases at exorbitant rents.[29] And a young Italian cleric wrote back to his family that the toughest thing about Paris was finding a place to live.[30]

The theologian Stephen Langton comments that student hostels advertised as having comfortable beds actually offered no more than piles of straw.[31] And the city was so crowded, Jacques of Vitry reports with alarm, that masters often had to rent teaching space upstairs from brothels.[32] All this is evidence of a booming city, where even though there was still plenty of room for expansion, building was simply not able to keep pace with the rapid pace of growth—this, of course, meant high rents, overcrowding, and worsening tensions among the scholars themselves as well as between town and gown. The first steps taken to relieve the situation can be found in the Paris statutes of 1215, which stipulated that no scholar was to occupy a classroom or lodging without seeking the previous tenant's consent and which also gave the university the right to enter agreements setting the rents of hostels.[33] Rent control became one of the key privileges sought and acquired by the university in the thirteenth century.[34]

If lodging was expensive and in short supply, other amenities seem to have made up for the situation. Thanks to the agricultural wealth of the Paris region and the city's commercial development, food and—no less important—wine were abundant and reasonably priced.[35]

> Pro parvo vinum, pro parvo panis habetur,
> Pro parvo carnes, pro parvo piscis emetur.
>
> (For a little, wine and bread are to be had,
> For a little, meat and fish are to be bought.)

This little verse (attributed to John of Garland) was meant to describe Toulouse, not Paris, but what is telling is that it was used to try to induce the dispersed Paris masters and scholars to join the new *studium* founded in Toulouse in 1229.[36] Other cities trying to build up their own *studia* claimed the amenities that *Parisius-Paradisus* was known to have in such unusual and glorious abundance.[37]

Here the beneficent policies of the Capetians had been at work in transforming the city they had chosen as their capital into the greatest commercial center in northern France. It was perhaps inevitable that Paris would expand as the Capetian power and wealth grew. But the kings did not leave anything to chance. They deliberately worked to increase commercial activity in, around, and through Paris. As early as 1137 we find Louis VI negotiating with the bishop about their mutual rights in the then uninhabited and seemingly unimportant area of the Right Bank known as the Campellus or Champeaux. Within two years the Capetians' plans for the Champeaux became clear when it was chosen as the location of the city's newest market. Over the next decades an increasing number of merchants, artisans, and moneychangers moved—or were moved—there to conduct their business under royal surveillance and protection. And it was there, in 1182, that Philip Augustus built the first two covered and enclosed pavilions of Les Halles, Paris's wholesale food market until twenty years ago.[38]

No less important in ensuring that their capital had abundant food and commodities were the privileges the Capetians granted to the Paris *hanse,* the

mercatores acquae. In 1171 Louis VII confirmed the statutes of this merchant corporation and gave its members a monopoly over the transport of all
goods on the Seine between Paris and Mantes. And in 1192 Philip Augustus
added to the *hanse*'s monopoly by granting its merchants the exclusive right
to unload, store, and sell wine in Paris.[39]

In granting these commercial privileges to the Paris *hanse,* the Capetian
kings were doing for their capital what their rivals, the Angevin kings of England, had done for the merchants of Rouen, the capital of Normandy. The
threat posed by the English presence in nearby Normandy (and the Vexin)
also accounts for the massive new walls Philip Augustus built to enclose
Paris, first, before his departure on the Third Crusade in 1189–90, to protect
the commercially important Right Bank, and then twenty years later, to surround an area almost as large on the city's less densely populated Left Bank,
where scholars were to settle in increasing numbers.[40] There were obviously
sufficient military reasons alone to account for Philip's decision to enclose the
area of the Left Bank adjacent to the promontory of Mont Ste. Geneviève,
but the new walls also provided a considerable amount of protected space
within the walls for new building to accommodate masters and students. It
may even be that these walls helped to secure the unity of the nascent university by physically tying the interests of scholars already settled on the Left
Bank to those of their colleagues on the Ile-de-la-Cité.[41] The total area within
these new walls has been varyingly estimated to be between 250 and 275
hectares (roughly between 620 and 680 acres), an area ten times the size of
that enclosed within the ancient Roman walls of the Ile-de-la-Cité and two to
four times larger than any other French city with major schools.[42] It has been
estimated that a population of at least twenty-five to thirty thousand resided
in Paris at the time the walls were completed in the early thirteenth century,
including already some three to four thousand scholars.[43]

By now I hope it is clear how the policies of the Capetians in building
Paris into a secure and prosperous base for their royal ambitions also provided distinct advantages to the city's growth as an educational center. The
market, the walls, and the paving of the city's primary roads and squares
(begun in 1186)[44] all added to the physical amenities Paris could offer to
scholars. We can even see the hand of the Capetians indirectly behind the
first efforts made to alleviate the housing shortage. The earliest two charitable
foundations for poor scholars were founded under Capetian auspices: the
Collège des Dix-huit in 1180, by a prosperous London merchant who enjoyed the special protection of the royal court, and the Collège de St. Thomas
du Louvre in 1186, by Count Robert of Dreux, Louis VII's brother and King
Philip's uncle.[45] The kings also nurtured the growth of the schools in more
direct ways, by their patronage and by the privileges they granted to scholars.
These, perhaps more than anything else, were what made Paris, the Capetian
capital, so accommodating a city for the first university.

Let us look at patronage first. The Capetians—especially Louis VII and
Philip II—received much praise as great patrons of learning. "With such
kind favor," wrote the Welshman Walter Map in the 1190s, "did [Louis VII]

promote clerics that in his time they flocked to Paris from all quarters of Christendom and, nourished and protected under the shadow of his wings, have continued in the schools unto this day."[46] Coming from a Paris graduate who spent most of his career in service not to the Capetians but to the Angevin kings of England, Walter's praise might seem misdirected—all the more so when one can cite recent studies which show that the kings of England were far ahead of the French in providing government employment for scholars as well as in promoting masters to the episcopacy. Only two or three masters have been found in the employ of Louis VII and about a dozen in that of Philip Augustus. And it was not until Louis IX that the percentage of masters among the French episcopacy began to compare at all favorably with England.[47]

But here is a clear case in which appearance seems to have been more important than reality, and in which good public relations served the Capetians and, in turn, Paris so well. The French kings gained prestige as patrons of the schools less by the actual number of scholars they favored than by the visibility of the few appointments they did make. It was, in fact, on the basis of only a few very prudent promotions that the Capetians won their reputation as generous patrons of learning. And perhaps ironically, the very deliberateness of the French kings in bringing masters into the royal administration probably helped their reputations by shielding them from the criticisms the English kings received from scholars who, once employed in their service, failed to advance as quickly or as far as they believed they should. A slow but steady increase in the employment of scholars served the long-term political interests of the Capetians far better. It was also sufficient to keep ambitious young men coming to the French capital in ever-increasing numbers with the hope that their learning might be noticed and rewarded by the king.

As unlikely as our evidence shows the prospects for royal patronage actually to have been, the presence of the king and his court must still be regarded as a powerful magnet that drew many scholars to Paris. Once settled in Paris, however, the scholars seem to have looked to the king less as a potential patron than as a guardian of their privileges. This is especially true after July 1200, when Paris scholars received their first formal grant of privileges from Philip Augustus. But we make a mistake if we assume that this grant was unprecedented. Paris never could have grown into a great center of learning without royal support and approval. There must have been many times before 1200 when the king had interceded to defend the rights, privileges, or immunities of individual scholars who found themselves at odds with the city's other residents or the civil magistrates.

Housing was but one of the causes of tensions and disputes. The presence of thousands of young students, mostly foreigners between the ages of fourteen and twenty, not yet in any formal way supervised by their masters, created a chronic problem of disorder. In the sources of the period, we hear the expected complaints about battles between students of different nationalities, masters' rivalries spilling from the classrooms into the streets, violent attacks on the city's prostitutes, and sports contests turning into brawls.[48] It was in an open area of the Left Bank customarily used by the scholars for recreation—known as the Prato clericorum or the Pré-aux-Clercs—where in 1192 the first recorded town-gown brawl occurred, apparently after some sort of a pickup game in which one scholar was killed and several others injured by serfs of the nearby abbey of St.-Germain-des-Prés.[49] In this case, it was the scholars who were attacked, and, because the perpetrators belonged to a monastery, the matter was adjudicated by Rome, not by the king. But so many cases involving violent attacks by students came to the royal court that we are told that on at least one occasion Philip Augustus gave serious thought to closing down the schools and evicting the troublesome scholars from Paris.[50] "They are hardier and readier for battle than my knights," the king is reputed to have said when he heard of yet another melee involving the city's scholars.[51]

What happened in 1200 was that a relatively minor, probably commonplace dispute flared up into a citywide uproar. Angered by an attempt to overcharge a servant sent to buy some wine, a German student (Henry de Jacea, archdeacon and bishop-elect of Liège) and several of his compatriots wrecked a tavern and severely beat its keeper. In retaliation, the tavernkeeper and his neighbors sought the assistance of the royal provost of Paris, Thomas, who then led a bloody assault on the German hostel in which several students were killed. To the Paris masters it did not matter in the least that the students had initiated the violence or that it was the provost's duty to maintain order in the city. Quick to defend scholarly privileges, the masters suspended all lectures and threatened to leave Paris unless the king provided full redress and punished the royal provost and his accomplices.[52]

Whatever his previous doubts about having so many scholars in Paris, Philip acted swiftly and decisively to satisfy the masters' demands. Although the king did not agree to having the provost whipped *"more scholarium,"* as the masters had proposed, Thomas and his accomplices were to be imprisoned for life. According to the terms of the royal charter, those who had fled before arraignment were to be actively pursued throughout the kingdom and brought back to Paris for trial. Each of them was to be allowed the option of trial by the ordeal of water. If thereby proven guilty, they were to be hanged; if cleared, they were nevertheless to be permanently banished from the realm, unless the scholars were willing to intercede on their behalf.[53] This took care of the immediate issues—and I should add that no mention at all was made of punishing any of the student perpetrators who may have survived the attack.

For the protection of scholars in the future, the charter also stipulated, first, that all the citizens of Paris were thenceforth obligated to report any crimes they saw a layman perpetrate against a scholar, to help to apprehend and arrest the assailant, and to testify about the crime at the royal court.[54] In addition, the royal provost and the city's magistrates were prohibited from laying hands on scholars or on their chattels. Only in the case of the most heinous crime could a scholar be arrested, and even then no force was to be used unless he physically resisted arrest; moreover, he was not to be held in jail but turned over at once to church authorities or to the custody of another scholar.[55] To assure the scholars that these privileges would be recognized, the king ordered the provost and people of Paris to swear publicly to abide by the terms of the charter. Finally, the charter required each succeeding provost to take such an oath before an assembly of scholars no later than the second Sunday after taking office.[56] These provisions must have made it unambiguously clear to the people of Paris that in any future town-gown disputes the king's support would come down firmly on the side of the city's scholars.

Why was the French king so favorably inclined toward scholars and so obviously willing to concede these privileges and immunities to get them to remain in Paris? One at once thinks of the economic impact of having three to four thousand masters and scholars resident in the city, most of them—despite all the complaints we hear of poverty—receiving adequate funds from their families, from church prebends, or even from teaching to pay high rents and to buy food, wine, clothing, and other supplies from the city's merchants and artisans. The schools were an important source of revenue to the citizens of Paris and, in turn, through taxation, to the king. At the same time, against these economic advantages one must weigh the military disadvantages of having so many scholars resident in Paris. Because of both its location and its function as capital, the security of Paris was vital to the defense of the French kingdom. From this point of view, the presence of thousands of scholars, the vast majority of them probably from outside the realm,[57] must have seemed a mixed blessing to the Capetians, especially when they were threatened by invasion, as they so often were. On at least one occasion, Louis VII took the precaution of expelling foreign scholars from Paris.[58] The king can hardly be blamed either, if one recalls that scholars often went about the city armed with weapons which they, as the sons of feudal lords, well knew how to wield.[59]

In support of the idea of the value of learning per se, one would like to be able to argue that the Capetians, of necessity, wanted to keep the brightest young men coming to the Paris schools because of the proven usefulness of their education and skills to government service. But alas, as we have already seen, the French kings were very slow to give university graduates a significant place in the administration of the realm. As useful as the Capetians may have found the skills of the few masters they did employ, they apparently did not yet regard the employment of academics as vital to the public interest. Moreover, even if they had, this would not, in itself, account for why they would have wanted the scholars to remain in Paris. After all, the English kings, who employed many more graduates, recruited quite well without having schools in London.[60]

What, in fact, made the schools of Paris so important to the Capetians was not nearly as much a matter of the practical or professional training they provided as of the prestige they gave to the monarchy. There was, as the French kings found out early on, a great deal of praise to be gained from protecting and patronizing scholars. The learned have always—or, at least, until recently—been important shapers of attitudes toward public authorities.[61] But more was at work in the Capetian court than just good public relations. There was also an underlying ideology of kingship: the idea that the growth of political authority was inextricably linked to the progress of learning. According to the political theorists of the time, the divinely ordained course of history involved the progressive movement of power (the *translatio imperii*) and learning (the *translatio studii*) conjointly from East to West— from Egypt, to Greece, to Rome.[62] The preeminence of the schools in Paris was thus understood as a sign that France had now become the successor to the great world civilizations of the past. It was, we are told by Master Peter the Chanter, because Philip Augustus was convinced that his capital was heir to Athens and Rome that he had decided not to evict the troublesome scholars from Paris.[63] "Neither Athens nor Egypt ever had as many scholars as Paris now does," boasts the royal chronicler William the Breton, writing in 1210, and he especially praises the monarchy for fostering learning by giving the city scholars unusual freedom and special privileges.[64] Aware of the prestige to be gained by supporting scholars, the French kings chose to make Paris, their capital, the new Athens, the greatest center of learning in Europe. Ever cautious and frugal, the Capetians discovered moreover that praise as great patrons of learning could be bought cheaply. It took, as we have seen, no more than a few prudent promotions.[65] Others came up with the funds for the colleges founded under their auspices. Moreover, the privileges and immunities granted to scholars came largely at the expense of other lords and the citizens of Paris.

The scholars, the king, and the citizens—these have been the main characters in my account of Paris so far. To retain this focus, I think it advisable here simply to jump over the important events in the university's history from the granting of the royal charter in 1200 to the Great Dispersion of 1229–30. It was, as I have argued elsewhere, during these years that the four Paris "faculties" (law, medicine, theology, and the arts) joined together, began to act as a single corporation, and first gained papal recognition as the "university of Paris masters and scholars."[66] Depsite the nascent university's well-known troubles with the bishop and chancellor, the relations among scholars, citizens, and the king were, if not completely free of minor conflicts and problems, apparently devoid of any incidents severe enough to jeopardize the security and continued expansion of the schools. At some point during these years, we do know that scholars had gained jurisdiction over the Pré-aux-Clercs (where, you will recall, a scholar had been killed in 1192), apparently to bring an end to the lingering dispute over the meadow between them and the abbey of St.-Germain.[67] And a vicious attack on a woman by a group of armed scholars was probably one of the major precipitants of the bitter dispute between the university and the bishop of 1218–19.[68] Still, however much the rapidly growing student population might have been contributing to the worsening of town-gown tensions, the terrible violence of the events immediately preceding the Great Dispersion seems to have come as quite a shock to all concerned.

It all began, again, with a dispute over the cost of some wine, this time in the bourg St. Marcel, then a small rural village outside the city's wall on the Left Bank. According to the English chronicler Matthew Paris, who probably heard his version from the dispersed masters who settled at Oxford and Cambridge, the scholars got the worst of the fracas on the first day and were forced to flee when the men of the bourg rushed to the tavernkeeper's rescue. But the next day, the scholars returned armed with clubs and swords. First they broke into the tavern and demolished the wine supply, then they wildly ran through the streets of the bourg, attacking anyone they could find, man or woman, and left several people half dead.[69]

Furious about the harm done to his dependents, the prior of St. Marcel complained to the bishop, and together they went to the queen, Blanche of Castille, ruling as regent for her son Louis IX, urging that force be used to quell the disturbance. The queen, acting—according to Matthew Paris, a strong supporter of the schools and obviously also a misogynist—with "female impudence and impetuosity," ordered the city's provost to find and arrest the students responsible.[70] As it was a holiday (Carnival time, 26–27 February 1229), there were, we are told, numerous students out in the country, and the royal provost and his men attacked them indiscriminately. In the resulting melee several students were killed, many more were injured or carried off to jail, and—according to another English chronicler who no doubt was exaggerating—320 scholars were thrown into the Seine.[71]

Outraged by what they regarded as the wanton violation of the privileges guaranteed to scholars by the royal charter of 1200, the masters immediately suspended all lectures and disputations. A month later (27 March 1229) the university drew up a formal protest threatening to leave the city for a minimum of six years unless full redress was made for "the atrocious injuries" suffered by its students at the hands of the provost and his men.[72] When the specified deadline (15 May) passed without any satisfactory response to this protest, the masters, as they had threatened to do, began to leave the city en masse, taking many of their students with them. By the following autumn the Paris *studium* was no more; the university of Paris masters and scholars was now to be found in Angers, Orléans, Reims, and Toulouse, in Oxford and Cambridge, not in Paris.[73]

How could things have reached such an impasse? Matthew Paris is not alone in blaming Blanche of Castille.[74] It is, to be sure, hard to imagine the situation degenerating to this point under Philip Augustus or Louis VII. But as regent for her young son, the queen was in a more vulnerable position. Struggling against continued resistance to northern rule in Languedoc and, in 1229, confronting the imminent threat of an English invasion, she could ill afford to be distracted, and to have the security of the kingdom endangered, by discord or disorder in Paris. Blanche thus had good reason to have acted firmly to quell the disturbance. But although she appears to have resisted making any concessions to the masters and scholars during the critical weeks when they were threatening to leave Paris, she did not wait long, once it was clear that the threat was real, to reissue the royal charter of 1200. This was done, in the name of Louis IX, in August 1229.[75] Still, it took almost two full years to get the university to agree to return to Paris.

It would take far too long to tell of the complicated and difficult negotiations during these years. Suffice it to say that much of the problem had to do with the bad relations between the members of the university, on the one hand, and the bishop[76] and papal legate, on the other. (The legate, Cardinal Romano of Sant'Angelo, plays a prominent role in several accounts of the dispute, including that of Matthew Paris, in which he is accused of being the queen's lover and the father of an illegitimate child by her.[77] But having himself suffered violence at the hands of Paris scholars four years earlier, when under papal orders he had destroyed the university's first seal,[78] he probably had less sensational reasons for supporting Blanche's use of force.) Whatever their previous misunderstandings, the masters must have been surprised (and frightened) when, in a case involving the deaths of several students, neither the bishop nor the legate was willing to defend their clerical privileges and immunities. In turn, the two churchmen, even if they had been hoping for just such an opportunity to gain greater control over the Paris masters, who, in their view, had grown too independent, must have been no less surprised when the university acted with a single will, dispersed its members, and effectively closed down the *studium*.

The dispersion could not have been easy for the masters and scholars. There were few, if any, cities offering all of Paris's amenities, and the era of the wandering scholar was now far behind. But having proven the strength of its corporate will in leaving Paris, the university was prepared to wait until it received firm guarantees of its future security and independence before agreeing to return. The attitudes of the dispersed scholars hardened all the more when, as the months went by, the cities where they settled proved so accommodating. Anxious to attract their share of the dispersed masters and scholars, these cities did everything they could to match or better the amenities of Paris. In the first recorded university advertising campaign, Toulouse commissioned the poet John of Garland to draft the letter quoted earlier. Styling itself as the "second Troy"—recall that Paris was accustomed to calling itself the "second Athens"—Toulouse promised scholars not just plentiful food and cheap wine but also a plenary indulgence (for masters), no restrictions on what could be studied or taught, a courteous and respectful populace, and a prince prepared to guarantee protection of scholars' privileges, property, and immunities, as well as masters who were more committed to their teaching than those in Paris, and, last but not least (as we from California know) a milder climate.[79]

In the end, it took the will and the authority of the pope to get the university reestablished in Paris. The papacy had long favored the development of the Paris *studium,* and Gregory IX was not willing to see the work of his predecessors undone. Paris, the great river of learning which had so long and so richly irrigated the church, could not be allowed to go dry.[80] The needs of all Christendom could not be sacrified to a local squabble. On 13 April 1231 Gregory IX issued his famous bull, *Parens scientiarum,* formalizing the settlement negotiated by representatives of the king, the bishop, and the university during the previous months.[81]

There is no need to discuss the terms found in this bull; they are well known and largely concerned with the authority of the bishop and the chancellor over the university.[82] Much more pertinent to this symposium are several other bulls issued by Gregory IX at the same time, documents as important as *Parens scientiarum* but too often overlooked in accounts of the university's return to Paris. I am referring to the series of letters sent by the pope to the major ecclesiastical (land)lords of Paris—the abbot of St. Germain-des-Prés (13 April), the bishop (24 April), and the dean and chapter of St. Marcel (6 May)—ordering each of them to have the men living under their jurisdiction take the same oath required of the citizens of Paris (*cives Parisienses*) by the royal charter of 1200 that they would respect the rights and immunities of scholars.[83] By the authority of the pope, the provisions of the royal charter, which still (even after the reconfirmation of August 1229) applied only to those citizens directly under the jurisdiction of the king, were thereby extended to the subjects of the city's other important landlords.

Why the members of the university would have made the issuance of these bulls a precondition of their return to Paris should, I hope, be obvious. Physical security is no less vital to a university than academic freedom, a hostile populace no less troublesome than an encroaching bishop (or chancellor). To end the Great Dispersion there had to be a new accommodation between the city and the university, between town and gown. And in 1231 the pope joined the king to guarantee scholars peace and security throughout the city. Only then did the masters agree to return to Paris; only then was it assured that there would be a University of Paris in Paris in the future.

The episode of the Great Dispersion illustrates one of the themes proposed for this symposium: the fragility of the university in relation to its environment. We have seen how scholars could feel insecure and unwelcomed even in the "Paradise of Delights," as Gregory IX calls Paris in one of his 1229 bulls, repeating a play on the city's name (*Parisius-Paradisus*) which had originated with the Goliards, the wandering scholars, who a century earlier had found Paris so accommodating for their studies and had started the trend to the city's schools.[84] In tracing Paris's development into a major political, economic, and educational center, I have also touched upon several other important themes and issues. Many of these will be taken up again and discussed at greater length in subsequent essays. But before we move from Paris to Florence and from the Middle Ages to the Renaissance, I feel obliged to comment, if only very briefly, on some of these other aspects of the relationship between the university and the city.

My first point has to do with the political role and influence of the university. Here, as far as the period I have been talking about, simply let me say that I find myself in essential agreement with what Hastings Rashdall wrote a century ago, that "the university [of Paris] was too cosmopolitan to concern itself much with French politics."[85] That Paris was the capital of the French kingdom mattered little to the largely foreign population of masters and students of the twelfth and early thirteenth centuries whose allegiances and ambitions were focused elsewhere.

My other points have to do with the more general impact of the city on the university. First, it should be obvious enough that, if not for the concurrent economic development of Paris, the rapidly growing population of masters and students could never have been sustained. But beyond providing the material conditions for the rise of the university, the city's commercial expansion also created a new intellectual environment. With the concentration of greater numbers of masters and students in one place, competition increased and the methods of teaching changed. The city's busy streets and squares were the natural arenas for public debate and disputation. Those often-cited critics of the urban schools, such as Rupert of Deutz, Peter of Celle, Bernard of Clairvaux, and Stephen of Tournai, were not far from the truth when they blamed the city for giving rise to contentious disputations and accused Paris masters of having become "merchants of words."[86] The move from the seclusion and relative calm of the cloister to the hustle and bustle of the city fundamentally transformed the methods and the means of education.

The urban environment had no less of an impact on what was studied. It has often been noted that in the decades when the university was being formed, the scholarship of the Paris masters, especially the theologians, became less speculative and creative, more practical and routine, than before. This intellectual change has usually, and I think rightly, been attributed to the needs of the growing numbers of students who came to the schools seeking training for careers that would be spent in the administrative ranks of the church or secular rulers. But as another factor in accounting for changes in scholarship in teaching, we should not discount the masters' own concerns with what they saw going on in the city around them. On this point a reference to the title of John Baldwin's important book on the social views of late-twelfth-century Paris theologians will have to suffice; *Masters, Princes and Merchants* clearly shows how active and practical an interest these masters took in each of the three primary aspects of the city's development: education, government, and commerce.[87] Committed to applying their learning to social action and reform and drawing upon their observations of what was happening in and around the city, these Paris masters, as Baldwin so clearly demonstrates, helped to define the moral theology and canon law of the medieval church on such matters as usury, the conduct of war, and the morality of capital punishment.

The urban surroundings also helped the masters to define their own professional identity. It was in the city, by living and working independently and in close quarters with merchants and artisans, that scholars for the first time came to think of teaching as a business (*negotium*), as a way to make a living.[88] The idea of enriching or even supporting oneself by teaching was, however, at odds with the ancient ideal that knowledge was a spiritual gift which ought not to be sold. "Sell neither wisdom, instruction, nor understanding," says Solomon in Proverbs 23:23, a line cited over and over again in the formative years of the university.[89] That the masters of the time struggled but never succeeded in resolving this tension is part of the problematic heritage of the institution they formed. We, their successors, the members of modern universities, struggle with the same problem of balancing certain ideals of academic freedom and economic disinterest against the realities of life in the cities where we teach and conduct our research.

NOTES

1. The *locus classicus* of this idea is the description of Paris found in a letter of Gui of Bazoches dating from 1175–90. It can be found in H. Denifle and E. Chatelain, eds., *Chartularium universitatis Parisiensis*, 4 vols. (Paris, 1889–97), I, intro. no. 54, pp. 55–56. Hereafter abbreviated as *CUP*.

2. See n. 13.

3. On these migrations, see H. Rashdall, *The Universities of Europe in the Middle Ages*, rev. ed. by F. M. Powicke and A. B. Emden, 3 vols. (Oxford, 1936), I, 168–73 (Bologna); II, 11–13, 26–27 (Padua); III, 33–34 (Oxford).

4. On this legislation and the use of oaths to prevent migrations, see Ibid., pp. 168–71; and P. Kibre, *Scholarly Privileges in the Middle Ages* (Cambridge, Mass., 1962), pp. 18–19. In the cases of Oxford and Cambridge, it was the universities rather than the civic authorities which imposed such oaths on their faculty. From about 1260 Oxford masters were required to swear at the time of their inception not to teach "elsewhere in England than here or at Cambridge" (*Statuta antiqua universitatis oxoniensis*, ed. Strickland Gibson [Oxford, 1931], p. 19). An identical oath was imposed on Cambridge masters a few years later (ca. 1265). See M. B. Hackett, *The Original Statues of Cambridge University* (Cambridge, 1970), p. 312.

5. Rashdall, *Universities* I, 171 n. 7.

6. Ibid., pp. 172–73. On the impact of buildings in stabilizing the medieval university, see the remarks of Jacques Verger, *Les Universités au moyen âge* (Paris, 1973), pp. 181–82.

7. See Rashdall, *Universities*, I, 310–11. See also S. C. Ferruolo, "Philip the Chancellor and the University of Paris," in *Southern Festschrift*, ed. G. F. Lytle (forthcoming).

8. See later discussions in this essay.

9. The 1321 migration from Bologna, for example, came about after the execution of a scholar who had been caught trying to abduct a citizen's daughter. See Rashdall, *Universities*, I, 172.

10. S. C. Ferruolo, " 'Quid dant artes nisi luctum': Learning, Ambition and Careers in the Medieval University," *History of Education Quarterly* 28 (Spring 1988), 1–22, esp. n. 11, p. 6.

11. See P. Michaud-Quantin, *Universitas: Expressions du mouvement communautaire dans le moyen-âge latin* (Paris, 1970).

12. On the development of the university in Paris, see S. C. Ferruolo, *The Origins of the University: The Schools of Paris and Their Critics, 1100–1215* (Stanford, Calif., 1985), pp. 279–309. Cf. G. Post, "Paris Masters as a Corporation, 1200–1246," *Speculum* 9 (1934): 421–45.

13. The most thorough analysis of the divergent meanings of the term *studium generale* is G. Ermini, "Concetto di *studium generale*," *Archivio giuridico* 127 (1942): 3–24. Also helpful are the discussions found in Rashdall, *Universities*, I. 16–17; and A. C. Cobban, *The Medieval Universities: Their Development and Organization* (London, 1975), pp. 23–36.

14. On the city of Paris during this period, see J. Boussard, *Nouvelle histoire de Paris*. Vol. 2: *De la fin du siège de 885–886 à la mort de Philippe Auguste* (Paris, 1976); see also L. Halphen, *Paris sous les premiers Capétiens (987–1223)* (Paris, 1909). On the development of the Right Bank as the commercial center of the city, see A. Lombard-Jourdan, *Paris: Genèse de la "Ville": La Rive droite de la Seine des origines à 1223* (Paris, 1973).

15. Cf. R.-H. Bautier, "Quand et comment Paris devint capitale," *Bulletin de la Société de l'histoire de Paris et de l'Ile de France* 105 (1978): 17–46.

16. See R. Fawtier, *The Capetian Kings of France*, trans. L. Butler and R. J. Adam (London, 1960), pp. 185–87; F. Lot and R. Fawtier, *Histoire des institutions françaises au moyen âge*. Vol. 2: *Institutions royales* (Paris, 1962), pp. 133–252; and esp. E. Bournazel, *Le Gouvernement capétien au XIIe siècle, 1108–1180* (Limoges, 1975), pp. 18–27, 157–78.

17. W. M. Newman, *La Domaine royal sous les premiers Capétiens* (Paris, 1937), pp. 98–99.

18. It may have also mattered to the early Capetians—who were often more ardent hunters than defenders of their realm—that Paris was at the center of one of the greatest forested areas remaining in northern France. See Fawtier, *The Capetian Kings*, p. 187.

19. On Philip, see Boussard, *Nouvelle histoire de Paris*, II, 99–108.

20. See Boussard, *Nouvelle histoire de Paris*, II, 102–8.

21. See E. Lesne, *Histoire de la propriété ecclésiastique en France*. Vol. 5: *Les Ecoles de la fin du VIIIe siècle à la fin du XIIe siècle* (Lille, 1940).

22. See R. W. Southern, "The Schools of Paris and the School of Chartres," in R. L. Benson and G. Constable, eds., *Renaissance and Renewal in the Twelfth Century* (Cambridge, Mass., 1982), pp. 113–37; see also Ferruolo, *The Origins of the University*, pp. 11–25.

23. Southern ("The Schools of Paris," p. 119) estimates that there were at least twenty-five well-known schools within one hundred miles of Paris in the twelfth century.

24. In 1107 Pope Paschal II confirmed the privileges of the abbey. See *Cartulaire générale de Paris, 528–1180*, ed. R. de Lasteyrie (Paris, 1887), p. 160.

25. On the *licentia docendi*, see G. Post, "Alexander III, the *Licentia docendi*, and the Rise of the University," in C. H. Taylor, ed., *Anniversary Essays in Medieval History by the Students of Charles Homer Haskins* (Boston, 1920), pp. 255–77; see also P. Delhaye, "L'Organisation scolaire au XIIe siècle," *Traditio* 5 (1947): 253–60.

26. Paris masters quickly found ways of getting around the ancient proscription of profiting from teaching. On the principle that "Knowledge is a gift from

God and cannot be sold," see G. Post, K. Giocarinis, and R. Kay, "The Medieval Heritage of a Humanistic Ideal: 'Scientia donum dei est, unde vendi non potest,' " *Traditio* 11 (1955): 195–234. On the practice and justifications of charging fees for teaching, see G. Post, "Masters' Salaries and Student Fees in the Middle Ages," *Speculum* 7 (1932): 181–98; see also J. W. Baldwin, *Masters, Princes and Merchants: The Social Views of Peter the Chanter and His Circle,* 2 vols. (Princeton, N.J., 1970), I, 117–30. On the idea of teaching as a *negotium,* see n. 88.

27. *Cartulaire de l'église Notre-Dame de Paris,* ed. B. Guérard, 4 vols. (Paris, 1850), I, 339. See A. Gabriel, "The Cathedral Schools of Notre-Dame and the Beginning of the University of Paris," in *Garlandia: Studies in the History of the Mediaeval University* (Frankfurt, 1969), pp. 42–44.

28. *CUP,* I, intro. no. 55, p. 56.

29. *CUP,* I, intro. no. 19, pp. 17–18.

30 "Tanta est ibi studiorum copia quod summa difficultate possunt reperiri hospitia." A. Hofmeister, "Studien über Otto von Freising, I," *Neues Archiv der Gesellschaft für ältere deutsche Geschichtskunde* 37 (1912) : 125, n. 3.

31. F. M. Powicke, *Stephen Langton* (Oxford, 1928), p. 44.

32. *Historia Occidentalis,* ed. J. Hinnebusch (Fribourg, 1972), p. 91.

33. *CUP,* I, no. 20, p. 79. On this legislation, see S. C. Ferruolo, "The Paris Statutes of 1215 Reconsidered," *History of Universities* 5 (1986): 1–14.

34. Kibre, *Scholarly Privileges,* pp. 90–98.

35. See R. Cazelles, *Nouvelle histoire de Paris.* Vol. 3: *De la fin du règne de Philippe Auguste à la mort de Charles V (1223–1380)* (Paris, 1972), pp. 374–91. In his previously cited letter of 1164 (see n. 29), John of Salisbury contrasts the "abundance of provisions" with the shortage of housing. Cf. the description of Gui of Bazoches in *CUP,* I, intro. no. 54, pp. 55–56.

36. *CUP,* I, no. 72, p. 131.

37. Southern, "The Schools of Paris," p. 119.

38. On these developments, see Boussard, *Nouvelle histoire de Paris,* II, 169–70, 299–302; see also Lombard-Jourdan, *Paris: Genèse de la "Ville,"* pp. 59–121.

39. On this *hanse* and its privileges, see Boussard, *Nouvelle histoire de Paris,* II, 161–62, 302–5. Cf. Cazelles, *Nouvelle histoire de Paris,* III, 197–201.

40. Halphen, *Paris sous les premiers Capétiens,* pp. 27–50; Boussard, *Nouvelle histoire de Paris,* II, 319–27. These walls, according to Boussard (p. 327), made Paris "la plus grande place forte du royaume." On the building of the walls and Philip II's other contributions to the development of Paris, see Boussard, "Philippe Auguste et Paris," in *La France de Philippe Auguste: Le Temps des mutations,* ed. R. H. Bautier, Actes du colloque international organisé par le Centre National de la Recherche Scientifique, no. 602 (Paris, 1982), pp. 323–40, esp. p. 330; see also J. W. Baldwin, *Government of Philip Augustus: Foundations of French Royal Power in the Middle Ages* (Berkeley and Los Angeles, 1986), pp. 342–51.

41. L. Halphen, "Les Origines de l'Université de Paris," in L. Halphen et al., eds., *Aspects de l'Université de Paris* (Paris, 1949), p. 20; see also J. W. Baldwin, "Masters at Paris, 1179–1215," in Benson and Constable, eds., *Renaissance and Renewal,* pp. 140–41.

42. Lombard-Jourdan, *Paris: Genèse de la "Ville,"* pp. 52–53; Southern, "The Schools of Paris," p. 119.

43. Southern, "The Schools of Paris," p. 128, n. 44.

44. Boussard, *Nouvelle histoire de Paris,* II, 318–19.

45. *CUP*, I, intro. nos. 14, 18, 50, pp. 11, 15–16, 49–50, respectively. On these foundations, see Rashdall, *Universities*, I, 501–3; see also Baldwin, "Masters at Paris," p. 141.

46. Walter Map, *De nugis curialium 5.5*, trans. M. R. James (London, 1923), p. 248.

47. J. W. Baldwin, *"Studium et regnum:* The Penetration of University Personnel into French and English Administration at the Turn of the Twelfth and Thirteenth Centuries," *Revue des études islamiques* 44 (1976): 199–215. See also Baldwin, "Masters at Paris," pp. 151–58.

48. Ferruolo, *The Origins of the University*, pp. 260–65.

49. *CUP*, I, intro. no. 47, p. 47. On this meadow and the conflicts over it, see Halphen, *Paris sous les premiers Capétiens*, pp. 103–4; Boussard, *Nouvelle histoire de Paris*, II, 183; and Kibre, *Scholarly Privileges*, pp. 241–43.

50. This is intimated in a remark in a biblical commentary by Peter the Chanter, cited by Baldwin, *Masters, Princes and Merchants*, II, 51, n. 55.

51. A. Luchaire, *Social France at the Time of Philip Augustus*, trans. E. B. Krehbiel (New York, 1967), p. 83.

52. Roger of Hoveden, *Chronica*, ed. W. Stubbs, Rolls Series 51, 4 vols. (London, 1868–71), IV, 120–21.

53. *CUP*, I, no. 1, pp. 59–61. According to Roger of Hoveden (see n. 52), the provost spent a long time in the royal prison and ultimately lost his life while scaling the prison wall in a failed effort at escape. We have no evidence of how many other citizens were punished for their involvement in the riot.

54. *CUP*, I, no. 1, pp. 59–60. This provision recognized the scholars' *privilegium canonis*, the canonical privilege protecting a cleric from bodily harm. See Kibre, *Scholarly Privileges*, pp. 7–8, 85–87.

55. *CUP*, I, no. 1, p. 60. This was the *privilegium fori*, or "benefit of clergy." See, in addition to Kibre (n. 53), Baldwin, *Masters, Princes and Merchants*, I, 145–49; see also R. Genestal, *Le Privilegium fori en France du décret de Gratien à la fin du XIVᵉ siècle*, 2 vols. (Paris, 1921–24).

In 1210, Philip issued a new decree on clerical privileges stipulating the specific crimes justifying the arrest of clerics; these included homicide; adultery; rape; assault and battery with sticks, stones, or pointed weapons; and housebreaking. *CUP*, I, no. 13, pp. 72–73.

56. *CUP*, I, no. 1, p. 60. This oath (in French), as taken by the provost in 1230, can be found in *CUP*, I, no. 67, pp. 122–23.

57. On the number of foreign scholars in Paris, see A. Gabriel, "English Masters and Students in Paris during the Twelfth Century," in *Garlandia*, pp. 1–37. As evidence of the especially large number of foreign masters in the late twelfth century, Gabriel (p. 5) cites a remark of the court poet, Master Gilles of Paris, referring to the dominance of learning in the city by foreigners. For some numerical data corroborating this anecdotal evidence, see Baldwin, "Masters at Paris," pp. 149–51; and Ferruolo, "Learning, Ambition, and Careers," pp. 10–13. On the conflicts and disputes that broke out among the various nationalities in Paris, there is the well-known account found in Jacques de Vitry's *Historia Occidentalis*, ed. by J. F. Hinnebusch (Fribourg, 1972), p. 92. On the variety of nationalities in Paris, see the remark found in a commentary of Stephen Langton, cited by G. Lacombe and B. Smalley in "Studies on the Commentaries of Cardinal Stephen Langton," *Archives d'histoire doctrinale et littéraire du moyen âge* 5 (1930): 164.

58. Our only evidence of this action is from a letter of John of Salisbury, which can be found in *CUP*, I, intro. no. 20, p. 21.

59. Among the reasons Bishop Peter of Nemours gives for excommunicating members of the university in 1218 is the failure of the masters to curb the violence of armed bands of students who roamed the streets of the city every night. See *CUP*, I, no. 30, p. 88. For other complaints about the injuries done by armed scholars, see Ferruolo, "Philip the Chancellor," forthcoming.

60. Cf. J. Verger, "A propos de la naissance de l'université de Paris: Contexte social, enjeu politique, portée intellectuelle," in *Schulen und Studium im sozialen Wandel des hohen und späten Mittelalters*, ed. J. Fried (Sigmaringen, 1986), p. 89.

61. See S. d'Irsay, "L'Opinion publique dans les universités médiévales: Etude sur l'activité politique de l'Université de Paris à ses débuts," *Revue des études historiques* 99 (1932): 237–56; see also J. LeGoff, "The Universities and Public Authorities in the Middle Ages," in *Time, Work and Culture in the Middle Ages*, trans. A. Goldhammer (Chicago, 1980), pp. 135–49.

62. On the idea of the *translatio studii*, see Baldwin, *Masters, Princes and Merchants*, I, 72–73; see also A. G. Jongkees, "*Translatio Studii:* Les Avatars d'un thème médiéval," in *Miscellanea mediaevalia in memoriam Jan Frederik Niermeyer* (Groningen, 1967), pp. 41–51. On its association with the political ideology of the period, see W. Goez, *Translatio Imperii: Ein Beitrag zur Geschichte des Geschichtsdenkens und der politischen Theorien im Mittelalter und in der frühen Neuzeit* (Tübingen, 1958), pp. 104–37.

63. See n. 50.

64. *Historia de vita et gestis Philippi Augusti*, ed. H. F. Delaborde, *Oeuvres de Rigord et de Guillaume le Bréton*, 2 vols. (Paris, 1882–85), I, 230. As the royal chronicler also points out (pp. 296–97), the grateful scholars showed their appreciation to Philip by turning out en masse to greet the king after his great victory at Bouvines in 1214.

65. Notable among them was Louis VII's appointment of John of Salisbury, the esteemed humanist (and supporter of Thomas Becket) to the bishopric of Chartres in 1176.

66. On these developments, see Ferruolo, *The Origins of the University*, pp. 279–308. The term *facultas*, meaning an academic discipline, appears for the first time in papal bulls issued in 1219 (*CUP*, I, nos. 29, 31, pp. 87, 89, respectively). It was not until 1255 that the term was actually used to refer to an association of masters in one discipline (*CUP*, I, no. 246, pp. 277–79). On this term, see *CUP* I, intro., p. x.

67. The university's rights over the meadow were reconfirmed by the statutes promulgated by Cardinal Robert of Courson in 1215 (*CUP*, I, no. 20, p. 79). There is no evidence indicating when the original grant had taken place.

68. See Ferruolo, "Philip the Chancellor," forthcoming.

69. Matthew Paris, *Chronica majora*, ed. H. R. Luard, Rolls Series 57 (London, 1872–84), III, 166–67; Rashdall, *Universities* I, 334–39.

70. *Chronica majora*, III, 167.

71. Ralph of Coggeshall, *Chronicon Anglicanum*, ed. J. Stevenson, Rolls Series 66 (London, 1875), p. 192.

72. *CUP*, I, no. 62, p. 118.

73. Rashdall, *Universities*, I, 336–37.

74. See E. Berger, *Histoire de Blanche de Castille, Reine de France* (Paris, 1895), pp. 134–36.

75. *CUP,* I, no. 66, pp. 120–22.

76. Master William of Auvergne, who had become bishop of Paris in 1228. On his difficult relations with the university, see N. Valois, *Guillaume d'Auvergne, Evêque de Paris (1228–1249)* (Paris, 1880; rpt. 1964), pp. 47–64.

77. *Chronica majora,* III, 168–69.

78. *CUP,* I, no. 45, p. 104, n. 3.

79. *CUP,* I, no. 72, pp. 129–31. Cf. the invitation extended to Paris masters and scholars by Henry III of England (*CUP,* I, no. 64, p. 119).

80. See the pope's strongly worded bull to William of Auvergne (*CUP,* I, no. 69, pp. 125–27). Cf. *CUP,* I, nos. 70, 71, 75, pp. 127–29, 133–34, respectively.

81. *CUP,* I, no. 79, pp. 136–39. These neogtiations had been scheduled to begin the previous August See *CUP,* I, no. 75, pp. 133–34.

82. See Rashdall, *Universities,* I, 338–39; and Kibre, *Scholarly Privileges,* pp. 94–95. Cf. Ferruolo, "Philip the Chancellor," forthcoming.

83. *CUP,* I, nos. 81, 88, 92, pp. 139–40, 144, 146, respectively. A second set of bulls was apparently also sent to both the abbot of St. Germain-des-Prés and the bishop of Paris on 6 May; see *CUP,* I, nos. 93–94, p. 147. Innocent IV had the abbots of both St. Geneviève and St. Germain renew these oaths in 1246; see *CUP,* I, 159–60, pp. 191–92.

84. *CUP,* I, no. 70, p. 127. See J. LeGoff, *Les Intellectuels au moyen âge* (Paris, 1960), pp. 29–31.

85. Rashdall, *Universities,* I, 540–41.

86. See LeGoff, *Les Intellectuels,* pp. 67–68; and Ferruolo, *The Origins of the University,* pp. 25–26, 47–49, 269–77.

87. For the full citation, see n. 26.

88. LeGoff, *Les Intellectuels,* pp. 104–8; L. Boehm, "Die *negotio scholaris:* Zur Entstehung von Berufsbewusstsein und Rechtsstand des Universitäts-gelehrten im Mittelalter," in K. Schnith, ed., *Festiva Lanx: Johannes Spörl Festgabe* (Munich, 1966), pp. 29–52.

89. Post et al., "Medieval Heritage of a Humanistic Ideal," pp. 197–210; Baldwin, *Masters, Princes and Merchants,* I, 124–29.

II

EARLY MODERN
REVITALIZATION

4

Renaissance Florence: Who Needs a University?

Gene Brucker

Like their counterparts across the Alps, Italian universities in the Middle Ages and the Renaissance were very unstable institutions. Even the most renowned, and the most durable, at Bologna and Padua, experienced periods of closure, of migrations of teachers and students, during times of plague and civic unrest. A poignant letter from the 1390s has survived from a law student at Bologna, who was about to take his doctoral examination, and indeed had been assured by his professors that he would pass with distinction, when an outbreak of the plague forced the authorities to suspend all university activities.[1] But these disruptions of academic routines did not affect the educational process as seriously as would be the case today. Professors and students moved easily and frequently from one university to another, since the instructional program was based, in every discipline, on the same texts, upon which the professors expounded and which the students absorbed. One must remember, too, the small size of these schools, comprising usually no more than twenty or thirty professors and sometimes fewer, and only a few hundred students. This modest scale and the austerity of the school's administrative structure resulted in very low overhead. Decisions about a university's operation—opening or closing, expanding or contracting—could be made expeditiously by the officials responsible for these academic enterprises.

The history of Florence's university is no exception to these generalizations; its existence was always uncertain and problematical.[2] A *studium generale* was first established by the republic in 1321; it foundered soon afterward and was resurrected in 1348 in the aftermath of the Black Death. From the mid-fourteenth to the mid-fifteenth century the university survived fitfully, alternating between phases of prosperity and vitality, and periods of decline, stagnation and, occasionally, closure. Between 1371 and 1379 the teaching faculty consisted of only two professors of medicine; from 1379 to 1385 the school was completely shut down, as it was again from 1407 until 1413.[3] The university functioned but certainly did not flourish in the years

47

subsequent to 1413. In 1429 the civic officials in charge of the university candidly admitted that the school was an inferior institution. "It grieves us sorely," they reported, "that this glorious republic, which has surpassed the rest of Italy and earlier centuries in beauty and splendor, should be surpassed, in this one respect, by some of our neighboring cities, which in every other way are inferior to us."[4]

This candid and accurate evaluation of the Florentine Studio did not result in a revival of its fortunes. Under the Medici regime established in 1434, the university limped along, skimpily financed and poorly attended. Finally, in 1473, under the aegis of Lorenzo the Magnificent, the Studio was transferred to Pisa, where it enjoyed two decades of high academic distinction, rivaling the universities of Bologna and Padua. But in 1494, prompted by the French invasion, the city of Pisa rebelled against Florence, and the university was transferred to Pistoia, then to Prato, and finally back to Florence in 1496. It survived there for seven years, before it was suppressed in 1503. After the restoration of the Medici in 1512, the university was again reopened in Pisa (1515), where it remained, though with sporadic "vacations," throughout the period of the Medicean grand duchy.[5]

The vicissitudes of the Florentine Studio emphasize the instability and fragility of the institution and raise some obvious questions. Why were the citizens of Florence unwilling to provide more support for their university? Why did they acquiesce in its transfer to the city of Pisa in 1473? Can the failure of the university be attributed primarily to a lack of financial support, and so linked to the priorities of its political leadership; or was the problem linked to the university's ambiguous role in Florence's cultural life?

Before exploring these issues further, I shall provide some background on the distinctive character of Italian universities, which set them apart from the schools on the other side of the Alps. Perhaps their most unique feature was their predominantly lay quality, both in personnel (faculty and students) and in administrative structures. Except for the theologians, who were largely recruited from the mendicant orders, and a few canon lawyers, the majority of Italian university professors were laymen. So, too, were most students; in Pisa in the late fifteenth century, only 211 of 1,296 *matricolati,* or 16 percent, were in clerical orders.[6] With the sole exception of the *Studium urbis* in Rome, which was essentially under papal control (though technically administered by a municipal magistracy), Italian universities were controlled by secular governments, either communal or signorial. The Roman papacy exercised very little influence over these institutions as did the local bishops or clergy, except marginally in the faculties of theology. It is true that doctoral degrees were conferred on candidates by episcopal authority,[7] but the examinations that preceded the award of the doctorate were conducted either by committees of university professors or by representatives from colleges of lawyers and physicians. The selection of professors, their stipends, and the organization of the curriculum were the responsibilities of civic officials, such as the Florentine *Ufficiali dello Studio.* It was not uncommon in Florence for the city's supreme executive, the Signoria, to overrule its own officials and either cancel a professorial appointment or hire a scholar on its own authority, as, for example, it did in 1373 when it selected Boccaccio to lecture on Dante's *Divine Comedy;* and in 1396, when it appointed Manuel Chrysoloras to provide instruction in Greek.

Italian universities cannot properly be studied in isolation, for they were parts of a complex and interrelated network. In Tuscany and its contiguous regions, that network was exceptionally dense, with universities located in Florence, Bologna, Ferrara, Siena, Perugia, and Arezzo, and more distantly in Pavia, Padua, and Rome. In moving from one school to another, professors were constantly seeking higher salaries, greater prestige, and a more congenial intellectual environment. Students were as mobile as their instructors. The more serious sought out the most distinguished scholars in their discipline, while others, less highly motivated, sought diversion and a minimum of academic obligations. In his autobiography the lawyer and historian Francesco Guicciardini described his academic peregrinations in Italian universities. He began the study of civil law in Florence in 1498; three years later his father sent him to Ferrara. But Francesco found the legal instruction there to be of low quality, and in 1502 he transferred to Padua, where he studied under Filippo Decio, whose lectures he had attended four years before in Florence. Francesco did not take his doctoral degree in Padua but instead in his native city, in the cloisters of San Lorenzo, where the Studio was then located.[8]

As Guicciardini's academic career demonstrates, Florentine students could obtain a solid university education away from home. The city did not need to subsidize a *studio* to train its young men for professional careers. This fact undoubtedly explains the unwillingness of many citizens to support a local university. But the issue was not simply a matter of convenience or utility, although pragmatic Florentines never lost sight of that dimension. Considerations of honor (*onore*) were also involved; no one challenged the truism that a distinguished university, and the scholars who comprised its faculty, redounded to a city's fame and reputation. In their deliberations on the value and importance of a municipal university, citizens considered both *utile* and *onore* and sought to balance those interests. In January 1460 the Florentine Signoria convened a group of citizens to give advice on the proposal to transfer the Florentine Studio to the subject city of Pisa, which was then in desperate need of a stimulus for its stagnant economy. The proposal was controversial, and the debate over its merits touched on fundamental issues of the university's role in an urban society.[9]

The speakers in this debate who opposed the Studio's transfer to Pisa used traditional and conservative arguments to support their position. Since universities contributed both to a city's cultural life and to its economy, the Studio should remain in Florence and not be moved to a subject city whose residents remained bitterly hostile to Florentine rule. Why benefit that nest of vipers; why contribute to the prosperity and reputation of a rival community? If, moreover, the Studio were shifted to Pisa, foreign students could matriculate there, not to study but to foment discord and rebellion. To this

political and economic analysis the defenders of the status quo added a pedagogical argument: adolescent students should remain at home, under the
watchful eyes of parents and relatives, rather than be exposed to the temptations that would inevitably corrupt them if they lived in a foreign community.

Most easily refuted by those who favored the school's transfer to Pisa
was the claim that the Studio would harbor political enemies of the republic
and thus constitute a threat to state security. They noted that the universities
of Pavia and Padua were located in subject cities of the dukes of Milan and
the republic of Venice, respectively, and neither school had ever been the focus
of political unrest. The advocates of the Studio's transfer also challenged the
view that university students who stayed at home studied harder and lived in a
better moral environment than did those who went abroad. They echoed the
opinion of Francesco Guicciardini's father, who (his son reported) "judged
that I would dedicate myself more fervently to my studies if I left home."[10]
Florence was a rich and worldly city, filled with traps and snares for adoles-
cents who, so one speaker asserted, "become inert and addicted to vice."
Florence was wealthy enough to support a university, but (the lawyer Otto
Niccolini argued) its citizens were so committed to making money that they
devoted neither time nor energy to the liberal arts. This lack of dedication
was the reason for the failure of the city's university to achieve distinction.
Scholars require solitude and an absence of distractions, Niccolini insisted;
Pisa but not Florence could provide those requirements.

The claim that Florentines, preoccupied with business and profit, had no
interest in learning cannot be accepted without qualification. But that such
statements could be made and believed suggests that the city's commitment to
culture was not total and that for every Niccolò Niccoli, and his passion for
antiquity, or a Giovanni Morelli, who advised his sons to read the classics
daily, there was an Andrea de' Pazzi, "who thought learning to be of little
value and had no desire that his son should spent time over it."[11] The city's
material contribution to its university was invariably modest and often niggardly. The yearly subsidy for the Studio in the early fifteenth century varied
between one thousand and three thousand florins, less than one-half of one
percent of the total state budget.[12] Significantly more civic money was spent
on the building of the cathedral or on subsidies to religious foundations, while
in the private sector Florentines invested far more on building and decorating
their palaces and on funerals and endowments for masses than for educational
purposes. Only one major bequest by a Florentine citizen to support the
university was made in these years: the banker Niccolò da Uzzano left the
bulk of his fortune to build a college for fifty poor scholars. For reasons that
have not been clarified, the Medici succeeded in obstructing the completion
of this project, so that sixty years after its beginning it was still incomplete.[13]
And while the neighboring towns of Prato and Pistoia provided university
fellowships for their native sons,[14] Florentines in their wills preferred to fund
dowries for indigent girls rather than stipends for poor students.

Though the university did not rank high in the catalogue of civic priorities, it did play a substantial role in the city's cultural life. To evaluate that

contribution, however, is no simple matter, since the Studio did not enjoy a monopoly in Florentine higher education. Schools of all kinds, at all levels, abounded in the city, from the basic instruction in the Tuscan *volgare* and in Latin to schools of business arithmetic, to the clerical schools in the cathedral and San Lorenzo, to the *studia* in the city's major convents: Santa Maria Novella, Santa Croce, Santo Spirito, Santa Maria del Carmine. Basic and advanced instruction in the humanities was provided by tutors in the households of the wealthy, and in those private homes men gathered around such luminaries as Coluccio Salutati, Niccolò Niccoli, and Leonardo Bruni (to mention only the most famous), none of whom had any formal connection with the Studio. Intellectual resources for autodidacts were also available, as the career of Leonardo da Vinci demonstrates.

The historiography of the Italian Renaissance has traditionally emphasized the *studia humanitatis* as the most important and creative element in that culture, eclipsing the scholastic tradition of the medieval period. Burckhardt's classic work reinforced and popularized that judgment, which today remains the standard interpretation enshrined in textbooks and popular works on the Renaissance. Paul Oskar Kristeller has long sought to correct this myopic view by stressing the importance and vitality of Aristotelian philosophy in Italian universities, as well as the survival of the scholastic method of instruction.[15] But lost in this dispute over primacy and priority is the fact that law was the unchallenged queen of academic disciplines in Italy—more important, more prestigious than either Aristotelian philosophy or Ciceronian rhetoric. The jurist Bartolus once said that lawyers were as important to the state as soldiers, and (he would surely have added) as poets and rhetoricians.[16] Humanists, philosophers, and theologians might have challenged that claim, but the evidence for the primacy of civil and canon law is overwhelming. At the Studium *urbis* in Rome, for example, the faculty in 1514 consisted of thirty-one professors of law, eighteen of rhetoric, thirteen of philosophy, four of theology, two of mathematics, and one each of astrology and botany.[17] Law professors invariably commanded the highest salaries; they led university processions, and they sat on higher benches in academic assemblies than did their colleagues in other disciplines.

In his pioneering work, *Lawyers and Statecraft in Renaissance Florence,* Lauro Martines wrote: "The pre-eminence of lawyers in the political life of the Republic was largely a function of the exalted state of legal science and of the type of oligarchy Florence was."[18] Lawyers were found in every segment of the political system. They filled all civic offices. They regularly gave advice and counsel to the city's chief executive officials. Every important diplomatic mission included one lawyer. They were constantly asked to provide legal opinions in jurisdictional disputes and to be involved in litigation concerning the state. The guild of lawyers and notaries was accorded the highest rank among the city's professional corporations. In public ceremonies and wedding processions, lawyers were placed just after knights and ahead of representatives from the other orders of society. The pervasive hostility to lawyers, so common among intellectuals—for example, Rabelais—in trans-alpine Europe, found few echoes in Florence, or indeed anywhere in Italy in these centuries.

While the major role of lawyers in Florence's political world has been well established, the influence of legal science on the city's cultural life has received less attention. Italian legal historians have concentrated so intensely on their texts that they have neglected to study the relationship between law and culture. As Julius Kirshner has remarked, the period "has not yet attracted its Paul Oskar Kristeller to excavate its textual treasures, nor its Heiko Oberman to transform the metaphor of decadence into a harvest."[19] Kirshner himself, and his student Thomas Kuehn, have made some promising forays,[20] but the field and its unpublished sources are so vast that it will require a monumental effort to bring our understanding of law and culture into some rough equivalence with that of humanism. Given the skimpy state of our knowledge in this area, only some cautious and tentative suggestions can be made, and in formulating these notions I must acknowledge my debt to my colleague William Bouwsma and the views expressed in his seminal article, "Lawyers and Early Modern Culture."[21] A significant number of Florentine lawyers were active scholars and teachers, holding professorships in the Studio and writing treatises and *consilia,* most of which remain unpublished and unstudied. Some of these legal scholars were also students of antiquity and thus linked to the humanists by a community of scholarly interest. They were also continuously involved with the practical aspects of life; to quote Bouwsma, "not only incidentally and occasionally, like the majority of men, but in the most concentrated form imaginable, at every moment of their working lives."[22] Thus, they were constantly forced to confront the gap between ideal and reality, and the relationship between the general and the specific. Their academic background and their professional activity fostered a spirit of pragmatism and practicality, and also of secularism. Their intellectual orientation and temperament are illustrated very well by an aphorism penned by Francesco Guicciardini:

> Common men find the variety of opinions that exists among lawyers quite reprehensible, without realizing that it proceeds not from any defects in the men but from the nature of the subject. General rules cannot possibly comprehend all particular cases. Often, specific cases cannot be decided on this basis of law, but must rather be dealt with by the opinions of men, which are not always in harmony. We see the same thing happen with physicians, philosophers, commercial arbitrators, and in the discourses of those who govern the state, among whom there is no less variety of judgment than among lawyers.[23]

Given the proximity of Bologna, Europe's preeminent center of legal scholarship, it would be difficult to prove that the existence of a university in Florence was essential for the study and practice of law there. Perhaps the most that can be claimed would be the enhanced opportunity for Florentine lawyers to pursue their scholarly interests while teaching and to participate in disputations and examinations. Florentines expected their lawyers to be competent and knowledgeable about contemporary legal scholarship, not only for practical purposes, both personal and collective, but also for their views on controversial moral problems, such as the licitness of interest payment on public bonds. In his recent article on the *novellista* Franco Sacchetti, Julius Kirshner has shown how Florentine lawyers and theologians struggled for more than a century to resolve that thorny issue. His evidence also showed that these topics were commonly debated by theologians in the churches and that the audiences attending those sermons were quite familiar with the problems and with the mode of argumentation.[24] Sacchetti himself— a merchant, an investor in civic bonds, a statesman as well as a writer—had no formal training in law or theology, but he was able in his writings to couch his arguments in the scholastic mode utilized by canonists and theologians.

I noted earlier that there exists no general synthesis of the role of legal studies in Florentine culture. Until very recently that would also have been true of medicine, but that lacuna has now been filled by Katherine Park's excellent monograph *Doctors and Medicine in Early Renaissance Florence.*[25] She argues convincingly that the discipline of medicine was an integral part of Florentine culture and that university-trained physicians, many of whom taught in the Studio, played an active and creative role in that culture through their teaching, writing, and private practice. Professors of medicine combined academic instruction (which included dissections) with the care of patients, whom they were accustomed to visit surrounded by their students. The most renowned scholars also wrote medical treatises and *consilia*. Park's analysis of these writings reveals the intellectual vitality of the medical discipline which, she insists, was a dynamic and progressive field and not, as scholastic learning has so often been described in this period, hopelessly sterile and moribund. It was from that scholarly writing that physicians such as Tommaso del Garbo and Paolo Toscanelli achieved Italian, indeed European, renown, becoming (in Park's phrase) "culture heroes." Florence treated its doctors "not only as a reservoir of cultural judgment and taste but also as part of its intellectual patrimony and a source of communal honor."[26] Conversely, foreign physicians were attracted to the city not only by its Studio and the opportunities for a lucrative practice but also by the cultural amenities to be found there. Perhaps more than any other academic discipline, medicine prospered from the presence of the Studio, and so was damaged by its periodic closures and its permanent transfer to Pisa in 1473.

If the role of the scholastic disciplines (law, medicine, theology) in Florence's cultural matrix has not received sufficient emphasis, that of the *studia humanitatis* has been the focus of intense scrutiny. The corpus of scholarship on Florentine humanism is so large and so rich that it must daunt the nonspecialist. Fortunately, scholars such as Paul Oskar Kristeller, Hans Baron, Eugenio Garin, and George Holmes have written valuable books of synthesis.[27] These general works have demonstrated the vitality of humanistic studies in fifteenth-century Florence and the establishment of a remarkable group of scholars based in the city, who were passionately dedicated to the exploration of the literary and artistic works of antiquity. The development of this cultural tradition owed very little to the university. Petrarch's hostility to his law school experience and his refusal to accept a professorship in the Florentine Studio were indicative of the attitude of most humanists, who viewed the universities as strongholds of barbarous Latin and intellectual obscurantism. The professors in the Florentine Studio who taught rhetoric and moral philosophy were not distinguished scholars, and their low salaries reflected their modest reputations. The only exceptions to this generalization were the elections to Studio professorships of Francesco Filelfo (1428–34) and Carlo Marsuppini (1431–42).[28] But none of the other prominent figures in the movement—Leonardo Bruni, Poggio Bracciolini, Niccolò Niccoli, Leon Battista Alberti—ever taught in the university, nor did they have significant intellectual contacts with the professoriate. Humanism was peculiarly suited to develop and flourish outside of an institutional context, with its loose networks of devotees and its informal colloquia and symposia, which figure so prominently in humanist dialogues.

In the field of Greek studies the Studio did play a more significant role. The appointment in 1396 of the Greek scholar Manuel Chrysoloras to a university professorship has rightly been seen as a critical moment in the revival of Greek in Italy. Even though Chrysoloras stayed in Florence for only three years, he attracted a coterie of young scholars—Bruni, Niccoli, Roberto de' Rossi, Palla Strozzi, Pier Paolo Vergerio—who pursued their studies of Greek and integrated that language and its literature into their cultural world.[29] But quite as important for this development was the election in 1456 of Joannes Argyropulos to a chair in Greek philosophy at the Studio. Argyropulos was the most distinguished intellectual who taught at the university in its last years in Florence, prior to its transfer to Pisa. He was a specialist in the philosophical writings of Plato and Aristotle, and recent scholarship has emphasized his critical role in the shift in late-fifteenth-century Florence from the rhetorical interests of Salutati and Bruni to the metaphysical concerns of Ficino and Pico della Mirandola.[30]

Florence in the Laurentian era—a golden age, so proclaimed by Angelo Poliziano, whose wide-ranging intellectual interests (philology, philosophy, history, poetry, law, theology) were so characteristic of this *ambiente*. In Eugenio Garin's judgment, Florence in the Laurentian age was the cultural capital of Europe. "It is difficult," he writes "to find any moment in history that could come close to that remarkable alloy of image and concept, of reason and incarnation, of number and body, which the Florentines had by then achieved."[31] The university had moved to Pisa, but the classics were still taught in Florence by Poliziano and Cristoforo Landino. In his villa at Careggi, Marsilio Ficino attracted an international clientele of scholars interested in Neoplatonic philosophy: the young Pico della Mirandola, the French humanist Lefebvre d'Etaples, the Englishman John Colet. Paolo Toscanelli represented most faithfully that tradition which cultivated an interest in the physical world, a tradition nourished by Florentine artists, from Brunelleschi and Alberti to Leonardo and Michelangelo. Leonardo described himself as *un omo sanza lettere,* without formal education. Yet he taught himself enough Latin to read scientific and philosophical works, as his notebooks attest. He had conversations with the philosopher Argyropulos and with Toscanelli, and doubtless with other intellectuals who met in the streets, squares, and cloisters of the city and in private homes.[32] From these oral and written sources, and from Leonardo's own fertile mind, came those brilliant and original insights that startle us by their prescience, such as the following example:

> They say that knowledge born of experience is mechanical, but that knowledge born and consummated in the mind is scientific. But to me it seems that all sciences are vain and full of errors that are not born of experience, mother of all certainty, and that are not tested by experience, that is to say, that do not at their origin, middle or end pass through any of the five senses. For if we are doubtful about the certainty of things that pass through the senses, how much more should we question the many things against which these senses rebel, such as the nature of God and the soul. . . . Experience does not feed investigators on dreams, but always proceeds from accurately determined first principles, step by step in true sequences to the end: as can be seen in the elements of mathematics founded on numbers and measures called arithmetic and geometry. . . .[33]

The most distinctive features of Florentine culture in the Laurentian age were, as Eugenio Garin has suggested, its diversity, its pluralism, and its remarkable degree of toleration. Though it has been argued that Ficino's Platonic Academy represented the dominant force in the city's intellectual life in these years, Neoplatonism was only one of several lively and competing traditions. These included Aristotelian philosophy, Thomist theology taught in the Dominican convents of Santa Maria Novella and Savonarola's San Marco, the humanist disciplines represented by Landino and Poliziano, and, finally, a rich literary tradition in the *volgare* cultivated by Lorenzo himself. He could compose elegant Latin epistles on philosophical topics which he sent to Ficino; he also wrote, in the vernacular, love sonnets, *laudi* on religious themes, pastoral verse, and carnival songs.[34] Lorenzo epitomized that brilliant and transitory moment in Florentine—and Italian—culture when intellectual options and choices were so varied and the opportunities for human achievement seemed (to many, at least) so boundless.

It is appropriate to terminate this story of Florence and its university at that moment, during Lorenzo's mature years, when the city he governed so skillfully basked in its cultural preeminence, blithely ignorant of the tragic events soon to be unleashed by the French invasion. The university at Pisa was Lorenzo's creation, designed to be the preeminent academic establishment for his dominion, and not for his city. In Florence the writings of Latin poets and Greek philosophers were regularly taught by distinguished scholars. Ficino's Platonic Academy became the prototype for the sixteenth-century academies that proliferated in Florence and in other Italian cities, providing intellectual stimulation and nourishment in those disciplines that were not recognized by the conservative scholars who taught in the peninsula's universities.

To recall, in conclusion, the subtitle of this paper, did Renaissance Florence need a university? If that question is interpreted strictly to mean, did Florence need a university in situ, the answer must be negative. Many significant strands of that city's culture developed outside an institutional and academic context, for example, its oral and vernacular literary traditions, its strong interest in quantification (though the *scuole d'abbaco* were certainly important), and its civic image, in both its historical and its eschatological aspects.[35] So rich and multifacted was this culture that Florentines scarcely missed their Studio when it was transferred to Pisa in 1473. The city's professional needs—for lawyers, physicians, and theologians—were amply filled by Pisa, and by Bologna and Padua, while humanistic studies flourished in both academic and private contexts. But the intellectual traditions of the university cannot be dismissed as irrelevant to the development of Florence's cultural life. From Dante and Petrarch to Machiavelli and Guicciardini, Florentine intellectuals absorbed more scholastic thought and methodology than many were willing to concede. From sermons in churches, from debates in law courts and political assemblies, and from private discussions, that academic tradition filtered down to those literate groups in the society that were not university-trained, influencing their thought as profoundly as did the study of antiquity. How these traditions interacted with each other and how the tensions between them were resolved are issues still to be fully clarified and understood.

NOTES

1. Archivio di Stato, Florence, *Carte Del Bene,* vol. 52, unpaginated, from Antonio (?) in Bologna to Messer Ricciardo del Bene in Florence, 22 August 1390.

2. The standard source for the early history of the Studio: *Statuti della Università e Studio fiorentino dell'anno MCCCLXXXVII al MCCCCLXXII,* ed. A. Gherardi (Florence, 1881). Recent studies include G. Brucker, "Florence and Its University, 1348–1434," in *Action and Conviction in Early Modern Europe: Essays in Memory of E. H. Harbison,* ed. T. K. Rabb and J. E. Seigel (Princeton, N.J., 1969), pp. 220–36; E. Spagnesi, *Utiliter edoceri. Atti inediti degli Studio fiorentino (1391–96),* (Milan, 1979); K. Park, "The Readers at the Florentine Studio according to Communal Fiscal Records (1357–1380, 1413–1446)," *Rinascimento* 20 (1980), 249–310.

3. Park, "Readers," pp. 251, 268.

4. Brucker, "Florence and Its University," p. 221.

5. The vicissitudes of the Studio can be traced in A. Fabroni, *Historia Academie Pisanae,* 2 vols. (Pisa, 1791–95), I; and in G. B. Picotti, "Lo studio di Pisa

dalle origini a Cosimo duca," in his *Scritti vari di storia pisana e toscana* (Pisa, 1968).

6. A. Verde, *Lo Studio fiorentino 1473–1503: Ricerche e documenti*, 6 vols. (Pistoia and Florence, 1977–85), III, xxiii.

7. This was the case in Florence but not in those universities (such as Arezzo) established by imperial license; see R. Black, "The *Studio aretino* in the Fifteenth and Early Sixteenth Centuries," *History of Universities* 5 (1985): 61.

8. Verde, *Lo Studio*, III, 293–94.

9. G. Brucker, "A Civic Debate on Florentine Higher Education (1460)," *Renaissance Quarterly* 34 (1982): 517–33.

10. Verde, *Lo Studio*, III, 294.

11. Vespasiano da Bisticci, *The Vespasiano Memoirs*, trans. W. George and E. Waters (New York, 1963), p. 310.

12. Brucker, "Florence and Its University," pp. 222–23.

13. U. Mazzone, *"El buon governo": Un projetto di riforma generale nella Firenze savonaroliana* (Florence, 1978), p. 124.

14. For examples of these *borsisti*, see Verde, *Lo Studio*, III, 237, 244, 247, 276, 291.

15. Most succinctly in *Renaissance Thought: The Classic, Scholastic and Humanist Strains* (New York, 1961).

16. J. Kirshner, review of works by Manlio Bellomo, in *The American Journal of Legal History* 25 (1981): 165.

17. E. Kai-kee, "Social Order and Rhetoric in the Rome of Julius II (1503–1513)," (Ph.D. diss., Univ. of California, Berkeley, 1983), p. 32.

18. Lauro Martines, *Lawyers and Statecraft in Renaissance Florence* (Princeton, 1968), p. 387.

19. J. Kirshner, book review in *American Journal of Legal History* 25 (1981): 164.

20. See J. Kirshner, "Some Problems in the Interpretation of Legal Texts *re* the Italian City-States," *Archiv für Begriffsgeschichte* 19 (1975): 16–27; T. Kuehn, *Emancipation in Late Medieval Florence* (New Brunswick, N.J., 1982).

21. William Bouwsma, "Lawyers and Early Modern Culture," *American Historical Review* 78 (1973): 303–27.

22. Ibid., p. 311.

23. F. Guicciardini, *Maxims and Reflections of a Renaissance Statesman*, trans. M. Domandi (New York, 1965), p. 69.

24. J. Kirshner, " 'Ubi est ille?' Franco Sacchetti on the *Monte Comune* of Florence," *Speculum* 59 (1984): 556–84.

25. Katherine Park, *Doctors and Medicine in Early Renaissance Florence* (Princeton, 1985).

26. Ibid., p. 188.

27. Kristeller, cited above, n. 15; H. Baron, *The Crisis of the Early Italian Renaissance*, 2nd ed. (Princeton, N.J., 1966); E. Garin, *Italian Humanism* (New York, 1966); G. Holmes, *The Florentine Enlightenment, 1400–50* (London, 1969).

28. Park, "Readers," 287–300.

29. Holmes, *The Florentine Enlightenment*, pp. 9–19.

30. J. E. Seigel, "The Teaching of Argyopulos and the Rhetoric of the First Humanists," *Action and Conviction*, pp. 237–60.

31. E. Garin, *Portraits from the Quattrocento* (New York, 1972), p. 197.

32. Ibid., pp. 244–67.

33. Leonardo da Vinci, *Paragone,* trans. I. Richter (London, 1949), pp. 25–26.

34. J. R. Hale, *Florence and the Medici: The Pattern of Control* (London, 1977), pp. 53–54.

35. D. Weinstein, *Savonarola and Florence* (Princeton, N.J., 1970), pp. 27–66.

5

Civic Humanism and Scientific Scholarship at Leiden

Anthony Grafton

In 1619 that intrepid traveler James Howell visited Leiden to see the university. He was not impressed. True, he appreciated the faculty, with its many scholars of European reputation. "Apollo," he admitted, "hath a strong influence here." But he found the buildings laughable by comparison with the great stone colleges that had transformed Oxford since the mid-sixteenth century: "Here are no Colleges at all, God-wot . . . nor scarce the face of an University." And he found the climate and situation no laughing matter: "The Heaven here has always some Cloud in his Countenance, and from this grossness and spissitude of Air proceeds the slow nature of the Inhabitants."[1] Thirty years before, Fynes Moryson had been more impressed by the lectures, but he too had criticized the "ruinous College" where the estates of Holland maintained poor scholars and public plays and festivals "poorely" represented the Spanish siege that preceded the founding of the university.[2] Twenty years later, John Evelyn found even more to say against the "college and schools, which are nothing extraordinary," and the so-called "magnificus Professor" who accepted a fee of one rix-dollar for taking Evelyn's oath and entering him as a student of the university.[3]

Yet the view from England was parochial, then as now. Throughout the seventeenth and eighteenth centuries most continental scholars saw Leiden as the greatest of their universities. German polyhistors wrote doggerel about that Parnassus of late humanism:

> Wo der Phoenix aller Zeiten
> Scaliger, der Wunder-Mann,
> Und der ihm stund an der Seiten,
> Lipsius hat viel gethan,
> Und auch derer Creaturen,
> Mehr als Menschliche Naturen.[4]

Even French *philosophes* respected this one institution of the ancien régime. The *Encyclopédie* itself called Leiden "the first Academy in all of Europe."[5]

And students from the entire Protestant world—England and Scotland as well as Sweden and Prussia—ignored the snide English travelers and crowded into Leiden's few lecture halls and cramped lodging houses.

It is easy enough to account for individuals' divergent reactions. All universities are Rorschach blots. Their buildings, their statutes, and their customs evoke radically different evaluations from their visitors. Take, for example, the Leiden anatomy theater—that famous circular room, decorated in lurid Mannerist style with articulated skeletons and grinning skulls, where sixty human bodies, male and female, were dissected publicly in the twenty-two years after it was built in 1593. The English Baconian Evelyn saw this as an agglomeration of interesting natural objects and man-made implements, rich in that fascinating detail that obsessed philosophers of his ilk:

> I was much pleased with a sight of their anatomy-school, theatre and repository adjoining, which is well furnished with natural curiosities; skeletons, from the whale and elephant to the fly and spider, which last is a very delicate piece of art, to see how the bones (if I may so call them of so tender an insect) could be separated from the mucilaginous parts of that minute animal. Amongst a great variety of other things, I was shown the knife newly taken out of a drunken Dutchman's guts. . . . The pictures of the chirurgeon and his patient, both living, were there.[6]

The German poet Andreas Gryphius, later to be celebrated for his tragedies, those magnificent six- and seven-hour spectacles of dazzling erudition and ghoulish obscurity, read a different lesson into the natural wonders that the Dutch displayed: "He found such delight in the study [of anatomy] that he himself undertook some dissections. And who would not be delighted to see in the human body a quintessence and model of the great world?"[7]

The English vision of a cosmos ruled by law and accessible to human intervention and the German vision of a cosmos ruled by sympathies made visible by physical resemblances could both be projected into the same display, seen in the same year. And while modern prejudices may lead us to imagine that Evelyn's vision reproduced that of his Dutch hosts, recent research has shown that Gryphius in fact teased out the moral and cosmological lessons that the designers of the theater had meant to teach.[8]

But the difficulties of interpreting Leiden University are even more substantial than these first soundings suggest. The further one plunges into early sources and modern histories, the more one despairs of ever emerging from the depths of detail. It seems impossible to lay out a panorama of the university's life and thought that does not falsify perspective and proportion. I do not refer to the difficulties that confront all historians of universities— the clouds of flatulent rhetoric in which administrators hide like squids projecting ink; the taciturnity of teachers and students alike about just what they do all day in study and classroom. Nor do I refer to the standard period problems of the late Renaissance—the sheer obscurity and appalling variety of the curriculum with its efforts to include all texts, all subjects, and all periods in a single vast encyclopedia, and its heroes who could, as Gryphius did while a Privatdozent at Leiden, give a single course that covered "metaphysics, geography, and trigonometry, logic, physiognomics and tragedy." These obstacles rise up in changing form to terrify any traveler hardy enough to make the voyage up the river of sources and opinions to the dark and lurking realities of the early modern university.[9]

Leiden presents its own special obstacles to the historian's progress. The sources are so rich, the conclusions that historians have drawn from them so varied, that the scholar is more likely to feel surfeited than satiated after making a meal of them.[10] Most historians have singled out the modern and progressive aspects of the university for emphasis. They have pointed to its botanical garden, its anatomy theater, its observatory, and its laboratories. They have emphasized the university's desire to foster advanced research as well as traditional teaching—its willingness to pay two great scholars, Joseph Scaliger and Claude Saumaise, not to teach but simply to give "reputation and lustre" to the university's name by their presence and their publications. And they have zealously collected rich evidence to suggest that the faculty was as innovative in its thinking as in its institutional setting. They have called attention to the development of new subjects with a bearing on Holland's commercial expansion—above all, Oriental languages and international law. They have laid great stress on the faculty's sympathy for liberal traditions in thought and research—above all, the efforts of Paul Merula and Dominicus Baudius, guided in part by Scaliger, to publish vital documents about Erasmus's life, to defend his Christian orthodoxy, and to perpetuate his brand of Christian humanist scholarship.[11] They have savored the satires on orthodox bigotry and simple dullness that Leiden professors produced in some abundance. And indeed, one can still derive amusement from Petrus Cunaeus's rich mockery of the theologians' efforts to impose dogmatic positions about unknowable points on all other scholars and Daniel Heinsius's imaginative parody of the grammarians' pedantic concentration on minute points of grammar at the expense of larger ones of meaning (the latter takes the form of an imaginary confrontation between the Athenians at the time of the Persian Wars, trying to make sense of the Delphic oracle's instruction to trust their wooden walls, and a grammarian who offers to clear the oracle up by parsing it, word for word).[12] And they have enumerated dozens of the most innovative Europeans of the late sixteenth and seventeenth centuries, from the lawyer Hugo Grotius through natural scientists such as Snellius and Stevin, Descartes and Galileo, to poets such as Gryphius and Heinsius, who lived, taught, or at least published their works in the Batavian Helicon.[13] Such evidence, all of it valid, seems to substantiate Wilhelm Dilthey's imposing judgment: "Leiden became the first university in a modern sense. For the distinguishing mark of such a university is the combination of teaching with independent research as an express purpose of the university's operation. . . . More was done for the progress of the sciences here than in any other place in Europe."[14]

But historians of a different and newer stripe have hacked quite different paths through the facts and documents. They have drawn attention to the fencing school that occupied as much space as—and was probably open more hours a week than—the legendary library on the floor above it; to the vernacular-language engineering school opened by Stevin in 1600; to the strong curricular emphasis on politics and warfare. Leiden was less a unique center for advanced research than a supremely successful late-Renaissance academy of the type run by every pedagogue from the Jesuits to the Puritans—the pragmatic upper-class academy designed to turn out tough, literate, new-model officers for the new-model armies and states of the seventeenth century. They have used these severely practical considerations to explain the vast numbers of otherwise ordinary young men—11,076 between 1626 and 1650, more than half of them foreigners—who chose Leiden rather than the physically grand but intellectually old-fashioned colleges of Oxford and Cambridge.[15] And they have identified as the normal Leiden student not the eager young intellectuals such as Gryphius, who stayed for years, read widely, and even taught, but those anonymous and boisterous young German students of applied mathematics who celebrated the Dutch defeat of the English fleet in 1666 by sailing through the town's canals on a barge, setting off ingenious fireworks, and shouting "Vivant Batavi." They took much interest in their individual duels and drinking sprees as in intellectual pursuits.[16]

Still others have battered their way into the forbidding premises of the theological faculty. They have discovered that most Hebrew and New Testament scholarship in Leiden was designed not as an inquiry into "wie es eigentlich gewesen" but as a set of tools for training orthodox theologians.[17] They have listened with admirable patience to the debates of Arminians and Gomarists about the being and nature of God and man's ability to know him, and they have discovered a substantial persistence of Thomist and Scotist methods and attitudes, especially among those who held some natural knowledge of God to be allotted to rational adults.[18] They have found allies among the historians of some arts subjects—notably the historians of science, who have revealed that the Aristotelian cosmos was alive and well in seventeenth-century philosophy teaching—and have shown that by no means all Leiden scientists promoted observation and experiment.[19] They have suggested, accordingly, that Leiden and Oxford were not all that far apart in the intellectual map of Baroque Europe. And it is hard to resist their contentions wholeheartedly when one eavesdrops on the massed sages of the faculties of philosophy and medicine debating about whether suspected witches should be tied up and thrown into bodies of water—and condemned if they floated. True, one constantly sees the telltale signs of Dutch calmness and humanity even among the theologians. They explained the tendency of suspected witches to float in simple, natural terms. Many suspects suffered from melancholy and were therefore flatulent; the gases they produced, rather than the repugnance of the water into which they were thrown, were what made them float.[20] But most of these men clearly still lived in a solid and comfortable Aristotelian universe, perfect above the moon's sphere and corruptible below, with four elements, seven planets moved by solid spheres, and scripture a full and perfect source of information about life, the universe, and everything.

Thanks to this realization—and to the growing reaction against Whig histories of ideas—a number of Leiden scholars have been reevaluated by historians of the disciplines they practiced. Georg Hornius, for example, an influential historian, appears as a prototypically modern thinker in Adalbert Klempt's influential book of 1960, *Die Säkularisierung der universalhistorischen Auffassung*. After all, his *Arca Noae* (*Noah's Ark*) of 1666, a tiny but elaborate manual of world history, included not just the traditional four ancient monarchies but also China and the Meso-American civilizations. Evidently this Latin-writing professor had learned much from the Dutch sailors whose exploits he praised in his dedicatory letter—so Klempt argued. In fact, however, Erich Hassinger has pointed out that Hornius drew his information from classical writers wherever possible, even where the merchants had refuted or amended what they had to say and the Amsterdam atlas makers had incorporated the newest information in their maps. His history, moreover, enfolds even its novel contents in the traditional story of Noah's ark and Noah's progeny—as is clear from its title page, where the four beasts of the book of Daniel, the traditional symbols of the Four Monarchies, engage in a scramble for possession of the globe, which hangs illogically but vividly in the sky above Noah's ark. Not all the news was fit to teach, then, even in mid-seventeenth-century Leiden.[21]

In recent years, happily, both Dutch and foreign students of the university have tried to synthesize these different interpretations fairly—to accept the apparent paradoxes and contradictions rather than to explain them away. In the splendid quartercentenary Festschriften of 1975 and in numerous monographs, they have begun to portray an institution at once cosmopolitan and provincial, oriented toward research and dedicated to pedagogy, innovative and traditional. It is in this revisionist spirit that I take up the challenge offered by this colloquium—to put some of Leiden's early teachers and institutions back into the busy streets in which they flourished.[22]

To begin with the city and its larger setting, the province of Holland, both were caught up in one of the greatest—and longest—political upheavals in modern European history. The provinces of the north, with Holland as their leader, slid into revolution against their Spanish overlord, Philip II, from the 1560s onward. The bitter and self-assured Calvinist missionaries detested the equally bitter and self-assured Catholic king, who hoped to use his inquisition and his superb armies to wipe them out. The aristocrats and urban patricians, rich and tolerant, were as often Catholic as Calvinist in their sympathies, but they too loathed Philip, for the style as much as the substance of his regime. They disliked the rising toll of burned heretics, the imposition of new taxes, and the violation of old privileges. And they hated the austere and distant demeanor of that overlord who never left Spain, never laughed, and built his castle in the image of the gridiron on which his favorite saint was fried. The urban poor, periodically reduced to desperation by economic hardships and food shortages, were ready to riot when provoked or repressed. Unstable alliances took shape, never crystallizing, never quite dissolving. Cities were forced into rebellion, and in Holland, above all, they proved able to resist Spanish sieges. Leiden's university, the first in the north, was founded in 1575 as part of the rituals of celebration that attended the citizens' hard-won victory over the Spanish—a victory obtained by opening the dykes and flooding the fields with sea water. The founding, then, was a political as well as an intellectual event, even though the edge was slightly taken off it by the fact that the university was at once equipped with a forged charter in which King Philip was made to express his pleasure in the new enterprise—and to authenticate it with a genuine-looking seal.[23]

After 1575, immigrants poured in, particularly Protestant refugees from the south. Capital and skill came with them. The population of Leiden rose from around twelve thousand in 1581 to around 45,000 in 1622. The city became one of the industrial centers of Europe, rivaling Lyons in manufacturing productivity and threatening Amsterdam's commercial hegemony. Leiden was the center of the Dutch wool industry. It made clocks and lenses. It supported fifty to sixty printers at a given time. In short, it was new, rich, and vulgar. And this peculiar combination of circumstances also helped to shape the new university.[24]

On the one hand, the city did not expand beyond its medieval walls until 1610, and despite that and later expansions it remained desperately crowded. The price of land became extortionate, and space for new buildings was almost impossible to obtain. No wonder, then, that Leiden professors bitterly complained about the noise, squalor, and crowding of their surroundings— so inadequately represented by the contemporary engravings that show an orderly, cultivated agrarian world outside the walls and an equally orderly inhabited world of houses within them.[25]

No wonder, either, that the university never tried to assume a physical form as grand as those of the late-Renaissance colleges of Oxford and Cambridge—or, indeed, Altdorf and Helmstedt. Leiden had impressive buildings—the city hall with its richly decorated facade and its churches with their vast windows, fanciful spires, and chimes carefully not synchronized, so that, then as now, some Leiden church rang the quarter-hour at any moment. But educational funds were spent on salaries, which could win results and thus enhance the university's standing, rather than on bricks and mortar, which could not be effectively deployed.

On the other hand, the fact that students and faculty had to lodge in the town rather than live in separate quarters—the fact that university life could never be sealed off from urban life—had radical consequences of a different sort. The professors—a third of whom, and often the most prominent ones, came from foreign countries, above all France and Germany—had to deal with Dutch culture and society. Teaching in Leiden required learning of an informal but hardly unimportant kind, an involuntary Berlitz immersion course in the mores of a very unusual society, one that struck many outsiders as riven by tensions and contradictions. The Dutch houses, still familiar to us from the painted world of Vermeer, gleamed with the paint and varnish needed to protect them from the corrosive moistness of the air. But Dutch bodies went unwashed even at meals. And the Dutch way of handling human waste seemed to flout the otherwise basic preoccupation with keeping public and private spaces clean. According to Moryson, "At Leyden young wenches of 12 or 13 yeares age, after 9 of the Clocke in the morning, shamed not ordinarily to doe those neceessityes of nature in the open and fayre streetes, which our women will not be seene to doe in private houses."[26] The men, for their part, disfigured the town's two great churches by urinating at their doors, twenty at a time, while the congregation left on Sundays.[27] Dutch commercial honesty put the rest of Europe to shame; Dutch greediness and reserve made relations between sons and fathers, husbands and wives take place on what seemed a colder and less intimate level than anywhere else. The Dutch saved something every year, whatever hardships they had to undergo in order to do so, and they thus sustained their heavy taxes. But half the population of Leiden lived by seasonal work and needed a dole of food every year to survive. No European society set more store by reserve and decorum in adults. But Dutch children ran wild in the streets, howling insults at the students, and their parents would beat anyone who resisted them.[28]

The confrontation with this alien society naturally left indelible marks on the university and its members. The heavy drinking normal in Holland, for example, depleted the ranks of the faculty in both the short term (as when Daniel Heinsius's students had to post a sign reading *Heinsius non legit hodie propter hesternam crapulam*—"Heinsius is too hung over to teach today") and in the long term (as when alcoholism killed off Gerard Tuning, who died of apoplexy while riding his carriage *bene potus, ut dicebatur,* and Dominicus Baudius).[29] It also shocked foreigners. Scaliger, attending a doctoral promotion only a month after his arrival in Leiden in 1593, had as a colleague Everard Bronckhorst, who recalled, "I drank rather a lot, so much that I vomited; may God forgive me." (Three months later Bronckhorst suffered a three-day-long hangover after another party; he did not swear off drinking with students until the city guards shot a fellow party-goer at his side in 1607.)[30] No wonder that Scaliger, for all his love and admiration for Leiden, bitterly complained about the drunken Dutchmen who disturbed him at work and at rest: "my neighbors shout, I can't hinder them; they drink from early morning on a fast day."[31]

More serious shocks arose from the fault lines where different cultural and economic groups rubbed against one another in city and university, each trying to establish control, if not hegemony. The power of the predikants made itself felt in the university's emphasis on theology, the only field whose students had two tiny colleges to live in, the States' College and the Walloon College, and scholarships to live on. The provision of theologians and preachers to serve the Protestant cause—so one local official said in the 1590s—was the secret purpose for which the entire university was founded.[32] Yet the power—and very different goals and desires—of the local patriciate had as great an impact. Janus Dousa, a local nobleman who had made a great splash in the bracing waters of Parisian literary circles, knew the high talk of the great world, and had an international reputation as poet and philologist, led the city's defense against the Spanish. He and the other curators made certain to appoint scholars of distinction, from other countries when they had to. They resisted the clerics' demands for control over every level of schooling and insisted that the arts faculty must offer the high level of training in history and rhetoric needed to fit the local elite for its political and military functions. And even the earliest sketches of the university's curriculum reflect the strong desire of these patrons to produce statesmen as well as clerics.[33] Thus, some of Leiden's apparent contradictions can be economically explained, though not in economic terms. They stem from the conflict of well-defined groups, all powerful but none dominant, all wishing to manipulate the curriculum and appointments.

Naturally, neither preachers nor patricians can simply be dismissed as simpleminded followers of a group line. They were complex individuals, whose decisions cannot be accounted for by simple schemata. More important, they gradually influenced one another in complicated and subtle ways. The patrician humanists who defended scientific independence and theological diversity as curators also pored over the university's accounts with what now looks like a fine lower-middle-class attention to petty details. They demanded that professors of great distinction account for every absence from class and pay fines for those unexcused by vital business elsewhere, admittedly a reasonable course of action when the cause of the absence was a hangover. At one point they even censured a famous and well-established professor, Johannes Meursius, because his "writing of many books" (*het schrijven van veel boucken*) had interfered with his teaching and caused enrollments in his Greek course to fall.[34] Meanwhile, predikants took as much pride as curators in the addition of great men such as Scaliger and Salmasius to the faculty.

The most violent interaction between the two sides took place during the religious crisis of 1618–19. Two of the three curators were dismissed and replaced by men who favored the Predikants and Maurice of Nassau. Arminian professors were also dismissed, though some—such as Cunaeus—rode out the storm by promising insincerely to apologize for their errors, and others eventually found themselves restored to grace—and jobs. The "Genevan Inquisition," as earlier curators called the Calvinist system of control by ministers and lay elders, never won total control, to be sure. But the new Leiden was a quite orthodox institution and, as such, represented a partial victory for what had been only one party in the university's early years.[35] When a young German intellectual like Hermann Conring came to Leiden on scholarship in the 1620s, he learned an enormous amount about politics and medicine from his formal teachers. But it was in Amsterdam, not Leiden, that he sensed the existence of a unique *"ingenii libertas"* that made him long to resist his *Ruf* back to Germany and stay forever in Holland.[36]

Such experiences warn us not to overestimate Leiden's hospitality for varieties of conduct and opinion.[37]

The most profound interactions between university and city, however, took place at a less formal level. The university always remained—at least in the ideals of its professors—a cosmopolitan institution, part of the Europe-wide, Latin-speaking Republic of Letters. True, from Huizinga on, historians have emphasized that the university helped Holland become the great intellectual intermediary between northern and southern, eastern and western Europe. But they have sometimes done less to follow the impact of this very international university on its very provincial setting.[38] In many ways the university acted as a great cultural syringe, injecting new ideas and cultural forms into what had previously been a narrowly traditional culture. The university was the center of sustained efforts to develop classical genres in Dutch poetry as the French had already done.[39] It was the center of efforts to replace the crude vernacular chronicles of the later Middle Ages with a critical and reflective historiography in Latin. It was the center of efforts to devise a new system of international law to support the commercial and military expansion of Holland in Asia and the New World. A private scholar intimately associated with the university, Petrus Scriverius, offered crucial support to Rembrandt during his early career as a painter in Leiden. Scriverius's learning provided Rembrandt with the first of those classical themes and biblical subjects that set his artistic enterprise off so sharply from the better-known Dutch project of describing man and nature in all their insignificant but gloriously profuse detail.[40] Like patricians and predikants, university and society were locked together in a symbiosis that enriched both parties.

The cross-fertilization of city and university could be traced on many levels and through many sources. But to watch the process at its most complex, we should attend to what the university and most of its visitors agreed was its intellectual core: the work of its great classical philologists, whose rather forbidding portraits—and entirely terrifying bibliographies—are the chief adornment of Meursius's commemorative volume of 1625, *Athenae Batavae*.[41] Justus Lipsius, professor of history and law from 1578 to 1591, and Joseph Scaliger, research scholar from 1593 to 1609, gave Leiden the distinctive reputation it enjoyed until after 1800 as the greatest center in the world for classical studies. We turn now to watching them at work in their chosen city.

Lipsius was himself a Dutchman, from the south. Educated at Louvain and in Italy, he had made his name by the early 1570s as an expert on Roman history and the possessor of an incandescent Latin prose style. In particular, he had made himself *the* expert on the greatest Roman philosopher of the first century A.D., Seneca, and the greatest Roman historian, Tacitus. He had seen that the mad and corrupt Roman empire they had known offered a vivid premonitory image of his own time, with its monarchs absolutely corrupted by absolute power and its revolutionaries bent on turning the world upside down. He had shown that sensitive young patricians could learn from Tacitus's cynicism how to read the motives of their masters, and from Seneca's Stoicism how to put up with the situations that resulted. And he had set himself what turned out to be his lifelong tasks: editing these texts critically and explicating them effectively.[42]

In Leiden, Lipsius saw that his palette of skills could make one crucial addition to local resources, cultural and political. He realized that the Dutch, though far superior in seamanship to the Spanish, were inferior on land. Ordinary soldiers lacked skill and discipline, and their leaders, though brave, knew far too little about strategy and tactics. Lipsius decided that his brand of scholarship could supply exactly the tools that the Dutch needed. Going back to Greek texts—above all Polybius's history of Rome—he reconstructed those features of military organization and discipline that made the Romans so superior to their opponents. He praised their uniforms, their diet, their harsh code of military justice, and their clear chains of command. But above all he singled out their ability to deploy their soldiers flexibly in dozens of small cohesive units that could respond rapidly to changes in the situation of a battle.[43]

Lipsius urged the Dutch to adopt the Roman order of battle (and even some features of Roman arms). And his audience took him very seriously indeed. Maurice of Orange, who studied with Lipsius at Leiden, disciplined his soldiers sternly, made them spend their winter months in training, and became the first Dutch commander who could beat the Spanish in the field. The Estates General of the Netherlands took Lipsius's advice and made their soldiers dig their own ditches and raise their own palisades as the Romans had done. As late as 1595–96, when Lipsius had left Leiden and returned to his original Catholic faith, Maurice was still experimenting with what he had learned from him. Maurice made a troop of soldiers armed as Romans fight another troop armed as Spaniards, to see who would prevail—and then received a sharp message from Lipsius criticizing this absurdly mechanical application of his precepts.

At the same time, Lipsius continued his work in history and philosophy. His *De constantia* of 1584 summed up Stoic ethics for the young aristocrat. His *Politica* of 1589 summed up the lessons of Stoics and historians about politics and warfare. And as a brilliant lecturer as well as a fashionable writer, he did more than anyone else to attract students to the fledgling university (which had started, three years before his arrival, with an enrollment of two!). Leiden, in short, enabled Lipsius to update the enterprise of Renaissance humanism both intellectually and pedagogically, to show that classical sources still provided sure guidance for practical action in this world.[44]

Yet relations between Lipsius and Leiden were more complex than this simple list of facts may suggest. After all, Lipsius himself was no straightforward Protestant academic. In fact, recent work has revealed him to have been a plagiarist, a liar, and—worse still by the standards of the time—a heretic.[45] He changed his religious practices and professions almost as rapidly and easily as he changed his academic jobs. And he saw the last practice as justified, we now know, because for a long time he belonged to a heretical sect, the Family of Love. This group included rich merchants, learned scholars, and illiterate but charismatic prophets. It centered in the great printing and publishing house of Christopher Plantin, who himself lived in Leiden during the 1580s. Its members spread in thin but strangely powerful streams across geographical and confessional borders. One tiny group flourished under the nose of Philip II in the Escorial, a second in Leiden, the intellectual citadel of his Calvinist enemies. All members claimed a direct access to God's commandments. All felt that they could take part in the public ceremonies of any Christian church, since all external acts were secondary to the illumination that burned within them. In Leiden, Lipsius and Plantin heard their prophets explicate the dreams and visions of the Book of Revelation. They went on long walks in the country, and in those private moments they admitted to one another that all religions "have a lot of simulation and concealment, but they are not to be despised, provided they involve no crime, since they are useful to feebler minds. The common people have need of such elementary aids."[46] By coming to Leiden, then, Lipsius not only did his bit to add more stonework to the intellectual fortress of Calvinism but also carved a private niche within it for himself and other spiritualists.

The idyll did not last. Lipsius gradually lost faith both in the military abilities of his aristocratic pupils and in the spiritual powers of Plantin's unlettered prophets. He came under powerful attack from the predikants, who thought that his *De constantia* took a pagan view of providence, and from a noisy liberal, Dirck Volckertsz. Coornhert attacked his *Politica* for urging that religious dissenters who disturbed the peace be restrained by force. Lipsius, the moderate and spiritualist, became notorious as the man who told religious and lay authorities to "burn and cut" (*ure et seca*) when confronted by contumacious heretics. Alleging the failure of his health, Lipsius left for Germany in 1591. Soon he reappeared as a Catholic professor in Louvain, where he spent his declining years purging his earlier books to get them off the *Index of Forbidden Books* and writing tracts about wonder-working shrines of the Virgin Mary that had cured pious invalids of such minor ills as blindness and having one leg shorter than the other.[47]

If we now tried to cast a balance—to weigh up the effects of the scholar on the city and the city on the scholar—we would, I think, run directly into difficulties. Was Leiden a favorable or an unfavorable environment? Did it do more to shape or to distort Lipsius's thought? Which was his real self—the secret Leiden liberal or the overt Louvain reactionary? I have no firm answer to these hard questions. And my second exemplary figure, Joseph Scaliger, poses even harder ones.

In some ways, to be sure, Scaliger's case seems the simpler of the two. From his early twenties on, he was a strict and devout Calvinist, closer in theology to the rigorist Gomarus (who became his literary executor) than to the liberal Arminius.[48] His coming to Leiden marked a natural transition, from private Protestant intellectual (he had taught for only two years at Geneva, long before) to public Protestant leader. And his qualifications for his post were as patent as his religious views. He was a great master of Latin and Greek textual criticism. He was the greatest master of historical chronology, that strange Mannerist discipline, now almost forgotten, that used both astronomical and philological techniques to establish the armature of dates on which all the exemplary events of biblical and classical history must be properly spaced and ordered like beads on a string.[49] Dousa invited him to restore to the university the "noise and brilliance" it had lost when Lipsius departed. When he refused to teach, Dousa and his colleagues gave Scaliger the world's first Macarthur Fellowship, inviting him to stay in Leiden, supported by a lavish salary, a housing subvention, and tax concessions, while he pursued his research untroubled by the need to give lectures.[50]

Like other high-priced professors, Scaliger proved a disappointment at first. The first book he wrote in Leiden, a Latin panegyric to his supposed ancestors, the della Scala of Verona, backfired; it provoked his Catholic enemies to dig up the documentary evidence to prove that he was no della Scala, despite the purple robe he liked to wear, but the grandson of a manuscript illuminator and scribe named Bordon.[51] The book he had brought with him and published with much fanfare after arriving, a treatise on the squaring of the circle, electrified the small and hypersensitive community of mathematicians by claiming that every one of them from Archimedes on had misunderstood the problem and the nature of their science. This too had unexpected—and unfortunate—consequences, since the specialists found it easy to show that many elementary mistakes vitiated Scaliger's arguments.[52] Even Scaliger's well-known aristocratic manners did not always win respect. One early observer wrote to Lipsius, no doubt hoping to please him, that "he is vehement both in praise and in abuse, and often of the same man or thing. Those he calls scoundrels, asses, beasts and ignoramuses today, will be gentleman, learned and erudite another day. And he makes both the praise and the abuse public. Many would be offended had he not become more a figure of fun than a cause of hatred."[53]

Yet Scaliger soon became one of the stately humanists of Leiden. With extraordinary energy, he put out twenty-five hundred folio pages on chronology, which more than restored his eminent position as a scholar. With even more extraordinary prescience, he chose disciples from the native and foreign young. Hugo Grotius had Scaliger's aid when he published—at the age of fifteen—his first major work, an edition of the hideously obscure late-antique encyclopedia by Martianus Capella. Other students included Daniel Heinsius, the most influential critic of Greek tragedy of the seventeenth century; Philip Cluverius, the first great historical geographer; and Thomas Erpenius, the Arabist.[54] Scaliger never did lecture. But he became a well-known figure in Dutch political and cultural life and a celebrity among Leiden students and visitors, just the sort of imposing person who had to be wheeled out when the city guard shot and killed a student in December 1607, and Scaliger's presence—along with a three-hour speech in Latin by his colleague Dominicus Baudius—helped to calm the rest of the students.[55] Scaliger's most original Leiden creation was a unique but ambitious kind of teaching. What he offered was a direct initiation into research. The signs of this are everywhere evident. In the edition of the fragments—all that survive—of the Roman satirist Lucilius that Dousa's son Franciscus prepared, Scaliger pops up on every other page. He amended verbal corruptions. He explained difficulties of diction and content. He requested what amounted to brief seminar papers which Dousa meticulously produced. In a characteristic passage, Dousa says, "Scaliger suggested to me that this very fine line too should be assigned to Lucilius (its author has hitherto been unknown). Many things conspire to make me agree. First there are traces of archaic Latin . . . like the use of the dative for the ablative. Then there is the matter of chronology."[56] In Scaliger's letters to another favorite student, Janus Wowerius, we see him keeping the firm hand of a dissertation director on a particularly erratic doctorand. When Wowerius proposes to edit the ancient Latin translation by Germanicus of the Greek astronomical poem by Aratus, Scaliger steers him elsewhere at once. His other student Grotius, he explains, has already done a perfect job, and Wowerius's samples of his new text "offer nothing better than or different from Grotius's edition."[57] But Scaliger, like a good Doktorvater, did more than steer his pupil away from terra already cognita. He helped Wowerius enter one of the roughest but richest territories known to early modern or modern philology, the history of scholarship itself—a subject on which Wowerius published an elaborate treatise two years later, which both followed Scaliger's general approach and incorporated his specific suggestions. And like a good doctoral student, Wowerius showed his appreciation by giving Scaliger no credit at all where it was due.[58]

In normal Protestant universities, professors lectured on set texts and students disputed on set questions. Even those students who tried to prove their learning in the humanities normally did so by defending in public a printed dissertation written by their professor, who collected a fee for providing it and often reprinted his students' collected dissertations under his own name. In Leiden, where he had an elite to teach, an assured income, and no trivial lectures to give, Scaliger could cut new pedagogical paths as he liked. No wonder that Dilthey stressed the modernity of the world Scaliger helped to build.

If we examine the preeminent source for Scaliger's informal teaching, the table talk recorded by two of his students between 1603 and 1607, we will see that he did more than assign specific technical tasks. He also presented a new cumulative ideal of knowledge itself. He forecast the great collaborative enterprises of modern classical scholarship, such as the Corpora of Greek and Latin inscriptions, with their epoch-making recovery of the day-to-day life of the ancient world: "There are so many splendid wills and ancient documents in inscriptions . . . if some young man would take the trouble to collect them, and all the letters dispersed everywhere, he would do well. There is a lot in inscriptions."[59]

He suggested some of the deep intellectual problems that the study of the New Testament would pose in the centuries to come, as it established the later origins and undermined the textual reliability of the canon in its received form: "There are more than fifty additions or changes to the New Testament and the Gospels. It's a strange thing, I don't dare to say it. If it were a profane author I would speak of it very differently."[60]

It was Scaliger's work as a chronologer that led him to these conclusions. He assumed, as a good Calvinist, that the chronology in all the gospels must originally have been the same, that the chronology of Acts must match that of Paul's Epistles. He discovered, as a good scholar, that the texts lacked the harmony that his prejudices had wrongly led him to expect. Accordingly, he came from dogmatic premises to the historically correct conclusion that the New Testament had not been transmitted intact (naturally, he did not guess that the texts had originally disagreed). Teaching by hint and indirection in his chimney corner, Scaliger adumbrated many of the fierce debates that would rend the Republic of Letters for the next century and more.

Yet Leiden provided more than a fertile germ plasm in which the bacilli Scaliger injected could grow and multiply. He took as well as gave. One of his many Leiden projects—to take a simple case first—was a vast index, more than one hundred folio pages long, to the greatest corpus of Greek and Latin inscriptions published in his time (a project in fact carried out by a Heidelberg scholar, Janus Gruter, with Scaliger's epistolary support and direction). Scaliger's meticulous and elegant tool for retrieving the vast banks of information assembled by his colleague gave a clear and systematic order to the religious, historical, and antiquarian contents of thousands of documents. His work has long been praised as the first really modern work of epigraphy. Yet, in fact, Scaliger took both the general form of his indices and much of their specific content from an earlier work that he never mentioned, a manuscript index to an earlier corpus that happened to wind up in Leiden because Dousa bought it in time for Scaliger to use it. Thus, very local resources inspired a great international project.[61]

Some of Scaliger's debts to his Dutch milieu were both deeper and more complex than this one. From 1600 to 1606 he worked at the greatest of his historical enterprises, the *Thesaurus temporum* (Chronological Treasury). In compiling this, he stumbled across a Byzantine world chronicle that yielded up the first genuine sources ever discovered for the history of the ancient Near East. Scaliger became the first scholar for centuries to read the accounts of Babylonian antiquities and Egyptian dynastic history written in Greek in the third century B.C. by the Babylonian priest Berosus and the Egyptian priest Manetho. Both works posed serious problems to a good sixteenth-century Calvinist like Scaliger. Berosus made civilization begin when a great fishlike monster, Oannes, climbed out of the ocean and taught men the arts and sciences. Manetho made his thirty-one Egyptian dynasties begin not just before the Flood but before the Creation.[62] Yet Scaliger saw that neither text was simply fraudulent, even if both seemed impossible to explicate. He insisted that both refracted, in mythical form, the true events of early human history that the Bible and the Greek historians had not recorded. And he included both sets of sources in his great book.

Scaliger's new sources sent violent waves rolling across the normally placid waters of European scholarship. For the next century and more, philosophers like Spinoza, theologians like Simon, and scholars like Vico would debate the veracity of these strange texts. The notion that they offered a mythical account of real events—in essence, Scaliger's original solution— gradually prevailed. As Paolo Rossi has shown in a recent book of great importance, these debates provided both much of the impetus and much of the matter for Vico's *New Science* as well as for many lesser books now justly unread.[63]

The curious fact in this sequence of debates is the position Scaliger took in it. For in his earlier chronological work he had devoted almost no attention to figures (like Theseus) and writers (like Hermes Trismegistus) who flourished in what he called the "mythical" period before the Olympic Games began in 776 B.C. Unlike most of his contemporaries, he seems to have had little hope of giving such events and people firm dates and places. Myths, accordingly, received almost no attention in his chronological scholarship until he came to Leiden.

What sensitized Scaliger to the historical uses of myth was a local controversy. Throughout the sixteenth century the intellectuals of nearby Frisia had developed an astonishingly detailed and dramatic early history for their province. They argued that three Indian gentlemen, Friso, Saxo, and Bruno, had left their native country in the fourth century B.C. They studied with Plato, fought for Philip and Alexander of Macedon, and then settled—logically enough—in Frisia, where they drove off the giants who had previously inhabited northern Europe and founded Groningen. The image is enchanting: three gentlemen in frock coats sitting about a peat fire in the bogs, speaking perfect Sanskrit with their followers. But around 1600 it became the subject of a sharp controversy.[64] Ubbo Emmius, whom Scaliger knew and respected, attacked Friso & Co. as fabulous.[65] And Suffridus Petri, who had given these stories currency in learned Latin, mounted a brilliant defense. He claimed that the early history of Frisia could have been transmitted in genuine ancient texts now lost and in popular songs—such as the famous *carmina* that had preserved the tales of Roman and German origins in antiquity. And he insisted that even if such sources contained fables, they should be analyzed and purified, not abandoned: "Antiquities are one thing, the fables mixed up with them are another. A good historian should not simply abandon the antiquities because of the fables, but should cleanse the fables for the sake of the antiquities [they contain]."[66] From Petri's wrong but admirably ingenious defense of Frisian legends, which came out just as he attacked Berosus and Manetho, Scaliger took the tolerant and eclectic analytical principles that he applied. Thus, a debate literally provincial to the point of marginality—one that Scaliger encountered only because members of the

Leiden elite took part in it—produced a vital element of the vast historical structure Scaliger reared. Vico owed something of his concept of the aboriginal giants to the Frisian antiquaries Scaliger had read as well as to the Neapolitan *lazzaroni* he himself knew. For, as Rossi's evidence shows, it was Scaliger's new evidence and his insistence that it be taken seriously that shook European intellectuals' confidence in the primacy of the Bible as an account of man's early history. Had Scaliger not compiled, Vico would never have distilled his peculiar and visionary concoctions; and as we can now see, Scaliger's work rested in a fundamental sense on that of Petrus and others.

Scaliger's case also shows the futility of trying to impose neat causal schemes on this crowded but vital city and its learned but lively professors. Only a few morals emerge. In each case interaction took place in two directions, the city shaping its professor and the professor his city. In each case we can trace the interaction only if we abandon the registers of matriculated students and accounts of extracurricular high jinks that preoccupy most historians of education and plunge into the vast and terrifying Latin books that reveal these teachers' goals and methods in detail. In each case, in the end, we learn more from a complex image than from a deceptively simplified road map. City and university, scholar and society, come together in a constantly changing pattern that requires the skills of a choreographer rather than a cartographer to record it. The steps of the dance are complex and involuted, the tune so faint that not all its notes can be recovered. Yet our only hope of understanding the formal intellectual life of early modern Europe in its urban context is to abandon prejudices and formulas, plunge in, and join the dance ourselves.

NOTES

My thanks to Henk Jan de Jonge and Glenn Most for their detailed comments on earlier drafts of this essay.

1. *Epistolae Ho-Elianae: The Familiar Letters of James Howell,* ed. J. Jacobs (London, 1890), p. 32.

2. *Shakespeare's Europe: Unpublished Chapters of Fynes Moryson's Itinerary,* ed. C. Hughes (London, 1903), pp. 372–77.

3. *The Diary of John Evelyn,* ed. A. Dobson (London, 1908), p. 17.

4. Chr. Köler, quoted by H. Schneppen, *Niederländische Universitäten und Deutsches Geistesleben* (Münster Westfalen, 1960), p. 36.

5. Ibid., p. 7.

6. *Diary of John Evelyn,* pp. 17–18.

7. B. Siegmund von Stosch, *Danck-und Denck-Seule des Andreae Gryphii* (1665), in *Text und Kritik* 7/8 (n.d.): 6.

8. Th. H. Lunsingh Scheurleer, "Un amphithéâtre d'anatomie moralisée," in *Leiden University in the Seventeenth Century: An Exchange of Learning,* ed. Lunsingh Scheurleer et al. (Leiden, 1975), pp. 217–77.

9. See A. Grafton, "The World of the Polyhistors: Humanism and Encyclopedism," *Central European History* 18 (1985): 31–47.

10. For a full bibliography of earlier work, see R. E. O. Ekkart in *Bibliographie internationale de l'histoire des universités* (Geneva, 1976) II, 83–140.

11. A. Flitner, *Erasmus im Urteil seiner Nachwelt* (Tübingen, 1952), pp. 94–105; B. Mansfield, *Phoenix of His Age* (Toronto, 1979); and the exhibition catalogue *Erasmus en Leiden* (Leiden, 1986), esp. pp. 30–45.

12. P. Cunaeus, *Sardi venales* (1612), in *Two Neo-Latin Menippean Satires,* ed. C. Matheeussen and C. L. Heesakkers (Leiden, 1980); D. Heinsius, *Orationum editio nova* (Leiden, 1627), pp. 449–52.

13. See, for example, D. W. Davies, *The World of the Elseviers 1580–1712* (The Hague, 1954), chap. 1; C. R. Boxer, *The Dutch Seaborne Empire 1600–1800* (Harmondsworth, 1973), pp. 176–78.

14. W. Dilthey, *Weltanschauung und Analyse des Menschen seit Renaissance und Reformation,* 7th ed.; *Gesammelte Schriften* 2 (Stuttgart and Göttingen, 1964), pp. 443–44. The standard older compendium on the university also stresses the vital importance of its success in attracting world-famous scholars. G. D. J. Schotel, *De Academie te Leiden in de 16ᵉ, 17ᵉ en 18ᵉ eeuw* (Haarlem, 1875), chap. viii.

15. See, in general, G. Oestreich, *Neo-Stoicism and the Early Modern State* (Cambridge, 1982); and H. Wansink, *Politieke Wetenschappen aan de Leidse universiteit 1575–1650* (Utrecht, 1981).

16. See F. Lucä, "Memoirs," in *Deutsche Selbstzeugnisse* 6, ed. M. Beyer-Frölich (Leipzig, 1930), p. 132.

17. H. J. de Jonge, *De bestudering van het Nieuwe Testament aan de Noordnederlandse universiteiten en het Remonstrants Seminarie van 1575 tot 1700* (Amsterdam, 1980), pp. 11–18; idem, "The Study of the New Testament in the Dutch Universities," *History of Universities* 1 (1981): 113–29. For Hebrew scholarship, see the illuminating dissertation of P. T. van Rooden, *Constantijn L'Empereur (1591–1648), professor hebreeuws en theologie te Leiden* (Leiden, 1985).

18. J. Platt, *Reformed Thought and Scholasticism* (Leiden, 1982).

19. E. G. Ruestow, *Physics at Seventeenth- and Eighteenth-Century Leiden* (The Hague, 1973); A. M. Luyendijk-Elshout, "Oeconomia animalis, pores and particles," *Leiden University in the Seventeenth Century,* ed. by Lunsingh Scheurleer, pp. 295–307.

20. *Bronnen tot de geschiedenis der Leidsche Universiteit,* ed. P. C. Molhuysen. Vol. 1: *1574–7 Febr. 1610* (The Hague, 1913), doc. 258, pp. 289–91 (9 January 1594). See also R. Bartlett, *Trial by Fire and Water* (Oxford, 1986), pp. 146–52, for this incident and its larger context.

21. A. Klempt, *Die Säkularisierung der universalhistorischen Auffassung* (Göttingen, 1960), pp. 114–23; E. Hassinger, *Empirisch-rationaler Historismus* (Bern and Munich, 1978), pp. 127–36; G. Hornius, *Arca Noae* (Leiden and Rotterdam, 1666).

22. See, in general, J. J. Woltjer's introduction in *Leiden University in the Seventeenth Century,* pp. 3–19. In addition to this magnificent book, the quatercentenary produced anniversary volumes of the journals *Quarendo* 5 (1975) and *Lias* 2 (1975), and the extremely rich and informative Rijksmuseum Amsterdam exhibition catalog, *Leidse Universiteit 400. Stichting en eerste bloei 1575–ca. 1650* (Amsterdam, 1975).

23. M. Jurriaanse, *The Founding of Leiden University* (Leiden, 1965).

24. See, for example, P. Zumthor, *Daily Life in Rembrandt's Holland* (London, 1961); Boxer, *The Dutch Seaborne Empire,* pp. 60–61, 70, 322. S. Schama,

The Embarrassment of Riches (New York, 1987), which appeared after this essay was written, sheds a flood of light on many matters fitfully illuminated in what follows in this essay.

25. J. J. Scaliger, *Poemata anecdota*, ed. H. J. de Jonge (Leiden, 1980), p. 9. *Autobiography of Joseph Scaliger*, trans. G. W. Robinson (Cambridge, Mass., 1927), pp. 50–52.

26. *Shakespeare's Europe*, p. 382.

27. Lucä, "Memoirs," p. 132. Scaliger noted that the Walloons urinated against the inside as well as the outside walls of their churches.

28. W. Temple, *Observations upon the United Province of the Netherlands*, ed. G. Clark (Oxford, 1972), pp. 88–89; *Autobiography of Joseph Scaliger*, pp. 48–49; Lucä, "Memoirs," pp. 131–32.

29. E. Bronckhorst, *Diarium*, ed. J. C. van Slee (The Hague, 1898), pp. 122, 136; Schotel, *De Academie te Leiden*, pp. 230–32; D. J. H. ter Horst, *Daniel Heinsius (1580–1655)* (Utrecht, 1934), chap. ix. One of Heinsius's acquaintances described him in his later years as "no longer a man but an amphora."

30. Brockhorst, *Diarium*, pp. 64, 68, 118.

31. *Autobiography of Joseph Scaliger*, p. 49.

32. P. Dibon, *La Philosophie néerlandaise au siècle d'or* (Amsterdam, 1954), I, 4. See also G. H. M. Posthumus Meyjes, *Geschiedenis van het Waalse College te Leiden, 1606–1699* (Leiden, 1975), for the Walloon College. For evidence that William of Orange himself saw the promotion of theology as the chief aim of the university, see *Leidse Universiteit 400*, p. 76, item A 131.

33. Dibon, *La Philosophie néerlandaise*, pp. 7–11, on G. Feugueray's 1575 *Hypotyposis*, in *Bronnen*, ed. Molhuysen, I, doc. 26, pp. *39–*43 (which envisages training for the church, the state, and medicine, p. *40).

34. *Bronnen tot de geschiedenis der Leidsche Universiteit*, ed. P. C. Molhuysen (The Hague, 1916), II, 127; L. Holstenius, *Epistolae ad diversos*, ed. J. F. Boissonade (Paris, 1817), pp. 4–5. In fact, the curators objected to Meursius's religious views.

35. Dibon, *La Philosophie néerlandaise*, I, 80–90.

36. See the exhibition catalogue from the Herzog August Bibliothek, Wolfenbüttel: *Hermann Conring 1606–1681* (Wolfenbüttel, 1981), pp. 23–29.

37. The role of religious tolerance—and even Nicodemism—in the university's early history certainly deserves detailed study but may be slightly overemphasized in the important work of the late J. van Dorsten. See for example, his "Temporis filia veritas: Wetenschap en religievrede," *Tijdschrift voor Geschiedenis* 89 (1976): 413–19. A more nuanced view in A. Hamilton, *The Family of Love* (Cambridge, 1981), pp. 99–111.

38. J. Huizinga, *Dutch Civilization in the Seventeenth Century and Other Essays*, ed. P. Geyl, trans. A. Pomerans (New York, 1968), p. 151.

39. J. A. van Dorsten, *Poets, Patrons and Professors* (Leiden and London, 1961); P. Tuynman, "Petrus Scriverius, 12 January 1576–30 April 1660," *Quaerendo* 7 (1977): 5–45.

40. G. Schwartz, *Rembrandt* (New York, 1985), esp. chap. 4.

41. J. Meursius, *Athenae Batavae* (Leiden, 1625). This was adapted from the *Alma Academia Leidensis* of 1614, and much of its content is made up of autobiographies of the professors which retain great value. See, in general, S. Ridderbos, *De philologie aan de Leidsche Universiteit gedurende de eerste vijfentwintig jaren van haar bestaan* (Leiden, 1906); J. H. Waszink, "Classical Philology,"

Leiden University in the Seventeenth Century, ed. Scheurleer et al., pp. 160–75; "Lo sviluppo della filologia nei Paesi Bassi del nord dalla morte di Erasmo fino alla morte dello Scaligero," *Annali della Scuola Normale Superiore di Pisa,* cl. di lettere e filosofia, ser. 3, 8 (1978): 97–133.

42. See, in general, M. W. Croll, *Style, Rhetoric and Rhythm* (Princeton, N.J., 1966); A. Momigliano, *Essays in Ancient and Modern Historiography* (Oxford, 1977), chap. 13.

43. A. D. Momigliano, *Polybius between the English and the Turks,* 7th J. L. Myres Memorial Lecture (Oxford, 1974), pp. 10–12.

44. Wansink, *Politieke wetenschappen.*

45. J. Ruysschaert, *Juste Lipse et les Annales de Tacite* (Louvain, 1949).

46. B. Rekers, *Benito Arias Montano (1527–1598)* (London, 1972), p. 102. See also N. Mout, *Bohemen en de Nederlanden in de zestiende eeuw* (Leiden, 1975); Hamilton, *The Family of Love.*

47. G. Güldner, *Das Toleranz-Problem in den Niederlanden im Ausgang des 16. Jahrhunderts* (Lübeck and Hamburg, 1968). Lipsius insisted that his phrase *ure et seca* had been meant only as a call to use serious remedies (its sense in classical Latin), not as a demand for execution. But both his contemporaries and modern historians have differed about the plausibility of this effort to make the literal metaphorical when challenged. In addition to Güldner's careful study, which favors Lipsius, see H. Bonger, *Leven en werk van D.V. Coornhert* (Amsterdam, 1978), pp. 140–56, which favors Coornhert.

48. The standard biography remains J. Bernays, *Joseph Justus Scaliger* (Berlin, 1855); more recent literature is listed in A. Grafton and H. J. de Jonge, *Joseph Scaliger: A Bibliography 1852–1982* (The Hague, 1982). For details of Scaliger's life in Leiden, see H. J. de Jonge, "Josephus Scaliger in Leiden," *Jaarboekje voor geschiedenis en oudheidkunde van Leiden en omstreken* 71 (1979): 71–94.

49. A. Grafton, "From *De die natali* to *De emendatione temporum:* The origins and setting of Scaliger's chronology," *Journal of the Warburg and Courtauld Institutes* 48 (1985): 100–143.

50. See *Bronnen,* I, index s.n. Scaliger.

51. M. Billanovich, "Benedetto Bordon e Giulio Cesare Scaligero," *Italia Medioevale e Umanistica* 11 (1968): 187–256.

52. G. Crapulli, *Mathesis Universalis* (Rome, 1969), pp. 101–23. W. E. van Wijk, *Het eerste leerboek der technische tijdrekenkunde* (Leiden, 1954).

53. F. Raphelengius to Lipsius, November 1595, quoted by Bernays, *Joseph Justus Scaliger,* p. 174.

54. See, in general, Bernays, *Joseph Justus Scaliger;* for other cases in point, see A. L. Katchen, *Christian Hebraists and Dutch Rabbis* (Cambridge, Mass., 1984).

55. For the incident, see *Bronnen,* I, *443–*57. For Baudius's speech—the duration of which I infer from the length of the text—see his *Epistolarum centuriae tres,* new ed. (Amsterdam, 1647), pp. 555–608. For Scaliger's presence, see pp. 556–57, 608. Naturally, the timing is an approximation.

56. Lucilius, *Satyrarum quae supersunt reliquiae,* ed. F. Dousa (Padua, 1735), p. 236 (on a fragment now assigned to Ennius).

57. Scaliger to Wowerius, 12 December (Julian) 1602; Scaliger, *Epistolae,* ed. D. Heinsius (Leiden, 1627), p. 718.

58. Wowerius's interest in the comparison of Greek and Jewish (Masoretic) critical methods clearly comes from Scaliger. For specific points that reappear

compare Scaliger, *Epistolae,* pp. 718–19, with J. Wowerius, *De polymathia tractatio,* 18.4 and 24.6; *Thesaurus Graecarum Antiquitatum,* ed. Jac. Gronovius (Leiden, 1701), X, cols. 1080, 1114.

59. *Scaligerana,* ed. by P. Desmaizeaux (Amsterdam, 1740), pp. 395–96; see also de Jonge, "The Study of the New Testament," p. 84.

60. *Scaligerana,* p. 399; de Jonge, p. 82.

61. A. Grafton, "Joseph Scaliger's Indices to J. Gruter's *Inscriptiones Antiquae,*" *Lias* 2 (1975): 109–13.

62. Syncellus 29 M = *FrGrHist* 680 F 1; 59 M ff. = *FrGrHist* 609 F 2. See A. Grafton, "Joseph Scaliger and Historical Chronology: The Rise and Fall of a Discipline," *History & Theory* 14 (1975): 156–85.

63. P. Rossi, *The Dark Abyss of Time,* trans. L. Cochrane (Chicago, 1984).

64. E. H. Waterbolk, "Zeventiende-eeuwers in de Republiek over de grondslagen van het geschiedverhaal. Mondelinge of schriftelijke overlevering," *Bijdrage voor de Geschiedenis der Nederlanden* 12 (1957): 26–44; "Reacties op het historisch pyrrhonisme," ibid., 15 (1960): 81–102; both rpt. in *Mythe & Werkelijkheid,* ed. J. A. L. Lancée (Utrecht, 1979), pp. 9–24, 68–85; H. J. Erasmus, *The Origins of Rome in Historiography from Petrarch to Perizonius* (Assen, 1962). For a summary of the Frisian *Urgeschichte,* see S. Petrus, *Apologia . . . pro antiquitate et origine Frisiorum* (Franeker, 1603), pp. 15–17. See also Schama, *The Embarrassment of Riches,* chap. 2.

65. U. Emmius, *De origine atque antiquitatibus Frisiorum,* in his *Rerum Frisicarum historia* (Leiden, 1616), separately paginated, 7ff. See *Scaligerana,* p. 304 ("bon & rare").

66. Petrus, *Apologia,* pp. 40–41; previously quoted by Erasmus, *Origins of Rome,* p. 90.

6

The Geneva Academy in the Eighteenth Century: A Calvinist Seminary or a Civic University?

Michael Heyd

In February 1795 Thomas Jefferson made a somewhat startling suggestion to President George Washington. Speaking on behalf of François D'Ivernois, a Genevan publisher and intellectual living as a refugee in England, Jefferson suggested transferring the whole faculty of the Genevan Academy to America and thus establishing a national university in the new United States.[1] Geneva was in the grips of revolution at that time, and the future of the Academy seemed very uncertain. In America funds were available for such a purpose from the shares of the Potomac and James River companies. Jefferson, who knew D'Ivernois from his years in Paris, enthusiastically endorsed the idea. Having failed to convince the Virginia Legislature to adopt that plan, he wrote to Washington and urged him to allocate the funds of the Potomac shares to bring the Genevan faculty over. He stressed that Geneva, together with Edinburgh, "were considered the two eyes of Europe in matters of science," and that whereas Edinburgh had been most famous in medicine, Geneva was "most so in other branches of science."[2]

The president, however, remained skeptical. To transfer en masse the whole faculty of the Geneva Academy was not practical (especially as they did not speak English), not necessarily desirable (other European universities such as Edinburgh may have had better scholars in some disciplines), and, above all, politically dangerous: "[H]aving been at variance with the levelling party of their own country, the measure might be considered as an aristocratic movement by more than those who . . . are continually sounding the alarm bell of aristocracy."[3] Consequently, nothing came out of this plan, and Jefferson was later to concentrate his efforts on the establishment of a state university in Virginia.[4]

The episode is nevertheless significant for several reasons. First of all, it indicates that Geneva was considered to be one of the most important

79

universities in Europe in the eighteenth century (together with Leiden and Edinburgh, both discussed in this volume). Second, this episode reveals the extent to which the Genevan Academy was identified with the ancien régime in the city. This is a crucial point to which we shall have occasion to return in this essay. Finally, it is worth noting that Jefferson—who can hardly be suspected of Calvinist leanings—found Calvin's academy congenial to his intellectual tastes. By the end of the eighteenth century, the Genevan Academy was clearly a center of Enlightenment culture. To what extent had it indeed become a civic university rather than a Calvinist theological seminary, and what was the role of the city authorities in this process?

In discussing city-university relations in Geneva, we should bear in mind several particular characteristics peculiar to the Genevan case. First and foremost, Geneva of the early modern period was a city-state. The city authorities were thus *state* authorities as well. Second, unlike most other Protestant academies and universities, the academy founded by Calvin was up to the end of the seventeenth century largely under the control of the Company of Pastors (La Compagnie des Pasteurs), the Genevan Church, even though the city authorities provided its funds and had the right to approve or reject the nomination of professors. City-university relations thus closely involved a state-church relationship. Furthermore, with neither an imperial nor a papal charter, the academy could not give official degrees, and hence (like the Huguenot academies in France, the nonconformist academies in England, and the other Swiss academies in Zurich, Bern and Lausanne, with the important exception of the University of Basel) Geneva was not a university proper, nor did it have a medical faculty or even a regular and permanent law chair until the eighteenth century. Its main function in the seventeenth century was to train ministers not only for Geneva proper but for the international Calvinist movement in general.[5]

Not that Calvin and Beza envisaged the Academy *exclusively* as a theological seminary. Calvin regarded it also as an institution of liberal education for the Genevan youth and, following the humanistic model, conceived the Academy as consisting of chairs in the three languages (Hebrew, Greek, and Latin) in addition to the theology chairs. (The Latin chair was soon to develop into a philosophy chair.)[6] His disciple and successor, Théodore de Bèze, went further. He continually entertained the idea of establishing chairs of medicine and law in the Academy and took several steps toward the realization of this plan.[7] The Company of Pastors, however, was usually suspicious of such ideas, especially concerning the introduction of law studies in the Academy.[8] Consequently, though some prominent law professors were occasionally nominated in the Geneva Academy (such as François Hotman in the sixteenth century and Jacques Godefroy in the seventeenth), there was no continuous and regular law chair in the Academy. As for medicine, a short experience with an irascible Aristotelian physician by the name of Simon Simoni, who got entangled with one of the ministers in 1567, sealed the fate of medical studies in the Academy for many years.[9]

In the course of the seventeenth century, besides the propaedeutic chairs of Hebrew, Greek, and philosophy, the main thrust of academic teaching was toward theological studies. In midcentury, 60 percent of the students came to the Academy specifically to study theology, having done their propadeutic studies elsewhere. Eighty percent of the students graduated in theology, and 70 percent were later to become pastors. Most of the students (over 80 percent) came from other places, especially from France (over 40 percent).[10] The Academy thus clearly catered to an international Calvinist community, and its main function was the training of ministers. Not surprisingly, a third chair of theology was added in 1661. The lay authorities increasingly intervened in academic affairs, whether in matters of discipline or in the procedures concerning the election of professors, and also appointed three *scholarques* for these purposes. Nevertheless, the Venerable Company of Pastors was still largely in charge of the daily affairs of the Academy.[11] On the basis of the character of the student body which made the Academy an institution predominantly geared to the training of ministers, the pastors could rightly claim that the Academy should properly remain under their supervision.

Things began to change, however, in the last third of the seventeenth century. In 1669 a Cartesian professor of philosophy, Jean-Robert Chouet, was appointed to the Academy largely (though not exclusively) owing to the pressure of the town's Small Council.[12] The introduction of Cartesian philosophy may have attracted more philosophy students to the Academy since their numbers clearly rose, especially that of foreigners among them.[13] Even more important, the revocation of the Edict of Nantes in 1685 deprived the Academy of an important source of student recruitment, that of the French Huguenot community. Indeed, by the end of the seventeenth century and the early eighteenth the student body in Geneva—as in Basel and other Swiss academies—became far less international in character, thus reflecting the gradual disintegration of the international Calvinist movement, as well perhaps as the decline of the habit of the *peregrinatio academica*.[14] Like many other European universities, the Geneva Academy experienced a sharp fall in the number of its students around the turn of the century, caused also by the economic crisis of the 1690s. So serious was that decline in enrollment (in certain years, less than twenty students registered in the Livre du Recteur) that the very existence of the Academy seemed to be put in question.[15] It clearly needed a new identity and a new sense of vocation.

Geneva was not unique in undergoing such a crisis around the turn of the century. Universities such as Leiden and Edinburgh were similarly searching for a new identity and a more modern orientation about 1700. Peculiar to Geneva, however, was the fact that the Academy was still largely run by the Company of Pastors, whereas in Leiden, Edinburgh, or the other Swiss Academies the supervision over the university was firmly in secular hands, who had to contend mostly with the professors rather than the church.[16] The search for a new intellectual orientation, which would attract more students, was therefore closely linked in Geneva with the efforts of the city authorities to assume control over academic affairs. Already in the 1690s proposals were made in the Council of the Two Hundred to establish an Academic Senate which would include in addition to the professors and the *Scholarques* several physicians and lawyers from the Two Hundred and only two representatives of the Company of Pastors. The model they wished to imitate was the *Schulrat* in places like Zurich or Bern.[17] Such a senate, rather than the Company of Pastors, it was argued, should superintend the affairs of the Academy. In addition, it was proposed, new subjects such as mathematics and medicine should be introduced into the Academy in order to attract more foreign students.[18] The aim was clearly to turn the Academy from a Calvinist seminary to a lay university.

It is not by accident, however, that these proposals were made in the Council of the Two Hundred, a broader body than the Small Council which had been ruling the town since the late sixteenth century. Though largely composed of members of the ruling oligarchy, the Council of the Two Hundred came occasionally into conflict with the Small Council concerning its political and judicial privileges and could become an arena in which demands were aired to broaden the political process in town.[19] Indeed, those who raised the projects to "secularize" the Academy—Jacob de Normandie, Théodore Grenus, Abraham and François Mestrezat, and Pierre Fatio (three of them lawyers, one a physician)—were all to become leaders of the so-called Fatio revolt in 1707 against the town oligarchy.[20]

We come now to a crucial point. The crisis of the Academy at the turn of the century coincided with the beginning of political opposition to the oligarchic regime in the city. Both phenomena, in fact, were the result of the revocation of the Edict of Nantes, as well as the wars of Louis XIV and the economic crisis of the 1690s.[21] The War of the League of Augsburg, the subsistence crisis of 1693–94, and the economic competition in town caused by the influx of Huguenot refugees all contributed significantly to the growing social polarization in Geneva between the oligarchy, consisting of rich merchants and bankers who lived in the upper city, and the rest of the citizens, the *Bourgeoisie:* artisans, watchmakers, and small merchants living downtown. The War of the Spanish Succession (1702–13) exasperated these tensions still further and added an ideological dimension to them, since while the war and the official boycott on commerce with France created unemployment among the artisans, the big merchants and bankers found ways to circumvent that boycott and continued to do business with France.[22] The oligarchy increasingly allied itself economically with Catholic France, whereas the *Bourgeosie* regarded itself as "patriotic" and felt unduly discriminated against in the economic sphere. Under these circumstances, the oligarchic rule which was established in Geneva for well over a hundred years was no longer easily accepted by the citizens in town. Some of them sought to return to the "democratic" constitution which allegedly existed in Geneva in the first years after the Reformation. These tendencies found their first radical and ill-fated expression in the "revolt" of 1707 which sought to reestablish the defunct General Assembly (Conseil Général) of all citizens as the effective sovereign and legislative body in the city. The leaders of the revolt, primarily Jacob de

Normandie and Pierre Fatio, though members of the ruling families in town who sat in the Council of the Two Hundred, each had personal reasons to align themselves with the *Bourgeoisie*.[23] Fatio himself was ultimately charged with conspiracy, sentenced to death, and executed. In a more moderate form, the same tendencies may be seen in the plans to take the control over the Academy away from the Company of Pastors and to turn it into a civic, largely secular institution.

Faced with these challenges, the magistrates in town (among them the Cartesian Chouet, who was elected in the meantime to the Small Council and left the Academy) were obviously in a delicate situation.[24] On the one hand, they wished—like some of the members of the Two Hundred—to give the Academy a more secular orientation and to limit the role of the Company of Pastors in the running of the Academy. On the other hand, they did not want to open the door for too much intervention from "below," even from lawyers, physicians, and merchants who were sitting in the Council of the Two Hundred. Nor could the Small Council afford to break openly with the Company of Pastors, especially not after the Fatio affair of 1707. The steps taken in the first decade of the eighteenth century reflect this ambivalent stance. An academic assembly (later called sometimes an Academic Senate) of the professors and *scholarques* was indeed established, but no members of the Council of the Two Hundred participated in it. Nor was it a governing body of the Academy but rather a mediating body between the Company of Pastors and the Small Council concerning academic affairs. Although in the next generation the Small Council constantly tried to enhance the role of the academic assembly as a decision-making body, the Company of Pastors kept viewing it as merely a mediating factor.[25] An honorary chair of mathematics was also established in 1704, but this was done with full support and coopera-tion of the Company of Pastors, a significant point to which we shall return below.[26] The program for the "secularization" of the Academy was partially realized, however, with respect to the library. In 1702 a board of directors was constituted over the library, consisting of seven members: the Rector, one of the *scholarques* from the Small Council, three representatives of the Company of Pastors (two of whom were to serve as librarians), and two members of the Two Hundred (one a lawyer, the other a physician). Here, then, civic control over the library (which became the Bibliothè *publique*) was ensured. With regard to the location of the library, the city authorities had to give in, however. While they wanted to transfer the library to the Maison de Ville in the center of town, which would make it accessible to all citizens and clearly a *civic* institution, the Venerable Company insisted that it would be too noisy a place and should remain in the Collège (though moved to a greater hall). These considerations finally convinced the magis-trates, yet the lengthy debate over the location of the library is a nice exam-ple of city-university relationship, with all the practical, political, and sym-bolic connotations involved in such a seemingly prosaic matter.[27]

Finally, the most far-reaching idea, to turn the Academy into a full-fledged university, was not forgotten. It was raised in fact after the 1707 "revolt" by city officials who opposed the radical demands of Fatio and the General Assembly—by the lawyer and *procureur général* Jean Buisson in the Two Hundred and by Jean-Robert Chouet in the Academic Assembly.[28] Chouet stressed in his proposal the prestige such a university would confer upon the city and the ability to attract once again foreigners to town, with all the economic advantages such a flow would entail. He also believed that a charter for establishing a university could be obtained at that point from the emperor, Charles IV. The Company of Pastors, however, fiercely opposed that project, stressing that it would change the whole ecclesiastical constitution and deprive the church of its traditional responsibility over the Academy, an academy which had been established "pour fournir des Pasteurs, et non point pour créer des Docteurs en toutes les facultés." The pastors also tried to argue that the establishment of a university would not be in the interests of the city. Not only would it attract Catholics to town—"ce qui a toujours été regardé comme un grand mal"—but, they said, one knew only too well "combien les Ecoliers font de désordres dans les villes" where there are universities with extensive privileges.[29] Faced with such a determined opposition, the secular authorities gave in. The academic assembly rejected that proposal, and Chouet, Buisson, and other councillors decided that in a period when the rule of the oligarchy in town was threatened it was better not to alienate the Venerable Company. The idea of turning the Academy into a university did not die out, however. It was raised several times in the next generation. Thus, the lay professor of philosophy Jean-Antoine Gautier suggested that possibility in his inaugural address as Rector in 1719. He envisioned a university with chairs in natural law, medicine, anatomy, botany, and chemistry, probably taking the University of Leiden as his model.[30] The idea of a university was also mentioned, as we shall presently see, in connection with discussions concerning the establishment of new chairs in the Academy in the early 1720s and late 1730s. Yet nothing came out of these various proposals. Till the end of the ancien régime (and in fact until the second half of the nineteenth century), Geneva had an academy rather than a university proper.

Nevertheless, during the eighteenth century the Academy increasingly became a civic university, in essence if not in name. This can be seen in the type of students enrolled, in the new chairs that were founded, as well as in the growing control of the city councils over academic affairs. We shall limit ourselves here largely to the first few decades of the century. In terms of student enrollment, the Academy clearly overcame the severe crisis of the turn of the century. Both the literary sources and the quantitative data point to a moderate growth in the number of students from the early years of the century onward. Yet much of this growth came from Geneva proper. Indeed, whereas in the seventeenth century local students usually constituted less than 20 percent of the student body, by 1725 they were close to 50 percent. Concomitant with this rise was a relative decline in the number of theology students.[31] Such changes strengthened the claims of the city councils to have greater authority over the Academy. A similar "parochialization" is also noticeable in the recruitment of professors. In the seventeenth century non-Genevans were sometimes appointed to chairs in the Academy, and in the cases when a *concurs* was declared it was opened to Genevans and foreigners alike.[32] In the eighteenth century, by contrast, most regularly the *programme* for a *concours* was addressed only to Genevans, though foreigners were not explicitly excluded. It is interesting to note that the Company of Pastors repeatedly asked to open the competition officially for foreigners, too, whereas the Small Council felt that there were enough suitable candidates in town.[33] Evidently, the Venerable Company was still somewhat international in its orientation, but by the eighteenth century it no longer succeeded in impressing that character on the Academy.

The growing involvement of the city authorities in academic affairs is most noticeable, however, in the appointment of professors and especially in the establishment of new chairs, although the process was slower and more hesitant than the parallel founding of new chairs in the University of Edinburgh in that same generation.[34] The pastors in the eighteenth century did not object to the enlargement of the scope of studies in the Academy. In their values, culture, and education the pastors shared the "enlightened" outlook of the Genevan oligarchy. What bothered them was only the question of institutional control over the Academy. The Council of the Two Hundred, on its part, similarly pressed to gain a greater role in academic affairs. After it was purged of radical elements following the Fatio affair of 1707, the Two Hundred cooperated more closely with the Small Council. Both councils, after all, were constituted of members of the oligarchy, and in the eighteenth century they needed to establish a common front vis-à-vis the rest of the Bourgeoisie in town which grew increasingly radical. Consequently, the gradual "secularization" of the control over the Academy in the eighteenth century also meant growing involvement of the Two Hundred in academic matters. This becomes amply clear in the new chairs which were successfully founded in the 1720s and 1730s.

One major development was the reorganization of law instruction in the Academy in the early 1720s. As mentioned above, law instruction was never very regular in the Academy, and law students did not regard themselves as regular students.[35] The teaching of Pierre Mussard, the law professor since 1686, was apparently not very effective. In the 1710s there is evidence that informal teaching of law was done privately in town, often by foreigners who were not necessarily doctors of law.[36] Following the death of Mussard, the Syndics Chouet and Sartoris and the philosophy professor Gautier took the initiative to reform and reorganize law teaching in the Academy. A committee was formed in June 1722 which recommended establishing two chairs in which natural law and civil law would be taught.[37] The plan itself to expand law teaching and modernize it by including natural law in the curriculum did not cause any controversy. The Company of Pastors, in fact, congratulated the council on that decision, which would enable young Genevans to study law in their own city (*Patrie*) rather than seek it abroad and incur high expenses.[38] Indeed, the pastors stressed that this broadening of studies was the original aim of the founders of the Academy.[39] They even referred at a certain point to the wish to create "une florissante Université," adding, however, that it would render the Academy "plus célèbre et plus recommendable parmi tous les *Protestants*."[40] The problem arose rather concerning the manner of election of the law professors, their status and future relationship with the Company of Pastors. Although the Venerable Company did not claim, at this point, to elect the law professors (it would do so sixteen years later, as we shall see), it argued that it could not admit within its ranks professors whom it did not elect itself. Could the Company let such members participate in the election and censure of other professors who were often pastors as well? The pastors obviously feared that the law professors would act as a secular "fifth column" within the Company. At a certain point they even suggested to incorporate the law professors fully into the Company rather than let them participate only in the discussion of academic affairs. The Small Council insisted, however, that the law professors not be an integral part of the Venerable Company but should join it whenever academic matters were to be discussed. While they would not participate in the election and censure of the professors of theology and Oriental languages, they should definitely take part in the election and supervision over the professors of other lay disciplines, namely philosophy and belles lettres.[41] This last point is historically significant as it highlights the curious status of philosophy and belles lettres in Geneva. Traditionally viewed as propadeutic to theology, the holders of these chairs were regular members of the Company of Pastors and often (though not necessarily) pastors themselves. Yet the City Council viewed these subjects, together with law, as typically lay disciplines. Unable (or unwilling) to deprive the Venerable Company of its traditional right to elect the philosophy and belles lettres professors, the city authorities nevertheless managed to introduce their own nominees (the law professors and, soon, other law professors as well) to participate in these elections. After long debates the Venerable Company had no alternative but to accept these new arrangements and to admit the law professors within its ranks when academic matters were discussed and decided.

Simultaneously with the debate with the Venerable Company, the Small Council had to deal with another challenge, coming from the Council of the Two Hundred. Viewing the *règlement* concerning the law chairs as a new arrangement affecting the structure of the Academy, the Two Hundred demanded that it be brought before them for approval.[42] The Small Council, though initially it tried to belittle the novelty of the reorganization of the law chairs and although no precedent could be found to support the demand of the Two Hundred, finally decided to bring the *règlement* before them.[43] When the *règlement* was brought before the Two Hundred, however, they demanded not only to discuss the founding of the two chairs but also to elect the professors themselves.[44] A long and highly interesting debate followed in which political and professional considerations intermingled. Some pressed for a professional approach: a commission predominantly of lawyers would elect the law professors. Others claimed that such a procedure was contrary to the constitutional structure of the Academy and the city. Once a political approach was adopted, it was difficult to oppose the claims of the Two Hundred to elect the professors, especially since the Small Council included many relatives of the present candidates who would be barred from taking part in these elections. The decision was thus made to give this time to the Two Hundred the right to elect the law professors, without regarding it as a precedent for the future.[45] A joint committee of members of the Small Council and the Two Hundred actually handled the *concours,* published the *programme,* and examined the candidates, and the Two Hundred ultimately elected unanimously Jean-Jacques Burlamaqui and Jean Cramer to these chairs. Both were to be strong upholders of the oligarchic regime in the next generation, furnishing it with a new ideology based on natural law.[46]

It is important to stress, however, that this "political" approach to the election was adopted only since there was no academic senate with authority to run the Academy and elect its professors. In fact, in the course of the discussions concerning the law chairs, the Two Hundred raised once again the suggestion to form an effective academic senate which would elect the lay professors in the Academy and in which they would have their own representatives.[47] As before, nothing came out of this proposal, and the Genevan Academy continued to be run by a curious combination of the Company of Pastors and the city councils, with steady increase in the role of the Two Hundred in academic affairs.[48] Thus, the following year, in 1724, the Two Hundred were granted the right to approve the establishment of a regular chair of mathematics and the election of the two professors, Jean-Louis Calandrini and Gabriel Cramer, to that chair.[49] The Venerable Company, which was not even consulted on that issue, acquiesced this time, although it regarded mathematics as a branch of philosophy, the chair of which was still under its charge. Like the law professors, the professors of mathematics were to join the Company when it discussed academic affairs.[50] A pattern was already established according to which new chairs of lay disciplines were under the jurisdiction of the Council of the Two Hundred.

The growing role of the Council of the Two Hundred should once again be understood against the background of the political events in Geneva in the eighteenth century. As mentioned above, following the Fatio affair of 1707 the Council of the Two Hundred, now purged of its radical members, increasingly cooperated with the Small Council and was seen more and more as an ally in the struggle against the Bourgeoisie. Indeed, some spokesmen of the oligarchy were keen to stress after 1707 that the sovereign body in town was the Council of the Two Hundred rather than the General Assembly of all citizens.[51] On the other hand, in spite of the gradual decline in the prestige and importance of the Company of Pastors, it could not be dispensed with altogether. The ministers—most of whom were members of the ruling families but whose pastoral work brought them into daily contact with the citizens in town—held an important mediating function between the oligarchy and the town Bourgeoisie. This became clear in the course of the political tumults in Geneva between 1734 and 1738.[52] Nevertheless, faced with the growing radicalization and threats of violence on the part of the Bourgeoisie (now much better organized and unified than in 1707), the Venerable Company was quite helpless, and its influence declined. It was ultimately the mediating intervention of foreign powers, primarily France, not that of the pastors, which saved the rule of the oligarchy in town for another generation.[53]

It is in this context that academic developments in the late 1730s should be seen. First, an honorary chair of experimental physics was founded in 1737. Interestingly enough, the proposal was made by two staunch opponents of the radical Bourgeoisie, Jean-Jacques Trembley in the Council of the Two Hundred and Gabriel Grenus in the Small Council.[54] The proposal was enthusiastically supported by the philosophy professors (two of whom, Cramer and Calandrini, were ardent Newtonians) in a detailed memorandum they had submitted to the council.[55] The Company of Pastors similarly supported this establishment, the more so since the candidate in question (Jean Jallabert) was himself a minister. Consequently, his membership in the Company was not a problem either.[56] Once again, it was the oligarchic regime which supported the new experimental science and created a special chair for that purpose in the Academy, and on that issue the pastors were in complete agreement with the magistrates.[57]

The Venerable Company was less submissive, however, a year and a half later when the Small Council decided in January 1739 to nominate Jean-Pierre Cromelin as honorary professor of civil history. Though acquiescing with that particular decision, the pastors took the occasion to look into the whole issue not only of honorary professorships but of academic nominations by the city councils in general. They formed a commission which produced the following April a long and detailed memorandum.[58] The memorandum clearly aimed at regaining for the Venerable Company those privileges of election which were recently lost to the secular bodies, especially to the Council of the Two Hundred. In the first part of the document, entitled "Raisons de Droit," the commission argued that the various *ordonnances* dealing with the Academy clearly entrusted the Company of Pastors with the privilege to elect *all* professors of the Academy. The City Council had only the authority to approve or to reject the decision of the Company.[59] The second part put forward the "Raisons de Convenance" in favor of keeping the elections of all professors in the hands of the Company.[60] The commission portrayed the Company of Pastors and Professors as a body of experts not only in theology but also in philosophical matters and in the humanistic sciences. They were the ones who could judge the methods, the eloquence and erudition, as well as the linguistic abilities (i.e., Latin) of the various candidates. The Venerable Company projected itself in typically "enlightened" terms, as a company of *gens de lettres,* both ecclesiastical and lay, who could learn from each other. While maintaining that "in a city such as ours, it is extremely important that the human sciences should be taught in a manner useful to religion," the commission argued that only within the Venerable Company could the harmony between the various disciplines and the different types of scholars be maintained.[61] Finally, in the last part of the memorandum the commission claimed that even in disciplines such as law and mathematics the Venerable Company was the appropriate body to elect the professors—in mathematics, because it was clearly a branch of philosophy, traditionally under the jurisdiction of the Company; and in law, because they had enough knowledge in natural law (though admittedly they were not experts in civil law) and were most capable to judge the method, philosophical background, and linguistic knowledge of the candidates.[62]

The pastors' conception of culture was hence very much that of the Protestant Enlightenment of the period. Nonetheless, it is highly significant that this detailed memorandum was hardly discussed after it was submitted to the Small Council. The pastors' claim to regain the privilege to elect all professors was apparently not heeded, and the existing complicated division of the control over the Academy remained. Since the political crisis in the fall of 1737 was quieted by external French intervention, not by the Venerable Company, the pastors lost quite a bit of their leverage power. From the 1740s on, the Council of the Two Hundred was regularly in charge of the election of the law professors, the professors of mathematics, and the occasional honorary professors.[63]

The point that the Company of Pastors did not oppose the broadening of secular subjects in the Academy, only the "secularization" of the institutional control over it, may be finally illustrated by examining the question of a chair of medicine. The proposal to open medical teaching in the Academy was first made in the eighteenth century by Pierre Fatio and Jean Buisson in the Council of the Two Hundred in 1704 and 1706, before Fatio became openly involved in radical politics.[64] The idea was later picked up by Rector Gautier, as mentioned above, by the theologian Jean-Alphonse Turrettini, and by Daniel Le Clerc, one of the prominent physicians in town.[65] The opposition to such a project came, surprisingly enough, from the Corps de Médecine, the guild of practicing physicians, surgeons, and apothecaries in the city. Within this guild (also called the Faculté de Médecine), two doctors used to give instruction in anatomy, surgery, and pharmacology for the surgeons, pharmacists, and their assistants. The *faculté,* headed by a Doyen—the oldest doctor—was also responsible for the licensing of doctors, surgeons, and pharmacists, and it feared that a professor of medicine would cast a shadow over its professional authority and assume control over medical affairs in town.[66] In 1713, Daniel Le Clerc, who was mentioned above, formed a Société de Médecine under the auspices of the Small Council. The society was to meet weekly and discuss medical questions in a way which would be instructive for young physicians and other "aspirants à la médecine." The council urged opening those meetings to the public at large so as the society "feroit honneur à cette Ville." Yet such a society could not be a substitute for regular medical teaching, and in any case it did not survive its founders.[67]

Only in 1755 was an honorary professor of medicine appointed in the Academy, Théodore Tronchin, the disciple and successor of Boerhaave and celebrated physician of Voltaire.[68] Not much came out of this nomination.

The Faculté de Médecine kept trying to obstruct such medical teaching in the Academy, Tronchin himself hardly gave systematic lectures, and in 1766 he left for Paris. Since it was a personal chair, no successor was appointed and no medical teaching was established in the Academy during the ancien régime. Yet the episode is important primarily because the Company of Pastors was the initiator for Tronchin's appointment. The memorandum it presented to the Small Council on this issue is highly revealing since it shows the extent to which the pastors themselves wanted by the middle of the eighteenth century to give the Academy a civic character. Indeed, they stressed that the establishment of a chair of medicine was a constant wish of those responsible for the Academy from Calvin himself onward, and they mentioned specifically Gautier and Turrettini in the early eighteenth century. Moreover, the pastors emphasized the importance of such a chair for improving the health and welfare of the citizens, for attracting foreign students to Geneva, and for the honor of the Republic. Indeed, they added "cette chaire est la seule qui manque à l'Académie dans l'ordre des Facultés. Ce relief nous fera marcher de pair avec les autres Académies et les Universités Ordinaires."[69]

This last quotation reveals once again the ambivalent attitude of the Genevan Company of Pastors to the idea of a complete university in town. Intellectually they were very much in favor of such a university, provided, however, that they would maintain control over it. The secular authorities, on the other hand, wished to turn the Academy into a civic university in terms of the constitutional bodies which would run it, but not all groups in town were in favor of establishing a complete cycle of studies in such a university. The medical corporation adamantly opposed any attempt to introduce regular medical teaching into the Academy. Hence, the obstacles in the way of turning Calvin's Academy into a full-fledged civic university cannot be explained merely on the basis of simple church-state tensions.

Finally, it should be borne in mind that the Genevan Academy of the eighteenth century was by no means the exclusive center of intellectual activity in town. Important intellectuals and scientists remained outside it. Some of them, like Charles Bonnet, the most important Genevan scientist in that period, were members of the oligarchy and could live on the income of their estates.[70] Some preferred another job rather than an academic post. Thus, the well-known scholar, theologian, and historian Firmin Abauzit declined an offer of the philosophy chair in 1723 but accepted a post as librarian in 1727. Toward the end of his life, in fact, he got involved to some extent in radical politics, following the condemnation of Rousseau's *Contrat Social* in 1762.[71] Other scientists and intellectuals were also clearly connected with radical circles in town. Jean-André Deluc, the future geologist, was the son of Jacques-François Deluc, a leader of the radical opposition in the 1760s. Jean-André was engaged in commerce, and, although elected to the Two Hundred in 1770, he left Geneva in 1773 when his business failed.[72] The scientist Georges-Louis Le Sage, who tried to develop a mechanistic account of gravitation, was the son of another radical thinker, Georges-Louis Le Sage Sr. whose work *L'Esprit des loix* was condemned in Geneva in 1652. Being a *natif* (he received his Bourgeoisie gratis only in 1770), Le Sage Jr. could not practice medicine as his father hoped he would, nor could he teach in the Academy, and had to make a living by private teaching.[73] It is not accidental that Abauzit, the Delucs father and son, and Le Sage Sr. and Jr. were in contact and correspondence with the greatest Genevan radical of all, Jean-Jacques Rousseau, though Deluc Jr. and Le Sage Jr. tried to disengage themselves somewhat from radical politics.[74] The relationship between the Academy, embodying the values of the "Magisterial Enlightenment," and the more radical intellectuals outside it is a separate subject, however. The purpose here was to highlight the curious constitution of the Genevan Academy in the eighteenth century, which was no longer an international Calvinist Academy but not quite a civic university either. That constitution reflected the various social, political, and institutional tensions in Geneva of that period. It also shows that neither "university" nor "city" is a homogeneous entity. The relationship between them is necessarily complex.

NOTES

This article was written while I was a research fellow at the Institute for Advanced Studies, The Hebrew University, Jerusalem. I wish to thank the staff of the Institute, as well as all my colleagues there, for their unfailing assistance and cordial advice. I also wish to thank the staff of the *Archives d'Etat* and the *Bibliothèque publique et universitaire* in Geneva for their constant help, and the members of the *Institute d'histoire de la réformation* for their regular hospitality. Finally, thanks are due to Bernard Lescaze from Geneva, with whom I had fruitful conversations concerning the subject of this paper, and to the other participants of the colloquium on "The City and the University," particularly Professor Thomas Bender, for their important and helpful comments. Needless to say, I alone am responsible for whatever faults still remain in this article.

1. D'Ivernois first made this suggestion to John Adams in a memorandum he wrote in August 1794. He sent a similar memorandum to Jefferson on 5 September of that year. It is worth pointing out that the Genevan-born Albert Gallatin (1761–1849), then already an important Republican politician and later secretary of the Treasury and diplomat, was also approached by D'Ivernois, though he was quite skeptical about the plan from the start. On François D'Ivernois (1757–1842) and the whole project of transferring the Genevan Academy to America, see O. Karmin, *Sir Francis D'Ivernois, 1757–1842: Sa vie, son oeuvre et son temps* (Geneva, 1920), pp. 273–92, and pp. 640–48 for D'Ivernois's original memorandum to Adams. Jefferson's letter to Washington may be found in Jared Sparks, ed., *The Writings of George Washington: Being His Correspondence, Addresses, Messages, and Other Papers, Official and Private* (Boston, 1836), XI, 473–76. His earlier letter to D'Ivernois of 6 February may be found in Paul Leicester Ford, ed., *The Writings of Thomas Jefferson*, 12 vols. (New York and London, 1896), VII, 2–6. On this affair, see also Herbert B. Adams, "The College of William and Mary: A Contribution to the History of Higher Education, with Suggestions for Its National Promotion," in *Circulars of Information of the U.S. Bureau of Education,*

no. 1 (Washington, 1887); and idem, "Thomas Jefferson and the University of Virginia," in *Circulars of Information of the U.S. Bureau of Education*, no. 1 (Washington, 1888). See also Charles Borgeaud, *Histoire de l'Université de Genève*. Vol. I: *L'Académie de Calvin 1559–1798* (Geneva, 1900), pp. 611–13.

2. Sparks, *The Writings of George Washington*, XI, 473.

3. Letter of George Washington to Thomas Jefferson, 15 March 1795, in John C. Fitzpatrick, ed., *The Writings of George Washington from the Original Manuscript Sources, 1744–1799* (Washington: U.S. Government Printing Office, 1940), XXXIV, 146–49, quotation from p. 148. It should be stressed, however, that Jefferson himself expressed similar reservations concerning the political orientation of the Genevan Academy already in 1785 in a letter to J. Bannister. See Karmin, *Sir Francis D'Ivernois*, pp. 273–74.

4. See also Merril D. Peterson, *Thomas Jefferson and the New Nation, A Biography* (New York, 1970), pp. 961–88. Peterson is mistaken, however, in calling the Genevan Academy a "seminary" (p. 963).

5. For the history of Geneva and its special characteristics at the time of the Reformation, see William E. Monter, *Calvin's Geneva* (New York, 1967), and his earlier work, *Studies in Genevan Government: 1536–1605* (Geneva, 1964). On the history of the Academy, the standard history is the magisterial study of Borgeaud, *Histoire de l'Université de Genève*. Vol. I: *L'Académie de Calvin, 1559–1798*. For the history of the Academy in the late seventeenth and early eighteenth centuries, particularly the introduction of Cartesian science in the Academy, see Michael Heyd, *Between Orthodoxy and the Enlightenment: Jean-Robert Chouet and the Introduction of Cartesian Science in the Academy of Geneva* (The Hague, and Jerusalem, 1982).

6. See Borgeaud, *L'Académie de Calvin*, pp. 29–63, esp. pp. 51–53.

7. Ibid., pp. 87–101. See also the introduction which Beza added to the *Leges Academicae* published by Borgeaud, p. 626. For Beza's correspondence in the 1560s concerning these plans, see *Correspondance de Théodore de Bèze*, ed. H. Aubert et al. (Geneva, 1970) VI, 93–94, and ed. H. Aubert et al., (Geneva, 1976), VIII, 86–89. See also Paul E. Geisendorf, *Théodore de Bèze* (Geneva, 1949), pp. 261–63, 327–30.

8. On Calvin's deep suspicions toward lawyers, whom he viewed as adversaries and challengers to the authority of the ministers, see his letter to Gaspard Olevianus in Heidelberg on 27 October 1562, in *Joannis Calvini Opera quae supersunt omnia*, ed. G. Baum et al., XIX, 564, in *Corpus Reformatorum* (Brunswick: Schwetschke, 1863–1900), XLVII.

9. For the sporadic instruction of law in Geneva in the sixteenth and seventeenth centuries, see Borgeaud, *L'Académie de Calvin*, pp. 87–93, 277–312, 368–71. On Simon Simoni and the abortive attempts to establish a medical chair in the sixteenth century, see pp. 94–101.

10. See Heyd, *Between Orthodoxy and the Enlightenment*, pp. 145–57. For the quantitative data, see also Appendix II, Table 16, p. 276.

11. See ibid., pp. 157–65. In this respect, Geneva was exceptional in comparison to other Swiss academies, where the *scholarques*, together with the professor and only a few ecclesiastics, were in charge of academic affairs in the seventeenth century. See Ulrich Im Hof, "Die reformierten Hohen Schulen und ihre schweizerischen Stadtstaaten," in E. Maschke and J. Sydow, *Stadt und Universität im Mittelalter und in der früheren Neuzeit*, Veröffentlichungen des Südwestdeutschen Arbeitskreises für Stadtgeschichtsforschung, no. 3 (Sigmaringen, 1977).

12. See Heyd, *Between Orthodoxy and the Enlightenment*, pp. 37–54.

13. Ibid., pp. 154–57.

14. See ibid., pp. 175–78, 228–35, and App. II. For the Swiss universities, see Im Hof, "Die reformierten Hohen Schulen," pp. 60–61, 64.

15. Heyd, *Between Orthodoxy and the Enlightenment*, pp. 175–78. For the decline in student enrollment in other European universities, see Lawrence Stone, "The Size and Composition of the Oxford Student Body, 1580–1909," in Lawrence Stone, ed., *The University in Society* (Princeton, N.J., 1974), I, 37–59; and Henry Kamen, *The Iron Century: Social Change in Europe, 1550–1660* (London, 1971), pp. 289–92.

16. For Leiden, see Edward G. Ruestow, *Physics at Seventeenth and Eighteenth Century Leiden: Philosophy and the New Science in the University* (The Hague, 1973), intro. For Edinburgh, see Nicholas Phillipson, "Culture and Society in the 18th Century Province: The Case of Edinburgh and the Scottish Enlightenment," in Stone, *The University in Society*, II, 407–48, and his article in this volume. See also Ronald C. Cant, "Origins of the Enlightenment in Scotland: The Universities," in R. H. Campbell and Andrew S. Skinner, eds., *The Origins and Nature of the Scottish Enlightenment* (Edinburgh, 1982), pp. 42–64; as well as the older thesis by Isabel Kenrick, "The University of Edinburgh 1660–1715: A Study in the Transformation of Teaching Methods and Curriculum" (Ph.D. diss., Bryn Mawr, Penn., 1956), chap. 3. See also Alexander Morgan and Robert Keer Hannay, eds., *University of Edinburgh: Charters, Statutes, and Acts of the Town Council and the Senatus, 1583–1858* (Edinburgh and London, 1937), pp. 136–39. On the Swiss academies, see Im Hof, "Die reformierten Hohen Schulen," pp. 58–59.

17. Heyd, *Between Orthodoxy and the Enlightenment*, pp. 178–89. For the *Schulrat* in Swiss cities like Zurich or Bern, see Im Hof, "Die reformierten Hohen Schulen," pp. 58–60.

18. Heyd, *Between Orthodoxy and the Enlightenment*, pp. 180–82.

19. The most serious occasion on which there developed a confrontation between the Two Hundred and the Small Council in that period was the Sarasin affair of 1667, a confrontation which concerned judicial and formal issues and in which the Bourgeoisie clearly supported the Two Hundred. The pastors played an important mediatory role in that affair. Once it was resolved, however, all sides did their best to suppress the memory of this event, and no mention of it was made in the official registers. See the old but still important article of E. Mallet, "Conflit entre le Petit Conseil et le Conseil des Deux Cents en 1667, ou Episode de l'Auditeur Sarasin," *Mémoires et documents de la Société d'histoire et d'archéologie de Genève* (1840–1842), I, 277–320.

20. On the Fatio revolt of 1707, the only book-length study is still André Corbaz, *Pierre Fatio, précurseur et martyr de la démocratie genevoise, 1662–1707* (Geneva, 1923). See also, however, J.-P. Ferrier, "Le XVIIIe siecle. Politique intérieure et extérieur," in Paul E. Martin, ed., *Histoire de Genève des origines à 1798* (Geneva, 1951); and Robert Félalime, *La Genève de mes ancêtres* (Geneva, 1979), chaps. VIII, IX.

21. See, on these topics, Pierre Bertrand, *Genève et la revocation de l'Edit de Nantes* (Geneva, 1935); Anne-Marie Piuz, *Affairs et politiques: Recherches sur le commerce de Genève au XVIIe siècle* (Paris, 1966), pp. 384–91, as well as her article, "La Disette de 1693–1694 à Genève et ses conséquences démographiques," *Mélanges publiés par la Faculté des Sciences Economiques et Sociales de l'Uni-*

versité de Genève (Geneva, 1965), pp. 175–85; Heyd, *Between Orthodoxy and the Enlightenment*, pp. 175–78; and, finally, the recent collective work by O. Reverdin, J. Sautier, et al., *Genève et la Révocation de l'Edit de Nantes. Mémoires et documents publiés par la Société d'histoire et d'archéologie de Genève*, Vol. L (Geneva and Paris, 1985), particularly the monographs of Jérôme Sautier (esp. pp. 123–58), Olivier Fatio (esp. pp. 278–81), and Liliane Mottu-Weber (esp. pp. 324–28, 383–86).

22. See René Guerdan, *Histoire de Genève* (Paris, 1981), pp. 169–86.

23. On the motivations of Pierre Fatio, see ibid., pp. 178–79; and Félalime, *La Genève de mes ancêtres*, p. 75.

24. Chouet, it should be stressed, was the one who responded to Fatio in the fateful session of the Conseil Général of 5 May, 1707. On this speech, which expressed the moderate line of the oligarchy, and some important extracts from it, see W. A. Liebeskind, "Le Discours du Syndic Chouet sur la nature du gouvernement de l'Etat de Genève" and "Un Débat sur la démocratie Genevoise: Chouet et Fatio au Conseil Général (5 Mai 1707)," both published in his *Institutions politiques et traditions nationales* (Geneva, 1973), pp. 188–204.

25. The register of the academic assembly of *scholarques* and professors is kept at the Bibliotèque Publique et Universitaire in Geneva, Ms. francais, Vol. 985. It begins in 1702, and the first volume ends in 1719. The assembly convened apparently several years before 1702, too, but no registers have been found of these years. For the simultaneous use of the terms "assemblée académique" and "sénat académique," see, for example, the discussion in the Venerable Company of Pastors on 20 and 27 June 1721, Registres de la Vénérable, Compagnie des Pasteur in the Archives d'Etat in Geneva, R 21, pp. 77–78. On the conflicting views concerning the status and role of this assembly, see, for instance, the discussions around the elections of a philosophy professor in 1723. Although there was no debate between the Venerable Company and the Small Council on substantive issues—the Council approved the request of the pastors to postpone the *concours* for a new professor and to let Ezéchiel Gallatin fulfill these functions in the meantime—it nevertheless reprimanded the Company for not mentioning the prior resolution of the Sénat Académique, a reticence which did not pay due honor to that body. See minutes of the Petit Conseil, 20 January 1723, in *Registres du Conseil* (henceforth *RC*) in the Archives d'Etat in Geneva, 222, pp. 83–85.

26. See Heyd, *Between Orthodoxy and the Enlightenment*, pp. 218–28.

27. Ibid., pp. 204–12.

28. Jean Buisson made his proposal on 5 December 1707 and on 4 June 1708. On the first of these occasions he coupled this proposal with suggestions to take harsh measures against those who participated with Pierre Fatio in the radical proposals to establish a secret ballot in the General Assembly the previous year. See *RC*, Vol. 207, pp. 835–36, and Vol. 208, p. 350. On the latter day Chouet raised the same issue in the Academic Assembly; see Ms. Fr. 985, fols. 80–83. The text of his proposals was published by Borgeaud, *L'Académie de Calvin*, pp. 497–99. Jean Buisson, a doctor of law, belonged to one of the richest families in town. See J. A. Galiffe et al., *Notices généalogiques sur les familles genevoises*, (1892), II, 511.

29. See Ms. Fr. 985, fols. 80–83; and Borgeaud, *L'Académie de Calvin*, p. 498. Interestingly enough, however, the registers of the Venerable Company do not mention these propositions at all, neither following Buisson's proposal in De-

cember 1707 nor after Chouet's proposals in June 1708. See RCP, Vol. R 19, pp. 235–37, 293–95.

30. See Borgeaud, *L'Académie de Calvin*, p. 586.

31. Heyd, *Between Orthodoxy and the Enlightenment*, pp. 228–35 and App. II. Among the literary sources for these developments are the minutes of the academic assembly, Ms. Fr. 985, pp. 96, 100, 104, 110; and the report of the Rector before the Small Council in 1724, *RC*, Vol. 223, p. 338. The numbers given in these sources are usually higher than the quantitative data we have since many students did not register in the Livre du Recteur on which our quantitative study was largely based. See Heyd, App. I. For similar developments in the Swiss Academies and in Basel, see Im Hof, "Die reformierten Hohen Schulen," pp. 60–61, 64.

32. Most of the foreigners, however, usually had some previous connection in town. Among the cases which can be mentioned are Nicholas Vedel, from the Palatinate, who was elected as a philosophy professor in 1618 (he was, however, in town since the previous year); Friederich Spanheim, also from the Palatinate, the theology professor between 1631 and 1642 (though he was a former student in the Academy); the Scotsman Alexandre Morus, who was first Greek professor (1639–1642) and later nominated as Spanheim's successor; Philippe Reynard Vitriarius, of the Palatinate, who was nominated as a professor of law in 1675 and soon married into a Genevan family; or the German Jean-Melchoir Steinberg (though born in Geneva), who was elected as a philosophy professor in 1650 together with the Genevan Puerari, following a *concours*. See Borgeaud, *L'Académie de Calvin*, pp. 348–53 (Spanheim), 353–57 (Morus), 404–5 (Steinberg), 386–89 (Vitriarius), 398–99 (Vedel).

33. In 1719, for example, it was decided in the academic assembly that only Genevans would be invited to the *concours* for a professor of belles lettres (Ms. Fr. 985, fol. 121). A similar decision was made by the Venerable Company in 1723 concerning the *concours* for a philosophy professor (*RCP*, R 21, p. 244), and in 1724 with regards to a new candidate for the chair of Hebrew and Oriental languages (*RC*, Vol. 223, p. 367). By contrast, when the second philosophy chair became vacant in 1723, the pastors asked that foreigners be invited as well, yet the Council, after a long discussion, decided that only Genevans would be invited, though it included *habitants* (people living in Geneva who were born abroad and had not received citizenship) (*RCP*, R 21, p. 351; *RC*, Vol. 222, pp. 538–39, 575). Interestingly enough, after the decision was made, an anonymous placard was posted denouncing the exclusion of foreigners from the competition (*RCP*, R 21, pp. 393–94; *RC*, Vol. 223, p. 120). The issue was raised once again in 1734, on the occasion of the election of a new philosophy professor to succeed Gallatin, who was nominated in 1723 and died in 1733. Once again the pastors pressed to invite foreigners, or at least to let those who heard about it participate. This later compromise was indeed adopted by the Council (*RCP*, R. 24, pp. 12–14, 19–22; *RC*, Vol. 234, 8 February 1734). In 1738, however, when the need to elect a new law professor came up, the council decided to invite foreigners as well (*RC*, Vol. 238, 12 December 1738). In other Swiss academies and universities the tendency to appoint only local professors is clear already in the seventeenth century. See Im Hof, "Die reformierten Hohen Schulen," p. 62.

34. An honorary chair of civil law was established in Edinburgh in 1709, a regular chair in 1716. Formal instruction in chemistry, mathematics, and moral philosophy began in 1715, and a chair of universal history was established in 1719.

In the 1720s the faculty of medicine was reconstructed, linking it more closely with clinical teaching; finally, in 1738, a chair of botany was founded. See I. Kenrick, "The University of Edinburgh," chap. IV; and Anand C. Chitnis, "Provost Drummond and the Origins of Edinburgh Medicine," in Campbell and Skinner, eds., *The Origins and Nature of the Scottish Enlightenment,* pp. 86–98. Similar increase in the number of chairs is also noticeable in the Swiss academies in the eighteenth century. See Im Hof, "Die reformierten Hohen Schuler," pp. 61–62.

35. For efforts in the years 1710–1713 to oblige law students to matriculate as regular students, to be examined at the end of their studies, and to receive a formal certificate from the Rector, see Ms. Fr. 985, pp. 98, 101, 103. Similar efforts were renewed in 1722; see Ms. Fr. 986, session of 29 April 1722; and *RCP,* R 21, pp. 150–51 (1 May 1722). On the status of law students in Geneva in the seventeenth and early eighteenth centuries, see also Heyd, *Between Orthodoxy and the Enlightenment,* pp. 246–48; Borgeaud, *L'Académie de Calvin,* p. 450; S. Stelling-Michaud, ed., *Le Livre du Recteur de l'Académie de Genève,* (Geneva, 1959), I, 31–32.

36. Ms. Fr. 98, p. 99.

37. *RC,* Vol. 221, pp. 281–82 (7 June 1722), and the minutes of the committee meeting (26 June 1722), between pp. 446–47 and pp. 447–48, for the Council's decision. The decision was to create two chairs because there were two appropriate candidates, Jean-Jacques Burlamaqui (who served already as an honorary professor since 1720) and Jean Cramer. On both of them, see n. 46.

38. The representation of the pastors of 30 October 1722 concerning this matter is in *RCP,* R 21, pp. 206–9. A second representation, of 12 November 1722, is on pp. 214–16, and the copy presented to the council is in *RC,* Vol. 221, between pp. 586 and 587. For previous discussions of this subject by the Company of Pastors, see *RCP,* R 21, pp. 187, 191–92, 195 (2, 9, 30 October 1722). In fact, already in 1707, the theologian Jean Alphonse Turrettini had tried to bring to Geneva the famous natural law jurist Barbeyrac (who was also the teacher of Jean-Jacques Burlamaqui, the professor nominated in 1722).

39. They quoted the notice which Beza added at the beginning of the *Leges Academicae,* published by Estienne in 1559. See Borgeaud, *L'Académie de Calvin,* p. 626, for that text.

40. Borgeaud, *L'Académie de Calvin,* p. 206; my italics.

41. *RC,* Vol. 221, pp. 546–48, 587. The Council relied in its decision on the precedent of Benigne Mussard, who was joined to the Venerable Company in 1695 (though, it should be stressed, he was elected a pastor a few months earlier), and of Jacques Godefroy in 1631 (though he did not participate in the election of the theology and Hebrew professors).

42. The representation of the *Procureur Général* before the Small Council is in *RC,* Vol. 221, pp. 160–61.

43. *RC,* Vol. 221, pp. 463–64 (26, September 1722), and pp. 555–57 (30 November 1722).

44. *RC,* Vol. 221, pp. 601–2 (23 December 1722).

45. *RC,* Vol. 222, pp. 77–83 (19 January 1723).

46. *RC,* Vol. 222, pp. 194, 209–11 (15, 16, 29, 30 March 1723). On Burlamaqui (1694–1748), his role in the political affairs of Geneva, and his political theories in defense of the oligarchic regime as an "elected aristocracy," see Bernard Gagnebin, *Burlamaqui et le droit naturel* (Geneva, 1944), esp. pp. 51–65, 176–82; as well as Walther J. Habscheid, "Jean-Jacques Burlamaqui (1694–1748) und

seine *Principes du droit naturel,"* in *Staat und Geselschaft: Festgabe für Günther Küchenhoff* (Göttingen, 1967). There is also a Ph.D. dissertation which compares Burlamaqui's theories with those of Rousseau: Gary Lew Barnet, "A Comparison of the Moral and Political Ideas of Jean-Jacques Rousseau and Jean-Jacques Burlamaqui" (Ph.D. diss., Univ. of Arizona, 1970), esp. pp. 271–89. Barnet tends, however, to stress the similarities rather than the deep difference between the two. See also Robert Delathé, *"Jean-Jacques Rousseau et la science politique de son temps,* 2nd ed. (Paris, 1979), pp. 84–89, for the argument that Burlamaqui had very little influence on Rousseau.

On Jean Cramer, see Gottfried Partsch, "Jean Cramer et son précis de l'histoire du droit Genevois (1761)," *Bulletin de la Société d'histoire et d'archéologie de Genève* 13 (1964): 13–87, which consists mostly of Cramer's "Recherches historiques sur les loix de Genève." But see pp. 15–16 for biographical information and pp. 61–62 for Cramer's views concerning the political tumults of 1707 and 1734–1738 and their outcomes.

47. *RC,* Vol. 222, p. 78 (19 January 1723), p. 211 (29 March 1723). For the worries of the Venerable Company concerning this renewed project (they formed a commission which was supposed to follow any developments concerning such a plan), see *RCP,* R 21, pp. 233–34 (22 January 1723).

48. The involvement of the Council of the Two Hundred in law teaching was made clear, for example, in 1724, when the law professors wished to change the curriculum, realizing that they could not teach natural law and the *Institutes* in the same year. The academic assembly rejected their request, pointing out that only the Two Hundred could approve such a change. Ms. Fr. 986, fols. 13r–13v (21 March 1724).

49. *RC,* Vol. 223, pp. 398–99 (18 September 1724).

50. *RCP,* R 22, pp. 9–17 (15, 22 September 1724).

51. See on that subject J. Sautier, "La Médiation de 1737–1738: Contribution à l'histoire des institutions politiques de Genève," thèse d'Etat, Université de Droit, d'Economie et des Sciences Sociales de Paris, 1979, pp. 207–13.

52. See Jacob E. Cellerier, "Du rôle politique de la Vénérable Compagnie dans l'ancienne République de Genève. Spécialement dans la crise de 1734 et années suivantes," *Société d'histoire et d'archéologie de Genève; Mémoires et Documents* (1860), XII, 189–307; for the personal composition of the Venerable Company and its family links with the Council, see App. C, p. 277. The crisis began in 1734 following the debate over the right to impose new taxes for fortifications and the need to convene the General Assembly. It reached an explosion point with the famous *affaire de tamponnement,* when some members of the oligarchy secretly plugged the cannons downtown to prevent them from being used by the Bourgeoisie against the government.

53. On the French intervention in 1737–38 and the political crisis in the 1730s in general, see Sautier, "La Médiation de 1737–1738."

54. The Council decided that such a foundation would indeed be "très utile à notre ville et à notre Académie." *RC,* Vol. 237, pp. 120, 197–98 (4 April, 25 May 1737). Jean-Jacques Trembley (1705–53) was the son of Marc-Conrad Trembley, one of the councilors who were deposed after the *affaire du tamponnement.* See *Dictionnaire historique et biographique de la Suisse,* VI, 662. Another Jean-Jacques Trembley, 1676–1763, a distant relative of the former and the brother of the Syndic Jean Trembley, was himself deposed from the Two Hundred in 1734. See Galiffe, *Notices généalogiques,* II, 394. On Gabriel Grenus Jr. and

his role in the political crisis of 1737–38, see Le Baron de Grenus, *Notices biographiques sur Mm. Jacques, Theodore, Pierre, Gabriel et Jean-Louis Grenus* (Geneva, 1849), pp. 17–23, 81–103; and Sautier, "La Médiation de 1737–1738."

55. *RC*, Vol. 237, between pp. 198 and 199. Calandrini performed some important mediating functions during the crisis in 1734. Cramer was the brother of the law professor who was shortly to become a member of the Small Council and a key politician in town.

56. *RCP*, R 25, pp. 13, 17–19 (31 May, 7 June 1737); *RC*, Vol. 237, pp. 214–15 (6 June 1737).

57. In his inaugural lecture two years later, Jean Jallabert clearly expressed his gratitude to the oligarchic regime in town, to both the secular and ecclesiastical authorities. Especially noteworthy was his reverential reference to Gabriel Grenus, who had died in the meantime. Jean Jallabert, *De Philosophiae Experimentalis ultilitate, illiusque et Matheseos Concordia* (Geneva, 1740), esp. pp. 2, 12–13.

58. The original document is in *RCP*, R 25, between pp. 249 and 250: "Mémoire Dressé par Mess. les Commissaires de la V.C. Sur la Part qu'elle doit avoir à l'Election des Professeurs." A handwritten copy may also be found in the *Archives d'Etat*, *Académie* Aa 2 bis 4. Both copies are unpaginated.

59. The commission based itself on the 1576 edition of the *Ordonnances Ecclésiastiques* and on the *Odre des Ecoles*, its first Latin edition of 1559 (*Leges Academiae*), but especially its French edition of 1609. The pastors argued that this latter version had the status of a constitutional document and was the only text according to which the issue of electing professors had to be determined.

60. *RCP*, R 25, ibid., 2nd part. This part of the text was also quoted by Borgeaud, *L'Académie de Calvin*, pp. 521–25.

61. *RCP*, R 25, ibid., 2nd part. The quotation in the original reads as follows: "il importe extrêmement, sur tout dans une Ville comme la nôtre, que les Sciences humaines soient enseignées d'une manière utile à la Religion." Ibid., 2nd part, sec. V.

62. *RCP*, R 25, ibid., 3rd part. This section was not quoted by Borgeaud.

63. See Borgeaud, *L'Académie de Calvin*, pp. 525–28.

64. *RC*, Vol. 204, p. 373 (7 July 1704); *RC*, Vol. 206, p. 160 (5 April 1706).

65. Ms. Fr. 986, 27 June 1719, 11 June 1720. On Daniel Le Clerc, see Leon Gautier, *La Médecine à Genève jusqu'à la fin du dix-huitième siècle* (Geneva, 1906), pp. 331–35, 341–43, 433, and 533–34 for a list of his writings. See also P. Röthlisberger, "Daniel Le Clerc (1652–1728) und seine *Histoire de la médicine*," *Gesnerus* 21 (1964): 126–41, esp. 126–132 for biographical information.

66. See Borgeaud, *L'Académie de Calvin*, pp. 583–85; and Gautier, *La Médecine à Genève*, pp. 336–40. It is worth comparing the developments in Geneva concerning a chair of medicine to the reforms of medical teaching in Edinburgh in the early eighteenth century. There, the College of Surgeons and the College of Physicians closely cooperated with the university faculty of medicine. See Anand C. Chitnis, "Provost Drummond and the Origins of Edinburgh Medicine," in Campbell and Skinner, eds., *The Origins and Nature of the Scottish Enlightenment*, pp. 86–98.

67. Borgeaud, *L'Académie de Calvin*, pp. 585–86, Gautier, *La Médecine à Genève*, pp. 333–35.

68. On Théodore Tronchin (1709–81), see Borgeaud, *L'Académie de Calvin*, pp. 587–88; Gautier, *La Médecine à Genève*, pp. 337–38, 435, 553–54. See also

Henry Tronchin, *Théodore Tronchin (1709–1781): Un médecin du XVIIIe siècle: D'apres des documents inédits* (Paris and Geneva, 1906).

69. *RC,* Vol. 255 (24 February 1755). The *mémoire* is between pp. 116–17, signed by Ami Lullin, the rector and professor of ecclesiastical history.

70. On Bonnet, see *Dictionary of Scientific Biography* (henceforth *DSB*), II, 286–87; Borgeaud, *L'Académie de Calvin,* pp. 564–67; and Jacques Marx, *Charles Bonnet contre les Lumières,* in *Studies on Voltaire and the Eighteenth Century* 156–57 (1976).

71. Firmin Abauzit (1679–1767), whom Rousseau regarded as the only true philosopher of the century and whose religious views clearly influenced *La Profession de foi du Vicaire Savoyard,* has not yet received the modern scholarly attention he deserves. Among the older studies, see Eugène and Emile Haag, eds., *La France Protestante,* 2nd ed. (1877), Vol. I, cols. 1–8; Clément Montfajon, *Firmin Abauzit: Réfugié Français à Genève après la Révocation de l'Edit de Nantes, 1679–1767,* (thèse, Le Vigan, 1890); Marcel Fabre, *Firmin Abauzit et J.-J. Rousseau* (Uzès, 1929). See also Borgeaud, *L'Académie de Calvin,* p. 597. For Abauzit's response to Rousseau's eulogy of him, see his letter to Rousseau of 7 March 1761, in R. A. Leigh, ed., *Correspondance complète de Jean-Jacques Rousseau* (Geneva and Madison, Wisc., 1969), VIII, Letter 1345, pp. 230–31. For two of Rousseau's letters to Abauzit (one doubtful), see ibid., XV (1972), Letter 2555, pp. 308–9, and XXII (1974), Letter 3722, pp. 198–99.

72. On DeLuc, see *DSB,* IV, 27–29.

73. On Le Sage Jr., there is an old biographical note by his disciple and former associate Pierre Prévost, *Notice de la vie et des écrits de George-Louis Le Sage de Genève* (Geneva, 1805). On the political affair concerning the *L'Espirt des Loix* of Le Sage Sr., see Andre Gür, "Un Précédent à la condamnation du 'Contrat Social': L'Affaire Georges-Louis Le Sage (1752)," *Bulletin de la Société d'histoire et d'archéologie de Genève* (1968): 77–94.

74. On Le Sage Jr.'s conversations with Rousseau in 1754, see Leigh, ed., *Correspondance Complète,* III, 14–15, and App. 135, pp. 331–34. On the political attitudes of Le Sage Jr. and Deluc Jr. in the 1760s, see *Correspondance Complète,* XXX, 267–70, and XXXI, 35–36.

7

Commerce and Culture: Edinburgh, Edinburgh University, and the Scottish Enlightenment

Nicholas Phillipson

For the first three centuries of its existence Edinburgh University was a civic university in the strictest sense of the term.[1] The Royal Charter of 1582 which authorized the Town Council of Edinburgh to establish schools and colleges in the city ("with advice, however, of the ministers") also gave it extensive if vaguely defined powers to regulate the affairs of the new Tounis College. From the outset these powers were widely interpreted, were jealously guarded, and became a source of constant friction between town and gown. Thus, the Town Council quickly established its absolute control over the finances and buildings of the college; over the apointment of principals, professors, and regents; over discipline; and, above all, over the curriculum. All attempts on the part of the faculty to establish a *senatus academicus* were firmly resisted until 1772, and even then it was to be little more than a committee of a Town Council which even insisted on presenting new professors formally to the *senatus*. "Our duty," said Principal Baird in 1826, "is to receive the Professor when they bring him to our table."[2] As the royal commissioners who were appointed to visit the Scottish universities in 1826 commented, "The most striking circumstance as to the College of Edinburgh is, that it is not erected into an independent Seminary, but it is plainly, as to all essential parts, subjected to the Provost, Magistrates and Council of the City."[3]

It was as a civic university that the college eked out the first inglorious 120 years of its existence. It was as such that its academic structure was drastically redesigned in the early decades of the eighteenth century. And it was as such that the Tounis College rather unexpectedly emerged in the second half of the century as the most important and innovative university in the Western world in the age of the late Enlightenment. It became a place of pilgrimage for students from the Continent and the Anglo-Saxon worlds in search of a modern liberal education or medical training, a source of widely used textbooks of philosophy, literature, and medicine. And it was entirely appropriate, if somewhat reckless, of the Town Council and the professors to immortalize their achievement in a vast, grandiose, ruinously expensive new building, designed by Robert Adam. Together with the great new neoclassical Exchange, Register House, and Law Courts, the new building was intended to present the modern university as an integral part of the public life of the capital city of a country whose fortunes were being transformed by commerce and politeness.[4]

We are only just beginning to realize how important the academic culture of the newly enlightened college of Edinburgh was to the contemporary world, its philosophical culture in particular. By the turn of the eighteenth and nineteenth centuries, the textbooks, treatises, and histories of professors such as Adam Ferguson, Dugald Stewart, Hugh Blair, William Robertson, and their masters and followers were being used in an astonishing number of universities at home and overseas. They are to be found in the states of northern and southern Germany and northern and southern Italy. They are to be found in Switzerland, Holland, even in Oxford and Cambridge and in the new University College of London which opened in 1826. Above all, Scottish philosophy flourished in the colleges and universities of Restoration France and in the newly independent republic of America, where it was to exert what many have felt was a stranglehold on its academic culture until the Civil War. Like the teaching of Ramus in the sixteenth and early seventeenth centuries, like that of Grotius and Pufendorf a century later, the pedagogy of Scottish professors in general and those of Edinburgh in particular had become the most powerful educational machine for training young men destined for public life in church and state. And it did so at a time when the fabric of the Western world was being transformed by war, revolution, and massive demographic and economic change.[5]

This essay is about the origins of that system of liberal or philosophical education. And although, as we shall see, it was primarily the work of a handful of professors, their achievement can only be properly understood as part of the history of a city whose citizens were deeply preoccupied with the reconstruction of their country's institutions and culture. For it was all part of an elaborate exercise in Scottish *peristroika* which was designed to turn Scotland into a prosperous, virtuous, and godly nation and an integral part of a free British polity.

For its first 120 years, the college can scarcely be described as a model of a civic university. By 1690 it was composed of a principal, three professors of divinity, a professor of humanity, a professor of mathematics (whose teaching was of ornamental rather than structural significance to the curriculum), and four regents of philosophy on whom the weight of teaching the three hundred or so students depended.[6] Like the Academy of Geneva, its primary purpose was to serve as an educational engine of reformed religion and to harness an essentially Erasmian curriculum to the needs of a Presbyterian theological education.[7] At first it had been hoped that the new college would attract the sons of the nobility and gentry as well as prospective divinity students, but that was not to be. There was little the Town Council could do to prevent the continual intrusion of the church, whether Presbyterian or Episcopalian, into the affairs of the college, and it conspicuously failed to encourage the teaching of law or medicine. Thus, from the very first, the college became a seminary whose primary function was to train boys for the church and to give some of the sons of the laity a smattering of classical and philosophical education before departing for the Continent and, above all, for Holland, for the sort of liberal education which was not available to them at home. As we shall see, by 1700 this was a situation that would no longer be tolerated, and the Genevan phase of the college's history would give place to a Dutch one.

In fact, the pressure to reconstruct the college at the end of the seventeenth century was symptomatic of a much wider concern with the state of Scotland's civil and ecclesiastical institutions, and the story of the reconstruction of the college is an important part of the quite remarkable institutional revolution which occurred between 1688 and the 1740s. It was a period that saw the restoration of the Presbyterian kirk after thirty years of Episcopalian rule and a sustained and bitter struggle for control of the new kirk by high-flying and moderate Presbyterians. It was a period that saw Scottish political institutions crumble under the pressure of aristocratic faction, economic crisis, and a rapidly deteriorating pattern of Anglo-Scottish relations. It was a period that saw the creation of the Anglo-Scottish Union of 1707 and the start of a massive exercise in adapting Scotland's political, religious, financial, and cultural institutions to service the needs of the new British polity. But, above all, it was a period that saw a transformation of the political fortunes of the middling ranks of Scottish society, the landed gentry, the professional classes, and the merchants; and in the status of Edinburgh, which was to be the focal point of their political, religious, and cultural life for the next century.[8]

It cannot be stressed too strongly how profoundly the collective life of the middling ranks was affected by these events. It was they, after all, who were primarily responsible for managing the local affairs of a country whose religious life was in turmoil and which was stricken with acute problems of poverty and underemployment in a periously underdeveloped economy. It was they who controlled much of the legal system and the kirk. It was they who had debated the condition of Scotland with notable sophistication in the decade before the Union. And it was they who became deeply involved in the political transformations which followed it. For it was to this class that the court and nobility looked for men to manage their affairs in Scotland now that the center of power had shifted from Edinburgh to London. And it was they who would dominate the social and cultural life of post-Union Edinburgh, a city which had lost its parliament and its nobility and had become a provincial capital. Under their governance the city would emerge as a modern Athens, whose citizens would become increasingly preoccupied with economic engineering, with manners and politeness, and with encouraging the growth of that philosophic, scientific, and literary culture which turned the city into one of the major sources of enlightenment in the Western world.

By the 1690s these men of middling rank already formed a highly educated elite. But this was by virtue of education they had received in Dutch, not Scottish, universities and above all in Leiden. We do not know exactly how many Scots studied in Holland between the 1690s and the 1740s, but the evidence is suggestive if patchy. Some went for two or three years, the poorer for only so many months. Some went to study law, medicine, and theology; richer and more ambitious young men such as John Clerk of Penicuick were able to study painting, music, modern languages, and especially the classics, which formed the foundation on which the liberal arts curriculum of Leiden was based. Taken as a whole, it seems that Dutch education was becoming part of the normal education of at least one son of those landed and professional families who could afford it.[9]

For those who were left at home there were exiguous but interesting educational consolations to be found in Edinburgh, not in the college but in the classrooms of private teachers or professors of such subjects as Italian and French and even, on one occasion in 1671, German and Polish; fencing and dancing; and, more important, anatomy, botany, Scots, and civil law. As Town Council minutes show, these teachers were licensed to ply their trades in the city by the Town Council which sometimes even allowed them to teach in the college classrooms.[10] Some of these licensed teachers were men of enterprise who were anxious to tap the lively market for polite education which existed among those who could not afford the delights of Holland. In 1704 John Spottiswoode was given permission to found a little academy to teach law, mathematics, grammar, logic, and rhetoric, not to mention history and philology, in the hope that this would "cultivate in your minds and actions, religion and vertue."[11] A year later William Cockburn proposed to set up "a College or lecture on Moral and Political Learning" to serve as a "Solid foundation for Law or Divinity and endue Gentlemen with many Conspicuous Qualifications suitable to their Characters."[12] Such a state of affairs simply threw into relief the uncomfortable fact that the college was simply unable to satisfy the educational needs of the country's governing elite, a fact that was underlined by the remarkable and disastrous experiments in university reform which were being undertaken by the strict Presbyterian clergy who had hijacked the General Assembly in 1690 and were engaged in an elaborate exercise in attempting to turn Scotland into a godly, neocovenanting polity. So far as the universities were concerned, they were to be purged of Episcopalians and nonjurors, and their teaching was to be radically reformed by means of a tightly controlled, neoscholastic system of education. The philosophy curriculum would be held together by a new textbook of philosophy which would be written by the regents of philosophy of the Scottish universities and authorized by Act of Parliament. And its intellectual purpose would be to harness the philosophy of the ancients and moderns to the needs of the neoscholastic, federal theology of the covenanters.[13] This remarkable, radical experiment came to very little. The new textbook was never completed. The universities of Glasgow, Aberdeen, and St. Andrew's, which were under the protection of relatively friendly chancellors, were only lightly scarred by the experiment. But Edinburgh, which was in the hands of a malleable Town Council, was less fortunate. In 1690 its Episcopalian principal was replaced by Gilbert Rule, the architect of this neoconvenanting experiment. The university promptly slid into a state of financial crisis as all but the strictest Presbyterian students fled to other pastures, and patriots such as Andrew Fletcher of Saltoun complained of the priestcraft which was destroying the nation's virtue and liberty.[14] By 1700 the professors and regents were complaining that falling student numbers meant that their salaries were only half of those their colleagues enjoyed elsewhere in Scotland and that they were "despised and falling into contempt."[15] It was clear that the Genevan era had ended.

By now the college was ripe for radical reform. The crown needed a college that could train a new generation of more moderate Presbyterian ministers. The Town Council wanted a new system of education to attract more students, improve the college's finances, and help to rationalize the complicated educational system that had grown up in the city. The result was a series of far-reaching institutional reforms which began in 1708 and were more or less completed by the 1740s. The intention was simple; the college itself was to be remodeled on the model of Leiden in the hope that this would turn what had been little more than a seminary into a college catering to sons of gentlemen as well as boys destined for the church. Regents who had taught the quadrivium and the classics to prepare students to enter Divinity Hall were turned into professors of Latin, Greek, and philosophy who would confine their teaching to a single discipline so that "all the parts of philosophy be taught in two years, as they are in the most famous universities abroad."[16] The crown founded new regius chairs in divinity and public law. Finally, the Town Council set out to tackle the problem of rationalizing the city's educational system by the simple expedient of turning some of the private teachers it had licensed to teach in the city into college professors. By the 1740s the Town Council had appointed college professors of anatomy, botany, materia medica, clinical medicine, civil history, Scots and civil law, the latter, for example, being justified because "through want of professors of the Civil Law in this Kingdom the youth who have applied themselves to that studie have been necessitate to travell and remain abroad a considerable time for their education to the prejudice of the Nation by the necessarie charges occasioned thereby untill of late some gentlemen having undertaken that profession altho' only in a private capacity have given convincing proofs how advantageously that study might be prosecute at home if countenanced and encouraged by publick authority."[17] It was a Dutch system designed to attract the sons of the nobility and gentry and even dissenters as well as boys destined for the kirk. It was intended to ensure that divinity, like law and medicine, would be taught as a liberal profession. If all went well, a clergy and a laity taught on such principles would develop that consensual understanding of the relations between the church and civil society on which the future of a godly, free, and prosperous modern polity depended.

This remarkable exercise in turning Edinburgh into a Scoto-Dutch college had the most important implications for its intellectual history. At one level the whole exercise had been nothing more than a crude exercise in modernization, Dutch institutions had been imported simply because they were Dutch, because a Dutch college seemed to be the most likely to attract well-bred, fee-paying students, and because it might conceivably provide the city with a reputable college. Much of the Dutch curriculum was imported wholesale as well. As a fascinating curriculum which was published in 1741 makes clear, the backbone of the teaching in the law, medical, and divinity faculties was supplied by standard Dutch textbooks.[18] In one crucial respect, however, simple imitation proved to be impossible. As Anthony Grafton points out in this volume, from the seventeenth until the early nineteenth centuries the crowning glory of the Leiden curriculum was its classical curriculum. It was this that held the entire system of education together and provided students with a point of entry to the study of philosophy, literature, and even the arts of war.

But however important the classics were to the structure of Leiden education and, indeed, to the classical education of generations of Scots noblemen and gentlemen who had been educated in the Low Countries, a classical famework was quite inappropriate to Scottish needs. For one thing, the teaching of divinity had always been based on philosophy. For another, the classics were, always had been, and would always remain the Achilles' heel of the Scottish system of parochial education, constantly exposing the Scots to the charge that, for all their philosophy, they were a half-educated nation.[19] The traditional claims of the old quadrivium, reinforced by the weaknesses of popular classical education and the embarrassing declension of the chairs of Latin and Greek into little more than sources of remedial education for future divinity students, presented the town councilors and professors with the problem of trying to construct a philosophy curriculum which could hold the new system of education together.

Once again, the magistrates and professors responded in an entirely predictable way, by proposing to use the texts and textbooks of Grotius and Pufendorf, the authors of the most admired, comprehensive, and widely used system of moral philosophy in the universities of the Western world. But the problem of introducing these fashionable textbooks into the Edinburgh curriculum was far from easily solved. As I have shown elsewhere, they had to come to terms with the fact that Grotius's philosophy was Arminian and heretical according to the provisions of the Westminster Confession of Faith.[20] Worse still, so far as the kirk was concerned, Pufendorf's attempts to contain this problem smacked not only of materialism but of absolute monarchy as well. Between the late 1690s and 1746, two Glasgow philosophers, Gersholm Carmichael and the great moralist Francis Hutcheson, had produced classic answers to these problems and in doing so had laid important foundation stones for that remarkable enquiry into man, society, and history which remains one of the glories of the Scottish Enlightenment. Pedagogically speaking, however, the Glasgow experiments were thoroughly alarming. Carmichael's answers were too Augustinian for moderate Presbyterians, and Hutcheson's were too Arminian for high-flyers. What was worse, by the 1750s the extraordinary writings of David Hume and Adam Smith had showed all too clearly how easily modern philosophy could degenerate into a morass of what Christians saw as skepticism and materialism.

The first Edinburgh professors had no convincing answers to these problems. Some seemed to have dreamed of a neo-Shaftesburian system of moral philosophy, which would have reconciled the interests of religion and virtue, but nothing seems to have come of it.[21] Most contented themselves with the safe but inglorious expedient of providing a modern introduction to the insecure truths of Grotius and Pufendorf. Not until the 1760s would Edinburgh's academic philosophers come to grips with the problem of laying the foundations of that new system of philosophy on which the college's intellectual reputation would be found. From 1708 until the middle decades of the century Edinburgh University was an uneasy hybrid, belonging to the worlds of the old, decayed Genevan university, the low-level system of civic education which had grown up under the city's patronage in the latter decades of the seventeenth century, and the formidably sophisticated world of Leiden. Not until it had developed a coherent curriculum and the philosophical underpinning necessary to support it would it be in a position to rival Leiden's position in the academic life of the West. That it did so is because of the remarkable behavior of the students and professors who inhabited the university between the 1720s and 1740s. It was they who were to lay the intellectual foundations of the academic culture on which the university's reputation was to be founded in the later decades of the century. And they were to do so by creating a system of liberal education based on the principles of politeness. It was these quintessentially urban values which would eventually turn the hybrid university of the early eighteenth century into an enlightened one.

By the 1720s it is clear that the flow of well-born students to the Dutch universities had been checked. However, it is also clear that the new curriculum did not satisfy their expectations. It was generally accepted that classical teaching was rudimentary, and enterprising students such as the future Lord Kames took private tuition in the classics before embarking on the study of civil law with the new professor, James Craig, "a very dull man" from whom he learned his law by rote.[22] Students like the young Alexander Carlyle, who attended Sir John Pringle's moral philosophy lectures in 1737, complained that they were "chiefly a Compilation from Ld. Bacon's Works and had it not been for Puffendorfs [sic] Small Book which he made his Text, we should not have been instructed in the Rudiments of the Science."[23] Natural philosophy was ill taught by a professor who, he thought, quite wrongly, never had excelled in his subject, and as for the teaching of divinity, it was, as we shall see, "Dull and Dutch and prolix."[24] Indeed, he found it a relief to travel to

Glasgow, "coarse and vulgar" though its society was, in order to hear the celebrated moral philosophy and divinity lectures of Francis Hutcheson and William Leechman.[25] Not even the new medical faculty, which so many historians have seen as the crowning glory of the reformed university, was immune from criticism. Some students found Boerheave's medical curriculum, on which that of Edinburgh was based, out of date intellectually and better suited to the artisanal needs of the apothecaries' and surgeons' apprentices who filled the lecture rooms than those of the gentlemanly medical students who sought to turn medicine into a polite and philosophical discipline.[26] Overall, and notwithstanding the generally admired teaching of peripheral subjects such as mathematics and rhetoric and belles lettres, the students' attitudes to the curriculum students was clear; it was a curriculum that was dull and tediously taught, bearing the stamp of the low-level city teaching from which it was derived. It was, in short, better suited to the needs of clerks, apothecaries and country clergy than to gentlemen.

Some professors were clearly sensitive to "the comparatively inefficient state of the University of Edinburgh" which the young Thomas Somerville noted in the philosophy and divinity though not significantly in the medical faculties, as late as 1759.[27] Some were in correspondence with Viscount Molesworth, the most august of British Classical Republicans, about the problems of designing a system of philosophical education which would encourage the spread of virtue and religion in a modern polity.[28] Some offered special "colleges" to those who could afford it to provide them with the sort of teaching their parents had received in Holland. Thus, the professor of logic John Stevenson offered the classes in rhetoric and belles lettres that Carlyle enjoyed.[29] Charles Macky, the first professor of civil history and a pupil and disciple of Gronovius, taught ancient history and philosophy, presumably in the manner of his master.[30] The professor of mathematics Colin McLaurin offered a course in experimental philosophy.[31]

But more important by far was what I shall call the alternative academic culture the professors and students created outside the college and in the city. The Rankenian Club, which flourished from 1717 to the Forty-Five, and the Medical (later the Philosophical) Society, which was founded in 1731 and flourished for the rest of the century, were clubs in which professors of divinity, philosophy, and medicine met with the lawyers, ministers, men of letters, and local noblemen and gentlemen in order to discuss moral, natural, and medical philosophy. What is more, they did so because they connected the pursuit of learning with the improvement of manners and with the patriotic business of furthering the interests of modern Scotland.[32] As the historian of the Rankenian Club put it, their object was "mutual improvement by liberal conversation and rational enquiry," and it was reckoned that the society had been "highly instrumental in disseminating through Scotland, freedom of thought, boldness of disquisition, liberality of sentiment, accuracy of reasoning, correctness of taste, and attention to composition"; polite accomplishments which had done much to establish "the exalted rank which Scotsmen hold at present in the republic of letters."[33]

Students behaved in exactly the same way, sometimes with the open help and connivance of their professors. In the 1720s the future Lord Kames seems to have belonged to a "Society for Improving in Classical Lore" in order to help make good the deficiencies of his classical education.[34] The Physiological Library (to which the young David Hume seems to have belonged) was founded in 1724 with the support of the professor of natural philosophy whom Carlyle thought incompetent, and it aimed at a level of discussion of modern natural philosophy that was plainly beyond anything attempted in the classroom.[35] The students' medical society went further, launching a direct critique of the new medical school in the name of a new philosophical medicine, by debating such questions as "Is an acquaintance with Metaphysics, Mathematics and the different Branches of Natural Philosophy necessary to the study of medicine."[36] "By these means," Andrew Duncan recalled in 1771, "were the foundations of the Boerhaavian doctrine first shaken."[37] In the late 1730s the future historian and principal of the university William Robertson belonged to a society of divinity students which was intended to encourage public speaking.[38] As Carlyle recalled, it was part of a reaction to an inadequate divinity professor who "could form no school and the Students were left entirely to themselves and naturally form'd Opinions more Liberal than those they Got from the Professor." He continued, "This was the answer I gave to Pat. Ld. Elibank . . . when he asked me one day . . . What could be the Reason that the young Clergymen of that Period so far Surpass'd their Predecessors of his Early Days, in usefull Accomplishments and Liberality of Mind, viz. That the Professor of Theology was Dull and Dutch, and prolix. His Ldship said he perfectly understood me, and that this entirely accounted for the Change."[39]

It goes without saying that these were the reactions of a small, distinctive group of students. But they were students who had clear expectations of what a modern education should be, and, as we shall see, they spoke with the same voice as those who were to reconstruct the university curriculum a generation later. In linking the culture of the college with that of the city, in attempting to link the arts and sciences with each other and with ideas of public utility and even patriotism, the professors and students with whom we are concerned were using a distinctive, neo-Ciceronian, civic language whose roots lay in the enormously popular and influential writings of two great moral journalists, Joseph Addison and Richard Steele, and in their *Tatler* and *Spectator* essays in particular. These essays were first published between 1709 and 1713 and were constantly republished, imitated, and read throughout the century in the towns and cities of the Anglo-Saxon world for the next century. They were to be one of the most potent influences on contemporary urban culture at a formative stage of its development.[40] What is more, they were to form one of the most important ideological foundation stones on which the pedagogy of the enlightened university was to rest.

Addison and Steele wrote for ordinary citizens who were bewildered by the demands of urban life at a time when cities were expanding rapidly in size and complexity. They wrote as satirists who ridiculed the disruptive, high-flying pretensions of religious and political zealots, the fops who infected the social world with mindless and malicious tittle-tattle, the country gentlemen and bumpkins who were trapped in an outdated rustic culture. They took stock of the extraordinary mushroom growth of often extravagant, absurd, and constantly changing opinions about manners, morals, politics, and religion which seemed to be a function of the increased specialization and commercialization of modern society. Above all, they set out to show anxious modern citizens how they could acquire the sort of moral integrity or ego which was needed if they were ever to live useful and happy lives in a modern commercial city. Addison and Steele taught that it was foolish to turn one's back on the values of ordinary life as so many Christian and Stoic moralists had taught. It was perfectly possible to live virtuously and happily in the modern world if one learned the principles of politeness. That meant learning how to improve one's judgment of men and ideas and, above all, learning how to curb one's enthusiasms. They thought that this could best be done by cultivating the arts of conversation and friendship. Friendly conversation was the most effective and pleasant way of learning to be attentive to the opinions of others and to moderate one's own enthusiasm accordingly. And although modern politeness clearly would not encourage the high heroic virtues advocated by so many Stoic or Christian moralists, they did encourage the growth of social propriety and that sort of low-level social consensus which made ordinary life pleasant as well as possible. As Addison and Steele described it, politeness was a set of skills which were best acquired away from the hustle and bustle of the world of business, politics, and fashion, in the coffee house, in the tavern, or around the tea table. It was in these clubbable institutions that modern men and women would learn how to lead virtuous, happy, and useful lives.

As I have shown elsewhere, Edinburgh citizens were deeply attracted by Addisonian politeness and saw it as a powerful resource for rebuilding their civic culture. From the 1720s on, the city was to generate a club life of extraordinary range and variety which its historian D. D. McElroy has described as an integral part of Scotland's age of improvement.[41] For Edinburgh's clubs and societies were to be devoted to the improvement of the country's public life as well as to the improvement of its citizens' manners. By the middle decades of the century there were clubs, largely recruited from the middling ranks of Scottish society, which were devoted to elaborate projects of political, economic, and religious engineering and to the improvement of the arts and sciences. All of this was to be of the greatest importance to Scottish liberal education and to that of Edinburgh in particular. This was the culture in which David Hume was raised, in which he lost his Christian faith and embarked on the construction of a new, skeptical science of man which would demonstrate the critical importance of politeness and philosophy to maintaining the fabric of a modern commercial polity.[42] It was also the culture in which many of the medical professors who would redesign the Edinburgh medical curriculum were raised—William Cullen, Robert Whytt, Alexander Munro II, and Joseph Black in particular. Above all, it was the culture which shaped the education of that little band of moderate clergy who were to play the crucial role in designing the system of liberal education with which we are concerned—the historian William Robertson, the philosopher Adam Ferguson, and the literary critic and moral theologian Hugh Blair.

By the 1750s this group had hijacked the General Assembly with the help of the crown and many landed proprietors, and it was playing an increasingly prominent part in shaping the cultural life of a city that was becoming known as a modern Athens.[43] They were not only celebrated preachers whose sermons sought to encourage the consensual relationship between the kirk and civil society that was to be the special preoccupation of moderate theologians. They were active proponents of improvement in all its forms. They were among the founding fathers of the Select Society, the most formidable and august of the midcentury improvement societies, which sought to train up a new generation of legislators who were versed in the modern arts and sciences and anxious to harness them to the problems of maintaining a great commercial polity. They campaigned vigorously for a Scottish militia on account of the libertarian virtues with which it was associated. It was they who did most to encourage the search for the poems of Ossian, which would demonstrate that Celtic Scotland had once been the home of a Scottish Homer and of a civilization that was less barbaric, more inclined to receive the monotheistic truths of Christian religion than the fierce and passionate polytheists of ancient Greece. And all of this was done in the name of a new Presbyterianism which would turn modern Scotland into a free, godly, commercial polity regulated by the principles of philosophy and politeness. David Hume, who, for all his infidelity, knew the moderates and liked them well, wrote the following of them:

> It is happy for the inhabitants of this metropolis [Edinburgh], which has naturally a great influence on the country, that the same persons, who can make such a figure in profane learning, are entrusted with the guidance of the people in their spiritual concerns, which are of such superior, and indeed of unspeakable importance! These illustrious examples, if anything, must make the infidel abashed of his vain cavils, and put a stop to that torrent of vice, profaneness, and immorality, by which the age is so unhappily distinguished.[44]

By the mid-1760s and with the help of the crown and Town Council, this moderate elite had taken virtual control of the university, Robertson as principal, Ferguson as professor of moral philosophy, and Blair as the first regius professor of rhetoric and belles lettres. Within a decade these same forces had succeeded in colonizing the university with a new generation of philosophers, theologians, and doctors who formed a remarkable network of friends and relations, often of considerable intellectual talent and always sympathetic to the new moderatism. Intellectually their primary task was to construct the philosophical foundations on which a coherent system of liberal education could be built which would show how modern philosophy, history, and letters could be put to the service of politeness and true religion. It was a formidable task. As intelligent, strict Presbyterians like John Witherspoon, the future president of Princeton, pointed out, the general tendency of polite morality was to reduce religion and morality to good manners and the dictates of fashion.[45] Indeed it was a tendency whose disastrous consequences were all too evident in the polite skepticism of David Hume and in the dangerously materialist tendencies of Adam Smith's moral philosophy teaching at Glasgow University.

But the young moderates were too committed, too *engagées,* as citizens and patriots to be able to turn their backs on the sociable popular ethics of politeness. That system of ethics had, after all, proved to be a powerful mechanism for curbing the religious enthusiasm and zealotry which they were committed to destroy. What is more, it was a system of popular ethics which, for better or worse, had begun to take a powerful hold on the social culture of contemporary Britain and had begun to acquire a peculiar significance for Edinburgh citizens who were committed to the reconstruction of their country's culture. The task the moderate professors faced was to find ways of containing the skepticism and materialism with which Addisonian politeness and Glaswegian moral philosophy were associated and of creating a philosophy which could be turned to educational purposes and used to build a modern, commercial, Christian polity.

The moderate professors thought that the skepticism and materialism which seemed to be inherent in modern culture could best be contained by invoking that neo-Stoic love of perfection which moralists such as Shaftesbury thought was an essential part of the "constitution of the mind" and was activated by the pressures of ordinary life and by the natural desire to reflect on the wilder purposes of life. Properly cultivated, this natural instinct would enable men and women to acquire more extensive views of morality and of divine providence, and this in turn would induce a new reverence for the deity and his creation and activate a new interest in seeking to improve the world the deity had created for us.

There is, alas, only time to glance at the way in which the moderate professors explored this important agenda, which is, incidentally, of very much more importance to the intellectual history of the Scottish Enlightenment than is commonly realized. It seems likely, however, that the system of liberal pedagogy that concerns us here was its most durable by-product. Adam Ferguson's moral philosophy lectures were probably the most important foundation stones on which the new pedagogy rested. Ferguson was anxious, above all, to discover how classical republican values could be recaptured in a modern, commercial polity. So far as he was concerned, the task of the moral philosopher was to show, by examining the constitution of the mind and the principles of social organization, that men were naturally active, restless, sociable beings whose natural ambition, love of independence, and perfection could all too easily be stifled by ignorance, luxury, and idleness, and a false respect for propriety and social approval. Indeed, without the pressures of "great occasions" men could all too easily fall victim to "their own imbecility under the name of politeness" and even devalue the ardor and generosity of spirit that were so characteristic of ancient and primitive forms of civilization.[46] And just as the great classicists of Leiden had used the classics as a doorway to the study of history, so Ferguson turned from philosophy to the history of Rome to study "the great revolution by which the republican form of government was exchanged for despotism" so that modern citizens could learn to identify the forces which threatened liberty in a free polity.[47]

According to his biographer and friend Dugald Stewart, Principal William Robertson was, like Ferguson, a man who was "formed for action, no less than speculation."[48] He was a man of "good sense" whose life embodied the qualities of friendliness, moderation, and prudence so revered by Addisonians, and his historical writings and sermons "were directed to the great sciences of political action." As a historian, cleric, and lifelong admirer of the ancient Stoics, he thought that the principal purpose of history was to show the unfolding of a providential order as men learned how to use the mental and moral resources the creator had given them to exploit their material environment and to turn it to their own purposes and to those of their fellows and the deity. In the process, as Edward Gibbon liked to point out, he was able to show that modern history need not necessarily be skeptical.[49] Like his brethren, Hugh Blair, the immensely popular and wealthy professor of rhetoric and belles lettres, was frequently apostophized for the good sense and taste he displayed in his sermons which succeeded in "uniting in the most perfect form the attractions of utility and beauty [by giving] a new and better tone to the style of instruction from the pulpit; and contributed, in a remarkable degree, to correct and refine the religious, the moral, and the literary taste of the times in which he lived."[50] In his celebrated lectures on rhetoric and belles lettres, which his biographer described as "a most judicious, elegant and comprehensive system of rules for forming the style, and cultivating the taste of the youth" and a German admirer called "Blair's blooming rhetorications," students were taught to attend to the content as well as the form of literature in order to learn how the rules of literary criticism could be applied to morality.[51]

In all of this the moderate professors were drawing politeness and its problems into the classroom in order to harness its values to philosophy, literature, and science and to create an academic culture which would prepare boys destined for public life in a godly, free commercial polity. However, it was left to Dugald Stewart, Ferguson and Blair's pupil, to complete the pedagogical edifice during his long tenure of the Edinburgh moral philosophy chair from 1785 to 1810. For Stewart was to attempt the *grand synthese* of Scottish academic philosophy by means of a sympathetic but critical review of its strengths and weaknesses. As I have shown elsewhere, Stewart had learned from Adam Smith how easy it was to explain the roots of mankind's love of perfection in materialist terms, as something we learn in the course of ordinary life.[52] But he had also learned from the lectures of Thomas Reid, Smith's successor in the Glasgow moral philosophy chair, that by reflecting carefully and systematically on the contents of one's mind, one could learn how to distinguish between those ideas which were the product of prejudice and experience and those which were part of the constitution of a mind that had been constructed by a benevolent deity. Students would soon learn that the business of understanding themselves and the world in which they lived was simply a matter of good sense which could be acquired by cultivating their taste and judgment. What is more, it would teach them that the imagination, once constrained by good sense, was the key to improving one's own behavior and that of society at large. As he once put it,

> Good sense . . . is unquestionably of all the qualities of the understanding, that which essentially constitutes superiority of mind; for although we are sometimes apt to appropriate the appellation of genius to certain peculiarities in the intellectual habits [sic], it is he only who distinguishes himself from the rest of mankind by thinking better than they on some subjects, who fairly brings his powers into comparison with others.[53]

For all practical purposes the publication of Stewart's lectures on moral philosophy in 1792–93 marks the completion of the system of polite pedagogy that had been developed in Edinburgh University during the eighteenth century. The moderates had constructed a system of liberal education whose roots lay in a polite philosophy rooted in the values of commerce and of the city. It was an academic culture which was designed to contain the problems posed by skepticism, materialism, and religious enthusiasm and to do so in the name of a society which was anxious to show how religion, commerce, and philosophy could be used to secure liberty and happiness, and, as we saw at the outset of this essay, it was a pedagogy which was to be extraordinarily attractive to the civilized world at a crucial stage of its development. What I have shown here is that although that academic culture was the invention of a small group of men, their achievement can only be understood as part of the history of a university which was experiencing great difficulty in adapting itself to a modern age. And all of this is part of the history of a city which became a modern Athens.

NOTES

1. There are three general histories of Edinburgh University, all outdated but all usable: T. Craufurd, *History of the University of Edinburgh from 1580–1646* (Edinburgh 1808); A. Bower, *The History of the University of Edinburgh,* 2 vols. (Edinburgh, 1817); A. Grant, *The Story of the University of Edinburgh,* 2 vols. (London, 1884). A. Dalzel's posthumous *History of the University of Edinburgh from Its Foundation* (Edinburgh, 1862) is not to be trusted. The only modern histories are D. B. Horn's short but informative *A Short History of the University of Edinburgh, 1556–1889* and I. Kenrick's useful *The University of Edinburgh, 1660–1715: A Study in the Transformation of Teaching Methods and Curriculum* (Ph.D. diss., Bryn Mawr, Penn., 1956).

2. *The Universities Commission—Scotland. Edinburgh Evidence* (Parlt. Papers, 1837), XXXV, 82.

3. *General Report of Commissioners on the Universities and College of Scotland* (Parlt. Papers, 1831), XII, 99.

4. Horn, *A Short History*, chaps. 2–3. See also A. J. Youngson, *The Making of Classical Edinburgh* (Edinburgh, 1966).

5. The full story of the transmission of Scottish academic culture has yet to be told. However, see H. May, *The Enlightenment in America* (New York, 1976), pp. 341–50; D. Meyer, *The Instructed Conscience* (Philadelphia, 1972); P. P. Dockwrey, "Dugald Stewart and the Early French Eclectics, 1796–1820" (Ph.D. diss., Cambridge, 1976); M. Kuehn, *Scottish Common Sense in Germany, 1768–1800: A Contribution to the History of Critical Philosophy* (Kingston and Montreal, 1987).

6. There are no reliable statistics about the size of the matriculated student population at this time. The estimate is given in Horn's *A Short History*, p. 30. See also R. L. Emerson, "Scottish Universities in the Eighteenth Century, 1690–1800," *Studies on Voltaire and the Eighteenth Century* 167 (1977): 453–74.

7. J. McConica, "The Fate of Erasmian Humanism," in *Universities, Society and the Future*, ed. N. T. Phillipson (Edinburgh, 1983), pp. 37–61.

8. This and the following paragraph summarize a line of argument developed in the following essays: "Culture and Society in the Eighteenth Century Province: The Case of Edinburgh and the Scottish Enlightenment," in *The University in Society*, ed. L. Stone, 2 vols. (Princeton, N.J., 1974), II, 407–48; "The Scottish Enlightenment," in *The Enlightenment in National Context*, eds. R. Porter and M. Teich (Cambridge, 1981), pp. 19–40; "Politeness, Anglicisation and the Union," *Scotland and England, 1286–1815*, ed. by R. A. Mason (Edinburgh, 1987), pp. 226–46.

9. See my "Lawyers, Landowners and the Civic Leadership of Post-Union Scotland," *Juridical Review* (1976) 107, 120. R. Feenstra "Scottish Dutch Legal Relations in the Seventeenth and Eighteenth Centuries," in *Scotland and Europe 1200–1850*, ed. T. C. Smout (Edinburgh, 1986), pp. 128–42.

10. *Extracts from the Records of the Burgh of Edinburgh*, 3 vols.: 1681–88, 1689–1701, 1702–18 (Edinburgh, 1954–67). See esp. the indexes, under "College," "Schools," "Surgeons," and "Physicians."

11. J. Spottiswood, *A Discourse Showing the Necessary Qualifications of a Student of the Laws: And What Is Propos'd in the Colleges of the Laws, History & Philology, Establish'd at Edinburgh* (Edinburgh, 1704).

12. *A Letter from Mr. Cockburn. To the Right Honorable John, Earl of Roxburgh* . . . (Edinburgh, 1705).

13. This remarkable story is chronicled in the minutes of the Commissioners of the Visitation of Colleges, a selection of which is published in the *Munimenta Alme Universitatis Glasquensis*, Maitland Club (Glasgow, 1854). See also R. K. Hannay, "The Visitation of the College of Edinburgh, 1690," in *Book of the Old Edinburgh Club* (Edinburgh, 1916), VIII, 79–100.

14. Andrew Fletcher's republican anticlericalism forms a *leitmotif* to his *Political Works* and comes into focus in *Proposals for the Reformation of Schools and Universities in Order to the Better Education of Youth. Humbly Offer'd to the Serious Consideration of the High Court of Parliament* (Edinburgh, 1704). The provenance of this pamphlet is argued bibliographically by R. S. McFee, "A Bibliography of Andrew Fletcher of Saltoun," *Papers of the Edinburgh Bibliographical Society* 4 (1901): 117–48.

15. *Acts of the Parliament of Scotland*, 1707, XI, App. 120(b).

16. *Extracts from the Records of the Burgh of Edinburgh 1701–8*, 16 June 1708, pp. 154–55.

17. Ibid., 18 October 1710, pp. 201–2. It is interesting to notice that the first professor of anatomy, Alexander Monro *primus,* who was appointed in 1720, was described as "Professor of Anatomy in this City and College." Grant, *The Story of the University of Edinburgh,* I, 300.

18. *Scots Magazine* 3 (1741): 371–74.

19. See, for example, D. J. Withrington, "Education and Society in the Eighteenth Century," in *Scotland in the Age of Improvement,* ed. N. T. Phillipson and R. M. Mitchiison (Edinburgh, 1970). The problem persisted long into the nineteenth century. See R. D. Anderson, *Education and Opportunity in Victorian Scotland: Schools and Universities* (Oxford, 1983), chaps. 1, 4.

20. See my "The Pursuit of Virtue in Scottish University Education: Dugald Stewart and Scottish Moral Philosophy in the Enlightenment," in *Universities, Society and the Future,* ed. N. T. Phillipson (Edinburgh, 1983), pp. 82–101.

21. Or so a cogent and striking memorandum in Principal Wishart's papers suggests. Unclassified document, *Wishart MSS,* Edinburgh University Library.

22. I. S. Ross, *Lord Kames and the Scotland of His Day* (Oxford, 1972), p. 14.

23. A. Carlyle, *Anecdotes and Characters of the Times,* ed. J. Kinsley (London, 1973), p. 25.

24. Ibid., pp. 24, 30.

25. Ibid., pp. 35–37.

26. There is a substantial literature on the Dutch origins of the Edinburgh Medical School. Of particular relevance here are J. R. R. Christie, "The Origins and Development of the Scottish Scientific Community, 1680–1760," *History of Science* 12 (1974): 122–41; A. L. Donovan, *Philosophical Chemistry in the Scottish Enlightenment* (Edinburgh, 1975); C. J. Lawrence, "Early Edinburgh Medicine: Theory and Practice," in *The Early Years of the Edinburgh Medical School,* ed. R. G. W. Anderson and A. D. C. Simpson (Edinburgh, 1976), pp. 81–94; R. M. Scott, "The Origins of the Edinburgh Medical School 1696–1775" (Ph.D. diss., Edinburgh, 1984).

27. T. Somerville, *My Own Life and Times, 1741–1814* (Edinburgh, 1861), p. 19.

28. P. Jones, "The Scottish Professoriate and the Polite Academy," in *Wealth and Virtue: The Shaping of Political Economy in the Scottish Enlightenment,* ed. I. Hont and M. Ignatieff (Cambridge, 1983), pp. 89–117. And "The Polite Academy and the Presbyterians," in *New Perspectives on the Politics and Culture of Early Modern Scotland,* ed. J. Dwyer, R. A. Mason, and A. Murdoch (Edinburgh, 1982), pp. 156–78.

29. Jones, "The Scottish Professoriate," pp. 99–100.

30. L. W. Sharp, "Charles Makie, the First Professor of History at Edinburgh University," *Scottish Historical Review* 41 (1961): 23–45.

31. *Scots Magazine* (1741): 372.

32. I have discussed the club life of Edinburgh in the articles cited in n. 8.

33. *Scots Magazine* (1771): 340–44.

34. Ross, *Lord Kames,* p. 71n.

35. M. M. Barfoot, *Hume and the Culture of Science in Early Eighteenth Century Britain,* Oxford Studies in the History of Philosophy, 1988–89.

36. Donovan, *Philosophical Chemistry,* p. 41.

37. J. Gray, *History of the Royal Medical Society 1737–1937* (Edinburgh, 1952), pp. 30–32.

38. D. Stewart, *Account of the Life and Writings of Dr. Robertson* (London, 1802), pp. 8–9.

39. Carlyle, *Anecdotes and Characters*, pp. 29–30.

40. What follows develops the discussion set out in my essays cited in note 8. See also J. B. A. Pocock, *Virtue, Commerce and History* (Cambridge, 1985), pp. 234–39; M. G. Ketcham, *Transparent Designs: Reading, Performance and Forms in the Spector Papers* (Athens, Ga., 1985).

41. D. D. McElroy, *Scotland's Age of Improvement* (Pullman, Wash., 1969).

42. N. T. Phillipson, "Hume as Moralist: A Social Historian's Perspective," in *The Philosophers of the Enlightenment*, ed. S. C. Brown (Hassock, Sussex, 1979), pp. 140–61. See also my forthcoming *Hume as Historian*.

43. Our understanding of the moderate clergy and therefore of the social history of the Scottish Enlightenment has been transformed by R. B. Sher, *Church and University in the Scottish Enlightenment: The Moderate Literati of Edinburgh* (Edinburgh, 1985). What follows, and indeed much of what has been argued earlier, owes much to Sher's discussion. In general terms, I draw here on Sher's research in order to develop an interpretation of the intellectual history of moderatism that moves in a somewhat different direction from his.

44. E. C. Mossner, "Hume as Literary Patron: A Suppressed Review of Robert Henry's History of Great Britain 1773," *Modern Philology* 39 (May 1942): 361–82.

45. [J. Witherspoon], *Ecclesiastical Characteristics; or, The Arcana of Church Policy*, 5th ed. (Edinburgh, 1762).

46. A. Ferguson, *An Essay on the History of Civil Society*, ed. D. Forbes (Edinburgh, 1967).

47. A. Ferguson, *The History of the Progress and Termination of the Roman Republic* (London, 1827), p. 2.

48. What follows is based on D. Stewart, *Account of the Life and Writings of William Robertson*, 2nd ed. (London, 1802).

49. In 1826 the professor of divinity at Edinburgh, William Ritchie, was asked by the Parliamentary Visitors what the learned on the Continent thought of the works of men like Robertson. He replied, "High when I was there. I was at Mr. Gibbon's one day when a French Duke was with him. The Duke made a pause, and said 'Gibbon, I recollect no excellent historian who has not been a sceptic.' Gibbon pulled out his snuff-box and tapped it, for he did not like the speech. He said 'I recollect to have heard nothing of the scepticism of doctor Robertson'; and the first man he suggested as a great historian was Doctor Robertson." *Universities Commission—Scotland* (Parlt. Papers, 1837), XXXV, 150.

50. J. Finlayson, ed., "A Short Account of the Life and Character of Dr. Hugh Blair," in *Sermons by Hugh Blair, D.D., F.R.S.*, 3 vols. (London, 1825), I, xviii.

51. Ibid., X. Dalzel, *History of the University of Edinburgh*, I, xviii.

52. What follows summarizes my argument in "The Pursuit of Virtue in Scottish University Education."

53. Stewart, *Account of the Life and Writings of William Robertson*, p. 205.

III

THE METROPOLITAN UNIVERSITY

8

London: A Metropolitan University?

Sheldon Rothblatt

The London University began life as a solitary college. In a decade it was a federation, and it has never ceased to be a federation, if different now from then. Its past and present, although a logical extrapolation from its history, could not be predicted and becomes, therefore, yet another instance of the wise assumption that no institution, least of all a university, exists apart from a much larger social and cultural whole.

Three particular themes or threads run through the course of the following discussion. The first is the relationship of the London University to its specific urban environment at the time of its founding, meaning the relationship of the university to an actual or potential local market for students, resources, and services. The second is its relationship to other preexisting educational institutions against which, inevitably, it was compared and measured. And the third is the position of the new university with respect to certain special features of Britain's urban and national cultural history. Taken together, the three themes illustrate how different national and urban conflicts and traditions produce different conceptions of an urban university.

Conceived in 1826, the London University was only the third university to be created in England, although smaller Scotland had four. It was established as an alternative but not as a rival to Oxford and Cambridge, whose curriculum and socially exclusive intake had long been under attack. The fortunes of those institutions were actually on the rise. Matriculations were up, and the beginnings of a quite significant internal reform movement centered on certain of the colleges were evident; but the ancient universities were costly and remained socially exclusive. They were sufficiently protected by the Established Church of England to retain their religious restrictions for another thirty years. The excluded had to look elsewhere.

The London University was founded in a period when urban populations were expanding throughout the island, as they were in western Europe generally, when town elites were improving their political influence in England, and when the besetting problems of cities—housing, expansion of the built-up areas, sanitation, poverty, crime, popular education—were continually dis-

119

cussed.[1] Cities, in sum, were moving to the forefront of social thought, and it was therefore only natural that they should become the home of educational experiments. City-based universities were appearing in Germany and new universities generally in the United States, and the only major question for England was not whether a new university should be founded, but where and of what type. The most rapidly growing population areas of England were the new manufacturing districts of the Midlands and the North. The resources for establishing a provincial university of some kind were probably available, but selection of London was more appropriate since only the capital was the home of numerous interests whose combined strength could be effective against the Anglican university monopoly. London was the only city whose prestige could give a university in its midst something of the importance attached to Oxford and Cambridge.

Furthermore, London was changing. Its population increased by at least three-quarters of a million in the first three decades of the nineteenth century, and at no point in the first fifty years did the decadal rate of growth fall below 17 percent.[2] Spectacular building programs associated with the regency and reign of George IV dramatized the increases. Residents of the vast and fragmented capital were beginning to think of themselves collectively as having a common identity and purpose, of being part of a great city of unprecedented scale. The disparate and hitherto separate and even isolated nodes of the capital—its financial district or "City," its royal enclave, West End fashionable streets, developing inner suburbs, and older commuter villages—were being thought of as a greater London or "metropolis."[3] Supporters of a new university believed that London Town had now reached a stage of development where it needed and could maintain an institution of higher education. It was more than once observed that the capital was the only major European city without one, an anomaly in view of London's size and ranking world importance in finance, shipping, and representative government.

Beginnings

It is well to begin by disposing of a confusion in nomenclature. Historically, there are two Universities of London. The first is the small institution of some thirty chairs situated in Gower Street that went by the name of the "University of London" or the "London University." Many of the chairs were the nuclei of what much later became academic departments. Chairs in the biological sciences were grouped together to form a medical "school" or "department" which almost immediately sought a suitable location for a teaching hospital.

The university was founded as a nonsectarian proprietary company rather than as a charitable endowment, presumably to avoid jurisdiction by the Ecclesiastical Commissioners and the Church of England. Its doors were opened in 1828. It was supported initially by the proceeds from the public sale of shares in a joint-stock company, but a cap of 4 percent was put on the returns to shareholders to counter the reproach that profit, not education, was the true object of the new institution.[4] There was an additional risk. Since limited-liability companies were illegal, shareholders were individually responsible for all debts. Unlike Oxford and Cambridge or the Scottish universities, the new university in London did not possess degree-granting authority, which could only be conferred by royal charter, an uncertain prospect for a non-sectarian foundation at a time when all universities were historically if not legally connected to religious establishments, whether north or south of the River Tweed, and tied to them by golden strands of patronage and mutual advantage.

The second University of London was the entity created by Parliament and royal charter in 1836. Constitutional changes were made in 1850 but particularly in 1858, and yet another constitution was adopted in the early twentieth century. The second University of London was not a university as commonly understood but a peculiar creation, an agency of the state staffed by a minuscule administrative body of perhaps three civil servants backed by a governing body or senate of some three dozen members. The sole function of the new entity was to set examinations, collect fees for them, appoint examiners, and award degrees to successful candidates—in sum, to furnish the degree-granting capability denied the original University of London. Any fee surplus was returned to the state. By the Act of 1836 the original University of London was reduced to "college" status and was henceforth to be known as "University College" or "University College London." Legally separate from the examining university, retaining independent financial status, and possessing its own governing council, this body had the option of offering nondegree courses or preparing students to read for those recognized by the degree-giving university.

Another university college, called and still called "King's College" or "King's College London," was founded shortly after the first by a group of supporters representing the Established Church interest. Situated in the Strand, it was opened to students in 1831. It too raised capital through the sale of shares, but subscriptions were also solicited. Its capital base was nearly identical to that of the first college. King's stood in exactly the same relationship as University College to the examining university of 1836. The constitution made provision for affiliating other institutions to the center as they arose and for granting degrees to them through the mechanism of independent examinations.

A Capital Market

Access and cost were the two most unambiguous policies of University College. Ambitious, the founders talked about attracting some two thousand full- and part-time students from London's diverse and comfortable but not necessarily affluent population. London families certainly could not afford the third or more of their annual incomes required for residence in costly Oxford and Cambridge.[5]

In the language of the day, the university's constituency was to be the "middling classes" (or "middling orders" or "middling rich"), whom the poet Thomas Campbell, perhaps the university's original publicist, identified as the "small, comfortable trading fortunes," the large indeterminate group that stretched from skilled workers, shopkeepers, and clerks in commercial houses to *rentiers,* business, and professional men but did not include the establishment, that is, the great barristers, the upper officers of the armed services, leading medical practitioners, and the landed and financial aristocracy and clergy. Today we might call the middling classes a middle-income group. They were a politically active and influential body in the rather unsettled social climate of early-nineteenth-century London.[6]

Religiously, some of the original shareholders were evangelical or latitudinarian Anglicans who could see the benefits to their children of a low-cost alternative to the ancient universities, but the expected pool consisted primarily of families of dissenting or nonconforming Protestants and secondarily of others, such as freethinking intellectuals, the small numbers of Roman Catholics, whose political emancipation occurred at the end of the 1820s, and the even smaller numbers of Jews, who remained unemancipated for several decades more. As a representative of the tiny Jewish community, the City financier Isaac Goldsmid, a friend of Henry Brougham, the brilliant parliamentarian most responsible for securing support for the upstart institution, was particularly effective in bringing coalitions together and keeping alive the principle of a nonsectarian university.[7]

The Dissenters were not a unified body. Some had close effective economic and political ties to the governing elites, while others were marginalized intellectuals; but insofar as there was a distinct culture of dissent, as inherited from the political awakening of the late eighteenth century, it tended to be individualistic, market-oriented, utilitarian, "rational" in the Enlightenment meaning of the word, and consequently secular or at least nonsectarian and tolerant.[8] In the eighteenth century the educational needs of Dissenters had been met by a series of experimental establishments called dissenting academies, and their intellectual interests had led them to create a famous urban network of "Lit and Phil" societies. But the great age of the academies was virtually over when discussions about a city university began, and interest shifted from the model of the academy, which was essentially a *Hochschule,* to the model of the university, where a wider range of subjects could be taught and professional training obtained.

There were several schemes afoot in the 1820s for a nondenominational university. Besides the London University, a plan was sketched out in 1826 for a university in the North, quite possibly in Liverpool, to which denominational colleges could be subordinated.[9] It is possible that for many proponents of a new university the issue was not necessarily a university of and for the metropolis of London, not a "Cockney University" as the Tory writers of the satirical journal *John Bull* scoffed, but a national university for

Dissenters in some convenient and appropriate location, and it can therefore be surmised that a potential "national" mission shadowed the first decade's history of the University of London even as the founders set about to create an urban institution in the capital. Campbell had once stated that he did not favor a "mere Dissenters' University,"[10] but some sentiment in favor of such an institution remained. Wording suggesting that the London University had been especially founded for Dissenters was actually introduced into the draft preamble to the charter that created the examining London University of 1836, but Lord Melbourne as prime minister cautioned that the statement was unnecessary (and probably harmful).[11]

The question of whether a new university should be for Dissenters or whether it should be secular figured in the earliest discussions. A majority of the Christian supporters of the London University would have preferred some religious teaching, but the nature of the political alliance prevented such a policy, and the new foundation, like Thomas Jefferson's University of Virginia (founded in 1819), was consequently called an "infidel" or "godless" university and joked about in a student publication as a "metropolitan pesthouse."[12]

The founding coalition was even more mixed politically than religiously. It included radicals of the left—Benthamites and upper-working-class reformers like Francis Place—who were joined to liberal aristocratic Whigs and Scottish democrats. It included single-issue groups, such as evangelical Anglicans, generally conservative and philanthropically high-minded or humanitarian, who, if they were in the forefront of movements to suppress public vice, were also active in the campaign to abolish the slave trade throughout the empire. Socially, all of the groups, secular as well as religious, represented a broad if not exhaustive section of the population of the capital and can be accurately described as embodying the spirit and energy of the metropolis.

No single body represented the government of the capital, however, for despite some effort at rationalizing London's administration, a large number of separate local authorities remained in existence, no less than thirty-eight in the year 1855, and consolidation did not occur until the last decade of the century, when the first of a number of metropolitan jurisdictions was created.[13] There was consequently no center for a new university to affix itself to, no identifiable municipality which could serve as a source of support and encouragement for a young institution facing the uncertainties of the market and the hostility of the clerical establishment. (By the same token, the new institution was "free" from political interference.) However, the Court of Common Council of the autonomous City of London very demonstrably took the side of the new university during the battle over the granting of a royal charter in the 1830s. The City, which has retained its independence to this day, had a history of supporting higher education efforts dating as far back as the late seventeenth century, when proposals for a university first circulated, and in the nineteenth century the City retained some endowments collected for that purpose and used them to support public lectures. Later in the century great livery companies representing the City's merchant community—the clothworkers, for example, or the drapers—were strong benefactors of the London colleges at shaky financial moments.[14]

Urban Models of a University

No urban type of university existed in England. The closest native models were Scottish, particularly the sixteenth-century foundations of the "College of Edinburgh" and Marischal College, Aberdeen. Edinburgh itself was modeled on the Protestant academy in Geneva with which many Scots had been associated. The ties between college and municipality at Edinburgh were so close that what was to become the university was often referred to as the Town College. The city powers of Edinburgh even authorized the college to grant degrees (before an act of Parliament was passed in 1621). However, by the nineteenth century the Scottish universities did not regard themselves in any sense as municipal or civic universities. They identified with the northern kingdom, with its history and with Scottish culture generally, with a Presbyterian inheritance, Enlightenment traditions of thought, and a certain conception of humanist education which traveled well, having crossed the Atlantic and implanted itself in the colonial colleges of America. They thought of themselves as a system or group of universities, even, it might be suggested, a state system. Long before the practice began in England, they were receiving regular parliamentary grants. Furthermore, they permitted a certain element of student transfer among the four institutions. The medical schools of the Scottish universities had distinguished themselves in the eighteenth century, attracting students from other parts of the kingdom and earning in this respect a national and even European reputation still very viable in the early decades of the nineteenth century.[15]

Nevertheless, from the Scottish universities the new university colleges of London took a great deal. They borrowed a set of far-ranging mechanisms for achieving relatively open access, a curriculum responsive to market demand and amenable to change, flexible programs of study including part-time, a low-cost system of professorial lecturing, and a particular spirit of general and professional education, focused more on the well-educated student of a service culture than on the potential social, political, and religious leader of society that was the traditional English university concern. A university should produce "useful men," Professor George Jardine of Glasgow had once stated, not "great men," and Jardine was greatly admired by Campbell.[16] The Scottish model convinced the leaders of the movement to found a new university that a nonresidential institution could be successful in the capital.

Those leaders, it has often been remarked, were themselves largely Scottish or had been educated in Scotland, men such as Brougham and Campbell, prominent evangelicals such as the Macaulays, or intellectuals such as James Mill. One of the leading Dissenters, F. A. Cox, the Baptist minister at Hackney Academy, was a Scottish graduate. Liberal Whigs with an antiestablishment bent such as Lord John Russell had spent some time at Edinburgh, home of the great polemical journal *The Edinburgh Review,* which had launched a famous attack on the education offered at Oxford and Cambridge in the first decade of the new century, and Scotland was the source of the revolution in economic thought which made possible a market view of education. It has often been pointed out that Scots predominated among the first selections of London University's professors. In the words of a detractor, the University of London was

> a north country production; the land of mountain and of flood has contributed, her poet Campbell, and her accountant Hume; she will give them a M'Culloch, and all the Macs of Celtic birth who inundate England. . . . It will be something like a Scottish University in London, and a nursery for Scottish seedling merit.[17]

The Scottish example and market economics were featured in the educational plan adopted by University College. Professors were paid from fees collected from classroom attendance instead of from endowments or recurrent income, and the absence of salary guarantees (beyond the first year of appointment) actually made recruitment difficult.[18] Undergraduates were expected to live at home. In a famous published letter Campbell had specified a catchment area of two miles in all directions from the university, which was virtually coterminous with the residential neighborhoods of the "middling classes." (Although they were within Campbell's catchment area, the prosperous West Enders, occupying Mayfair houses and terraces, had higher hopes for their sons and were not likely to be patrons of the new institution.)[19] Provision was made for half and summer courses, part-time or regular attendance, with a graded schedule of fees. Regular students could take either a four-year program of general studies or a professional course; and students who matriculated at what might be considered advanced levels were granted appropriate credit. While degrees were not available, credentials could be awarded to certify completion of the various programs of study. One other feature of the early curriculum is worth noting as indicating a consumer orientation—one is tempted to call it American. The council of the university strongly advised potential students to consult beforehand with individual professors whose courses they planned to take. This had the double advantage of enabling undergraduates to anticipate workloads and standards and of providing professors with a chance to assess a student's preparation. Teaching and expectations could be accordingly adjusted.[20]

The founders had at one time considered establishing a high school, such as existed in the Scottish capital, rather than a university, being sensitive to the costs of prolonging entry into the labor market beyond age nineteen or twenty. The Scottish universities had addressed this problem by simply matriculating undergraduates of secondary-school age, and Campbell had suggested a similar approach. The extreme youth of many of London's first undergraduates does account for some of the new institution's earliest pedagogical features. The famous mathematician Augustus De Morgan found his students so disorderly, behaving "like ill-regulated schoolboys," that he set them "impositions" as punishments, a decision that drove many of them out of the classroom even though attendance was reported monthly to parents and guardians.[21] "Continuous assessment" was introduced, as in schools. Individual professors examined the students in their courses, sometimes every week or even more often, on the grounds that not only was the practice educationally sound, but it also gave students needed preparation for the General Certificate in literature and science.[22]

The inexpensive Scottish conception of a nonresidential unitary university featuring compensation pegged to attendance rather than the English idea of an expensive residential collegiate university with tutorial instruction was unquestionably the inspiration of the University of London, but foreign models were also considered—the German universities, as represented by the two new foundations of Bonn and Berlin, and an American state institution, the University of Virginia, which, while founded in 1819, opened its doors in 1826. Campbell had twice visited Germany to study its university structure, and the plans for Virginia were well known in London because the Rockfish Gap Report was being flogged around the capital in an effort to attract talent. However, foreign models did not really provide the fledgling institution with a workable urban model. That would have been difficult, for Virginia was not an urban university, and the German universities were more closely tied to state and state objectives than to cities. At best foreign models only reinforced certain directions in London's early history—the system of professorial lecturing supported partly or wholly out of fees, for example, and some freedom of student choice in selecting courses. These were probably most useful as part of the public relations effort undertaken to attract backers to the scheme.

Curriculum

An urban theme is apparent in the curriculum of both teaching colleges, but most obviously in the professional divisions. It has often been remarked that cities foster a division of labor and generate a demand for specialized services.[23] Cities growing rapidly encounter problems that require some element of expert knowledge, although problem-solving methods will inevitably vary according to time and place. In the case of late-Regency and early-Victorian London, it was the state of the capital's sanitation and physical condition generally that led the founders to promote the foundation of a medical department. The university's trump card from the first was medical education, which supporters hoped could be improved by the addition of scientific instruction to what by tradition was clinical training based on the hospital ward. The opening of the medical school at University College was in fact the official opening of the university. Possibly no other feature of the curriculum caused the pre- or post-1836 University of London more difficulty than medicine.

Rivalries with existing teaching hospitals and medical royal societies continually hampered efforts at reorganization and accounted for a number of the structural peculiarities of London that remain to this day. The medical profession caused the university as much trouble as the Established Church during the 1830s controversies over the granting of a royal charter empowering the institution to grant degrees.

King's College also had a medical school, but it surpassed University College as a source of innovation when a department of civil engineering was established in 1838. Engineering, too, was thought to be a crucial way of addressing the problems of urban sanitation and of controlling the spread of disease and epidemics, such as the dreaded cholera which returned to the kingdom in the early 1830s. Civil engineers were less in demand for industrial purposes because the scale of enterprise in the lower Thames Valley was largely handicraft. Approximately 80 percent of London's manufacturing establishments employed four workers or fewer as late as 1851, in contrast to the very large factories of the company towns to the North. A network of small workshops were scattered throughout the metropolis, with a heavy concentration in the eastern and northeastern districts. The capital did not take the lead in the great transportation revolution that rapidly covered the kingdom with a system of railroads. That honor belongs to places like Stockton, Darlington, Liverpool, and Manchester, but by the 1850s London was indisputably the hub of the kingdom's communications network,[24] and railroads were well able to absorb the engineering skills being certified by the new university.

In particular, the utilitarian intellectuals backing the new institution in Gower Street certainly approved of professional or "useful" education, as did the representatives of rational dissent, and science and applied science received their blessings, as we might expect, since these subjects were connected to professional education and regarded as progressive. Both university colleges also provided a general or arts course, but these are not easy to characterize as "urban" in conception. Borrowed from the late-Enlightenment Scottish universities and the old dissenting academies, the curriculum was a mixture of modern subjects such as English language and literature or modern history, foreign languages, logic and moral philosophy, and traditional subjects such as Latin and Greek. Classical learning not only remained in the curriculum; it actually predominated in the first two years of the four-year general course at University College.[25]

Quite probably we should not expect radical departures in every respect whenever a new university is created, nor should we suppose that new urban institutions will automatically reject conventional courses of study merely because the new clientele are city dwellers whose needs are presumed special to their circumstances. Universities by their very nature as depositories of learning are loathe to break completely with past practice, nor are they always able to do so, whether they are land-grant institutions in American states or new universities in Britain and its empire. Their faculty have normally been educated conventionally and owe some loyalty to the basic disciplines that stand at the foundations of any curriculum, no matter how innovative. The existing knowledge base is therefore ipso facto constraining. Furthermore, there is usually a certain expectation on the part of potential users that while departures from convention may be desirable, a university should not completely abandon the traditions that have given it strength, prestige, and, above all, legitimacy. There is always the additional likelihood that newer uses will be found for older fields of learning.

As important as the actual curriculum, at least in London's case, was the spirit in which the professors were to approach the arts course. Here we can certainly identify an urban influence or connection. In the first place the professional curriculum partly drove the general curriculum. An obvious case was medicine, which required the colleges to invest resources in the teaching of the biological and physical sciences, and another was engineering, which required mathematics. But other subjects fulfilled some of the aims of the backers. Political economy, a favorite of London's utilitarians, was thought to be essential for the training of civil servants, and a chair of Hindustani established at University College could be justified as preparation for bureaucratic positions in the East India Company, the public monopoly located in the metropolis and chartered by the government for the administration of British-controlled areas of the Indian subcontinent. Jurisprudence and mathematics were claimed to be useful for such widely differing but not unrelated activities as commerce, foreign affairs, and law.[26]

Utility was also emphasized at the rival institution in the Strand, but with a notable exception: the teaching of English language and literature. At University College, English was taught conventionally, that is, with the same broad goals as classical languages. Grammar, composition, and the structure of literature were stressed in order to strengthen the powers of written and oral expression. The ultimate objective was success in the material world. Language teaching had followed this pattern for centuries, although in some historical periods logic and dialectic rather than composition and declamation were emphasized.

In the Strand the purposes were different. Literature rather than language was at the center of attention. Individual authors were scrutinized and studied in association with the development of modern history. The originators of this pioneering approach were the poet Robert Southey, who was offered but declined a chair, and F. D. Maurice, the famous theologian and Christian Socialist. Maurice connected England's special national virtues, discernible in its literature, to the middle class and commercial success. At the same time, fearing that his London students would be too eager to embrace the narrower aspects of that inheritance, he taught duty and responsibility and respect for national purpose as reflected in literature and history. His aims were also those of the Broad Church movement: self-sacrifice, community, a sense of the larger whole. To underscore the importance of this approach, the English course was made a regular part of the full-time curriculum, whereas at the rival college it remained optional.[27]

In Gower Street the message of material gain and career was not similarly restrained. The founding of the first London University was part of the same popular or mass education movement that had produced the monitorial system advocated by the educators Lancaster and Bell, the mechanics' institutes, and the Society for the Diffusion of Popular Knowledge, all of which, as a practical necessity, accepted cost cutting as a first step and utility as a second. But cheap education and "merely" useful knowledge were poor education and by their very nature supremely self-serving without higher reference—such, at least, were the public accusations of critics.

The accusations were not generous, but they had a point or two in their favor. The educational theory behind all popular education was more or less the same: the Lockean/utilitarian assumption of empty mind spaces which had only to be "furnished" or "stocked" with information by a process of associating ideas. A complicated epistemological theory, refined over the course of a century, was vulgarized into a crude method of mind cramming, and the teacher to whom Maurice had assigned an elevated role had often to be content with lesser employment.

The teaching of English at the first two constituent colleges of the University of London demonstrates the effect a particular urban environment may have on pedagogy, but as the illustrations show, there is no slavish relationship between the two. Other variables and influences enter the picture, and all that can be confidently said—and it may be saying a great deal—is that the urban context forced the colleges or individual professors to seriously consider or reconsider the grander or larger objectives of their teaching.

An urban preoccupation or concern was and continued to be important for both of the new colleges. It is certainly reflected in the relatively early provision made for educating young women. The more open life of the city, its diverse influences, and the greater accessibility of schools in urban as opposed to rural settings created a demand for the further education of women and gave to University College the distinction of being one of the leaders in the nineteenth-century movement for coeducation. As early as 1832 women were admitted to lectures on electricity. Thirty years later a special course of thirteen lectures on animal physiology attracted 113 women—in fact, the lectures had been requested by several London-based women's associations. Between 1869 and 1878 changes were introduced which allowed University College to become the pioneering coeducational institution in the kingdom.[28]

At King's in the 1850s an annual course of lectures on the physical condition of the poor was instituted to aid clergy working in city parishes. "[L]ittle progress can be made in the attempt to persuade men to be Christians," reads an entry in the council minutes, "so long as their physical condition is degraded below the level of humanity."[29] In the Department of General Literature and Science a professorship of the "Principles and Practice of Commerce" was reinstituted in 1852 when the chair was given to the famous statistician Leone Levi, who agreed to give a course of evening lectures on commercial and banking law "which has attracted a large class, including the chief Managers of the principal banking firms."[30]

As the century progressed both institutions undertook work for London-based industrial enterprises as the city's economic infrastructure underwent change. The earliest contributions were in chemistry. Largely technical at first, of a low level and oriented to the needs of London manufacturers in the food, soap, glass, and cement industries, contributions after the 1880s became increasingly part of a major applied science and research effort second to none in the kingdom. Sir William Ramsay at University College was a consultant to the British Radium Corporation in London and was involved in the beginnings of what became the great chemical firm of Courtauld's located in Kew. The establishment of the Imperial College of Technology in 1907 greatly extended the University of London's capacity for high-level technology in such fields as electrical engineering, gas, industrial dyestuffs, and petroleum. By 1914 the university was actively involved in agriculture and aeronautics, but not marine engineering, navigation, and nautical astronomy despite the capital's Thameside location.[31]

However, the new research undertakings were not necessarily restricted to London markets, especially toward the end of the century. Secret work was performed for the national steel industry, as well as for government, and London professors had connections to firms in places like Huddersfield, Warrington, and Manchester. The historian who has done the most to advance our understanding of the relationships between British industry and universities has stated that the ties between researchers in the University of London and manufacturers located in the capital were actually not as strong as those between civic universities and their cities, especially in the North, and he lays the proximate blame at the feet of local industrialists rather than the university and the ultimate blame on the nature of the metropolis. "London," he concludes, "was too large to generate a cohesive movement of loyal support to its own university."[32]

Upward Academic Drift

Today higher education institutions are defined as urban if their location is in a city, if their student body is recruited locally, if improved access is emphasized, if professional or specialized programs of study are featured, and if the institution repeatedly shows itself sensitive to urban social and economic problems.[33] By all of these criteria both University and King's Colleges were urban in conception and commitment. The first two university colleges of the University of London are remarkable examples of the new social forces at work in England in the third and fourth decades of the nineteenth century. The early educational policies adopted by both were strongly oriented to the local market and were in this respect, as in so many others, conscious departures from the historic model offered by the ancient universities. Yet we must be prepared for a paradox. Despite these undeniable facts, the subsequent development of the University of London is a history of "upward academic drift." Rivalries between the first two university colleges were certainly a principal factor in that drift, but we must also remember that underlying the earliest speculations concerning the expansion of higher education in England was the question of a "national" university mission for Dissenters, whose political strength and numbers actually lay outside London. As long as there was some hope that the connections between Oxford and Cambridge and the Church of England could be relaxed, the matter of a national university was secondary. But despite its great constitutional victories of 1828 to 1832, the dissenting community failed in its efforts to use Parliament to remove subscription to the Thirty-Nine Articles of the Church as a virtual condition of attendance at the ancient universities. The House of Lords, where the bishops sat, could not be brought around, and the ancient foundations were able to hold tightly fast to their monopoly despite strong support for Dissenters in the Commons. Failure reopened interest in the possibility of a "national" university for Dissenters, but the secular direction of University College had already been established.

The question of a national university for Dissenters and others brought up the related issue of whether the new institution would be empowered to grant degrees. The degree problem had been shelved in the 1820s because Brougham, anxious to see the new enterprise launched, wanted to avoid unnecessary controversy. Everyone knew, however, that the issue would reappear. Of little use to the landed aristocracy whose sons attended Oxford and Cambridge, since their careers and fortunes were otherwise ensured, degrees were valued by Dissenters and others in need of a certification of competence. Degrees were also necessary for fellowships in the royal medical societies, although this privilege could only be bestowed upon Oxbridge graduates.

The degree in Britain was protected from market forces. As such it was presumed to be relatively free of precisely the kind of local pressures to which the new self-styled "university" was responding. It could not be created virtually at will as in the American case but represented, no matter how imperfectly, a standard of learning and especially "discipline." It was a privilege bestowed by the center and specified in the grant of a royal charter obtained by "prayer" to the crown in council.

The Privy Council was divided on the issue of a London University degree, but the House of Commons was strongly in favor and voted a memorial to the crown. Many members of the government also supported the new institution, but in the complicated and protracted process of deliberation, which covered the years from 1831 to 1836, the church lobby was able to rally its supporters. The education offered by the new institution was faulty and suspect, opponents said. The standard was lower and would be driven still lower by a helpless dependence on consumer preference. This could be shown in the first instance by the absence of theological instruction. But there was also no teaching of religious ethics as part of moral philosophy, no required attendance at chapel, and no reference whatsoever to even the most broadly defined Christian heritage. At stake, therefore, was a particular definition or conception of university education in England that it had, via history and law, a close and inextricable connection with the Church of England,

and that the crown, to which the Privy Council was advisory, was bound to that law and was itself part of the Church of England, the head and supreme governor, in fact, and could not, however well disposed to the new University of London, contradict itself. The bachelor's degree carried certain privileges largely related to ecclesiastical purposes, and to grant these to graduates of a "metropolitan pest-house" was unthinkable.[34]

Since no secular university had ever been founded in Britain before the 1820s, the law governing the title "university" was actually unclear and uncertain. The issue had simply never arisen, but in a period of intense religious rivalries and evangelical and High Church revival, an attempt was made by the church party to attach a narrow and precise legal definition to a vague historical word. Happily, the church found an unlikely but invaluable ally in the opposition of the organized medical profession, whose strength and resources lay in the capital. The teaching hospitals and royal medical societies did not want control over the education of doctors shifted to a new institution, and to give the London University power to award degrees, including medical degrees, meant the potential loss of medical recruits for themselves.[35]

Learning was inseparable from discipline, and the standards of both had to be maintained. Universities in Britain existed to teach undergraduates (medical students were usually undergraduates as well), and undergraduates, whether at English or at Scottish universities, were under the tutelage of teachers concerned with their moral superintendence. The new University of London was more than "godless." It had (so opponents claimed) shamefully abandoned students to the extreme dangers of the London streets and temptations of the nearby West End theaters. These charges were irritating, especially in light of the notorious conduct of Oxbridge sporting hearties, and they were countered by arguments pointing out the virtues of home residence. Yet supporters of the audacious London University were sensitive to the accusation that they were no more than a licensed business offering a mechanical or utilitarian education indifferent to the moral development of the whole person—a particular view of liberal education that had come to be closely associated with residential forms of higher education. The first warden of London University himself made a compromising analogy when he (proudly) informed Brougham in 1828 that the new institution in Gower Street was "a great machine. . . . Your pleasure would be something like Watts' when he first saw the steady majestic motion of a great engine."[36] This unfortunate image was used at a time when the mechanistic language of the eighteenth-century Enlightenment was being replaced by organic metaphors of nurturing, growth, and development. A university education was supposed to form and shape character and inculcate a sense of high responsibility to society. It was not, as Maurice would inform his students at King's College, an instrument for selfishly advancing one's social and economic position in society.

Given the influence enjoyed by the college in Gower Street, a compromise was inevitable, but some avenue had to be found for ensuring that if granted degrees, or allowed access to degrees, undergraduates at the new university would receive a sound education of an acceptable standard. There followed the famous solution of 1836. The title "university" was reserved for a new entity which alone was empowered to award degrees. The new "royal university" was denominated a "public" institution, but the original foundations were to be considered "private," as were Oxford and Cambridge colleges. Private bodies could impose religious tests or make any other disciplinary arrangements for students, and therefore King's College could keep religious tests for its students (which it did for only full-time students). University College could retain its secular status, but in the act of preparing students for degrees the infidel college would not have control over the university curriculum and standards. University College was unhappy but bowed to the inevitable. The new constitution did not altogether suit King's College either. No religious instruction was necessary to pass the university's examinations, and degrees were not awarded in divinity. For several years King's boycotted the university's examinations altogether, finally submitting to student pressure.[37]

The solution of 1836 divided the responsibility for teaching and examining between two very different kinds of institutions—colleges and university—but a connection was maintained through the stipulation that candidates for degrees show proof of attendance at lectures in officially recognized or "affiliated" institutions. In 1850 new colleges in the empire were allowed to affiliate, but in 1858 the whole idea of affiliation was dropped, with the sole exception of candidates for medical degrees. The university was now permitted to grant degrees to anyone who had successfully taken and passed its examinations. It no longer mattered whether candidates had actually attended lectures at King's and University colleges. It no longer mattered whether candidates had been tutored at recognized or "affiliated" institutions. They could be taught privately, attend cramming sessions, sign up for courses in new civic colleges such as Owens College, Manchester, attend extension courses, or be tutored by clergymen in remote imperial territories. They could sit examinations with only the equivalent of a sixth-form school preparation. All of this was of no consequence in deciding who could take the London University degree examinations. Thus the first steps were taken toward the "external degree" that became famous in the twentieth century and in time would attract more students than the "internal degree,"[38] and thus triumphed the most extreme version of the English principle of the separation of teaching and examining, a perfect example of the mid-Victorian belief in the validation of merit through an impersonal and objective system of competitive examinations. By the end of the century the external degree function of the university was so pronounced that a bill in Parliament to strengthen the position of resident teachers was opposed on the grounds that it would "Londonize" the university.[39]

The controversy over degrees and the creation of a national university under state control with headquarters in London brings us to a major theme, the origin and purpose of the federal principle in British higher education, by which is meant a network of teaching joined to an administrative center through students preparing for examinations, as in the London case of 1858, or through actual institutional affiliation, as in the London case of 1836 and the other nineteenth-century federations. The division of labor between a set of teaching institutions and a central administrative body represented a brilliant compromise among deeply opposed religious, professional, and social interests, between entrenched institutions and upstarts. It was a compromise between a local and a national conception of a university's responsibility to society, since it appears plausible that the strict separation of center and periphery was intended to forestall some of the implications of a free market for higher education. Weakly endowed, created by shareholders, and driven by fees, the godless institution in Gower Street was highly vulnerable. The founders were willing to offer part-time courses, evening classes, and remedial education to accommodate the occasional and, as we now say, the "mature" student and to make still other adjustments to the requirements of the urban London market. Charges that standards would be sacrificed in an effort to attract students were not totally malicious, as even parliamentary supporters of University College were willing to admit.[40] To prevent downward drift in the quality of the degree, the architects of the compromise of 1836 took examining out of the hands of professors, who were thereby no longer free to set the standards of achievement for degree candidates.

It was, of course, a considerable exaggeration to suggest by comparison that the academic standard at the Oxbridge colleges was particularly noteworthy when only a small number of their undergraduates in the 1820s and 1830s showed an inclination to compete for distinction, but at least it could be argued that a semblance of quality existed thanks to the creation of the honors degree, first instituted at Cambridge in the mid-eighteenth century and at Oxford in 1800.

While the precise requirements of 1836 were not altogether satisfactory for King's College, the compromise fulfilled some of its earlier aspirations. King's had been searching for ways of embracing a national mission and mitigating its relationship to the local open market. It is true that in much of its curriculum and in its establishment of departments of medicine and engineering the college in the Strand had followed the lead of University College in appealing to a London constituency. It had similarly made provision for part-time students, but at the same time it had endeavored to follow the example of the two senior English universities and attach itself to the establishment. In order to attract the patronage of the court of King George IV (with some minor success), it had named itself after the monarch and obtained a royal charter of incorporation in 1829, although without the right to grant degrees. From the start it had connected itself to the Church of England. The principal was to be in holy orders; professors, with a few exceptions, were expected to be members of the Established Church; and outside ecclesiastical leaders were part of the structure of governance. The college's loyalties were caught between a market and an elite conception of education, which is where King's remained for the rest of the century.[41]

The establishment of a second and different University of London was a solution to the problem of quality control, as it was at the same time a compromise between rival conceptions of a university education. The two colleges, or any other affiliated institutions, remained free to establish their own working relationships with the local market, to include admissions, the level of fees, staffing, and nondegree courses; but insofar as they wished their undergraduates to obtain degrees, they had to submit their teaching to an impartial audit in the form of external examinations. A meritocratic top pressed down on a mass-market base to allow access while controlling the output of graduates, leading to protracted disputes between the colleges and the university, between the professors who wanted to teach (or conduct research) in their own way and a body of outside examiners who were primarily interested in guaranteeing the degree standard and the uniform quality of undergraduate teaching.

The exact origins of the examining university of 1836 remain obscure. Relevant documents, the discussions in the Privy Council, for example, and correspondence that might cast light on the negotiations either do not exist or are extremely difficult to locate.[42] Quite possibly, the idea that an independent board of examiners be created to control degrees was first suggested by physicians and surgeons in 1833 as part of a general parliamentary interest in the standards of medical practice.[43] There is, however, a longer history. It may be argued that the idea of a division of functions between a teaching college and an examining center owes its inspiration to a similar if not identical set of responsibilities that had developed at the collegiate University of Cambridge. For present purposes it is not necessary to pursue the partition back beyond the eighteenth century when the university assumed responsibility for the administration of a new type of examination—written, not oral, and honors not "ordinary"—called the tripos. Some two dozen autonomous colleges with powers of admission and extensive financial resources monopolized teaching, as they had since the sixteenth century. The division of labor was particularly satisfactory because it did not in any way alter existing privileges. No student was required to read for honors, but anyone anxious to distinguish himself academically could prepare for a rigorous examination administered by an impartial and distant body of university examiners. Impartiality was valued because eighteenth-century English society was dominated by a far-reaching and effective system of aristocratic patronage from which the universities were hardly immune. Historians have therefore correctly identified the Cambridge tripos as the beginnings of a meritocratic system of educational achievement that in time became a model of its kind in Britain, and it is not surprising that the senate of the post-1836 University of London was dominated by graduates and faculty from Cambridge, particularly Trinity College, the largest and the leading college, or that the Royal Charter of 1836 should mention a "Board of Examiners . . . to perform all the functions of the examiners in the Senate House [the administrative headquarters] of Cambridge."[44] Unlike Cambridge, however, where the examiners were all internal, the London University solution extended the principle of the separation of functions by using examiners who were not required to hold collegiate appointments. They thus had no personal or pecuniary interest in the success of individual degree candidates as did faculty whose livelihood was based on their ability to attract students to the lecture hall.

The compromise of 1836 had another effect on the future history of the London federation: it introduced the possibility of a radically new mission for British higher education whose logical outcome was the constitutional changes introduced in 1850 and 1858. It was in the 1830s and 1840s that the idea of federation as a way of uniting the disparate parts of a political system began to spread, and in the 1840s it was applied to the Canadian provinces, which became in that decade a federation of dominions. The principle of federation was applied to higher education. Many embryonic colleges had arisen in Canada and in fact elsewhere from the 1790s on. They were now cobbled together by the device of the London-originated examinations. Thus, the London University was substituted for Cambridge University, the Burlington House examinations for the Senate House examinations, as examples to be followed for new universities in the United Kingdom and the empire. Federation replaced confederation. Although variations on the principle of federation would continue to be made, as in the case of the Irish university system, all new higher education institutions began life as university colleges tied into a dominant examining university, until the end of the century when the University of Birmingham was founded on a unitary or Scottish plan.

Federations, especially federations with strong centers, had a number of distinct advantages and features. They protected young colleges during the early years when they might fail, instead of allowing them to go under as often happened in the United States, and minimized their exposure to the pressure for open access and easy degrees. They kept administrative costs to a minimum, for an examining university had small staffs and low overhead. This was an important political objective of mid-Victorian liberalism, which favored low-cost administration and high consumer choice, but at the same time accepted a minimal regulatory role for the state in such matters as education, the protection of minors in industry, and the adulteration of food. The constitution of 1858 had been adopted because the University of London found itself without the resources to determine whether certificates of attendance in affiliated institutions were genuine and reflected a serious level of instruction.[45] It was simply more practical and economical to affirm the principle of minimal governmental interference by controlling examinations, which could be made as stringent as desired. Indeed, after 1858 the examination noticeably stiffened, and in the 1860s nearly half the candidates for degrees were failed.[46]

From the middle of the nineteenth century until the last decades, when a noisy campaign was waged for what was called a "teaching university" in the capital, the University of London had a confused relationship with the metropolitan area that had been its original home. A "Cockney University" it may have been, but from the start a wider mission was hinted at. An early statement looked forward to a time when the university's draw would be worldwide, and Lord Auckland, who had been the first president of the council of the original University of London, had predicted that his institution would become imperial, that colonial students would journey to London to study in Gower Street.[47] It is in the middle years of the nineteenth century that the sources first begin to mention actual imperial responsibilities. Thus, the council of King's College referred to the need for civil engineers to build railroads "in the various dependencies of the British Crown, particularly in the East Indies, in Canada, and in Australia," and fully expected King's students to seek such opportunities, recalling in their service "at home and abroad, the sound religious principles, as well as the science, the industrious habits, and the practical skill which they have learnt within the walls."[48]

Having thus begun as an experiment in higher education to establish a new type of university called "metropolitan," London University rapidly acquired a national mission and almost concurrently an imperial one. Local ties and services were certainly maintained, as already enumerated, but the London University was not a "municipal" institution as sixteenth-century Edinburgh had been a Town College, responsible to a well-defined local authority and incorporating Renaissance and Reformation theories of public responsibility. It was not even a "civic" one, to draw a further distinction between universities that are municipal and maintained by local authorities and those that are independent but in a more general way represent the principal interests of specific urban communities. Although London is sometimes called a civic university, credit for being Britain's first such institution must go to Birmingham. Given the association between a university and the nation that existed in the 1830s and beyond, given the nature of the capital—its patchwork system of internal governance; its increasing economic, political, and cultural domination of the kingdom; and its position as (to use a geographer's phrase) a "primate" city—civic status would have been far too limiting.

For many the supercession of the original university by a different conception was perfectly consistent with the character of the metropolis as the center of a proud island kingdom and as a global city or, as so many of its inhabitants were pleased to say, the "Metropolis of the world."[49] But others phrased it differently. Less pleased, the principal of King's College said in 1888 that the University of London was not a university and was not of London.[50]

London: The Unique City

London was a great city, possessing the population, the human and capital resources, the communications infrastructure, the cultural institutions, and the grandeur and style that great cities possess, but it was also a special kind of urban creation. To appreciate that dimension of its history and to grasp its importance for understanding the place of the London University in nineteenth-century Britain, we need to view the metropolis's morphology and cultural traits from another, a broader, and, to begin with, a comparative and offshore perspective.

London has often struck continental visitors as the least European of great cities. A classic work by a Danish architect and city planner approvingly calls London unique because of its human scale, represented principally by its special morphology of a central core of Georgian squares, low-rise prospect, and endless suburban villages separated by green spaces.[51] The latter features have also led some critics to call the metropolis antiurban. A second continental observer provides us with one typical elaboration of this view. The Englishman, he says, "has no feeling for the beauty of the town. . . . [H]e has no scruples about destroying monuments of architecture, but is up in arms as soon as anyone proposes to fell a tree."[52] The real love of the English is the garden, the garden square, the park—that is, space use historically associated with the stately home, the cathedral town, the hamlet, the country cottage, the village green, the churchyard overgrown with grass and wildflowers, common land, lovers' lanes, and hedgerows filled with game and songbirds. The English prefer low-rise buildings and detached or semi-detached houses—in a word, the suburb, particularly and especially that great Victorian creation, the garden suburb, which crossed the Atlantic and appears at such places as Forest Hills. London is the anticity because the suburb is what matters, the periphery, not the center. The two interpenetrate in a carefully defined manner. The periphery is the private and separate world of home and family. The center is the public world of work, competition, and strain. The animation of city streets is a fact of daylight. At night one nurses the soul in the isolation of the suburb.[53]

Historically it was not always this way. In the eighteenth century, men of letters, critics, Grub Street journalists, people of fashion, and habitués of the theaters regarded London as the embodiment of civilization or civility. There was, of course, a darker side—the mob, the idle and debauched, the stews and rookeries, the thieving and physical squalor—but even these drawbacks contributed to the unique thrill and adventure that was a city. The concentration of population and resources, elegant structures, pace, and perpetual novelty stimulated conversation, broadened one's understanding of human affairs and the human condition, and extended the range and possibilities of personal achievement. A city and London especially were places that excited the imagination and heightened perceptions, and some nineteenth-century commentators, still under this spell, even applied to the capital the word *sublime*, normally reserved for natural and supernatural phenomena.[54] A great city was the Enlightenment itself, a source of hopeful ideas about human potential and material progress. It followed that a city did not necessarily require a university because the city itself was a university, at least according to litterateurs such as Joseph Addison, the Oxford graduate, for whom a superior education was acquired in the corner of a London coffee shop affording an outlook upon the vibrant, laughing town.

These sentiments did not vanish in the next century, nor have they vanished today. They still exist everywhere as part of the mental baggage citizens carry with them into daily life. However, against the view that London was urbane and civilized there arose a different opinion in the nineteenth century, namely, that a city had the defects of its merits. If it was a source of lively invention, it did not necessarily respect tradition and custom. If it encouraged experiment, it deprecated the old ways. The desire to embrace the very latest in news and fashion inclined the successful to ignore the unsuccessful, as did competition for the city's considerable resources. It was easy enough, in a community of large numbers of strangers, to feel lost or marginal, handicapped or disadvantaged. Sublime for some in the eighteenth century, London became pandemonium for others in the nineteenth century, an infernal city or Babylon. "Even Dickens," writes Richard Shannon, "the first major imaginative writer to accept the unavoidable reality of the city, never reconciled himself to it as the primary source of moral energy."[55]

From the 1860s on, when the underground and overground railroads began to transport Londoners farther out into the pastoral regions of the greater metropolitan environment, London was sharply transformed from a city that had once been strongly influenced by Italian Renaissance ideas of central town planning to a city ringed and interpenetrated by suburban villas and gardens. The financial district closed down at night. Centrally located flats—of which a few were built at midcentury—were occupied only by *boulevardiers,* bachelors, and others suspected of loose conduct. No respectable family lived in the center. The slums spread and were shut off from the more fortunately situated residential areas. Neither the city nor its more fashionable population continued to orient itself to the street, as inclined to do when the fine public squares of the preceding century were laid out, as Paris and Vienna still did.

The Victorians (and Edwardians) preferred cities that evoked villa and countryside, and most of nineteenth-century London, as well as provincial factory cities and seaports, drifted toward a suburban configuration. The result was many Londons rolled into one. There was the London of fogs, crime, and horrifying slums stretching from Aldgate eastward along the Thames and northward into Middlesex. There was the London of the two historic "cities," the City of Westminster, royal and glamorous (but once also the home of the radical utilitarians who helped in the establishment of University College), and the City of London, the greatest capital market in the world. There was the London of the garden suburbs, country villages in the city, plantations of fine and pleasant houses such as Regent's Park and Swiss Cottage or Bedford Park, or modest but desirable districts such as Camberwell south of the river, the new home of the lower middle class, especially clerks from London's expanding office economy.

A Capital University

The new University of London corresponded more to the ideals of the older eighteenth-century city than to the nineteenth. The equation of cities with civilization in Enlightenment Europe, the public conception of city life that led to the proliferation of open squares and public gathering places, the orientation to the street, and the feeling that the Town was a source of social and intellectual emancipation were closer to the vision of an interconnected university and city held by the founders of the infidel university than later Victorian views. The neoclassical facade of University College, designed by the same architect who was building the British Museum, at once declared its affiliation with the grand tradition and demanded a prominent place in the cityscape. (King's was laid out as a set of Palladian terraces forming a cloister approached through an arch. The site constraints were serious, but the difference in orientation to the street and city remains significant.) By one of history's ironies, the university was founded at precisely the moment when the pressures and problems of city life were beginning to attract considerable critical attention, when the Romantic exaltation of village and field was influential, and when the flight to the suburbs was about to commence. Raymond Williams has called this major reorientation in the topographical sensibility of the English a "rentier's or dormitory dream."[56] A different view of the ideal university was emerging and found its home in the reviving fortunes of Oxford and Cambridge, whose residential colleges and tutors in loco parentis more closely approximated suburban aspirations than did the aims of the new colleges in the geographical center of the capital. The revival of Oxford and Cambridge, the midcentury "Young Oxford" and "Young Cambridge" spirit that accompanied the reform movement, and the ensuing golden age of the colleges corresponded exactly to the suburban juxtaposition of beauty, young manhood or womanhod, innocence, and segregation. The ideal university was situated among giant horse chestnut trees and fields of asphodel, and in quiet cloisters were heard the sound of chapel bells through the soft nights of summer. Such, at any event, was the mythos first advanced during the Romantic period of the early nineteenth century and disseminated in countless nineteenth-century recollections of college life on the banks of the rivers Cam and Isis.[57]

The ideal university, then, did not lie in London districts such as Bloomsbury, where University College and its medical school were to be found, or in South Kensington, where the Imperial College was to have its home, although Egham, where in the 1880s Thomas Holloway had used the immense profits from the sale of quack medicines to build a storybook French chateau as a college for women, was pleasantly suburban and had real possibilities. The genuine article lay much farther afield, well beyond the edges of London's northernmost suburbs, across the ridges of hills where Roman soldiers had marched, and past country churches. It was to be found in the busy market towns that still embody one of the most alluring dreams in the repertory of universities. For the moment we can capture the essence of that dream by saying that it is (or was) fundamentally antiurban. It rejected the laboratory of experiment that is the city for the assurance of tradition. For the city view that the socialization of the young is the joint responsibility of many institutions, it substituted faith in a "Plan of St. Gall," with trust in the powers of a "total" institution,[58] and it took its inspiration from an ancient belief in the importance of educating young people to be "whole," that is, to possess a rounded outlook on human affairs rather than "mere" competence in a professional or specialized field.

The Victorian debate on higher education, therefore, was also connected to an ongoing larger cultural debate on the merits of the city and the country and whether cities could even provide the kind of nurturing environment from which strong and self-confident personalities came forth. Something of the flavor of that debate is preserved in these well-known remarks about two undergraduates who attended University College in the 1840s:

> It is sometimes said that it needs the quiet of a country town, remote from the capital, to foster the love of genuine study in young men. But of this at least I am sure: that Gower Street, and Oxford Street, and the New Road, and the dreary chain of squares from Euston to Bloomsbury, were the scenes of discussions as eager and as abstract as ever were the sedate cloisters or the flowery river meadows of Cambridge or Oxford.[59]

This is Richard Holt Hutton recounting the day that he and Walter Bagehot, the renowned editor of *The Economist,* being lost in philosophic argument, were unable to locate Regent Street after many hours of wandering. The anecdote is intended to illustrate the exciting early days of the University of London and to suggest the positive effect on learning that a city can have. The anecdote is also a eulogy of intellectual life and the power of ideas and debate, and these, it may be argued, are particularly characteristic of a great city. They derive from the energy of the city, its open and inquisitive character, and its abstract or distancing nature. The Oxbridge idyll, however, was not about distancing but about intimacy. It was more than the life of the mind. It was also about friendships, tradition, associations, and loyalties, about the very fact of being young and hopeful. One spoke as did Cardinal Newman about the genius loci of the university. The English idea of a university was that it was insulated from external influences, that it was self-contained or a milieu.[60] When Durham University was founded in the early 1830s, virtually on the heels of the London University, it was located in a cathedral town on a bluff overlooking a delightful English river. All the correct historical associations were present. (Durham's lack of success despite these advantages is another story.)

Youth was presumed to be responsive to the symbols of association, tradition, and beauty celebrated in Victorian neohistoricism. In the London University there was to be

> no melodramatic pageantry, no ancient ceremonial, no silver mace, no gowns either black or red, no hoods either of fur or of satin, no public

orator to make speeches which nobody hears, no oaths sworn only to be broken. Nobody thought of emulating the cloisters, the organs, the painted glass, the withered mummies, the busts of great men, and the pictures of naked women, which attract visitors from every part of the Island to the banks of Isis and Cam.

But the same sardonic writer, a talented and confident graduate of Trinity College, Cambridge, converted to London's cause, was prepared to sweep away the romantic cobwebs concealing the truth that "Young academicians venture to get drunk within a few yards of the grave of Newton, and to commit solecisms, though the awful eye of Erasmus frowns upon them from the canvas."[61] Nevertheless, just as the metropolis was a "Grete Wen" to detractors like the rural apologist William Cobbett, who in a famous image of the 1820s compared it to a swollen, suppurating, repulsive blemish on the face of England, meaning also that it was a tissue of unhappy and indissolubly connected social relationships, so was it stated that the university founded there was unsuitable for educating the young.[62] Urban attachments in Victorian England were not as strong as pastoral ones and could not be similarly sentimentalized. In short, "[a] Metropolitan University, whose students live at home or in lodgings, cannot under any conceivable arrangements offer an exact equivalent of the camaraderie, 'studious cloisters pale' and 'the elms which shaded Newton or Milton,' " wrote *The Quarterly Review* in 1887.[63] Walking about London, Bagehot and Holt found the squares and streets of Bloomsbury second to none as places for animated intellectual talk, but on another occasion Bagehot defined a university education as the "impact of young thought upon young thought, of fresh thought on fresh thought, of hot thought on hot thought,"[64] words that describe the close friendships and schoollike environment of isolated English (or American) colleges, not universities open to the world. During the University of London reorganization controversy of the 1890s a writer for the *Spectator* was led to praise private American universities such as Harvard for retaining the kind of aesthetic environment long considered essential for educating young people while adopting a research function. Without lawns, rivers, and quadrangles, without a "campus," without separate space, there was no such thing as a university.[65]

Against this history and in relation to it, the first University of London had undertaken a formidable assignment. A university for the capital had been discussed since the seventeenth century but had never been achieved. Once achieved, it had encountered two types of opposition: the clerical and religious establishment, in alliance with the entrenched interests of the older liberal professions, accustomed to privileges and monopolies; and the equally effective and widespread sentiment that cities were inherently threatening and competitive, dangerous to mental and bodily health alike.[66] The history of nineteenth-century London University, therefore, is the history of a new type of institution attempting to discover a mission for itself unique and special enough to avoid unflattering comparisons to Oxford and Cambridge.

That search was full of unexpected twists and turns, many of them outside the control of the first University of London but a logical or at least understandable result of the larger cultural and institutional history of England. Once the title "university" was taken from a privately funded college and delivered to an agency of the state—restored, that is, to the "public" sector where by tradition and dubiously by law universities belonged—it could be predicted that a change of mission and ethos would follow. "Public" educational institutions had wider responsibilities than private ones. Such was certainly the history of those historic grammar schools that had once been the source of local pride and initiative but had gone "public" in the eighteenth century, expanding their intake to regions well outside their original catchment areas. Such was to be the history of those early- and mid-nineteenth-century proprietary schools that had also become great Victorian boarding schools in their own right, proud of their role in producing political and military leaders for the empire.[67] Here certainly was a conjunction of purposes. Glamour was always available in an imperial dimension. Lord Rosebery, the sometime liberal foreign secretary, opined in 1903 that the London University should stand to the British empire as the great technological institution in Berlin, the Charlottenburg, stood to the German empire.[68] For that purpose, for professional education, for scientific research, for the development of the applied social sciences, if not for a traditional English undergraduate education, the new university was perfectly situated. It was a capital university. What other outcome was possible?

At Home

It has been said that great universities do not make much difference to capital cities.[69] The university in a metropolis is no more obvious than great courts of law, than organs of government, than the headquarters of global corporations, than the intellectual and artistic life that may in fact go on without it. The university is no more visible than other giant edifices. The sudden vision of Magdalen Tower in the High or the fantastic appearance of screen, porter's lodge, and chapel of the college in the King's Parade at Cambridge best achieve their theatrical effect without competition. Imagine an eighteenth-century *capriccio* of Oxbridge colleges placed in London settings. What would be the impact? The charming irresistible collegiate courts and spires would no more dominate the metropolis than does the London law school of Lincoln's Inn which resembles them. Perhaps in 1828 there was a chance. The capital was still advancing. The great public buildings, hotels, banks, and insurance companies were yet to be built. Even so, the effect of University College's handsome front was limited. There was no campus of walks, gardens, and meadows and no soaring campanile. As the century moved along, the University of London's fiefdoms were not concentrated in a single spot or neighborhood but scattered throughout the capital. Sir William Beveridge understood the difficulty when in 1928 he called for a new central administration building that would replace Burlington House and provide the University of London with a clear statement of its relation to the metropolis:

> The University of London is at once civic and national and international, federal and collegiate, though not residential, a poor man's University in a city of boundless wealth. . . . The central symbol of the Bloomsbury site can not fittingly look like an imitation of any other University; it must not be a replica from the middle ages. It should be something that . . . can only be at home in London.[70]

When completed, the Senate House was the tallest building in London.[71] It is not so today. Most assuredly it is not a replica of the Middle Ages. It is not a college masquerading as a Cotswold village. Whether it is "at home" in London is for the observer to decide, unless nobbled by the mischievous suggestion that in a great city no building, as no person, is truly ever at home.

NOTES

I would like to thank Martin Trow, Gunther Barth, Elizabeth Morse, and Nina Robinson of the University of California at Berkeley for their truly invaluable assistance in preparing this study.

1. Andrew Lees, *Cities Perceived: Urban Society in European and American Thought, 1820–1940* (New York, 1985), chap. II.

2. Statistics calculated from B. R. Mitchell, *Abstract of British Historical Statistics* (Cambridge, 1962), p. 19.

3. Historically, a *metropolis* was an archiepiscopal see, a capital city generally, or the center of some activity. It was used in the 1780s to describe a monster, but the more neutral meaning to indicate a conurbation appears in the 1820s and 1830s. One of the "founders" of the University of London called the capital "our gigantic metropolis." Thomas Lloyd Humberstone, *University Reform in London* (London, 1926), p. 25. See also H. J. Dyos, "Greater and Greater London: Notes on Metropolis and Provinces in the Nineteenth and Twentieth Centuries," in *Britain and the Netherlands*, ed. J. S. Bromley and E. H. Kossman (The Hague, 1971), p. 93; Anthony Sutcliffe, *Metropolis 1890–1940* (Chicago, 1984), pp. 67, 256 n.; Raymond Williams, *The Country and the City* (London, 1973), p. 146.

4. However, no interest was ever paid on the shares. H. Hale Bellot, *University College London, 1826–1926* (London, 1929), p. 305.

5. Ibid., p. 51; and Donald Olsen, intro. to David Owen, *The Government of Victorian London, 1855–1889: The Metropolitan Board of Works, the Vestries and the City Corporation* (Cambridge, Mass., 1982), p. 3. Total costs at Oxford and Cambridge were habitually estimated at between 250 and 300 pounds per annum, and it was claimed that attendance at London University would reduce those figures by about two-thirds. Cyrus Redding, *Literary Reminiscences and Memoirs of Thomas Campbell* (London, 1860), II, 12. George B. Jeffery, *The Unity of Knowledge: Some Reflections on the Universities of Cambridge and London* (Cambridge, 1950), p. 10, says that there were six hundred full-time

students at University College in its first year, but attendance may have dropped considerably by 1835 if William Tooke's remarks to the House of Commons, 20 May 1835, col. 281, are correct.

6. Bellot, *University College London*, pp. 47–48; R. S. Neale, *Class and Ideology in the Nineteenth Century* (London, 1972), p. 30.

7. Bellot, *University College London*, pp. 29–30; Chester New, *Life of Henry Brougham to 1830* (Oxford, 1961), p. 360.

8. John Seed, "Gentlemen Dissenters: The Social and Political Meanings of Rational Dissent in the 1770s and 1780s," *Historical Journal* 28 (June 1985): 299–325. Dissent grew rapidly between 1770 and 1810. The Wesleyans, for example, increased fivefold and the Baptists fourfold. The Dissenters have been estimated at about 312,000 in 1810, 437,000 in 1820, and 600,000 in 1830, and their growth in numbers can be correlated with their political influence. See Robert Currie, Alan Gilbert, and Lee Horslay, *Churches and Churchgoers* (Oxford, 1977), pp. 23–25.

9. N. R. Tempest, "An Early Scheme for an Undenominational University," *Universities Review* 32 (February 1960): 45–49.

10. William Beattie, *Life and Letters of Thomas Campbell*, 2nd ed. (London, 1850), II, 411.

11. W. M. Torrens, *Memoirs of the Right Honourable William, Second Viscount Melbourne* (London, 1878), II, 158.

12. *First Book for the Instruction of Students in the King's College London* (London, 183?), p. 8. For Virginia, see Jennings Wagoner, "Constraint and Variety in Virginia Higher Education, *History of Education Quarterly* 25 (Spring–Summer 1985): 184; and "Honor and Dishonor at Mr. Jefferson's University," *History of Education Quarterly* 26 (Summer 1986): 157.

13. Francis Sheppard, "London and the Nation in the Nineteenth Century," *Transactions of the Royal Historical Society*, 5th ser., 35 (1985): 60.

14. Gordon Heulin, *King's College London, 1828–1978* (London, 1978), pp. 29, 42.

15. For the Scottish universities, see Paul Robertson, "Scottish Universities and Industry, 1860–1914," *Scottish Economic and Social History* 4 (1984): 53; Douglas Sloan, *The Scottish Enlightenment and the American College Ideal* (New York, 1971), pp. 19–28. I am further indebted to correspondence with Robert Anderson and conversations with Nicholas Phillipson, both of the University of Edinburgh, and to their writings.

16. Redding, *Literary Reminiscences*, pp. 19–21. My colleague Gunther Barth suggests that the aim of producing "useful men" is particularly urban in outlook.

17. *Observations on the Probable Failure of the London University* (London, 1825), p. 10; New, *Life of Henry Brougham*, p. 378. The second largest group of professors were from Cambridge, generally regarded as more sympathetic to dissent than Oxford.

18. Bellot, *University College London*, pp. 37–38, 40, 251.

19. Redding, *Literary Reminiscences*, p. 11; Heulin, *King's College London*, p. 7.

20. *Second Statement of the Council of the University of London* (London, 1828), p. 19.

21. Henry Solly, *These Eighty Years, or the Story of an Unfinished Life* (London, 1893), I, 143–44. Shephard T. Taylor, *The Diary of a Medical Student during the Mid-Victorian Period, 1860–64* (Norwich, 1927), mentions the noisy

classes of medical students, continually having to be reprimanded by their teachers. The inability of professors at both colleges to keep order was often noted. See Alan Bacon, "English Literature Becomes a Subject: King's College, London as Pioneer," *Victorian Studies* 29 (Summer 1986): 605–6. F. D. Maurice referred to his students at King's College as "boys," as indeed they often were. Campbell, in his famous open letter to the *Times* of 9 February 1825 addressed to Brougham, spoke of attracting a student body of fifteen- or sixteen- to twenty-year-olds (and at one time may have been considering an even younger distribution). See Bellot, *University College London,* p. 52; and Redding, *Literary Reminiscences,* p. 9.

22. *Second Statement,* pp. 26–27.

23. George Simmel, *On Individuality and Social Forms* (Chicago and London, 1971), pp. 337, 325–37.

24. Sheppard, "London and the Nation," pp. 56–57.

25. James Henderson Burns, *Jeremy Bentham and University College* (London, 1962), p. 10.

26. Liberal or general education, it has been pointed out, survives in urban-based universities despite the heavy demand for basic skills and vocational education because urban environments requires highly developed arts of communication, negotiation, and mediation. See Park R. Kolbe, *Urban Influences on Higher Education in England and the United States* (New York, 1928), pp. 123–24.

27. Bacon, "English Literature," pp. 600–12.

28. Negley Harte, *The Admission of Women to University College London: A Centenary Lecture* (London, 1979), p. 5.

29. *King's College London Calendar* (1850–51), pp. 22–23.

30. Ibid. (1856–57), p. 40.

31. Michael Sanderson, *The Universities and British Industry 1850–1970* (London, 1972), pp. 106–20.

32. Ibid., p. 118. Sanderson, "The Professor as Industrial Consultant: Oliver Arnold and the British Steel Industry, 1900–1914," *Economic History Review* 31 (November 1978): 585–600.

33. Title XI of the U.S. Higher Education Act of 1980. See Henry R. Winkler, "Higher Education in an Urban Context," in *Preparation for Life? The Paradox of Education in the Late Twentieth Century,* ed. Joan N. Burstyn (Lewes and Philadelphia, 1986), pp. 58–76.

34. For the establishment argument, see Sir Charles Wetherell, *Substance of the Speech of Sir Charles Wetherell before the Lords of the Privy Council on the Subject of Incorporating the London University* (London, 1834).

35. Bellot, *University College London,* pp. 236–37.

36. New, *Life of Henry Brougham,* p. 383.

37. Heulin, *King's College London,* p. 15. The religious issue as a national issue is well illustrated by Dr. Thomas Arnold's indignation at the compromise of 1836. Although a liberal or Broad Church Anglican, he was far from being a secularist. "There is no difficulty," he wrote from Rugby School in 1837, "with Dissenters of any denomination," but "are we really for the sake of a few Jews, who may like to have a Degree in Arts,—or for the sake of one or two Mahomedans, who may possibly have the same wish, or for the sake of English unbelievers . . .—are we to destroy our only chance of our being even either useful or respected as an Institution of national education?" Arthur Penrhyn Stanley, *The Life and Correspondence of Thomas Arnold,* 9th ed. (London, 1868), II, 9, 82, 85.

38. Technically, the Act of 1836 made all degrees external, but a de facto dis-

tinction could be drawn between degrees awarded to students in attendance at London colleges or schools and those who were taught in the provinces and overseas. Careful statistics are difficult to acquire, but according to one calculation for the years 1889, 1890, and 1891, a total of 138 first degrees were awarded to students from London institutions, 240 to students from national institutions, and 552 to candidates from elsewhere. Therefore, approximately 15 percent took what may be called "internal" first degrees. Humberstone, *University Reform*, p. 67. In 1903, when a formal distinction between inside and outside degrees was made, there were 912 external candidates for all degrees as compared to 160 internal candidates. Royal Commission on University Education in London (1911), Appendix to Second Report, p. 240.

39. Humberstone, *University Reform*, p. 70.

40. Dr. Lushington in Parliamentary Papers, House of Commons Debates, 26 March 1835, cols. 285–86. A hint that King's College did not perform university-level work in the arts and divinity courses appears in the *King's College London Calendar* (1846), p. 12. For a detailed discussion of the federal principle, see Sheldon Rothblatt, "Historical and Comparative Remarks on the Federal Principle in Higher Education," *History of Education* 16 (1987): 151–80.

41. For the definition of an elite institution, see Martin Trow, "Problems in the Transition from Elite to Mass Higher Education," in *Policies for Higher Education,* General Report of the Organisation for Economic Co-operation and Development (Paris, 1974), pp. 55–101, esp. 80–81.

42. Negley Harte, *The University of London, 1836–1986* (London, 1986), p. 74, credits Thomas Spring Rice, chancellor of the Exchequer, with playing the leading part in creating the University of London of 1836 but provides no account of the genesis of his ideas or his precise role. Judging by a hilarious obituary notice in the *Times* for 9 February 1866, p. 10, the Irish-born chancellor had few contemporary admirers, but new work is uncovering his role in many important educational enterprises. See, for example, Ian D. C. Newbould, "The Whigs, the Church, and Education, 1839," *Journal of British Studies* 26 (July 1987): 333, 333 n.

43. Bellot, *University College London*, pp. 236–37, 246.

44. W. A. Allchin, *An Account of the Reconstruction of the University of London* (London, 1905), I, 7; Harte, *The University of London*, p. 86.

45. Harte, *The University of London*, p. 105.

46. Ibid., p. 106.

47. Arthur Percival Newton, *The Universities and the Educational Systems of the British Empire* (London, 1924), p. 18. Bellot, *University College London*, p. 48.

48. *King's College London Calendar* (1856–57), p. 41.

49. *Spectator* 18 (18 June 1898): 851. London's nineteenth-century domination over English provincial cities is illuminatingly discussed in Donald Read, *The English Provinces, 1769–1960: A Study in Influence* (London, 1964), pp. 232–61.

50. Harte, *The University of London*, p. 120.

51. Steen Eiler Rasmussen, *London: The Unique City* (London, 1948).

52. Paul Cohen-Portheim, *England, The Unknown Isle* (New York, 1931), pp. 87–88.

53. For the Victorian suburbs, see Williams, *The Country and the City*, p. 47; D. A. Reeder, "A Theatre of Suburbs: Some Patterns of Development in West London, 1801–1911," in *The Study of Urban History*, ed. H. J. Dyos (London, 1968); H. J. Dyos, *Victorian Suburb* (Leicester, 1973); Donald J. Olsen, *The*

Growth of Victorian London (London, 1976), and "Victorian London: Specialization, Segregation, and Privacy," in *Victorian Studies* 17 (March 1974): 265–78; Alan A. Jackson, *Semi-Detached London* (London, 1973); and Nicholas Taylor, *The Village in the City* (London, 1973).

54. Nicholas Taylor, "The Awful Sublimity of the Victorian City," in *The Victorian City: Images and Realities,* ed. H. J. Dyos and Michael Wolff (London and Boston, 1973), II. See also Sheldon Rothblatt, "Nineteenth-Century London," in *People and Communities in the Western World,* ed. Gene Brucker (Homewood, Ill., 1979), pp. 199–206.

55. Richard Shannon, *The Crisis of Imperialism, 1865–1915* (St. Albans, Herts., 1976), p. 270.

56. Williams, *The Country and the City,* pp. 47, 297. The suburban perspective imposed on the tradition of rustic painting is discussed in Ann Bermingham, *Landscape and Ideology: The English Rustic Tradition, 1740–1860* (Berkeley, Calif., 1986).

57. Kolbe, *Urban Influences,* p. 127, speaks of an impairment of the aesthetic sense as one of the drawbacks of urban-based education: "[Y]outh of the college age is particularly susceptible to beauty of surroundings. . . . The memories of a college life spent among beautiful surroundings form an intangible treasure which is not the least of the benefits of higher education."

58. The phrase is Erving Goffman's to describe "encompassing" or "closed" institutions such as asylums, hospitals, prisons, and boarding schools.

59. *The Works of Walter Bagehot,* ed. Forrest Morgan (Hartford, Conn., 1891), I, xxvii–viii.

60. *Milieu* is an excellent rendition of John Henry Newman's *place.* It is used by Jacques Dreze and Jean Debelle in *Conceptions de l'université* (Paris, 1968), p. 46. Newman uses *genius loci* in relation to both Oxford and Cambridge in *A Packet of Letters,* ed. Joyce Sugg (Oxford, 1983), pp. 12–13, and *The Idea of a University,* ed. I. T. Ker (Oxford, 1976), p. 130.

61. [Thomas Babington Macaulay], "Thoughts on the Advancement of Academical Education in England," *Edinburgh Review* 43 (1826): 316, 324.

62. Cobbett was by no means the first writer to use the word *wen* in relation to London. See Williams, *The Country and the City,* p. 146.

63. *Quarterly Review* (January 1887): 57–8.

64. *The Works of Walter Bagehot,* pp. xcii–iii.

65. *Spectator* 18 (12 February 1898): 231.

66. See Bruce Haley, *The Healthy Body and Victorian Culture* (Cambridge, Mass., 1978); and for fears about the health of undergraduates, see Sheldon Rothblatt, "Failure in Early Nineteenth-Century Oxford and Cambridge," *History of Education* (March 1982): 1–21. In his diary Shephard Taylor describes the violence and dangers of London during his days as a King's College medical student in the 1860s. He attended about three or four public hangings, repulsed the advances of prostitutes, and was several times the victim of pickpockets. He mentions a number of grisly murders, one of them the garroting of a fellow student.

67. For the public schools and empire, see J. A. Mangan, *The Games Ethic and Imperialism* (Harmondsworth, 1986).

68. Humberstone, *University Reform,* p. 168.

69. Cohen-Portheim, *England, The Unknown Isle,* p. 95. A similar thought has occurred to Daniel Bell. In *The Reforming of General Education* (New York, 1966), pp. 3–4, he writes: "In its traditions and public character, Columbia has

ambitiously sought to be the great university in the great city, though never wholly succeeding in that task. (What single institution can dominate this city?)"

70. Sir William Beveridge, *The Physical Relation of a University to a City* (16 November 1928), p. 16.

71. Harte, *The University of London,* pp. 219–21.

9

Preparing for Public Life:
The Collegiate Students at
New York University
1832-1881

Louise L. Stevenson

Commencement Song, No. 1

And we must be good citizens,
And spout in Congress Halls,
And we must be good citizens,
Fight wrong—give right to all.

Commencement Song, No. 2

But now New York I leave, sir,
To breast the waves of life;
I'm going to serve my country,
And sport a pretty wife.[1]

From 1832 to 1881 New York City grew and developed as it climbed to rank with the great European capitals—London, Paris, Vienna, and Rome. By midcentury the former walking city had become the home of more than half a million people, 60 percent of whom had been born somewhere else. With the completion of the Erie Canal and the beginning of regularly scheduled packet service to Europe, New York became the leading commercial and financial center in the nation, outpacing its previous rivals Philadelphia, Boston, and Baltimore. New York also became an intellectual and artistic center. Here were to be found the National Academy of Design and the studios of famous and about-to-be famous artists such as Samuel F. B. Morse and Eastman Johnson. Boston had to cede its title as literary capital of the United States as book and magazine publishers located themselves in the burgeoning city. New Yorkers could even claim that their city was becoming the religious capital of the country, for many Protestant voluntary and benevolent organizations had chosen the city for their headquarters.[2]

At New York University, then called the University of the City of New York, the collegiate department did not develop in an equally dynamic fashion. It neither grew in number of students nor basked in the glory of its professors' attainments. In fact, New Yorkers who considered themselves in the forefront of literary culture gave the college little respect. In his novel *Cecil Dreeme,* Theodore Winthrop described a classroom as containing "a swarm of collegians buzzing for such drops of the honey of learning as they could get from a lank plant of a professor."³ And a writer in *Putnam's Monthly* said:

> The University building, an idealized affair of white marble, buttressed and pinnacled like a student's dream of the Middle Ages, stands, lovely to the eye, on the eastern side of Washington Square, fine old trees waving before its windows and the tall fountain adding the last grace of the academic grove; but the halls, which would give convenient room to six hundred students, echo to the steps of less than one hundred, and the place, with all its delicate beauty, looks melancholy and deserted.⁴

Even the college's own distinguished professor John William Draper often complained that the college "was conducting . . . [its] business on an egregiously wrong principle" and that it offered an education for which there were no buyers. The usual class had about thirty students, and in the 1870s the number of graduates in one year fell as low as fifteen.⁵ Nevertheless, the historical significance of an institution is not always found in its size or in the ways that its key figures' achievements anticipate the future, such as professors' anticipating the rise of the research university. Some institutions, including New York University, have historical significance because they provide a more profound understanding of the culture to which they belonged. So it is for the collegiate department in New York University, for it fitted young men to enter and to influence the midcentury world of Victorian America. The social situation that midcentury young men encountered as college graduates and the education that had prepared them for it were far different from those of graduates of either 1800 or 1900. A college in 1800 prepared graduates to be citizens of the republic; a college in 1900 usually prepared them to enter a profession. Halfway between, the midcentury college prepared students for public life.

In this essay I define public life, show its place in Victorian culture, and then explain how the New York University collegiate department readied students to engage it. In the college's classical curriculum and extracurriculum of literary-society debates and independently pursued activities, students found an entryway into the newly forming middle class. As the century progressed students' commitment to public life declined as their concerns shifted from those of republicanism to those of liberalism.

In the late eighteenth century college graduates, whether of Yale, Princeton, or one of the newer colleges such as Franklin or Dickinson in south-central Pennsylvania, were exposed to a set of concerns that we recognize as republican. Whether young men received an education of mental discipline at Yale or studied a reformed curriculum that included the study of agricultural science, history, and modern languages, they imbibed through literary-society debates, addresses from professors, and sermons a belief that the future of the nation rested in their hands. They responded to these issues by drawing on a republican frame of reference. Classical times supplied seemingly apt lessons for the contemporary world by teaching that the common good was achieved through virtue and sublimation of personal ambition to the welfare of the community. Specifically, literary-society members pondered questions such as whether the accumulation of wealth threatened the future of the republic, whether literature and the arts presaged national decadence, and whether party spirit compromised the survival of the republic.[6] College graduates who desired to become professionals most likely completed their education in the offices of established professionals. Then the young doctor, lawyer, or minister entered the life of a local community probably under the aegis of one of its members. As a professional he enjoyed a certain standing within his community simply because of his profession, and he could speak and expect a hearing on public issues.

The professional became involved with the life of his times through a local learned or literary society. A society might be as famous as Philadelphia's American Philosophical Society or Boston's Anthology Society or a small, unknown, and relatively informal group that assembled to discuss questions of literary merit and civic betterment, such as the Club, which met in New York during the 1820s.[7] In these societies college-educated men formed a vital group providing intellectual leadership and a living connection to the organized collegiate world of ideas. These societies also provided a location where the son of a small farmer, now a college-educated professional, could share ideas with a gentleman of leisure or merchant who may not have been a college graduate.[8]

The graduate of 1900 also looked forward to entering a well-defined world, but now it was one of professional expectations and not of community life. While a student in 1800 had encountered significant questions of national concern through a general discourse of debates, addresses, and sermons, in the turn-of-the-century college he encountered controversial issues in specific academic classes taught by professionals trained as specialists.[9] How students approached questions of public interest changed as well. By the last third of the century republican concerns and references no longer supplied the content for their discourse. Students spoke for the liberal position that individual achievement promoted the common good. The forum for student discussions of public issues changed, too, as the popularity of literary societies declined. The few students who wished to debate were more likely to join a debating club which faced intercollegiate opponents. Other, more popular activities such as fraternities and sports teams occupied the time of most college men. As fraternity members and members of a team, students learned skills that they would need later in hierarchically organized bureaucracies. Students also could elect activities that gave informal preprofessional training; writing for the college newspaper, for example, often was a step toward a career in journalism.

In the post–Civil War years a young man chose a specific major as preparation for graduate school. This major might be in one of the older professions of law, medicine, or theology, or it could lead to a Ph.D. degree. Or it could train him in one of the many new fields opening to professional study such as business or architecture. A college degree helped in the search for a job. The newly instituted Civil Service exams tested *what* one knew and not *whom* one knew. To connect his knowledge with the problems of society, the turn-of-the-century professional had to rely on his professional organization, and he was correspondingly less involved with his local community and its own leaders. In fact, the history of social scientific organizations and academic departments between the years of 1880 and 1920 shows that an academic who wished to advance in his own institution or to develop a reputation in his chosen field had to make a choice. He had to devote himself to specialized research problems and eschew broad-gauge efforts for social reform.[10]

Young men of the midcentury years encountered neither the coherent community structure of 1800 nor the well-marked professional road to respect and reward of 1900. Noah Porter, who graduated from Yale in 1831 and who ended his career as president of Yale in 1886, started his working life as an academy teacher. He then prepared for the ministry, contemplated becoming an editor, and finally became a college professor and pursued advanced study in Germany. Such career mobility was typical of the midcentury world. Qualifications for specific positions were not yet fixed. Men viewed careers not as lifelong commitments but as means to self-improvement, to be followed only while they were the most promising among possible alternatives. In this undefined world specific credentials for a specific career did not exist, and if they had they would have been counterproductive.

Without the stamp of institutional approval that a degree represents, young men had to rely on themselves and thus sought to cultivate desirable personal attributes that Victorians referred to as character and manliness. They needed and founded institutions for self-improvement such as young men's associations, library societies, and lyceums. These institutions, especially the lyceums, not only fostered self-cultivation but gave a young man an opportunity publicly to make his mark. The young lawyer speaking before a lyceum could show off his learning and gain the confidence of prospective clients. He could also demonstrate his concern for the welfare of the community, win its trust, and qualify himself to be one of its leaders, as Abraham Lincoln did when he was widening his political horizons as a young politician on the make in Springfield, Illinois.[11] Public lectures and lyceums touched the lives of far more aspiring young men than did colleges. At midcentury a mere 1.18 percent of the American population were college graduates, whereas most northern towns "of 1000 or more people" had "at least one association sponsoring lectures," according to historian Donald Scott. In New York City during the 1850s and 1860s advertisements announced more than three thousand lectures. Even if the audience for each was tiny, say ten, the total number of people who attended these lectures was vastly larger than the number of graduates from the New York University collegiate department. In the twenty years after the admission of the first classes in

1832, only 455 men graduated.[12] Nevertheless, despite the disparity in the size of their audiences, both colleges and public lectures prepared young men for public life in Victorian America.

The idea for the New York University appears to have been hatched in the meetings of a small but influential literary society known as the Club, composed of three lawyers, three Columbia College professors, two ministers, two merchants, and a medical doctor. Interested in civic betterment and raising cultural standards, this group was inspired in 1829 by the reports of Dr. Benjamin McVickar, brother of Club member Professor John McVikar of Columbia College, about the recently founded University of London. Designed to serve students from the "middling ranks," namely upper-level artisans, small tradesmen, and modestly prosperous merchants, it was a nonresidential, nonsectarian institution composed of both a collegiate department and professional schools. Club members recruited support for their project from other learned institutions—the New-York Historical Society, the Lyceum of Natural History, and the Mercantile Library.[13] In the sense that the new university was meant to coordinate, direct, and energize existing learned societies, it was building on the past. But other decisions made by the founders opened the new university to the forces of the future.

By far the most important of these decisions, in terms of the history of American higher education, was enunciated by the Rev. Dr. Milner at the inauguration of J. M. Mathews, the first chancellor: the new institution was to be "not a sectarian, but a Christian University." Though by present-day standards this decision seems limiting in its exclusion of all non-Christians, in the 1830s, when New York City was primarily Protestant, the decision opened the university to a broad audience. In fact, since most prestigious American colleges of the period were sectarian, this step appears as a bold move to embrace the pluralism of American antebellum life and especially of American urban life. As New York University historian Paul H. Mattingly points out, the university was merely one agency "of a widespread moral fervor that encompassed the host of rehabilitating agencies from the frontier revival, the state public school system, the asylums for the blind and insane, prisons for the criminal, and the work of missionaries in foreign countries."[14] The university excluded only those, as Mathews said, "to whom everything is Sectarian, but infidelity and irreligion." But other decisions concerning the curriculum of the collegiate department limited its appeal to those aspiring for membership in the new middle class composed of professionals, proprietors, and their white-collar employees.

A prospectus for the new college that was to open in 1832 explained that its curriculum was designed with an eye to both the character of New York City, which was "the scene of so many arts, and such extensive commerce," and the wants of young men "who are designed for the more practical pursuits of life; and who would desire to become masters of those branches of knowledge most immediately connected with their respective professions or employments."[15] The curriculum included courses in Latin and Greek language and literature, natural science, moral philosophy and belles lettres, history, geography, and literature.

Though it is hazardous to make too close a comparison with the University of London given the peculiarities of the British and the American class structure, it seems safe to say that the New York University curriculum addressed the more socially and culturally ambitious members of the "middling ranks." In antebellum America college graduates drew on the literary and classical references of their college studies to impress their auditors and confirm their membership in middle-class culture. New York's sizable population of artisans and mechanics, however, wanted a different sort of education and patronized the New York Mechanics Institute, founded in 1822. Its students came from the families of low-status professionals such as chemists, master craftsmen, and small masters. At the institute they imbibed "the ethic of self-improvement and study" recommended by moderate labor reformers. Radical self-appointed spokesmen for Jacksonian working men found all educational programs irrelevant to the needs of working men. Critical of both the New York University collegiate department and the Mechanics Institute, Fanny Wright and Thomas Skidmore drew on an antievangelical deist tradition to deny the value of a religiously based classical education and saw education adapted to the needs of working men as a palliative for true reform.[16]

In establishing New York University its founders drew on their religious imagination. They came to terms with the religious pluralism of the American city by making the new college nonsectarian. They neither abandoned religious belief and practice, as disciples of Enlightenment deist tradition would have preferred, nor privatized religious belief and practice, as moderns would consider logical. The university's founders embraced the diversity of the city while giving the college an active role in the millennial progress described by believers. The founders also expected that a classical education would properly educate leaders for this Christian future. Chancellor Mathews believed that the question of the moment was whether New York would produce leaders such as "a Chalmers, an Edwards, or a Dwight in the persons of those who might have been Humes, Voltaires, or Paines." In short, would the university be "a fountain of health and safety to the public mind," helping to produce a civilization "combining all the delicacy and beauty of the Grecian age, with the strong and enduring worth of a better, because a Christian era."[17]

The urban university represented by New York University made its mark by broadening its appeal to a Protestant population bound on achieving respectability and status in mid-nineteenth-century America. Thus the university remained within one of the traditions of American education; collegiate education always had been for a small number of men who wished to enter a cosmopolitan world of knowledge and depart from their inherited culture. This was true for aspiring ministers who entered seventeenth-century Harvard, for farm boys who left their rural backgrounds to enter nineteenth-century Yale, and for students who entered the collegiate department in New York University. It reached out to that expanding population that we know as the middle class. From one point of view the founders of New York University were forward-looking when they chose this audience. Over the course of the century artisan shops slowly disappeared, to be replaced by manufactures with owners and workers who disagreed over the nature of the republic and the value of labor. The owners became members of the new middle class, and from their numbers came the clientele of the New York University. A nonsectarian college with a classical curriculum could embrace this new class but at the expense of isolating its discourse from that of other social groups. The intentional omission of the artisan interest from collegiate education reminds us that the new middle class was self-confident. Its members assumed that they should arbitrate the content and standards of educated discourse. But the omission was momentous for nineteenth-century culture, for it presaged that the most notable educational institutions would be of and for the new middle class.[18]

Students came to the collegiate department from New York City as well as from the small towns and cities of Long Island, New Jersey, and the Hudson River Valley. Of the 134 students in ten classes sampled from 1836 to 1881 whose places of original residence are known, 45 or 34 percent came from New York City.[19] Though the evidence is slight, it is possible that students from the city may have enjoyed a slightly higher income level than students from small cities, towns, and rural backgrounds.[20] In 1833 Chancellor Mathews reported that the college had "at once become the resort of young men whose names have long been identified with the history of our State and of our country."[21] Students, however, imagined themselves not as belonging to the New York social or economic elites but as being "men of moderate means" from the city or "surrounding cities and towns." They looked down both on City College, with its free tuition, as "a kind of upper high school, intended for boys who could not afford a *real* education," and on Columbia, with its exorbitant tuition (one hundred fifty dollars in 1881), as an institution "attended only by aristocrats with fancy canes and kid gloves." The collegiate department at the university thus appeared to offer "a liberal education at a small expense."[22] Though the eighty-dollar tuition in the collegiate department was always less than Columbia's and that of some prestigious colleges (one hundred four dollars at Harvard in 1865), it still exceeded the tuition at other prestigious colleges (thirty-nine dollars at Yale in 1860) and exceeded the means of large numbers of students. The university awarded scholarships to every "meritorious and suitably qualified young man" regardless of his professional ambitions.[23] In 1846, of the one hundred forty-five students in the college sixty-four received scholarships; in 1860 forty-five out of one hundred ten.[24] Most of these young men intended to enter the ministries of various Protestant denominations, and the chancellor often described them in admiring words, such as "an influential body of pious young men" with "mature minds" whom the college was favored in having.[25]

The backgrounds and careers of the students who entered the ministry suggest how an urban college such as New York University's collegiate department functioned as a conduit in midcentury America to move men from small-town or rural life into professional life. About three-fifths of the forty-seven students from the ten sampled classes who became ministers came to the collegiate department from outside New York City, some from places such as Plattekill, Finchville, and Homer, New York, and Bristol and Rush, Pennsylvania. The future ministers were more likely than other students in the collegiate department to have matriculated in college when they were older than twenty-one. The profile of these students seems to match other historians' descriptions of antebellum ministerial students, who usually had modest backgrounds. For many young rural men moved by the religious currents of the day and faced with the prospect of earning a marginal living on the farm, a liberal education and entrance into the ministry must have appeared as an opportunity for a decently compensated and useful life. And in the fluid occupational world of midcentury the ministry often was a stepping stone to opportunities in other fields such as secondary or collegiate education, reform work, or publishing. The ministry also promoted geographic mobility. The records of the Zeta Psi fraternity of the collegiate department show that its members who became ministers moved as far west as Indiana; as far south as Louisiana; to larger cities such as Philadelphia, Savannah, and Albany; and to small cities or towns such as Meadville, Pennsylvania, or Glen Cove, New York, or South Orange, New Jersey.[26] Despite Draper's claim that the collegiate department was not serving the needs of students aspiring to mobility in midcentury America, quite the opposite seems true.

As the religious enthusiasms of the 1830s declined and the linkage between a college education and other professions became stronger, the collegiate department prepared fewer students for the ministry and more students for other professions. Of the ten sample years, 1836 represents a high: seven out of thirteen, or 54 percent, of the graduates whose professions are known prepared for the ministry. The low point occurred in 1856 with one out of ten. This decline also took place in New England colleges of all sizes. In the 1830s 43 percent of the graduates of the newer, smaller New England colleges entered the ministry; in the 1850s 28 percent did. At Yale the comparable figures are 36 percent and 23 percent, and at Harvard 18 versus 9 percent.[27]

In the ten sampled classes approximately the same number of graduates whose professions are known (159) entered the law as entered the ministry (27.7 percent versus 29.6 percent). Business, including, trade, manufacturing, and finance, was the third most popular career choice, attracting 13.8 percent of the graduates. This figure may be understated, however, because each year two or three students left the college to start business careers. An equal number of students also left the collegiate department each year to transfer to other colleges, to start professional studies, or to recover their health.[28] Medicine was the fourth most popular career choice, attracting 12.5 percent of the graduates. Education, including higher education, was fifth, claiming 6 percent. The percentage of graduates entering the law and business is about the same as the percentage of graduates from small Middle Atlantic colleges who pursued law and business careers. Still a higher percentage of graduates of smaller New England institutions pursued business careers. Perhaps, as Colin Burke suggests, students from New England colleges and larger colleges had greater "access to finance, banking, and the emerging railroad and manufacturing enterprises" because of their "family backgrounds and urban connections."[29] Possibly because of the existence of the university medical department, the percentage of graduates becoming doctors approached the 15 percent rate of large Middle Atlantic institutions. Thus, the collegiate department graduate appears to have had career options similar to those of the graduates of other institutions. Because most of these institutions offered a classical curriculum, it can be concluded that by itself the curriculum in the collegiate department offered neither special advantage nor disadvantage as preparation for the ministry, law, business, or medicine. Curriculum thus may not have determined a young man's choice of college. The decision to attend college was the decision to acquire a classical education. Family ties, religious affiliation, and the location of the college probably determined which college a young man attended.

Over the course of the period from 1832 to 1881 from the first sampled class to the last, there is no apparent pattern showing whether business, law, or education was increasing or decreasing in popularity as a career choice. After midcentury, however, college graduates increasingly entered new professions, such as civil engineering, and older professions, such as publishing, that previously had not had a strong association with collegiate education. These developments and the decreasing number of students entering the ministry show that the students were responding to the increasing diversity of white-collar work becoming available to college graduates.

At New York University collegiate students encountered an education that had two parts: faculty-organized college life and student-organized college life. The first included the formal curriculum, chapel attendance, and college-supervised oratory; the second comprised both the faculty-approved literary societies and those activities, such as fraternities and reading, that students pursued independently, without explicit faculty sanction but not necessarily with their disapproval.

Unlike students at other colleges, students in the collegiate department spent relatively little time each day attending required obligations. In their free time students apparently chose activities that did not violate the spirit of university regulations and that, in fact, often promoted its educational mission. Besides joining friends for a game of whist or chess, students enjoyed walking, sometimes to the reservoir at Forty-second Street, and sleighing after a fresh snow. They took advantage of the city's cultural attractions, attending the New York Gallery of Fine Arts and even buying season tickets to the National Gallery of Design. Apparently students did not draw a sharp line between what we call high and popular culture, for they also attended a concert by the black singing group Christy's Minstrels, which had a long run at Mechanics Hall in the spring of 1847. But student John Parsons, class of

1848, whose family was well connected in the city and who later joined the law firm of Abram S. Hewitt and helped to develop Cooper Union, "was little pleased" after a visit to P. T. Barnum's American Museum. One wonders which of Barnum's attractions offended him: the fortuneteller Madame Rockwell, the diorama of the removal of Napoleon's remains from St. Helena, the monster snakes, or the anatomical Venus, for which there was an additional shilling charge. Parsons also attended Sunday church regularly; in fact, he usually attended twice on Sunday.[30] Probably many other students did, too, not only future ministerial candidates but also pious students such as Parsons who later followed secular careers.

The only two organized activities that students pursued independently were the literary societies and fraternities. The first were sanctioned by the university; the second were not. Most students belonged to the societies, either the Eucleian or the Philomathean, or one of three fraternities, which each had from three to eight members. Fraternities comprised no more than half of the students until the 1850s, when the percentage began to increase, reaching more than 70 percent in some years of the 1870s and 1880s.[31] The faculty showed their approval of the societies by attending society meetings and anniversaries, when invited, and assigning the societies space for their meetings in rooms and libraries within the college building. Fraternities, at least until the 1870s, had no permanent meeting places, and a former fraternity member referred to them as nomadic.[32]

In spite of the faculty's approbation of the literary societies, both they and the fraternities engaged in hijinks. A society often raided and vandalized the rival society's meeting hall, and fraternity members might kidnap a prospective member or a member of a rival organization, steal his clothes, and release him on the streets of New York in blackface. At least in the years till 1881, fraternities and literary societies drew their members from the same kinds of students. Many students belonged to both; the God-fearing church attender Parsons spent one evening of each week at the Philomathean Society and another at the Sigma Phi fraternity. Members of both types of organizations held similar attitudes toward the collegiate department, its faculty, and its curriculum.[33]

Independent reading was an important adjunct to many students' education. Memoirs, diaries, and newspapers show how deeply engaged students were with different aspects of the nineteenth-century literary world. The titles reviewed in a student paper, the *University Quarterly,* suggest the career interest of some students in law, their general interest in Greek history and civilization, and some students' intent to remain abreast of scholarly religious commentary on the intellectual controversies of the age. Recommended were new editions of Blackstone's *Commentaries* and the *Aeneid* as well as recent numbers of the *Princeton Review.* A serious reader, Lyman Abbott, tells how he was determined to understand the "New England faith of [his] ancestors" and of his interest in the study of English history. After reading Macaulay's *History of England,* he continued to read Smollett, Hallam, Clarendon, and Hume, and he searched for religious conviction in the works of Bishop Pearson and Jonathan Edwards. A less serious reader, John Parsons, read novels almost exclusively, most by English authors such as Scott, Dickens, and Bulwer-Lytton, but occasionally by a contemporary popular American author such as Ellen Pickering, who wrote *The Quiet Husband* in 1845. His taste for romance apparently was insatiable as he started the Waverly series a week after vowing "to give up novels." An infrequent reader of nonfiction, Parsons chose Melville's *Typee* and *Omoo* after a sailing trip around Montauk and to the Connecticut shore of Long Island Sound. The trip had interested him in seafaring adventures; presumably Melville's critical account of Protestant missionaries had not attracted him to these travel books.[34]

To obtain books, a student depended rarely on the college library and more often on the library of his literary society. He also could join the Mercantile Library for five dollars a year, a fee within the reach of an aspiring ministerial candidate. For his novels Parsons patronized a number of the bookstores on Broadway. He did not confess to buying, or in fact did not buy, the more sensational cheap literature of the day that was available for less than half a dollar in soft cover. In the city, students had plenty of opportunity to practice the self-control that their mothers had taught them and that befitted future members of Victorian America.[35]

Because it was not a residential school, the New York University collegiate department had little control over its students' living arrangements and social life. The university had few rules, and even their enforcement was impractical. Students were required to live with their own families if they were New Yorkers or "with respectable private families" if they were not. The college threatened dismissal if students frequented "billiard-rooms, taverns, or other places of corrupting influence."[36] Despite its bark, the college did not bite. Lyman Abbott, class of 1853, remembers that he often ate in restaurants and "English chop houses, which were called taverns." He recalls that students "could eat and drink and amuse ourselves as we pleased, so long as we behaved ourselves with propriety in the three or four hours under the college roof."[37] Given the seething street life of New York City, one wonders if students really did behave. If they patronized saloons or, even worse, the houses of prostitution that the New York Female Moral Reform Society warned against, there is no official record or any record in known diaries and letters of students. Either students kept private the dark side of their lives or they lived up to the standards of morality, seriousness, and high purpose expected of proper Victorians.

Outside the classroom, students came under no disciplined surveillance; there was no attempt made to ascertain whether their living accommodations met university regulations or whether they avoided "places of corrupting influence." For the collegiate department itself, nevertheless, the lack of discipline outside the classroom may have been one of the reasons that there were no serious student-inspired disturbances during the antebellum years. Outside college hours students lived in New York City, not in a disciplined collegiate cloister, and they were free to investigate the city as they wished.[38]

The short college day started with required chapel at nine or nine-thirty;

then the students attended three classes that lasted till noon or one. The literary societies consumed Friday evening and perhaps Saturday morning for those who had been fined by the society censor for inappropriate behavior or unexcused absences. Required attendance at chapel and at daily recitations and the threat to inform parents of absences may have indirectly encouraged students to remain faithful to their academic obligations.

The required activities of the college day were linked. Although attendance was rarely universal and worship was often perfunctory, chapel gave explicit expression to the liberal Protestant belief that infused formal studies. Formal study supplied a theoretical understanding of religious beliefs and demonstrated that knowledge and piety were compatible. Finally, oratory gave students practical experience in applying their classroom theories and expounding on secular subjects that implicitly confirmed divine truth.

Little is known about the chapel service conducted by the chancellor or one of the professors. Absence from chapel was the main disciplinary problem that the chancellor noted in his annual report to the council. Lyman Abbott complained about the "so-called devotional exercise, which with most of us was not, I fear, very devotional."[39] Although all students did not share his opinion, their silence on the service suggests indifference.

In contrast, the students remembered their classroom experiences favorably. Abbott describes the "great teachers" whose classes he enjoyed. Never, he recalls, were students asked merely to recite; they were questioned on their understanding. For Abbott "one of the greatest teachers" was C. S. Henry, a professor of mental, moral, and political philosophy, who demanded that students be able to take a position, explain it clearly, and give a thorough reply to dissenters. "In short," Abbott found, "his object was not to give us information but to equip us with power." Henry's successor, Benjamin N. Martin, had the same ability: "not only did he teach facts but he taught men how to think." This intent—to teach students how to reason—seems to have been shared by professors in all fields. In the introduction to his text on natural philosophy, collegiate department professor Elias Loomis said that "the primary object in education should be to cultivate philosophical habits of mind; to teach the art of reasoning and of deducing correct conclusions from premises." When professors in the late 1870s began to change their teaching methods to a lecture format, editorials appeared in the student paper protesting "merely mechanical work."[40]

The curriculum of the collegiate department was what historians call a classical curriculum or a curriculum of mental discipline. Debate on its merits was heated. On one side there were contemporary critics such as Thomas Jefferson's former secretary of the treasury Albert Gallatin, first president of the governing council of the university, and John W. Draper. Drawing on an Enlightenment tradition that stressed the importance of scientific knowledge, they condemned the classical curriculum, and especially its component of classical languages, for establishing distinctions between an aristocracy of knowledge and people of common knowledge. They saw a classical education as perpetuating a state in which higher education did not serve the people, in this case the mechanics of the antebellum era, by meeting their needs and giving them systematic and scientific expression. "What nobler spectacle," Draper wrote, "could be offered than this chapel, crowded with those brave men who constitute our fire and military forces, listening to literary and scientific discourses, in their holiday dresses after the toils of the day." Instead classical education offered a useless and arcane body of knowledge. It addressed the interests of a small minority destined at best for the learned professions and at worst preparing themselves to engage in esoteric discourse.[41]

On the other side advocates of the classical curriculum offered variations on the justifications found in the well-known Yale Report. Advocates also drew on Enlightenment thought, but on the more conservative tradition of Scottish philosophy, which linked piety and learning. They were less concerned with the specific application of knowledge than with how education could shape a responsible and socially useful citizen. Yale-educated professor Benjamin N. Martin said that the course of study in the collegiate department "prepares men competent to select their course of life, and gives them the opportunity of prosecuting it with energy and wisdom." Recently historians have tried to discover why students believed, as many collegiate department students did, that "severe and steady mental discipline is the only sure source of success." Uncovering the career patterns of college graduates, historians are finding that the classical curriculum actually helped them cope with the vocational demands of a fluid society.[42]

Gallatin's and Draper's criticism of the classical curriculum appears democratic at first sight. But Draper's is not when it is seen as part of his entire social vision. Society, he thought, resembled an organism with differentiated parts, some superior and some subordinate. It was logical that a small number of people would conduct intellectual functions and guide the majority who performed "duties of a wholly material nature." They were ruled by the "hereditary instinct" of the mass: "Governed by external influences and by its own appetites, it can neither combine nor generalize." When these facts were understood by all, then the intellect of the nation could be properly organized, and there would be "no ignorant man" and therefore "no idle man and no poor man in the land."[43] Draper's vision was of a meritocracy of education. The common people might be educated up to a point, and their education might respect their inherited culture, but they would have little role in shaping the policy of the country according to their needs and desires. As an educational spokesman Draper seems to speak less for the educational aspirations of working men of the antebellum period and more as a harbinger of the reforms of the late nineteenth century that guaranteed to educated men a role in government as employees under civil service and appointed experts on regulatory agencies. Thus, Draper opposed intellectual leveling and believed that only properly educated men were qualified to be intellectual leaders of their society.

Advocates of classical education also wanted an educated elite to lead society. College would foster in its members certain characteristics of self and enable them to conduct a specialized discourse that excluded the uneducated.

As Victorians the culture advocates believed that prescription was necessary and not intrinsically bad. How someone learned to participate in the discourse of educated Victorians depended on his social origins. Outsiders who did not come from families caught up in the practice and spread of Victorianism had to educate themselves intentionally through reading or public institutions—schools, libraries, lyceums, and mechanics' institutes. Children of insiders naturally learned from their families how to enter this discourse. Schools then added to the education begun in the family. For a small fraction colleges brought this education to completion.[44]

All that remains of Victorian discourse is its written record. We are apt to think of Victorianism primarily as a written culture and forget that our written records had their origin in oral form—Emerson's addresses and Fuller's conversations, for example. As historian Daniel Walker Howe points out, antebellum Americans highly valued the spoken word, often considering it more persuasive and forceful than its later written version. They "had an appetite for eloquence," Howe thinks, "comparable only to the eagerness of the early Protestant Reformers to hear sermons." For our purposes Victorian discourse had two parts: method and content.[45]

Within the collegiate department, students learned the methods of Victorian discourse from the faculty and from participation in literary-society debates. Beyond their formal classes in rhetoric and composition, students until 1894–95 were required to make a presentation before the entire college once a term after chapel; upperclassmen presented original orations, and underclassmen read compositions. These presentations show the essential nature of an education for public life. Students were expected not merely to master a specific field of knowledge but to draw from all their college studies and be able to persuade other men. This requirement was not limited to men preparing for certain careers; it was required of all students, for all were expected to live a public life in Victorian America. As one student remarked, learning to orate prepared men "for public usefulness." In their literary societies, another student observed, they "perform[ed] in miniature the actions of the world." In rhetoric and composition classes and in literary-society debates students "exhibit[ed] the practical bearing of the knowledge" that they learned as theory in college classes.[46]

Students learned debate techniques and oratorical strategies particular to the mid-nineteenth century. These methods and strategies were familiar to politicians of the era, especially Whigs, and were practiced by literary-society members and citizens of towns and villages in their lyceums. Whereas modern debating strategy emphasizes the accumulation of fact and evidence, mid-nineteenth-century debate resembled a meandering discussion "in which opinion rather than evidence ruled." Instead of relying exclusively on facts, collegiate department debaters sought to persuade by combining ideas and feeling. As Martin, who taught rhetoric, said, "Rhetoric is the expression of emotion or of thought penetrated with emotion." To reach the imagination of an audience, he advised students to "use words for their force which add nothing to the meaning and suggest more than they express." This advice shows that the goal of antebellum oratory was more than to persuade men of what was right and appropriate in a given time or situation—in other words, what was true for the here and now. Instead, oratory had "for its object the discovery and statement of truth." To antebellum Protestants the word *truth* had transcendent meaning; it implied something with universal application through time and space and connections to the divine. God's natural creations could reveal truth. For instance, the viewers of a rock first placed it within geological history and then thought of its place in God's infinite universe.[47] Victorians also believed that God had created social institutions—the family, private property, and republican government, to name a crucial few— and they also were appreciated as being timeless, good, and true.

Students who learned to reveal truth gained mastery in a discourse that was not shared by all. New York City working men, for instance, defined truth differently. Beginning in the 1830s a broad audience that included laborers, artisans, mechanics, and clerks discovered this definition in the new penny press, which made newspaper reading part of the everyday life. Its writers helped readers see another version of truth: "Truth for its motto, Justice for its end, Revere the *Press, it is the Poor Man's Friend.*" Similar to middle-class Victorians, penny-press authors defined truth so that it was transcendent in meaning, universal in implication, and supportive of a democratic capitalist state. However, their definition also was specific because they thought of their state as one for working men and thus based on the tradition of equal rights. To expose abuses of power and infringements of working men's natural rights, penny-press writers drew on the rhetoric of equal rights that Tom Paine and artisan activists had used during the Revolution.[48]

The students' discourse also drew on a tradition of rhetoric. But in this case it was the classical tradition, which provided apt phrases and historical parallels to illuminate contemporary subjects. Student George H. Houghton began his chapel oration on 29 January 1842 by saying, "Let us turn to the nations of earth and see if we can find one, that having injured or wronged God's fleshly image or sinned against his higher self, that has not drunk of the cup of national retribution." Students shared with their time a historical imagination set within a framework of absolute morality. To explain their present they always consulted the past. They often drew cautionary lessons from the Greek and Roman past and also referred to European history, the Protestant Reformation, and the British and New England past. To find assurance that "all good is social and diffusive, especially that which relates to the public welfare of men and nations," they studied autocrats such as Napoleon, whose careers fascinated and whose selfish ambition decreed their downfall. The students' optimism that good would prevail and that it was represented by the United States formed part of the consensus that led some to the ethnocentric arrogance of missionary activities and territorial expansion, and others to sympathy with the plight of the American Indians, southern slaves, and Irish peasants.[49]

Oratory gave students not only knowledge of persuasion but also a sense of their future social and political role. They thought oratory linked their learning to public life. Eloquence and the role of educated men made democracy work. In the United States freedom of thought had led to a broadly diffused intelligence: "Where knowledge with the People deigns to dwell, / And shuns the Eremite's ascetic cell / To scatter far a broad intelligence; / Here is Thy home, triumphant *Eloquence!*" In European countries one might find superior poetry, music, and art, but these were the province of a "favored few." American democrats excelled in oratory: "We may not bring the public heart / With us to feel—with us to do; but Oratory throws her thrall— / Or breathes her influence—*Over all.*" In short, the students wanted "a cultured class" who would lead "the herd without their knowing . . . distinguished only by their being more perfect specimens of the people, and thence more popular."[50] These optimistic attitudes toward the role of educated men resembled Draper's views in several ways. First, there was the assumption that intelligence rather than wealth or numbers should have public influence. Second, Draper and the advocates of classical culture showed minimal appreciation for the opinions of the people. But Draper expected educated men to exercise their influence within specified areas of competence and through their profession, whereas the culture advocates looked to a more diffuse influence exercised through participation in public life.

As future participants in public life, students demonstrated their engagement with the times through their literary-society debates, orations, and newspapers. They addressed contemporary occurrences in New York City as well as foreign and national issues. Their choice of topics to debate and the debate decisions themselves indicate that their expectations about life beyond college were shifting. Students framed questions that identify them as carriers of a republican tradition, but their solutions show a liberal perspective. They moved toward embracing individual achievement and the wealth it produced and came to terms with the ethnic and religious pluralism so evident in New York City.

Throughout the period under discussion the student imagination was literary rather than scientific. Fewer than six literary-society debates concerned topics that can in any way be considered scientific. Charles Darwin's theory of evolution received notice only in 1883, long after it had become quite acceptable among many theists who argued that the universe of God included an evolving natural world. Many of the questions about literature that concerned students may be identified with traditional republican issues and date at least to the Revolutionary years. For example, they wondered if an aristocracy or a democracy was more favorable to literature and if the theater was beneficial to society. Some of their concerns about literature were new. Between the 1830s and the mid-1860s, students grappled with the relationship of the first amendment guarantee of freedom of the press to the vastly popular and often sensational journalism of the penny press. They debated whether "unrestrained freedom of the Public Press at the Present Day was conducive to the best interests of the country" and whether the liberty enjoyed by the penny press threatened freedom. They entertained the possibility of limiting the freedom of the press, but, except for one debate decision in 1860, possibly influenced by the rising tensions of sectional debate, they always decided that the press should remain unrestrained.[51] The penny press, as we have seen, supported opinions different from the students' opinions. Their concern shows that they were attending to a new phenomenon of antebellum society that challenged their potential authority as educated men in public life. Still, their commitment was explicitly to the Constitution and implicitly to a pluralistic society. Their commitment, nevertheless, did not rest on an "I'm okay, you're okay" sort of relativism. Rather, it rested on their confidence that in public life educated men could have influence. Through the power of oratory, society would come to have but one interest that might respect, though certainly not mirror, the demands of the penny press. The students' commitment to this sort of intermediate pluralism separates them most decisively from republicans of the past with their suspicions of party spirit and factionalism.

The students' acceptance of a pluralistic society is also apparent in their attitude toward immigration. Concern about the impact on the republic of a sizable non-English population is as old as Benjamin Franklin and Benjamin Rush's worries about the number of Germans in eighteenth-century Pennsylvania. While the students had reservations about unrestricted immigration, they rejected the extreme nativistic responses represented by the American Republican party of the 1840s and the Know Nothing party. In nine debates from 1836 to 1861 they decided against immigration only twice but decided five times that immigration should be encouraged or that no further legal restraints should be put in the way of immigrants' becoming citizens. The students' attitude toward the Irish is complex, nevertheless. Their support for immigration did not also imply acceptance of Catholicism. They saw this religion as a barrier to the practice of democratic politics. On many occasions from the 1830s to the Civil War, the relationship of Catholicism to liberty was the subject of debate. The students decided that in the present-day United States popery was incompatible with civil liberty and free institutions and that, in fact, it had been so even during the Middle Ages.[52]

In the students' attitude toward wealth lies another indication of a shift from republicanism. Men of the post-Revolutionary generation regarded wealth with some suspicion, for it could signal decadence and republican decline. These midcentury students still found the subject of wealth worth debating, but their responses show that they had lost their predecessors' uneasiness over the meaning of its accumulation. In debate students affirmed that it was best for society that wealth be unevenly distributed and that the accumulation of large amounts of wealth would not injure the commonwealth. The students opposed an active government when it limited the accumulation of wealth but supported an active government that created an area in which wealth could be accumulated. They opposed the income tax but supported the protective tariff. The way their debate questions were framed exposed their prejudices: Did the protective tariff lead to the rapid growth of wealth, and was free trade "a delusion and a snare?" Though the evidence is thin, the students seem to have favored a society in which a man could get ahead and identified his ability to prosper with the welfare of all. As one student writer said, "Hail the day when to all there shall be an equal chance; a fair field for the best men, let them start where they may, to get to the front."[53]

Even though student attitudes show a shift from the self-denial called for by republican virtue to the self-assertion called for by liberal individualism, they still placed limitations on that individualism. Students did not believe that the wealthy should rule society. They considered themselves, as professional men, more useful to society than mechanics, while mechanics were more important to prosperity than merchants. They were concerned for the poor and supported the public's responsibility to aid them. They responded to the changing nature of the antebellum work place and debated three times whether labor-saving machines benefited the working class, deciding in the affirmative twice. By the 1880s they had come to support labor unions, or at least consider them not injurious to laborers. In sum the collegiate-department students appear to have been socially responsible liberals. They recognized that "leisure, wealth, knowledge, influence, are means of doing good, not means of self-indulgence," and that the benefits they enjoyed were "divine trusts to be invested by us in charity for those among whom we are placed."[54]

Even as the students were learning to enter public life, social and intellectual changes were eroding the underpinnings of public life and its discourse. In the post–Civil War years positivism influenced social scientists, putting searchers for transcendent truth on the defensive. Comments by social scientist William Graham Sumner most concisely mark this change. He criticized the search for a transcendent truth as the enterprise of ministers, amateurs, and mystics; a credible enterprise was the search for "*reality* beyond everything else." Social scientists like himself wanted to examine "facts and build up inductions which shall have positive value." William James put the role of the scientist another way. He labeled psychologists who searched for a transcendent truth as metaphysicians; scientists collected facts and "ascertained the empirical correlation of the various sorts of thought or feeling with definite conditions of the brain." The same shift from a romantic definition occurred in other fields. For example, in history there is the shift from the purpose and method of George Bancroft to those of historians such as Herbert Baxter Adams. In more popular realms the shift can be noted in the changing style and goals of journalism. The founding of the *New York Times* in 1851 signaled the rise of an intentionally temperate journalistic style and showed the gradual ebbing of the passions that had fired the pro-workingmen writers of the penny press. The *Times*'s founder claimed that the paper's authors would not write "as if we were in a passion." As represented in New York by the *Times* and the *Herald,* the new journalism was based on the new ideal of objectivity that assumed, in historian Dan Schiller's words, "a world prior to all imposed values." Reporting the unalloyed facts allowed newspapermen to step beyond both sectarian and partisan differences that previously had divided the public; facts could lead "all men of all parties to rely upon [a paper's] statements." Within the student life of colleges the popularity of a pure-and-simple facticity was also felt. Antebellum literary-society debates had been judged by the standards of rhetoric and its search for truth. In the last quarter of the century debate topics were taken from the fields of sociology, politics, government, and economics, and judges looked for arguments based on facts that revealed complexity.[55]

At New York University transcendent truth as a goal of discourse disappeared slowly. In 1863 John W. Draper's son Henry used *true* in only its mundane sense in his physiology class; he referred to the destiny of food in the digestive system. Change, however, was slower to occur in history, literature, and the moral sciences. Professor of political science E. H. Gillett (1870–75) continued to believe that study of the facts of the past revealed God's plan. In his lectures on rhetoric Martin opposed the facticity of the new journalism: "A simple and barren assertion seldom has anything interesting in it." Some literary-society members resisted the change in debating and argued that the purpose of debate should still be to reveal truth and not merely to pile up facts to win an argument.[56]

With the tremendous burst of wealth that occurred during and after the Civil War and the arrival of non-English-speaking immigrants in the 1870s, students became more pessimistic about whether educated men could be effective in public life. They worried about materialism among prosperous groups and the political effects of immigration. For the first time, students doubted their power to counter the influence of materialism over public life in New York. To some the solution was a retreat to private life. "I am aware," one student wrote, "that civilization derives its name from the life of cities; but it is not in the noise and glitter of their public life, but in the profound retirement of their private life, that we must look for the elixir of civilization, settled of its dregs." They criticized the palaces on Fifth Avenue and the tenements on the Lower East Side. In the former lived men dominated by the almighty dollar, and in the latter lived men who were swayed by demagogic appeals. In literary-society debates, students in the postbellum years were three times as likely as those in the antebellum years to support immigration restriction. In a newspaper article a student condemned "the representative of the scum of European civilization, firm in his belief that where vice is useful it is a crime to be virtuous. . . . [U]nwilling to compete with honest men doing honest work for honest wages, . . . [he] soon occupies the seat of city alderman, yells 'Reform,' demands protection for the laboring classes and restriction of immigration for countries other than the land of his birth."[57]

As they lost confidence in public life, students began to modify their commitment to oratory. Now their affirmations of the value of oratory carried a bombastic tone that revealed their confidence as a pose: "the Pen and the Rostra have become the mightiest forces of our modern civilization, and he who would rise to a position of great influence must thoroughly understand their public working." The literary societies recruited few members; an editorial in the student paper attempted to arouse enthusiasm for the previously popular societies. As the percentage of students preparing for ministerial careers decreased, student discourse lost the piety of previous years and became moderately irreverent. Barnum's shows were ridiculed as "especially adapted to the young, to ministers and rigid Presbyterians." Whereas from 1841 to 1860 the literary societies had debated and affirmed eight times that "the pulpit does afford a greater field for eloquence than the bar," the subject came up merely twice in the next twenty-two years and was decided in the negative.[58]

As the commitment to public life declined, students found that they were dissatisfied with the collegiate department as it had been. Sometimes students of the 1870s and early 1880s expressed discontent with the classical curriculum. More frequently they called for the development of a college life at the university; fraternities and literary societies were no longer sufficient. In the mid-1870s intercollegiate activities began. The first intercollegiate debate is mentioned in a student paper in 1875. The students began to found clubs in sports and called for the building of a gymnasium. The more they participated with students at other colleges in intercollegiate events, the more they retreated from engagement with the city. Students began to call for the relocation of the college to the country, where they perceived greater possibilities for the development of a collegiate life. It fell to a graduate of earlier years, John E. Parsons, to defend the urban location of the college. In the city, he said, students had to confront a variety of "real and positive and pressing" experiences that prepared them for "practical life" and "practical contests." The removal of the college would also harm the city. "If New York is to take the lead only in that which is material," Parsons said, "it will stop short of true greatness."[59]

As students withdrew from commitment to public life, they lost their sense of how to influence society. Their comments on political issues contain no vision of how educated men could engage society. They merely rejected the radicalisms of the postbellum period, dismissing socialism as "a delusion in theory and a failure in practice." Or they affirmed the value of education. On the one hand the masses needed education to strengthen "public sentiment behind the law." On the other hand the wealthy needed to realize their responsibility to the community, for it was "the tendency of the present day to magnify the privileges and to neglect the rights of society." To problems of the 1870s and 1880s, students offered a minimal response when they affirmed the value of the political process. If illiterate immigrants had the ballot, they would come under the influence of "the American teacher. Voting makes every man consciously a part of the government, and gives him an interest in public affairs. . . . Unrestricted suffrage unites all classes, wins the love of every order-loving element of society, and makes us one nation, free from danger of treason within and consolidated against attack from without. It is the pledge and realization of our rights."[60]

Despite the change in student concerns, from the 1830s to 1880 the collegiate department was resistant to change. In this same period at Yale College, Harvard, the University of Michigan, and Cornell, educators were altering the rationale if not the content of the curriculum, introducing educational ideals imported from Germany, reforming the teaching of literature, abandoning the classical curriculum, and introducing electives. College was changing from preparation for public life to preparation for a career. Despite the fact that the New York University Council in 1858 attempted to broaden the appeal of the university by introducing a program for students who did not wish to earn a liberal arts diploma, the council never debated or reconsidered the curriculum of the collegiate department. To say the least, the collegiate department had a static quality about it that is remarkable given its New York City location and the midcentury time period, when change of every sort was erupting.

In sum, student sources from the collegiate department show that in the 1870s and 1880s faith in oratory and the power of public life declined. So did revelation of transcendent truth as a goal of discourse, the vitality and relevance of the classical tradition, and republicanism as a way of thinking about public issues. On the rise was the students' commitment to collegiate life, including sports, clubs, and fraternities. The students of the late nineteenth century became engaged with a youth culture of their own making and disengaged from the social and intellectual worlds that depended on the city for their vitality. In 1894 the removal of the collegiate department from Washington Square to University Heights symbolized the social and cultural shift already partially accomplished. The college itself was no longer a preparation for city life. Rather, a student gained entrance to particular areas of service needed within the city through the university's professional and graduate schools. At the University Heights campus the architecture of McKim, Mead, and White rather than the city itself was meant to inspire civic responsibility.[61]

The retreat from public life also implied that the meaning of professionalism had changed. For the students of the midcentury years, being a professional had been compatible with the attempt to exert influence through public life. Since the opening of the collegiate department in 1832 about 70 percent of its graduates had pursued graduate work to qualify for the ministry, the bar, or a medical career. In the last third of the century a culture of professionalism appeared that was at odds with commitment to public life. Now professionalism was a constricting force focused on "a set of learned values which structured the attitudes and responses of practitioners" and their clients. Literary-society records, student newspapers, and memoirs give the researcher no hint that this new culture was forming. Students continued to take on a whole range of urban problems. They never suggested that a professional should limit his audience and respond to only those problems which he had been trained to address. From the unfocused concerns of amateurs such as the collegiate-department students, professional social scientists such as Albion Small and Franklin H. Giddings found a haven in the supposedly scientific and professional practice of academic sociology.[62]

In contrast, the transition from republican to liberal thought that occurs during the midcentury years may be traced in sources of student thought and opinion. Professors rarely addressed questions of pluralism, wealth, immigration, and labor. So it can be assumed that students embraced liberal thought with its emphasis on equal opportunity, individual achievement, and public responsibility because of the influence of their reading, home life, previous education, contact with one another, and extracurricular influences in the city. Whereas formal college life apparently had no direct influence on the formation of this new way of thinking, it may have been supportive. In this case the much maligned classical curriculum appears to have nurtured change, of which even Gallatin might approve. In the development of their students' ideas, collegiate department professors probably had an indirect influence; their formal lessons lent implicit support to student positions. Evidence comes from the fact that students explicitly rejected professors' teachings when they contradicted a necessary tenet of liberal belief. For example, one student reviewer found that Draper's theory that climate determined human character made "man completely passive in his moral nature" and seemed to deny human ability.[63]

The larger significance of the New York University collegiate department arises from the insights it gives us into the cultural history of the American middle class. We need to remember that the nineteenth century was the century of migration from the countryside to the city—in Europe, from Europe to America, and within the United States as well. The majority of collegiate department students came to this urban college from rural or small-town backgrounds. From collegiate department courses, college life, and the city itself, the students learned ways of thinking and behaving that prepared them for public life, namely membership in and perhaps leadership of a national urban middle class. By definition this middle class was exclusive; the founders of New York University, for instance, never intended the collegiate department to respond to the educational needs of artisans and mechanics. Thus, the college was a doorway through which a small number of men passed to enter into the urban bourgeosie. If we recognize the middle class as a dynamic and progressive force in the nineteenth century, we must concede that for those who undertook it this move must have been momentous.

It would be wrong to think, however, that the collegiate department students can speak for the entire middle class. Nineteenth-century college students, of whom the collegiate department students are a sample, constitute a subset of the larger whole. Recruits entered the middle class from other directions. For instance, historian Sean Wilentz describes how the organization of manufacturing in New York City changed during the antebellum years. As artisan shops became owner-managed factories, some shop masters became proprietors and owners, or new members of the middle class. These middle-class shop owners and middle-class New York University students participated in a particular way of thinking that differentiated them from working men. Both groups believed in "The supposed harmony of interests between employer and employed, the reciprocity and essential fairness of the wage, the promise of social mobility and an independent competence for all industrious men, a model of private charity and benevolence, a nearly religious devotion to the market as an economic arbiter."[64] The students, however, would have been befuddled by the concept of an inclusive middle class. They saw themselves as distinctive—the group in society preparing themselves for leadership as they learned to participate in public life.

NOTES

I am indebted to Thomas J. Frusciano, university archivist, and Angela Chin for their assistance in guiding me to the sources for this article. John Andrew, Aileen Kraditor, and David Schuyler made helpful comments, and I thank them warmly. The expenses for research and preparation of this essay were defrayed by the Franklin and Marshall College Committee on Grants.

1. Eucleian Society, *The University Glee Book* (New York, 1860), pp, 7, 8–9.
2. Edward K. Spann, *The New Metropolis: New York City, 1840–1857* (New York, 1981), chap. 1, and pp. 23, 273; Neil Harris, *The Artist in American Society: The Formative Years, 1790–1860* (New York, 1966), chap. 10.
3. Theodore Winthrop, *Cecil Dreeme* (orig. published 1861; New York, 1876), p. 37.
4. "Educational Institutions in New-York," *Putnam's Monthly* 2, no. 7 (July 1853): 7–8.
5. John W. Draper to C. Noyes, 25 April 1850, Chancellor's Records, 1827–1888, New York University Archives. Unless otherwise noted, all manuscripts are from the New York University Archives.
6. Kenneth Silverman, *A Cultural History of the American Revolution* (New York, 1976); Linda K. Kerber, *Federalists in Dissent: Imagery and Ideology in Jeffersonian America* (Ithaca, N.Y., 1970); Joseph J. Ellis, *After the Revolution: Profiles of Early American Culture* (New York, 1979), chaps. 1, 2; Douglas Sloan, *The Scottish Enlightenment and the American College Ideal* (New York, 1971), pp. 194–213; Thomas S. Harding, *College Literary Societies: Their Contributions to Higher Education in the United States, 1815–1876* (New York, 1971); James McLachlan, "The *Choice of Hercules:* American Student Societies in the Early 19th Century," in *The University in Society,* ed. Lawrence Stone (Princeton, N.J., 1974), II, 449–95.
7. Lewis P. Simpson, ed., *The Federalist Literary Mind* (Baton Rouge, La., 1969), pp. 10–11; James T. Callow, *Kindred Spirits: Knickerbocker Writers and American Artists, 1807–1855* (Chapel Hill, N.C., 1967), chap. 1; John Brett Langstaff, *The Enterprising Life: John McVickar, 1787–1868* (New York, 1961), pp. 55–60.
8. James McLachlan, "The American College in the Nineteenth Century: Toward a Reappraisal," *Teachers College Record* 80 (1978): 292–95.
9. Burton J. Bledstein, *The Culture of Professionalism: The Middle Class and the Development of Higher Education in America* (New York, 1976), p. 327.
10. Mary O. Furner, *Advocacy and Objectivity: A Crisis in the Professionalization of American Social Science, 1865–1905* (Lexington, Ky., 1975); Rosalind Rosenberg, *Beyond Separate Spheres: The Intellectual Roots of Modern Feminism* (New Haven, Conn., 1982).
11. Abraham Lincoln, "Address before the Young Men's Lyceum of Spring-

field, Illinois," in Roy P. Basler, ed., *The Collected Works of Abraham Lincoln* (New Brunswick, N.J., 1953), I, 108–15.

12. In my discussion of midcentury careers I rely specifically on Donald M. Scott, "The Popular Lecture and the Creation of a Public in Mid-Nineteenth-Century America," *Journal of American History* 66 (1980): 795, 797, 794; and more generally on Colin Burke, *American Collegiate Populations: A Test of the Traditional View* (New York, 1982); and Joseph F. Kett, *Rites of Passage: Adolescence in America, 1790 to the Present* (New York, 1977), chaps. 1, 4. The statistics on college graduates come from Burke, p. 54, and the quote on the number of lyceums and lectures is from Scott, p. 791. For the number of graduates from NYU, see J. W. Draper, *The Indebtedness of the City of New-York to Its University* (New York, 1853), pp. 9–10.

13. Thomas Bender, *New York Intellect: A History of Intellectual Life in New York City, from 1750 to the Beginnings of Our Own Time* (New York, 1987), pp. 93–96, and chap. 3 generally. I thank Thomas Bender for generously sharing that chapter with me when it was in manuscript form. Bayrd Still, "A University for Its Times—The Formative Years: 1830–1870," unpublished paper, pp. 2–4; Langstaff, *The Enterprising Life*, pp. 55–65. The information on the University of London is derived from Sheldon Rothblatt's paper "London: A Metropolitan University?" which is included in this volume; also Rothblatt to Stevenson, 8 December 1986.

14. Paul H. Mattingly, "Why NYU Chose Gallaudet," *New York University Education Quarterly*, 13, no. 1 (Fall 1981): 9.

15. "Prospectus," *Commercial Advertiser*, 13 September 1832, transcript prepared by William R. Martin, William R. Martin Historical Collection, 1829–51.

16. Sean Wilentz, *Chants Democratic: New York City and the Rise of the American Working Class, 1788–1850* (New York, 1984), pp. 273 n., 272, 177–79, 187–88. Bender argues that it was not the original intent of the university's founders to exclude the educational interests of mechanics; *New York Intellect*, pp. 102–3; "To the Honourable the Legislature of the State of New York in Senate and Assembly Convened," 28 January 1831, Chancellor's Records.

17. James Mathews, "Baccalaureate Address at the Commencement of the New York University, July 17, 1834," Chancellor's Records; J. M. Mathews, *Recollections of Persons and Events Chiefly in the City of New York: Being Selections from His Journals* (New York, 1865), pp. 215, 217.

18. On the involvement of artisans with NYU in its formative years, see Bender, *New York Intellect*, pp. 95–96.

19. The classes were 1836, 1844, 1846, 1854, 1856, 1864, 1866, 1874, 1876, and 1881. Information about the graduates is taken from the *Biographical Catalogue of the Chancellors, Professors and Graduates of the Department of Arts and Science of the University of the City of New York* (New York, 1894). The statistics reported here are suggestive; they are not meant to be definitive. Researchers should consult the "Matriculation Books of the University of the City of New York," Vols. 1, 2, Student Records, 1832–1916. Volumes 1 and 2 cover 1832–43 and 1853–93, respectively, and include the names of students, their parents, and their residence plus other information such as a student's age, course of study, scholarships, and more.

20. Burke, *American Collegiate Populations*, pp. 135, 185–86.

21. Annual Report of Chancellor Mathews, 23 October 1833, Chancellor's Records, quoted in Still, "A University for Its Times," p. 14.

22. *University Quarterly* 4, no. 3 (May 1881): 111; Lyman Abbott, "Reminiscences: An American College in 1850," *Outlook* (28 March 1914): 688. Carl Kaestle collected a sample of twenty-five New Yorkers who graduated from the collegiate department from 1850 to 1855. He could ascertain the occupations of thirteen of the parents in the *New York Directory*, and they included "three physicians, three ministers, a merchant, a broker, an architect, a building materials dealer, a clerk, a grocer, and the secretary of a charitable organization. Carl F. Kaestle, *The Evolution of an Urban School System, New York City, 1750–1850* (Cambridge, Mass., 1973), p. 109. The tuition figures for Harvard and Yale are from McLachlan, "The American College in the Nineteenth Century," p. 296.

23. Report to Regents from the Council, Chancellor's Records, 1855–56, and 1855 and 1856.

24. See the Chancellor's Reports in the Chancellor's Records for appropriate years.

25. Chancellor's Reports, 19 October 1864, 26 October 1857, and Council Report to Regents, 1856–57, all in Chancellor's Records.

26. Burke, *American Collegiate Populations*, pp. 153–54, 191–92; David F. Allmendinger, Jr., *Paupers and Scholars: The Transformation of Student Life in Nineteenth-Century New England* (New York, 1975), chap. 1; Kett, *Rites of Passage*, pp. 32–33, 70; *Catalogue of the Zeta Psi Fraternity, 1847–1867* (New York, 1867).

27. Burke, *American Collegiate Populations*, pp. 140, 141.

28. For examples, see Council Reports to Regents, 1854–55, 1855–56, Chancellor's Records.

29. Burke, *American Collegiate Populations*, pp. 185–86.

30. "A Student at New York University in 1847: Excerpts from the Diary of John E. Parsons," *New-York Historical Society Quarterly* 38, no. 3 (July 1954): esp. 7, 23.

31. Howard Bement and Douglas Bement, *The Story of Zeta Psi: An Informal Chronicle of Eighty-four Years* (New York, 1932), pp. 219–23. The chancellor reported to the council that the literary societies "that embrace in their membership most of the students, are exacting a salutary influence upon the general discipline and improvements." Their meetings "incite to good scholarship and good conduct, and are thus important aids to the faculty," Chancellor's Report to the Council of the University, 25 October 1843.

32. Bement and Bement, *The Story of Zeta Psi*, pp. 220, 221.

33. Admittedly the evidence is skimpy. See the discussion that follows and the following fraternity newspaper: *The College Tablet*, 15 January 1850, 1 February 1850–15 March 1850. It also should be said that in the 1870s, with the development of intercollegiate activities and sports clubs, participation in the literary societies declined while fraternities prospered in the collegiate department as at most college and universities. For the earlier period, however, the collegiate department may have been an exception to the general rule claimed by other historians of higher education. They see fraternities and literary societies as antagonistic during all historical periods, not merely the last third of the nineteenth century. Frederic Rudolph hints at the antagonism, and Helen Lefkowitz Horowitz describes it in detail. See Rudolph's *Curriculum: A History of the American Undergraduate Course of Study since 1636* (San Francisco, 1981), p. 95; and Horowitz's *Campus Life: Undergraduate Cultures from the End of the Eighteenth Century to the Present* (New York, 1987), chaps. 2, 3. I am grateful to Professor Horowitz for send-

ing me a copy of her about-to-be-published manuscript; it was invaluable in providing a broad context for this essay.

34. For example, see the reviews in *University Quarterly* 1, no. 1 (February 1878): 38–40; 7, no. 1 (November 1883): 49; 3, no. 1 (October 1879): 36. Abbott, "Reminiscences," p. 690; "A Student at New York University in 1847," esp. p. 21.

35. Abbott, "Reminiscences," p. 679; "A Student at New York University in 1847."

36. See, for example, *Catalogue of the Officers, Alumni, and Students of the University of the City of New-York, 1839–40* (New York, 1840), pp. 17–18.

37. Abbott, "Reminiscences," p. 690.

38. Jean H. Baker, *Affairs of Party: The Political Culture of Northern Democrats in the Mid-Nineteenth Century* (Ithaca, N.Y., 1983), p. 99.

39. Abbott, "Reminiscences," pp. 678–79.

40. Ibid., pp. 686, 687, 688; *University Quarterly* 7, no. 3 (February 1884): 85; Elias Loomis, *Elements of Natural Philosophy Designed for Academies and High Schools* (orig. published 1858; New York, 1869), p. iii; *University Quarterly* 2, no. 2 (January 1879): 65–67; *University Quarterly* 1, no. 3 (July 1878): 116–17. The NYU students' favorable estimate of their college education was not unusual; see Wilson Smith, "Apologia pro Alma Mater: The College as Community in Antebellum America," in Eric McKitrick and Stanley Elkins, eds., *The Hofstadter Aegis: A Memorial* (New York, 1974), 140–41.

41. See Bender, *New York Intellect*, pp. 99–102; Draper, *The Indebtedness of the City*, pp. 28, 20–25.

42. Benjamin N. Martin, "American Education, or An Estimate of the System of College Education in the United States," address to the Alumni Association, 27 June 1854, New York University Archives; Robert Dodge, "Valedictory Address," 27 March 1840, Eucleian Society Records, Box 1; David B. Potts, "American Colleges in the Nineteenth Century: From Localism to Denominationalism," *History of Education Quarterly* 11 (1971): 368.

43. John W. Draper, *Thoughts on the Future Civil Policy of America*, 4th ed. (New York, 1865), pp. 260, 251, 269; idem, *Valedictory Lecture* (New York, 1842), p. 4.

44. For a useful definition of *discourse,* see David A. Hollinger, "Historians and the Discourse of Intellectuals," in John Higham and Paul K. Conkin, eds., *New Directions in American Intellectual History* (Baltimore, 1979), pp. 42–43.

45. Daniel Walker Howe, *The Political Culture of the American Whigs* (Chicago, 1979), pp. 25–27.

46. Mr. McLaughlin, "Valedictory Address," 31 May 1833; and M. V. B. Fowler, "Address," 28 June 1833, both in Adelphic Society Records in Eucleian Society Records, Box 1.

47. *Catalogue of the University of the City of New York, 1883–84, May 1884* (New York, 1884), p. 31; Egbert Ray Nichols, "A Historical Sketch of Intercollegiate Debating I," *Quarterly Journal of Speech* 22 (1936): 215; "Professor Martin's Lectures on Rhetoric," in Charles Henry Ludlum, "Student Notebooks of Charles Henry Ludlum," 1860–63, pp. 24, 25. For the definition of *truth,* see Theodore Dwight Bozeman, *Protestants in an Age of Science: The Baconian Ideal and Antebellum Religious Thought* (Chapel Hill, N.C., 1977), pp. 55–60.

48. Dan Schiller, *Objectivity and the News: The Public and the Rise of Commercial Journalism* (Philadelphia, 1981), pp. 39, 48, 54. The quotation is on

p. 36, and is from the *National Trades, Union,* 1 January 1836, as quoted in Philip S. Foner, *American Labor Songs of the Nineteenth Century* (Urbana, Ill., 1975), p. 17.

49. Howe, *The Political Culture,* p. 26; George H. Houghton, "Orations and Poetry," 1839–50, ms.; John Breckinridge, *An Address Delivered July 15, 1835, before the Eucleian and Philomathean Societies of the University of the City of New-York* (New York, 1836), pp. 9, 20; "William Salter—Philomathean," *Annals of Iowa,* 3rd series, 18 (1932): 295–312. Even a cursory reading of the *Biographical Catalogue* shows that many graduates acted on their convictions by joining voluntary societies and charitable organizations.

50. Howe, *The Political Culture,* p. 27; Delafield Smith, *Oratory: A Poem Delivered before the Literary Societies of the New-York University, June 28, 1852* (New York, 1852), pp. 11–12, 42; *University Quarterly* 2, no. 1 (October 1878): 12.

51. Eucleian Society Records, 28 April 1843, 26 February 1858, 10 June 1842, 26 April 1844, 28 January 1848, 25 September 1868; Philomathean Society Records, 19 February 1836, 28 May 1852, 11 October 1860, 9 October 1863.

52. On immigration and its restriction, see Philomathean Society Records, 5 February 1836; Eucleian Society Records, 13 December 1844, 21 November 1845, 10 December 1847, 8 June 1849, 17 May 1850, 8 November 1850, 4 November 1853, 23 October 1857, 19 March 1858. On Catholicism and its relationship to liberty, see Philomathean Society Records, 8 May 1835, and Eucleian Society Records, 28 May 1841, 20 February 1846, 25 May 1849.

53. Eucleian Society Records, 29 May 1857, 7 February 1873, 30 October 1868, 12 January 1884, 17 March 1882; *University Quarterly* 3, no. 4 (July 1880): 129.

54. Eucleian Society Records, 14 January 1842, 25 October 1844, 20 November 1863, 6 February 1852; Philomathean Society Records, 28 February 1861; Eucleian Society Records, 3 November 1882, 19 October 1883. See Wilentz, *Chants Democratic,* p. 285, for antebellum masters' negative opinion of unions.

55. William James, *The Principles of Psychology* (New York, 1890), I, vi, 1; II, 677; William Graham Sumner, *"The Challenge of Facts" and Other Essays,* ed. Albert Galloway Keller (New Haven, Conn., 1914), pp. 401, 425; idem, *Essays of William Graham Sumner,* ed. Albert Galloway Keller (New Haven, Conn., 1934), I, 44, 46. On the change of the definition of truth and its relation to science, see Louise L. Stevenson, *Scholarly Means to Evangelical Ends: The New Haven Scholars and the Transformation of Higher Learning in America, 1830–1890* (Baltimore, 1986), chap. 5. *New York Times,* 18 September 1851, quoted in Schiller, *Objectivity and the News,* p. 72; Schiller, *Objectivity and the News,* p. 87; *New York Times,* 22 March 1860, quoted in Schiller, *Objectivity and the News,* p. 87; Nichols, "Historical Sketch of Intercollegiate Debating," p. 217.

56. Henry Draper, "Lectures on Comparative Physiology," 1863, in Ludlum, "Student Notebooks," p. 33; E. H. Gillett, *Ancient Cities and Empires: Their Prophetic Doom, Read in the Light of History and Modern Research* (Philadelphia, 1867), p. 302; "Professor Martin's Lectures on Rhetoric," pp. 29, 30; "Debating," *Philomathean* 2, no. 4 (February 1875): 10. Admittedly, Draper made these remarks to his medical department students, but I can see no reason why he would not have made similar remarks to collegiate department students.

57. *University Quarterly* 2, no. 1 (October 1878): 14; Eucleian Society Rec-

ords, 5 February 1836–14 November 1883; Philomathean Society Records, 2 May 1861; *University Quarterly* 3, no. 3 (April 1980): 80.

58. *University Quarterly* 2, no. 1 (October 1878): 14; 3, no. 2 (January 1880): 55; *Philomathean* 1 (June 1874): 68; Eucleian Society Records, 29 October 1841–5 May 1882; Philomathean Society Records, 14 November 1856, 19 October 1857.

59. Support for the curriculum is still expressed in *University Quarterly* 1, no. 1 (February 1878) 20–22, but a slight grumbling can be sensed in the editorial in 3, no. 3 (April 1880): 97; Bayrd Still, "Student Life at New York University A Hundred Years Ago: The Student Scene in the Late 1870s and 1880s," unpublished paper, pp. 9–11; *University Quarterly* 6, no. 4 (July 1883): 148, 151.

60. *University Quarterly* 7, no. 4 (August 1884): 169, 173, 175; 4, no. 4 (July 1881): 137.

61. See the discussions in Bledstein, *Culture of Professionalism*, 178–202; Thomas Bender, "The Erosion of Public Culture: Cities, Discourses, and Professional Disciplines," in Thomas L. Haskell, ed., *The Authority of Experts: Studies in History and Theory* (Bloomington, Ind., 1984), pp. 98–101.

62. Bledstein, *The Culture of Professionalism*, p. 192; Bender, "The Erosion of Public Culture," pp. 99–100.

63. *Philomathean* 1, no. 4 (February 1874): 17. Draper's *History of the Conflict between Religion and Science* also received a poor notice: "the title presupposes the existence of a contest that never existed." *Philomathean* 2, no. 3 (January 1875). Another student rejected the teachings of an unnamed economist who said "that it is the duty of everyone to look out for himself" rather than to do good to others. *University Quarterly* 1, no. 1 (February 1878): 23.

64. Wilentz, *Chants Democratic*, p. 285.

IV

THE MODERN UNIVERSITY
AND THE MODERN CITY

10

"To Live for Science": Ideals and Realities at the University of Berlin

Charles E. McClelland

Der Wissenschaft leben—"to live for science" or, perhaps more accurately, for scholarship—represented the ideal of Wilhelm von Humboldt, not only for himself as a wealthy, aristocratic, and learned Prussian civil servant but for his major institutional creation, the University of Berlin. Not only he but also some of the brightest lights of the German intellectual and especially neohumanist firmament, such as Fichte and Schleiermacher, were deeply involved in planning and running the young university from its founding in 1810. Many of its first professors were already illustrious scholars borrowed from the Prussian Academy of Sciences. In the course of the nineteenth century this graft of searching intellect—what would come to be called research in a more institutionalized form—onto the pruned and rejuvenated trunk of the essentially teaching-oriented university tradition produced a new model for universities everywhere. And although Berlin was not the first university to try this experiment, it became so preeminent among German universities and had such good public relations agents that it usually got credit for being the pioneer of the "research university" model.

The new university would, in Humboldt's mind, provide a seat where young men could devote themselves to a new noble spirit of learning in leisure, with the search for new humane knowledge producing not merely "research results" but also the personal saturation in *Geist* that was essential for true *Bildung* or intellectual cultivation. Neohumanism would be spread through the land by a new breed of teachers, pastors, physicians, and civil servants. In the mind of Fichte a university open to talent and saturated with philosophy would lead to the regeneration of the German spirit and, ultimately, German life as well.

These were high ideals, rarely if ever achieved by traditional universities in the past. Universities, after all, have usually been professional training schools as well as seats of philosophical contemplation. Nevertheless, although the University of Berlin continued to mill out trained professionals in the four traditional faculties (or schools) of theology, law, medicine, and philosophy (or arts and sciences), just as its predecessors and competitors did, these professionals were held to be somehow better, more mature, and perhaps more saturated with German intellectual rigor. The quality of the Berlin professoriate contributed much to this reflected glory. Indeed, a higher percentage of students than elsewhere came to Berlin as the last stage in their peregrinations from one university to another, still common in the nineteenth century; it could therefore be considered the finishing school of the nation, a sort of super graduate school, the academic Parnassus of Germany.

These were indeed ideals, couched in the kind of high-minded and often hyperbolic language still to be found in many standard university histories and ritually dusted off at commencement time. The realities were somewhat different, though not completely at variance with the ideals. It might be less harsh to say that living up to Humboldt's or Fichte's ideals would have been impractical if not impossible but that the realities were rarely so compelling as to break all contact with their ideals. Then as now, universities had to respond to a variety of forces, including the governments that supported them, the institutions that hired their graduates, and the students themselves. The University of Berlin was no exception. But as such other German-speaking professors as Jakob Burckhardt (treated in Carl Schorske's essay in this volume) would later claim, it fell far short of its original pure neohumanist aims or transformed them to serve the interests of the Prussian "power state."

Berlin's history, like that of most German universities, can be approached in terms of institutional development, and that history has been explored, albeit as yet not thoroughly enough. The university also played an important role in the history of German and European knowledge, disciplines, and professions, a subject not yet adequately explored. Here, however, we must restrict ourselves to Berlin University in its urban context during its first century. Surprisingly, that relationship has hardly been explored at all, and this research gap, which I can only begin to fill in a sketchy way here, says much about the nature of the interaction between city and university in Berlin.

The official title of the university may serve as a symbol of the institution's role in the city. It was named the Friedrich-Wilhelms-Universität zu Berlin from its opening until 1949, when it had already suffered the secession of teachers and students to the Free University in West Berlin and renamed itself Humboldt-Universität. (Although Marx studied at Berlin and received his doctorate from Jena, his name was ironically reserved to rebaptize Leipzig, the oldest medieval university on the soil of the German Democratic Republic, four years later.) From the beginning Berlin's university not only took its name from one of Prussia's kings, but it served the Hohenzollern dynasty in a particularly close symbiosis and was even quartered in a royal palace. It was not an association of scholars with a guildlike organization, as in the case of the medieval foundations discussed in this volume, nor was it initiated by ecclesiastical bodies, as was often the case with foundations of the Reformation and Counterreformation in Germany. Nor was it, like the only other wholly new major German universities founded between 1800 and the Weimar period, Hamburg and Frankfurt (discussed by Martin Jay), a creation of city initiative. Founded by the Prussian state and located in the government quarter of a *Residenz* city, its character from the beginning was not merely urban (*städtisch*) but, for want of a better translation, capital-urban (*hauptstädtisch*).

The capital of 1810 was still largely also a creation of the Prussian crown, an administrative and garrison city whose preindustrial economic activity had been nursed along and controlled in state interests by royal mercantilism over the preceding century. About seventy years later it was a sprawling capitalist-industrial metropolis and the capital of a united Germany as well. The place of the university in this rapidly changing city might be called a story from Hegel to Bebel. The philosophical exalter of the supremacy of the Prussian *Machtstaat* arrived in 1818, symbolizing a shift away from the contemplative humanism of some of the founders. The appearance in the Reichstag in 1867 of the socialist leader committed to the overthrow of the conservative, militarist Prussian order symbolized the rise of the working masses. In that interval a second Berlin, essentially alien to the university, had taken recognizable shape. By the centenary of the university, near the end of Bebel's life, Berlin had a heavily "red" population, and the socialists were about to become the largest party in the Reichstag, much to the horror of the university. Let us begin by sketching the evolution of this remarkable city, then the growth of the university, and finally the interaction of city and university in the nineteenth century.

The city of Berlin traces its roots back into the Middle Ages. At this writing its leaders, East and West, are grappling with the problem of how to celebrate seven hundred fifty years of history in the contemporary world's only metropolis characterized by a guarded, living wall through it instead of nostalgic remnants of historic city walls around it.

In 1810, however, Berlin was in many respects a new city, visibly shaped through the presence of the Hohenzollern monarchy and its military and administrative apparatus. The city had little administrative autonomy even after the Stein-Hardenberg reforms of the Napoleonic period. Throughout most of the nineteenth century the city proper huddled inside its walls, a square mile encompassing the islands in the Spree River that had first hosted medieval fishing villages plus the immediate business, government, and residential quarters developed as late as the end of the eighteenth century. This area is roughly coterminous with today's Berlin Mitte, the central area of East Berlin, stretching from west to east only from the Brandenburg Gate, down Unter den Linden, across the huge Marx-Engels Square (formerly William II's royal palace), and on through the commercial district around Alexanderplatz to the beginning of the monumental residential street in Stalin-era socialist Gothic now known again as Frankfurter Strasse. Expanded to the north and west in the 1860s, when the city walls were also taken down, the municipal boundaries still only encompassed bits of what is now West Berlin.

Each part of the city and the settlements around it had a rather separate character, reflecting a high degree of socioeconomic segregation. Civic rights and duties reinforced this geographical division in a rough way. The actual "citizens"—those who had a vote in municipal elections—formed a tiny fraction of the inhabitants, most of whom were *Schutzverwandte* in the first half of the century, literally "protected relations." Even when these masses of "inhabitants" had been given a discounted vote and other citizenship rights in 1850 under the notorious Prussian three-class electoral law that weighted votes according to taxes paid by the voter, they were still effectively excluded from municipal influence. Only in Reichstag elections after 1867 did all males have a full vote. Berliners paid taxes, of course, chiefly on rent and commodities. But the municipal government was principally chosen by property owners, dominated by a rapidly changing plutocracy. These citizens were notoriously niggardly and small-minded in urban matters; even when they did have an urban vision and generosity, they often ran afoul of royal urban administrators who also had tenacious, if conflicting, agendas. A third and sizable group of residents was exempt from many taxes and municipal obligations and perhaps for this reason took a relatively minor role in urban matters. These were the military and civilian servants of the king, including the university professors and many university graduates, such as pastors and high school teachers. Such privileges underlined the special nearness of the university to the throne, as well as its special detachment from the broader life of the city.

Despite its compactness Berlin was already the second largest city in the Holy Roman Empire by 1800, with one hundred eighty-four thousand people, surpassed in population only by Vienna. By midcentury Berlin had almost caught up to Vienna with more than four hundred thousand souls. By 1871, when it became capital of the German Reich, Berlin's population had doubled again, making it considerably more populous than Vienna and the largest city in Germany, but still considerably smaller than London, Paris, or New York, the last of which served as an often-invoked and usually decried standard of feverish urban growth. By World War I Berlin had reached two million, and the annexation of its surrounding communities in 1920 raised Greater Berlin to a city of four million. By 1930 Berlin was the third largest city in the world.[1]

Like New York, Berlin grew chiefly through in-migration, but it drew heavily on its hinterland in Northeast Germany, producing less ethnic and cultural diversity than New York or Vienna. It was only during its period of hectic urban and industrial growth that Berlin produced a strongly identifiable urban style, with the characteristic toughness, wit, and even accent that marks Berliners (like New Yorkers) to this day. Nevertheless, since the arrival of Jews and French Huguenots at the invitation of the Hohenzollerns, themselves Calvinist rulers in a Lutheran land, ruling over a sizable Catholic population too after 1815, Berlin had attracted outsiders for its relatively tolerant religious atmosphere and its opportunities for work. Berlin in 1800 was already a considerable economic center, producing chiefly textiles and clothing. It experienced an explosive industrial growth after midcentury. But its working population remained geographically isolated, often outside the walls, living in the infamous *Mietskasernen* or "rental barracks" that rivaled the slums of London or New York for sheer human misery. A chronic housing shortage plagued the city throughout the nineteenth century. As other essays in this volume indicate, real estate and academia have never been as far apart as idealism supposes. But for Berlin as a city, unfettered building booms and land speculation did not solve the shortage problem; they only tended to further a continuing geographical dispersal of the population along familiar if increasingly complex lines of social stratification.

New York at least had an advanced transport network to aid its workers. Berlin lay far behind other world cities in this respect, partly because its active burghers and the royal bureaucracy could virtually walk to work or afford private transport. Constant disputes between cautious and cost-conscious municipal government and tenacious royal officials long delayed proper paving and lighting of streets, and open sewers were a noxious feature of city life through the first half of the century, causing, along with overcrowding, severe health hazards. Ironically, Hegel himself was a victim of the cholera epidemics that plagued the city. As late as the Bismarck era, it took the personal intervention of the Iron Chancellor himself to start the building of the Kurfürstendamm, today the very symbol of West Berlin, and even then he sighed that the effort had been more difficult than many of his complex international negotiations.

It is thus no wonder that Berlin struck many observers in the nineteenth century as provincial and narrow for a city of its size. Even after it had become the German capital in 1871, Berlin did not become "a central point which, like London or Paris, could attract all the best talents of the nation to itself."[2] The cosmopolitan Danish-born Prussian historian and statesman Carsten Georg Niebuhr, one of the most brilliant lights in the academy and university at its opening, called the city "a lifeless place in the worst area of the world" in 1810.[3] The city had little in the way of impressive architecture to awe the visitor, except the Potemkin-village façade of royal creations along Unter den Linden. Even that could be depressing, as Wilhelm Grimm, newly called to the city, wrote in 1841: "Since the whole street lies before one as soon as one turns into it, one immediately has a feeling in advance of the fatigue that will follow."[4] If Grimm missed the charm of his fairy tales in Berlin, a later observer, the novelist Theodor Fontane, sighed that the city was mainly useful as a place to make one's career.[5] Many other famous men and women who lived in Berlin could be cited, including Burckhardt and Dilthey, but few judged the city with unalloyed praise.

Provincialism can, of course, have its advantages, such as a closely knit intellectual community. Berlin did enjoy over the nineteenth century some of the advantages of compactness, along with a certain feeling of cultural inferiority to even smaller cities. It had in the first three or four decades a lively salon culture, succeeded for a couple of decades by a coffee-house culture, supplanted in turn by closed or floating intellectual groups that met in beer and wine cellars. Civic organizations also existed, but they were severely hampered by royal police authorities, suspicious of private clubs as breeding grounds of sedition, until the "liberal era" of the 1860s. Literary and aesthetic clubs, even charitable organizations, were tolerated or in some cases encouraged (particularly under Frederick William IV), but discussions that might spill over into politics were viewed with suspicion and frequently forbidden.

In the much freer political atmosphere from the 1860s onward, when the city government based on its narrow franchise came to be regularly dominated by liberal forces, civic humanism had to confront the increasingly grandiose patronage and intervention in the arts, literature, and architecture of the throne, particularly under William II.

As Berlin grew it seemed to have difficulty in rebuilding itself to generate the kind of unselfconscious civic pride common to Parisians and Viennese in the face of urban redevelopment under Napoleon III or Francis Joseph. Berlin had some daring urban planners, but they often went bankrupt, their visions swallowed in the tawdry reproduction of cramped streets and living quarters preferred by speculators. The city fathers and the king-emperor's government continued their struggles and delayed or canceled out important civic projects.

The fact that Berlin became the capital of the German Reich did not immediately alter its primary importance as the capital of Prussia. The national bureaucracy did grow slowly, and Berlin assumed more importance as an administrative capital; but so many important functions were left to the federal states, ever jealous of their sovereignty, that even this change did not cause a major caesura in the city. Industrial growth was certainly more important. Even the national parliament did not have a permanent home until a quarter-century after the unification but was originally quartered in an old, hastily made-over warehouse. The falling plaster that sometimes interrupted spirited debates reminded deputies of the real importance of the national parliament in the Hohenzollern Reich. The Reichstag's pompous new home, opened in the 1890s, was located, perhaps symbolically, outside the former walls of the city and away from the center of the government quarter, including the university.

The University of Berlin should perhaps in historical justice have been named the Napoleon Bonaparte University, for its founding is almost unimaginable without the reversals of Prussia's fortunes at the hands of the French emperor after the Battle of Jena in 1806. It is no small irony that Hegel spoke about "world-historical figures" from his lectern in Berlin and of the "cunning of reason" acting through them; he would have had no Berlin lectern otherwise, would have likely stayed in dreamy Tübingen, where any movements his philosophy indirectly inspired (including that of Marx and Bebel) would have likely had a different outcome for world history.

Berlin's university was founded, then, out of bleak necessity by a much-reduced Prussia shorn of its major university in Halle. Berlin was not lacking in institutions of higher learning, to be sure: it had an academy of sciences and excellent medical-training institutions (primarily for military surgeons), for example. There had been some discussions of opening a "general educational institution" (the word and concept *university* still stood in bad odor) before 1806, but no action had been taken. Now a shaken King Frederick William III went along with his new advisers and included a novel university in Prussia's reforming plans, to "replace with spiritual forces what we have lost in material ones."[6]

Many questions surround this founding. Should the new institution be a sort of *grande ecole superieure,* a super professional school, or should it continue the model of reformed universities (such as Humboldt's alma mater, Göttingen), include a large philosophical faculty, and draw on the advanced research ethos of the Prussian Academy of Sciences? What resulted was a compromise. The university format was retained but formally without many of the privileges for the faculties that had helped produce nepotism and torpor in many of Germany's older universities. The guildlike structures and autonomy of Europe's original universities, described elsewhere in this volume, had decayed so badly in the eighteenth century that they were in very ill repute. The original professors, chosen for their scholarly fame, were indeed impressive—members of the academy were entitled to lecture, and in 1810 some 12 percent of the teachers were academy members. This proportion of academy members who chose to lecture as well fell to 1 to 2 percent in subsequent decades, but by then a large number of professors were also elected to the academy. Hence there was always a considerable overlap between the full professors and the members of the academy.[7] The planning commissions, consisting of top people, eschewed more cronyism and tried to follow Humboldt's criteria of picking people who lived for learning.

But the more pragmatic traditions were not routed, and after the initial period of revolution from above, such founders as Humboldt, Fichte, and Schleiermacher were shunted aside in favor of more conservative and less illustrious colleagues. The university was rather starved for funds in contrast to the original plans, and it was really decades before Berlin achieved either the size or the scholarly distinction originally planned for it. It was, however, able to meet its minimal goal, the training of professionals for administrative, legal, clerical, medical, and educational careers.

The choice of Berlin for the new university was conditioned by the prior presence of institutions (such as medical schools, libraries, collections, and hospitals) and personnel rather than a consensus that a large city was an ideal location in which to inject students, either because they might be corrupted by urban life or, contrariwise, because they might cause headaches with their rowdy dueling and drinking behavior or penchant for not paying debts, whether financial or venereal. Even at the opposite end of the nineteenth century, worry about the inappropriate nature of the heart of the Reich capital caused the Prussian education ministry to consider plans for moving the university to the bucolic royal domain in Dahlem, many miles to the southwest of the central city, an area that actually became the home of the Free University in 1948. But in 1810 practicality prevailed, and the university was quartered in the grand if slightly dilapidated palace on Unter den Linden which Frederick the Great had built for his now-deceased brother Prince Henry. A similar sense of Prussian practicality had earlier placed the Academy of Sciences in the royal stables, next door to the future university, causing passersby to cite an imaginary dedication over the building: *musis et mulis,* "dedicated to muses and mules."[8]

The government designated two and a half of the central precincts of Berlin—Friedrichswerder, Dorotheenstadt, and the northern part of Friedrichsstadt—as the "university quarter." The king ordered that undesirable elements be ousted from this area by the police, and a housing bureau was set up to steer students toward respectable lodgings. Significantly, these parts of Berlin appear to have been consistently the living areas of the well-to-do, until the need for office space pushed many of them into newer residential areas to the west and southwest late in the century. One index for their prosperity is that only 5 to 15 percent of their inhabitants were classified as poor by the city government, compared with up to 50 percent in the industrializing suburbs.[9]

Nor was the social refinement of the university quarter unduly tarnished by student rowdiness, as originally feared. The old dueling fraternities which had served as nests of violence and dissoluteness at other universities were successfully discouraged at Berlin. Even patriotic, reformed fraternities such as the *Burschenschaften* were suppressed in the wake of the Carlsbad Decrees after 1819. Berlin quickly became known as an *Arbeitsuniversität,* a working university. As Ludwig Feuerbach wrote his father in 1824, "Drinking bouts, dueling, and outings are unthinkable here; at probably no other university are hard work, a sense for something higher than mere student pranks, such as striving for knowledge, and such peace and quiet generally so predominant as here. Other universities are truly taverns compared with this local work-house."[10]

A large percentage of students throughout the nineteenth century transferred to Berlin for the final semesters of study, contributing to a disproportionately mature student body. An index of this growing maturity is the number of semesters students stayed at Berlin. In 1820 the average number of semesters was three for the law and philosophical faculties and five for theology and medicine. Six to eight semesters were then normal for a university education. By the last decades of the century, when incidentally the number of semesters needed to complete university study had risen considerably, law students spent only two semesters at Berlin on average and members of the other faculties only three.[11] Partly because of the social atomization and quiet behavior of the student body, the university enjoyed a high degree of freedom from the otherwise strict censorship common in Prussia in the first half of the century.[12]

The university's faculty was recruited in the first decades largely from local and regional talent, another money-saving expedient of a government constantly strapped for funds. Some of this talent was extraordinary—one thinks of Fichte, Schleiermacher, Savigny, Ranke, and Reil, to name a few.

Some stellar names were recruited from far afield, such as Hegel and Schelling, but Berlin's was not a very cosmopolitan faculty in the first half-century of its existence. Some of the recruiting was dictated by political and religious motives of the government, sometimes resulting in dubious choices but just as often succeeding in attracting first-rate scholars. As conservative as such governmental recruiting influence was, particularly in the period down to the 1860s, it had the long-range salutary effect of breaking the traditions of nepotism and favoritism that had plagued and weakened German universities in previous centuries and thereby fostered a sort of professionalization of university teaching and research.

This professionalization of the faculties, which took many decades to complete, strengthened the basis of scholarly expertise, demonstrated increasingly by publications recognized as important by the community of *Wissenschaft,* which was becoming the sine qua non for entering the occupation of university teacher—a phenomenon neither unique to Berlin nor invented by it but one carried to new visibility by such a big, new university. Professors were increasingly called to Berlin as a reward for scholarly achievement, and that meant scholarly innovation. It was no longer sufficient for an aspiring professor to be merely *gelehrt,* or learned; he also had to have appeared to push along the methodological or substantive frontiers of knowledge. The researcher at the borders of new knowledge, not merely the master of old received knowledge, gradually became the ideal candidate for professorships and directorships of seminars and institutes, the rapidly multiplying cells of research and teaching within the older and increasingly meaningless four faculties.

This is not to say that there were no biases in such appointments. Most professorial appointments presupposed unswerving loyalty to throne and altar. Burckhardts and Nietzsches had either no chance or no taste for Berlin. At its most reactionary Berlin's theological faculty turned out ultra-conservative and orthodox pastors, just as its philosophical faculty produced thousands of rigid classicists to staff the new secondary schools spreading over Prussia. In a more liberal era after the 1860s the latitude for serious challenges to the reigning order remained circumscribed. Yet if at least lip service was paid to the Prussian monarchy and, later, the German national idea, professors had a wide degree of freedom within their seminars and laboratories. The freedom of inquiry in the name of science and scholarship balanced in practice the need for loyalty to the current regime, and indeed Berlin educated its fair share of radicals who wished to apply the critical scholarly method to contemporary social and political problems.

It is thus perhaps slightly misleading to cite the overheatedly patriotic 1870 speech of the then-rector of Berlin, famous physiologist Emil DuBois-Reymond, who called the university the "personal bodyguard of the Hohenzollern monarchy." Equally misleading would be the idea that there were hundreds of versions of Karl Marx lurking about, preparing the world for revolution. Most professors and students were happy to pay lip service or more to the dynasty and get on with their work. Physically, legally, and mentally set off to itself in the middle of the government buildings and, for much of the nineteenth century, across the street from the royal palace, the University of Berlin was far closer to the mentality of the well-educated and sometimes enlightened bureaucrats around them than to the mentality of the democratically elected Reichstag farther down the street or that of the masses taking up residence in tenements on the fringes of the city.

Since all senior professors were formally civil servants and most of the students were destined to be, this mentality is perfectly understandable. We should not overlook the fact, however, that a precondition for entering the university was the absolution of the classical *Gymnasium* or its equivalent. Students and professors shared with each other (as well as with the higher bureaucracy) the common heritage of the *Bildungsbürgertum*. This automatically set them off in many respects (not least in their own eyes) from the rest of the bourgeoisie, which typically did not finish *Gymnasium* but rather turned its attention to making money, as well as the mere artisans and workers whose education was rudimentary and vocational at best.

Thus, it would be more accurate to say that the university lived in symbiosis with its immediate "city," the *Residenzstadt* Berlin, but in a relationship of relative mutual indifference with the larger metropolis. Some examples can be given later to illustrate this peculiar situation. The symbiosis even with the *Residenz* was never complete, however; for all the administrative bureaucracy had in common with the university and for all the protection and indulgence many of the more influential cultural ministers of the nineteenth century granted to it, the spirit of "living for knowledge" and untrammeled research often conflicted with the more orthodox, fearful, overcautious views of the state administration. But with the exception of some obscurantists, the administration was also proud of the achievements of the university and its individual researchers and professors. The peer approval from outside Prussia and Germany also gave the latter a high degree of protection from arbitrary interventions. Prussia's policy in much of the nineteenth century was to take advantage of a climate of change while not appearing to be a radical innovator; this could be said of such questions as national unification, industrial and commercial progress, and even social legislation. Its premier university could be said to have followed this line to a large degree, changing with new trends in scholarship and science but never radically enough to call into question the fundamental tenets of Prussia and the university system. One might call this innovative conservatism, and the internal contradictions did not fully catch up with either state or university during most of the nineteenth century.

To be sure, by the 1880s Berlin University had begun to grow rapidly and to face the problem of specialization. From a manageably small institution of a few dozen professors "living for knowledge," Berlin was threatening, according to contemporaries by the end of the century, to turn into a "large-scale enterprise" or "factory" (*Grossbetrieb*) with thousands of students and hundreds of faculty members who could no longer possibly know each other personally. Under these conditions the university began to enter a crisis that was, again, not unique to Berlin but which was exacerbated by its being the largest German university. The potential for dictatorial rule by institute and seminar directors responsible only to the education ministry, the increasingly miserable and humiliating conditions under which advanced students and young professors had to work, and sheer size with its accompanying anomie were much more serious threats to the Humboldtian university ideal after 1880 than August Bebel's Social Democrats.

Having described in outline how the city and the university each developed in nineteenth-century Berlin, let me now turn to some interactions between them.

First, one should note that the number of faculty and students was always quite small in comparison to the population of Berlin: altogether there were barely a thousand by 1818, around two thousand by 1830, a high point not to be reached again permanently until the 1870s.[13] By comparison, the city had nearly two hundred thousand inhabitants in 1819 and more than eight hundred thousand in 1871. The state bureaucracy alone employed some four thousand civil servants around 1810.[14] Of the two hundred thousand in 1819, more than sixteen thousand were military personnel, and a garrison of that size or larger could always be found in the city.[15] Many students took advantage of the chance to become one-year volunteers while studying, a special dispensation for well-educated young men in lieu of the universal military draft.

Such fleeting contacts with the military seem to have created few permanent bonds between students on the one side and the professional army on the other. The students were being trained to be reserve officers and thus had little in common with the rank-and-file draftees. At the same time, the professional officer class tended to look down on these Sunday soldiers.

A more congenial surface for interaction of faculty and students with the Berliners lay in the social life of the larger *Bildungsbürgertum,* in the salons, cafés, and beer or wine cellars of the university quarter, but these appear to have been fairly limited. Some of the more famous professors (such as Droysen the historian and Dirichlet the mathematician) did appear in such salons as that of Varnhagen and Rahel von Ense and one or two others, but these largely literary and often rather aristocratic gatherings did not seem congenial to the majority of hardworking faculty, let alone most students. (Even Ranke, at that time considered to be something of a social climber, abandoned the salons when they started to become critical of the government's policies.) One privatdozent at the university, Theodor Mundt, maintained a somewhat more accessible salon, but it seemed to be frequented more by his journalist friends than his university colleagues.[16] Typically, one of the most famous novelists and chroniclers of Berlin in the nineteenth century and, as a young man, a founding member of one of the more memorable literary societies, Theodor Fontane, had little contact with the university.

In the late nineteenth century, particularly after 1880, when the university was achieving the pinnacle of its reputation as a world-class institution, the city was also becoming host again to lively intellectual currents. In the 1880s and 1890s Berlin was making a fair bid to become the cultural capital of Germany, wresting artistic primacy away from Munich and becoming the main center of "Germanic modernism," perhaps the first self-consciously modernist literary movement in Europe. But as one of its central figures, Heinrich Hart, recalled later, the university had little role in this cultural effervescence: "A time of study such as we have never known opened up for us. But it was not in the auditoria of the *alma mater* that we gratified our urge to study—for there we were rare visitors. Our auditoria were streets, drinking places, coffee houses, occasionally also the *Reichstag*."[17] Cafés, which substituted for the small, closed salon a public, inexpensive place to read and exchange views, always had some university visitors, but Spargnapani on Unter den Linden was the place academics were most commonly to be seen in the first half of the nineteenth century.[18]

Perhaps the most ambitious attempts by university members to interact with the public took the form of open lectures. In the first years of the university such scholars as the Roman historian Niebuhr, the theologian Fichte, and others held lectures which the fashionable public attended in considerable numbers. In later decades, however, public interest in university lectures was the exception rather than the rule. In 1841, with government approval, an Association for Scholarly Lectures came into being and included as members or lecturers a large number of Berlin professors. The association hoped to bring the latest results of scholarly and scientific reasearch to the educated lay public through popular discourses.[19]

University members were also prominent in various attempts to solve what throughout most of the century was called the "social question," that is, the plight of the poor. Viktor Aime Huber, a romantic conservative called to the Berlin faculty in the 1840s, busily wrote, spoke, and founded organizations to recapture the demoralized and impoverished, including a model housing project for them.[20] Berlin University also became a major center for the so-called socialists of the chair (*Kathedersozialisten*) from the 1870s on. Such economists as Adolph Wagner, Lujo Brentano, and later Gustav Schmoller feared that rapid industrialization threatened to dissolve the loyalties of the working class and propagated various solutions including the encouragement of labor unions or direct government intervention.[21] But their impact was more national than local.

Other individual professors were perhaps more effective in their direct intervention in the affairs of their city. Rudolf Virchow, for example, was not only one of the more radical Berlin professors in the 1848 revolution; his subsequent agitation had a profound effect on public hygiene in the city. Thanks partly to his enormous prestige in German medicine and partly to the fact that his brother-in-law was mayor of Berlin for more than a decade, Berlin's open sewers were finally replaced in the 1870s with a modern water and sanitation system, and Berlin's first public hospital was built at the same time.[22]

Another Berlin professor, Rudolf von Gneist, was active in the city parliament in the decades after the 1848 revolution. To be sure, a number of professors in the late nineteenth century were active in politics, but they tended, like the historian Treitschke and the economist Schmoller, to prefer office in the Reichstag or the Prussian House of Lords to a deeper involvement in urban affairs. In effect they thus represented German scholarship, rather than the city of Berlin, in Prussian or national bodies.

The ambivalence of the university toward the larger city could not be more clearly illustrated than by the events of the 1848 revolution. The younger professors—almost all excluded from influence and power by a system which placed all internal administrative decisions in the hands of the full professors—had harbored grievances that they tried to air and correct in the more open atmosphere of the first months of revolution; but their leaders, such as Gneist as Michelet, saw their support fade away as reaction set in.[23] A few students sided with the radicals and the people on the barricades in the early phases of the revolution, but contemporary estimates allege that only about 5 percent of the whole student body participated in these street battles and demonstrations. Far more joined the civic guard to ensure law and order in the university area.[24] Professors and students were far more active in other German university cities in 1848.[25]

If the University did not respond enthusiastically to the democratic or radical overtones of the 1848 revolution, it did, however, provide leadership for one of the burning issues of the nineteenth century—the "German question." The young university was emptied of students during the Wars of Liberation in 1813–14, when students followed their enthusiasm for a German nation-state by volunteering to fight Napoleon. This romantic nationalism was successfully curbed by the reaction after 1815, but it never completely disappeared, even at Berlin. After the creation of the German Reich in 1871, Berlin students and professors became for the larger part ardent nationalists, endorsing even such dubious causes as the *Kulturkampf* directed against "disloyal" Catholics in the 1870s, anti-Semitism in the 1880s, or imperialism and fleet building from the 1890s onward. Thundering against "enemies of the Reich" (who naturally included the growing socialist movement) became a flourishing cottage industry at the university as the century ground toward its close, although such activity was not limited to Berlin.[26]

Another factor in considering interactions between university and city is the geographical and social origins of the university members. Fairly consistently throughout the nineteenth century, about 20 percent of Berlin students came from Berlin or the surrounding province of Brandenburg, more from the city than the province. This factor can best be explained by the high degree of self-recruitment out of the social strata of civil servants, teachers, and professionals who lived in Berlin and in no way indicates recruitment from beyond the middle and upper-middle class that lived in the central area or, later in the century, increasingly in the west end. By contrast, Berlin became (except for its constant percentage of Berliners) a rather cosmopolitan university by the end of the century: whereas more than half of the original Berlin students had come from the old territories of Prussia, this figure fell to only a third by the end of the century. The rest of Germany provided a fifth of the students until 1880 and a quarter thereafter.[27]

By 1900 Berlin's university could arguably be called the best in the world, at least in terms of the scientific and scholarly prestige of its faculty members. The city in which it was located possessed an urban dynamism and spirit virtually unknown in central Europe since the sixteenth century. The university had helped the city and indeed the Prussian monarchy achieve a kind of cultural distinction both had sorely lacked in 1800. But the vitality of the city had eclipsed the importance of the university in many ways by the dawn of the twentieth century. By 1912 the largest political party in the Reichstag was that of the socialist followers of Bebel, even though they espoused a doctrine that derived heavily from Hegel. Whereas the university had been created in 1810 to "replace with spiritual forces what we have lost in material ones," the Reich capital of 1900 derived its force increasingly from factories, including those that built its military weapons. As if to recognize the importance of that kind of power and the technical knowledge that made it efficiently possible, William II awarded his technical colleges equality of rank with his universities in 1900, much to the chagrin of the latter. And Berlin's Technical College and Kaiser-Wilhelm-Gesellschaft research centers were located not in the old city but in the western suburbs of Charlottenburg and Dahlem.

The sheer size of both the university and the city provoked frequent complaints about the breakdown of community and communications. Specialization had already led to an irreversible sense that the university was an agglomeration of research institutes, final-semester students polishing their specialized knowledge after having studied in more *gemütlich* small university towns, and professors who could not possibly have a chance to get to know all their colleagues. At a time when American universities had already grafted much of the German university's professionalism onto their new graduate schools and referred constantly to Berlin, Friedrich Althoff, the czar of Prussian universities, was toying with the American idea of a campus university in Dahlem to escape the hurly-burly and crowding of the government quarter in central Berlin.

Germany, Prussia, and Berlin had never experienced a century of change like the preceding one. The university that had been conceived as a quiet place for contemplative scholarship, and to serve the state with a reliable corps of effective and thoughtful professionals, recapturing Prussia's prestige lost on the battlefield with knowledge, had become, in Adolf von Harnack's words, a large-scale industry. The loss of Humboldt's ideals, or, at least, the thread of their meaning, is perhaps symbolically best reflected in the mammoth history of Berlin University's first century by Max Lenz. In an otherwise impeccably documented and, for its time, exemplary university history, Lenz found it impossible to carry the story forward past 1870 with the same completeness he had demonstrated for earlier periods. The university had simply become too complicated and large for one scholar to encompass with the same care and attention he had lavished on its first sixty years.

At the same time, the city of Berlin had burst its seams with breakneck growth. The new Reich capital had also become the financial and manufacturing megalopolis of central Europe, nervous, rushing, and, in Dilthey's word, chaotic. The university was no longer the main intellectual beacon—although it was still a justifiably proud one—in the cityscape. Technological and scientific research, the hallmarks of the dawning century, lay elsewhere than Unter den Linden, in the booming technical college and in the nascent imperial research institutes.

Despite these problems the University of Berlin retained its identity and pride, perhaps because it remained loyal to the *Residenz* that had brought it into being and which it had served so well. It would have been truly miraculous if that university had been able to integrate itself fully with the workaday life of its surrounding city, particularly when Berlin became the industrial giant it had by 1900. It remained true to the dynasty that never lived far away from the university's own palace and saw itself to the end of that dynasty—even beyond—as the banner carrier in science and scholarship of royal Prussia.

Given its origins, not to mention the ambitions of its faculty and students, this is not surprising. Berlin may seem on the surface comparable to other great urban universities founded in the nineteenth century, such as London or New York University. In terms of its functional expectations, if only in that, it may be more comparable to the great American state universities founded in the nineteenth century, often in cities that were little more than villages at the time.

If one excludes the masses of Berliners who never had the aspiration or opportunity to attend a university and focuses instead on the bureaucratic and military functions of Old Berlin, one can perhaps see the parallel more clearly. Created from the top down without community support, nestled among the classical royal buildings of Unter den Linden, behind which were originally still the sandy lanes of the impoverished frontier outpost of the Mark Brandenburg, Berlin might be called the campus university of the geographically compact *Residenz* of Prussia.

Berlin changed, and Prussia is no more. It might be that the University of Berlin became the first modern "research university" precisely because of its closeness in every way to an ambitious modern state, not because of its happenstance location in one of the world's fastest-growing cities in the past century. Surely nothing could underline the sense of Berlin University's mission more than the official dissolution of the State of Prussia by the Allies in 1947, the creation of the West Berlin Free University in 1948, and the renaming of the rump university in East Berlin in 1949. Political dictates, more than the interests of all Berliners in a common distinguished urban institution, shaped both the beginning and the end of the Friedrich-Wilhelms-Universität. As a modern urban university its relationship to its host city was in many ways unique. If its distinguished albeit relatively brief history does not fit easily into the patterns of other institutions described in this colloquium, its nearness to power and its place in but not by or for its urban environment raises interesting points for reflection.

NOTES

1. Hans Herzfeld, "Allgemeine Entwicklung und Politische Geschichte," in Hans Herzfeld, ed., *Berlin und die Provinz Brandenburg im 19. und 20. Jahrhundert* [*Veröffentlichungen der Historischen Kommission zu Berlin*] (Berlin, 1968), xxv, 4.

2. Ibid., p. 5.

3. Letter from B. G. Niebuhr to his father, 18 August 1810, in D. Gerhard and W. Norvin, eds., *Die Briefe Bartold Georg Niebuhrs*, 2 vols. (Berlin, 1926–29), II, 137.

4. Letter from Wilhelm Grimm to Georg G. Gervinus, 27 May 1841, cited in Dora Mayer, *Das öffentliche Leben in Berlin im Jahr vor der Märzrevolution* [*Schriften des Vereins für die Geschichte Berlins*] (Berlin, 1912), XLVI, 5.

5. Herzfeld, "Allgemeine Entwicklung," p. 74.

6. Max Lenz, *Geschichte der königlichen Friedrich-Wilhelms-Universität zu Berlin*, 4 vols. in 5 (Halle, 1910–18), I, 78.

7. Ibid., III, 503; Adolf von Harnack, *Geschichte der königlichen preussischen Akademie der Wissenschaften*, 3 vols. in 4 (Berlin, 1900), I/2, 645–54, 963–73, 1044–53.

8. Werner Hegemann, *Das steinerne Berlin. Geschichte der grössten Mietskasernenstadt der Welt* (Lugano, 1930; new ed. Berlin, 1963), p. 140.

9. Günther Liebchen, "Zu den Lebensbedingungen der unteren Schichten im Berlin des Vormärz," in Otto Büsch, ed., *Untersuchungen zur Geschichte der frühen Industrialisierung vornehmlich im Wirtschaftsraum Berlin/Brandenburg* [*Einzelveröffentlichungen der Historischen Kommission zu Berlin*] (Berlin, 1971), VI, 310–11.

10. Lenz, *Geschichte*, II/1, 183.

11. Ibid., III, 515.

12. Ibid., II/1, 183.

13. Ibid., II/2, 358.

14. Herzfeld, "Allgemeine Entwicklung," pp. 3, 15.

15. Karin Weimann, "Bevölkerungsentwicklung und Frühindustrialisierung in Berlin," in Büsch, *Untersuchungen*, p. 161.

16. Mayer, *Das öffentliche Leben*, pp. 56–58.

17. Heinrich Hart, "Literarische Erinnerungen 1880–1905," in *Gesammelte Werke* (Berlin, 1907), III, 27, cited in James McFarlane, "Berlin and the Rise of Modernism, 1886–96," in Malcolm Bradbury and James McFarlane, eds., *Modernism* (New York, 1976), p. 107.

18. Mayer, *Das öffentliche Leben*, p. 52.

19. Ibid., p. 44.

20. Hegemann, *Das steinerne Berlin*, pp. 200–205.

21. Horst Berger, "Der Kathedersozialismus an der Universität zu Berlin in

der Zeit von 1870 bis 1880," *Wissenschaftliche Zeitschrift der Humboldt-Universität zu Berlin. Gesellschafts- und Sprachwissenschaftliche Reihe* 11 (1962): 309–32.

22. Herzfeld, "Allgemeine Entwicklung," pp. 78–79.

23. Erich J. C. Hahn, "The Junior Faculty in 'Revolt': Reform Plans for Berlin University in 1848," *American Historical Review* 82 (1977): 875–95.

24. Herzfeld, "Allgemeine Entwicklung," pp. 57–58.

25. Charles E. McClelland, "Deutsche Professoren im Vormärz," in Klaus Schwabe, ed., *Deutsche Professoren als Elite, 1815–1945* (Boppard/Rhine, 1987).

26. See, for example, Konrad H. Jarausch, *Students, Society and Politics in Imperial Germany* (Princeton, N.J., 1982), esp. chap. 1; and Charles E. McClelland, "Berlin Historians and German Politics," in Walter Laqueur and George L. Mosse, eds., *Historians in Politics* (London, 1974), pp. 191–221.

27. Lenz, *Geschichte*, II/2, 359. On social origins of Berlin students, see Lenz, *Geschichte*, III, 522. In no faculty was there a majority of students from modest middle-class backgrounds during the whole century.

11

Science as Vocation in
Burckhardt's Basel

Carl E. Schorske

Basel in the nineteenth century can best be understood as a viable anachronism. Surviving from the medieval era as a city-state, it managed to maintain a substantial measure of its political autonomy and much of its patrician-dominated social structure. From the Renaissance era it retained a humanistic cultural tradition within a new world of powerful modern nation-states, big cities, big business, and technological culture. Determination to remain small was essential to the Basel elite's successful defense of its civic tradition and, for a long time, its social power. In a modern world that worshiped growth as health and bigness as bounty, especially in cities, Basel long resisted expansion. In 1780 it had about 15,000 inhabitants—only 15 percent more than in 1600. In 1848 it had 25,000. Only slowly in the second half of the nineteenth century did the resolution of the entrenched merchant oligarchy weaken under the temptations of new economic opportunities and the pressures of sociopolitical demands from below to meet the conditions for urban expansion. Yet not until 1880 did Basel's population pass the 80,-000 mark.[1]

Basel stubbornly tried to cling not only to the scale but also to the character of a polis, a free city. The historian Jacob Burckhardt expressed the outlook of the Basel oligarchy to which he belonged as a general proposition: "The small state exists so that there may be one spot on earth where the largest possible proportion of the inhabitants are citizens in the fullest sense of the word."[2]

History and geography had schooled Basel well for its adaptive defense of its ancient civic tradition against modernity. Situated at the elbow of the Rhine between the navigable portion of the river and the Alpine passes to Italy, the city had always enjoyed an enviable position on Europe's greatest commercial highway. The reverse side of this economic advantage, however, was political and strategic vulnerability. Trade routes easily became the roads of war. Basel lay on the boundary between some of the deepest and strongest divisions of Europe: between the French and German language and cultural communities, between the often warring and expansionist French monarchy and the Holy Roman Empire, between Protestantism to the north in Germany and Catholicism to the west in France. Amid conflicting forces, all more powerful than itself, Basel learned to live by a paradoxical combination of sophisticated cosmopolitanism and narrow localism. Open in commerce and culture, the city-state was closed and aloof in its civic self-definition. Access to citizenship was tightly controlled, often requiring generations of family residence, in the interest of the guild corporations and a small oligarchy that held its power through the guilds.

To safeguard its position among stronger neighbors, Basel avoided war and eschewed alliances wherever possible (even when it sold mercenaries). Instead the city developed a remarkable capacity and reputation for mediation between conflicting states, cantons, or communes. In 1501, when Basel joined the Swiss Confederation, the constitutional contract (*Bundesbrief*) forbade the city the use of armed force in intra-Swiss disputes and at the same time enjoined it to use its diplomatic skill as broker and peacemaker in conflicts among other Confederation members. Basel's sons preserved their right to be themselves by learning the minds and ways of their neighbors and using their understanding to avoid friction and to moderate conflict. The city's behavior in the Reformation was characteristic. Although it adopted the new Reformed faith, it exercised in 1529 its creative diplomacy to prevent the Catholic cantons from going to war with the Protestant ones, establishing for Switzerland the principle, not always honored in practice, of confessional peace based on local choice. It was a principle Europe would adopt only after another century of devastating religious wars.

Basel's practical, irenic cosmopolitanism found early reinforcement in a culture of humanism that became crucial to the city's whole subsequent development. The University of Basel, founded in 1454, became a center of Christian humanism and a place of confluence of Italian and French learning. Characteristically integrating economic opportunity and intellectual values, Basel also became in the sixteenth century a center of paper production and, more important, one of Europe's leading scholarly publishing centers. While members of the university community became involved in editorial functions, the printers were admitted to university lectures to enhance their understanding of Latin texts. It was this vigorous culture of the book that attracted Erasmus to make Basel his home for much of the last two decades of his life. Erasmus himself exercised a powerful and lasting, if informal, influence on the city's intelligentsia. His kind of humanism, with a stronghold in the university and a foothold in the patriciate, tempered the zealotry of the Reformation, sparing the city the worst, though not all, of the fratricidal consequences of the religious crisis. A glance at the culture heroes of the great Swiss cities tells us much: Zurich remembers the militant religious leader Zwingli as the refounder of the city; Geneva recalls stern Calvin; Basel looks back to the compromising humanist Erasmus.

While in many ways Basel resembled other patrician-controlled imperial free cities of the Germanies, it was unique in the high value assigned by its elite to humanistic culture. It was unique also among free cities—especially those of the Rhineland—in maintaining until modern times a university as radiating center of its specifically civic values. The profession of learning, from the sixteenth century onward, was prized among the merchant families as the priesthood was in Ireland. By the nineteenth century no self-respecting patrician family could be without its "Onkel Professor." True, in the eighteenth century the university sank to a low ebb in both size and quality. The professors were chosen almost exclusively from local families. They were elected from a slate of three candidates by lot, as were other officials under Basel's narrow collegial constitution. Despite a few intellectual dynasties of high caliber, such as the Bernoullis in math and science and the Burckhardts in philology and theology, the local monopoly of academic posts had cost the university its European stature by the time of the French Revolution.

After the trauma of the Revolution, when Basel's ancient political culture had been threatened by the centralized Helvetic Republic and Napoleon, the patriciate set about refounding the city and its own power in it on a more solid basis. Restoration in the Basel context meant not only the return to power of the ruling elite but also the deliberate reanimation of the humanist cultural tradition as the center of the civic ethos. To accomplish this objective the university was seen as the primary instrument. A reform commission was instituted in 1813 to reconstitute the university on modern lines.[3] The reformers had a choice of new models: the French one of the *grandes écoles,* to produce functional professionals for the modern state—architects, bureaucrats, teachers, natural scientists, and so on; or the German university, as revitalized by Humboldt's educational countermovement to cultivate the citizen of *Bildung,* a new human person of moral and aesthetic sensibility, creativity, and sharpened understanding. Although the Basel commission was staffed with several French-style rationalists, they too were by local tradition sympathetic to the Humboldtian alternative, which easily prevailed in their recommendations.

The reformers did not, however, restore autonomy to the university. Patricians though they were, they had learned the lesson of the deterioration of the university when it was an uncontrolled preserve of their own class. The reformers built university government directly into civil government, in a way that must be unique in the annals of both politics and learning. As Rome had two consuls, so Basel had two burgomasters. Of these, one also served as chancellor of the university. Since turnover in this office was low, continuity in university leadership was ensured. The burgomaster-chancellor had to be academically qualified and had to enjoy the confidence of the faculty. Of the four incumbents from 1803 down to 1874, three were professors as well as city council members (*Ratsherren*). All were, of course, unpaid public officials, wealthy members of the elite enjoying the highest esteem among both citizens and academics—rather like James Bryan Conant at Harvard and in Boston. They combined, as one of the historians of the university said, "scientific culture, the gift of statesmanship, and *Baseler Civismus*."⁴ The burgomaster-chancellorship was no mere honorific post like the chancellorship of Oxford. The holder of the office chaired a three-man committee (*Kuratel*) which supervised curriculum and prepared recommendations of faculty appointments for the city's Educational Council (*Erziehungsrat*), which he served as president. Faculty members played an advisory role in the appointment of professors, but no more. Final authority was vested in the Small Council of the city government, in which the great patrician families predominated until the city government was democratized in 1874.

One of the faculty reformers expressed well the revitalized ethos of civic humanism: "The meaning and nature of man is first revealed in the state. . . . But the determining condition of the state is freedom, in which every energy [*Kraft*] can develop itself without restraint, and the mind [*Geist*] can make itself effective in its activity undisturbed."⁵ *Civismus,* as the Baselers like to call public spirit, and *Wissenschaft* went hand in hand.

Two consequences flowed almost at once from this organization of the university, one affecting the character and ethos of the faculty, the other shaping the very substance of Basel's creative contribution to European thought. I shall briefly sketch the first and then illustrate the second with the two individual cases of Bachofen and Burckhardt.

Scarcely had the new university statutes been put into effect in 1818 when the post-Napoleonic political reaction began to harden its grip on intellectual life in Germany to the north. As liberal professors were dismissed or began to think of fleeing government repression in German—especially Prussian—universities, Basel fished in the troubled waters, winning a fine catch of front-rank academic talent. C. J. Jung's grandfather, who came on the recommendation of Alexander von Humboldt, reformed the medical faculty, while another émigré, the Germanist Wilhelm Wackernagel, reinvigorated the philological curriculum. There were genuine radicals among the new German appointees, too, such as Karl Follen, later founder of German study at Harvard, who was wanted in Prussia for his association with the student militants of the *Burschenschaften*. Conservative Basel gave him house room and more. On his behalf, for the first time in history, Basel stood up to powerful Prussia. The city government resisted both the threats of Prussia and the pressures of the anxious Swiss Confederation and refused to extradite the "subversive" professor. From that time forward Basel had the reputation for giving refuge to maverick foreign professors, including "heaven stormers." Even the leading families, normally known for the closed character of their society, welcomed such professors into their homes.

Political reaction in the Germanies, and especially the rise of Prussian *Realpolitik,* gradually changed the definition of the scholar's function in Germany, with important consequences for the culture of Basel. In response to the French Revolution, Humboldt and the Prussian reformers had developed a neohumanistic cultural ideal which, through school and university, was to make ethically sensitive citizens of Prussian subjects. Beginning with the reaction, however, and increasingly as the *Machstaat* progressed, the vocation of learning for citizens was transmuted into the profession of science for the state. The professor became not the purveyor of humanistic culture but the learned specialist. Such were the premises on which Germany's positivistic scientific eminence was built.

Basel took another road in defining science as vocation. Just as the Prussians were abandoning Humboldtian neohumanism, Basel espoused it heart and soul. Education, not specialized production, became the aim of scholarship. The Basel professor after the reform was not just a university scholar and teacher. He was a *praeceptor urbi* in the fullest sense of the term. The 1820s university reform involved him in a demanding outreach program, animated especially by the theologian Wilhelm de Wette. Professors were expected to offer public lectures. They also edited journals aimed at the amateur. To their crucial lectures, such as inaugural lectures or rectoral addresses, the whole town was invited—and many came. For faculty members— especially the young and the newcomers—the presence of the general public at such occasions could be intimidating. Thus, the young theologian Franz Overbeck wrote to his colleague Friedrich Nietzsche before his inaugural address: "Tuesday I must speak in the great hall [*aula*]. Here the whole city is invited. Naturally, it's no laughing matter."[6] Above all, the members of the philosophical faculty were expected to teach in the *Pädogogium,* the public preparatory school, as part of their regular teaching load. What this burden could amount to is made clear in the case of Nietzsche's obligations in the summer semester of 1870: two three-hour lecture courses and a seminar at the university and a six-hour course in Greek tragedy and six hours of Latin and Greek language instruction at the *Pädagogium*—a total of twenty hours.[7] In short, the Basel *homo academicus,* though a free, protected, and socially appreciated intellectual explorer, was at the same time a kind of home missionary whose vocation was to develop cosmopolitan *Bildung* in allegiance to the local scene. The first generation of neohumanist scholars, reinforced by Prussian émigrés, enthusiastically put this commitment into place. The second, those who matured in the 1830s, were reared in it.

As luck would have it, just when Basel adopted fully the German idealist scholarship of *Bildung,* European *Wissenschaft* was becoming geared into the requirements of the modern nation-state. Connected as it was with the defense of a tradition of the polis and of the power of its patriciate, Basel's neohumanism was socially anachronistic. Yet by virtue of its critical *prise de position* in relation to scholarship's subservience to the more common state structures of modern power, it can also be seen as culturally futuristic, formulating antipositivistic ideas that became widespread only in our century.

No act of civic or cultural will could prevent the political and economic forces of nineteenth-century Europe from penetrating Basel. Under the contagious impact of the French liberal revolution of 1830, the underprivileged of Basel's Catholic rural-artisan countryside revolted against Protestant patrician rule. The oligarchy's attempt to repress the insurgent populace failed, and urban Basel (*Stadt*) had to accept the secession of rural Basel (*Basel-*

Landschaft) as an independent canton. Then, in the 1840s, while liberalism grew in strength within Basel, challenging the ancient elitist political regime, the city-state's political autonomy was further reduced by the reorganization of the Swiss Confederation on more centralistic and democratic lines. At the same time the advent of railroads knit Basel's economy more strongly to neighboring France and Germany, while industrialization, especially after 1850, changed the social basis of Basel's industry from a traditional artisanate to a modern working class. Here, too, demographic and democratic pressures weakened the deferential society from within, even as Basel's great industrial neighboring states communicated the tremors of their crises of growth in the revolutions of 1848 and the wars of unification and national rivalry of the midcentury decades.

To the internal and external challenges to the embattled patrician way of life Basel found intellectual and psychological defenses, if not political ones. Elsewhere in Europe cultural responses to the trauma of modern social change came from free or deracinated intelligentsia, often artists; in Basel they came from academic intellectuals, from professors.

We will now look at two Basel academics in order to sketch the relation between their role definitions as civic scholars and the intellectual substance of the work that they bequeathed to posterity.

J. J. Bachofen, historical anthropologist, and Jacob Burckhardt, cultural historian, were not only born to the Basel patriciate but were educated by the first generation of neohumanists. Where their teachers were tempered optimists, fulfilled in their mission, the younger men had to endure the change in the conditions of patrician power which robbed the idealism of their elders of its social promise and its philosophic force. Bachofen and Burckhardt, each in his own way, did battle to rescue humanistic science-as-vocation from what they saw as the new academic servants of power. Each found a way to reanimate the humanistic legacy by injecting into it a new, quasi-aesthetic form of social understanding and a stoical intellectual stance.

Johann Jacob Bachofen (1815–87) most vividly dramatizes in his life and thought the pressures of the nineteenth century on the patrician consciousness. Scion of one of Basel's wealthiest families, which made its fortune, as did the Burkhardts, in the manufacture of silk ribbons, Bachofen studied both law and philology in German universities as well as in Basel. He began his career in legal work, both scholarly and practical. In 1841 the City Council appointed him to a teaching post in the law faculty of the university. The liberals, however, increasingly strong since the patrician failure to prevent the independence of rural Basel in 1833, launched a press campaign against the young man's appointment, branding it as "the result of illegitimate preferment and special family influences." At this slight to his talents and integrity Bachofen took deepest offense; he refused both title and university salary. A year later the City Council persuaded him to accept the office of professor, although he would not accept the salary. Then, in 1844, he changed his mind again: he gave up his professorship and became a private scholar.[8] Bachofen continued to perform other civic duties. He played an important role for the university as a member of the municipal committee, the three-man *Kuratel,* that controlled it. He also served as a judge for several decades. But the hostile charge of patrician nepotism, with its inevitable reflection on his competence as a legal scholar, had struck a wound that would not heal. Bachofen not only withdrew from his formal academic career but, in 1845, also resigned his seat on the Great Council—an extraordinary step for a patrician only thirty years old.

Bachofen's civic disengagement did not imply diminished devotion to his native city. "One has firm roots only in one's native soil," he wrote. "The great experiences of life can be gone through only there, for the destinies of families and states are not played out in one life, but only in a whole series of generations following one upon the other."[9] He not only tolerated "boredom as always" in "our Lilliput,"[10] but he committed heart and mind to preserving and enhancing the humane values for which his city stood.

As a private scholar Bachofen embarked on a kind of exploration that would serve as cultural counterfoil to the modern politics and scholarship that threatened his polis and its humanist tradition. For inspiration in this scholarly mission Bachofen looked back to the Basel humanists of the fifteenth century and to the German scholars who, from Winckelmann through Creuzer, had defined out of the classical heritage the *Bildungsideal* in the era of Humboldt. For his intellectual targets Bachofen looked north too: his enemies were the new Prussian scholars—"the pygmies"—from Niehbuhr on, who turned classical learning from the cultural glory that was Greece to the political greatness that was Rome. "In our age," he wrote, "even men's minds have been put in uniform."

The great historian Theodor Mommsen incarnated for Bachofen all that he feared and despised in modern classical learning.[11] Nationalist, liberal champion of German unification under Prussia, Mommsen in his spectacular *History of Rome to the Death of Caesar* (1854–56) celebrated Rome as the state which, by combining just law and power, had succeeded in unifying ancient Italy. Bachofen saw in Mommsen's achievement only its contemporary essence. "Rome and the Romans are not Mommsen's real concern," he wrote. "The heart of the book is the application of the latest ideas of the times, . . . the apotheosis [in and through Rome] of the boundless radicalism of the new Prussia."[12]

Bachofen exhumed from the mists of prehistory another Rome to contrast with Mommsen's naked, masculine power-state. Using myths and funerary sculpture of pre-Roman cultures and placing them in the light of his sensitive anthropological imagination, Bachofen recovered a prepolitical antiquity: the creative communities of the Sabines and the Etruscans, who charted the first perilous passage of mankind from raw nature to culture. Law appeared among these primitives not as a product of power to organize domination but as a manifestation of the spirit, to canalize and sublimate man's chaotic libidinal and violent instincts through religion and law. It was not the male of the species who accomplished this feat of community creativity but the female. Woman, as the only visible source of new biological life, established the first system of law, *Mutterrecht*. It was a system of lineage and of family, enforced by codes of blood vengeance. Woman took these first steps in self-defense, to protect her child nurturing and to regulate unbridled sexual license. Matriarchy, succeeding to hetaeric promiscuity, sublimated natural love into the idea of the sacred and elevated procreative drives into marital bonding and religious culture. Through religious ritual and mystical exaltation, matriarchal society created an ennobling "erotic-spiritual culture." In the end, Bachofen maintained, the female principle limited the intellectual potentialities of man. The earth-mother principle was overcome by the sky-father principle, material and psychic nature by abstract and intellectual nature, Demeter by Apollo. "Motherright yields to the right of the state, *ius naturale* to *ius civile*. . . . Nowhere was patriarchal law so sternly carried through as in Rome."[13] But the ultimate fundamental service of woman to humankind remained: she founded culture to refine our nature, while the male created the state to rule it.

Bachofen did not, despite his hatred for imperial Rome and Prussian *Realpolitik,* deplore this victory of the male principle as such; for on it, in his view, the role of intellect and of the individualism necessary to the great achievements of European culture was ultimately based. But if his mind accepted the victors, his heart stayed with the vanquished: with the dead past, not the living present; with the culture of the mothers, not the civilization of the fathers; with the nurturing erotic bonding of community as against the rational regulations of society; with the religious care of souls rather than the state's promotion and protection of abstract rights.

If Bachofen succeeded in restoring a humanistic *Altertumswissenschaft* against the critical realism of the new German historical science, he did so on a terrain of the past which could not perform the moralistic educational functions of the earlier humanists. For the chthonic realm of the mothers, with its dark divinities, could scarcely match the pantheon of Olympian gods and heroes in providing ideal types for civic *Bildung*. In fact, Bachofen performed a more dangerous intellectual function in his anthropology. He opened the repressed world of eros and thanatos to the historical consciousness of modern man. He held up to sympathetic contemplation all the values that were sacrificed when the male-dominated state prevailed over the matriarchal order—love, religion, a sensuous spirituality, cultivation of life, pious acceptance of death. This inveterate patrician could not, as Nietzsche tried to do, draw strength from the realm of instinct for the regeneration of modern culture. Bachofen's archaizing vision could create elegiacally an appreciation for a world that was lost, reinforcing the values of nurturing culture against those of overmastering politics. But it could not refute the historical truth of the success of Mommsen's Rome. His lifetime scholarly polemic produced lament for the lost and an attitude of resignation, but not hope for its renewal.

During the 1850s, when Mommsen was producing his paean to political power in the Roman history and Bachofen his sympathetic recreation of prepolitical culture in *Motherright,* Jacob Burckhardt was at work on *The Culture of the Renaissance in Italy.* Perhaps the most important single contribution of Basel to European thought since Erasmus, Burckhardt's book addressed in historical terms the problem of the relationship of cultural creativity to social experience. The book can also be read, like Bachofen's, as part of the effort of the Basel intelligentsia to preserve its cosmopolitan tradition of *Bildung* under modern conditions that were hostile both to it and to the survival of the patriciate that had nurtured and sustained it.

In 1858 Bachofen, as a member of *Kuratel,* drafted the invitation to Burckhardt to return from Zurich to his native city as professor of history. Bachofen expressed himself in terms well calculated to appeal to Burckhardt's civic idea of the intellectual's vocation. Not only did the faculty and the city officials enthusiastically wish him to return, Bachofen wrote to the younger scholar, but he had remained, for his wonderful public lectures in the 1840s, "the darling of the [Basel] public." "Come back joyfully then, and help to develop intellectual life, to give it the freshness among us that— if we don't lose our courage—will still be granted it."[14] Could a Burckhardt resist such an appeal—a Burckhardt whose family had provided Basel with forty professors for its university and at least one of the city's two burgomasters continuously for one hundred fifty years?

Burckhardt's acceptance should not surprise us, then. But the way in which he carried out his "office" of Basel professor really must excite our wonder. Where Bachofen withdrew from teaching to fight his battle for *Bildung* only through writing, Burckhardt self-consciously gave up publishing after his *Renaissance* appeared in 1860 and dedicated himself wholly to teaching his fellow Baselers at every level. His classes in the *Pädagogium,* the public prep school for the university, were as important to him as his university lectures. For the educated amateur in the Junior Merchants' Society or at the Basel Museum, Burckhardt lectured on subjects ranging from "The Art of Cooking of the Later Greeks" to "The Letters of Madame de Sévigné," preparing his polished presentations with the same careful research and organization of sources as other historical scholars devoted to their writing.[15] Everywhere Burckhardt's pedagogic aim was the same: to teach men how to understand history through contemplation and reflection. "Listen to the secret of things. The contemplative mood. . . ." He respected professional specialism for the accurate knowledge it produced but rejected it for its narrowness and its failure to seek wisdom: "How is the collector of inscriptions to find time for contemplative work? Why, they don't even know their Thucydides." (This barb is directed at Mommsen and his energetic organization of teams to collect Roman inscriptions in Italy. Bachofen, too, inveighed against this Prussianization of research.) Burckhardt avoided learned association meetings "where they go and sniff each other like dogs."[16] He prided himself, in research as in teaching, on being "an arch-dilettante," committed to nurturing amateurs to be reflective about their own historical experience by entering vicariously into the staggering varieties of life in the past, where each culture revealed another aspect of human nature and destiny. It was the "special duty of the cultivated person," he believed, "to broaden the picture of the continuity of world development in himself"[17] and, as a thinking participant-observer in the flow of history, to preserve it.

To this stubborn negator of the nineteenth century's articles of faith, continuity was far from synonymous with progress. Here Burckhardt was at one with Bachofen. Burckhardt's greater worldliness enabled him to see the changing configurations of history not with his colleague's bitter ethical regret or metaphysical despair but with a fine mixture of irony and otherworldly aesthetic wonder. Skeptical of progress, he avoided a necessitarian pessimism as well, accepting the openness of history as a changing scene of creativity and spiritual achievement ironically linked to malevolence, stupidity, terror, and suffering. Such a concept of history's flow made it possible to cherish and even expand culture even while undergoing the traumas of social disorder and political defeat.

In *The Culture of the Renaissance* Burckhardt created a new kind of history much closer to the work of the anthropologist than to that of the traditional historian. Synchronic cross-sections replace diachronic phases or narrative sequences as the basic structural units of the book. Burckhardt examines Renaissance culture not dynamically for actions and events but statically for its character as a scene of interrelated aspects of human life and activity. Not literature but stagecraft seems to offer Burckhardt the formal language for his historical *tableau vivant*. In a series of great panels devoted to the nature and structure of politics, intellectual life, mores, and religious practices, he shows us the Renaissance, as he says, not in its motion (*Verlauf*) but in its states of being (*Zustände*). The sense of historical space supersedes that of historical time.

Yet Burckhardt has placed his spatial scene in a temporal frame that lends it not only perspective but historical meaning. It is here that Burckhardt's concerns as a Baseler—community, the state, and cultural creativity—are brought into focus in his historical theater. At the back of the Renaissance stage Burckhardt has hung a backdrop of medievalism; in front of it a scrim of modernity through which we view it. At the beginning of each part of the book the medieval backdrop is deftly sketched in a few sentences. Burckhardt portrays it as a unified culture in which politics and religion penetrate each other and in which the individual was conscious of himself only as part of a community organized for the salvation of mankind. The Renaissance, seen against this medieval backdrop, is an era of decadence, the end of medieval innocence and unity, disintegrating as religion and politics separate, as pope and emperor divide. By the same token the Renaissance is also "a civilization which is the mother of our own," an era in which, out of the destruction of community, modern individualism, with its incredible self-consciousness, was born. The scrim of modernity sharpens our vision of the action on the stage. In the new city-states and despotisms of Italy, "for the first time we detect the modern political spirit of Europe, . . . often displaying the worst features of an unbridled egotism, outraging every right, killing every germ of a healthier culture." Yet in consequence and compensation the creativity of man is activated: "a new fact appears in history—the State as an outcome of reflection and calculation, the State as a work of art."[18] That the state is not God-given but man-devised, an artifact posited against the chaos of existence, often brings new terrors in its train. In the artistic world, however, creativity is also unleashed, this time in a most positive way, to produce new and glorious images of man as the medieval bonds of faith dissolve. Where Enlightenment historians had associated the Renaissance flowering of art with social progress, Burckhardt connected it with ruthless political individualism and despotism, the chaos of autonomous states that was Italy. Burckhardt's vision linked the glory of cultural creativity with the curse of unconstrained self-assertiveness that the decay of medieval unity released. Terror and beauty, intellectual discovery and moral degradation went hand in hand at the birth of "modern" culture, where individual competition replaced human community and man became literally self-made. Such a view was beyond progress and regression. In contrast to the elegiac ideas of Bachofen, who lamented the lost "natural" culture of Italy's primordial mothers, Burckhardt offered his contemporaries, in the mirror of the Renaissance, an image of the beginning of their own civilization in which neither hope nor despair seemed justified. The warmest appreciation of man's achievements in the sphere of culture was interwoven with the most unsentimental sense of the realities of naked power. Such a complex and skeptical historical vision, harsh but sublime, could well accomplish the vocational aim of Burckhardt as *Wissenschaftler,* Basel-style: to make the man of *Bildung* in the threatening world of the mass state "not smarter for tomorrow but wiser forever."

NOTES

1. Hans Mauersberg, *Wirtschafts- und Sozialgeschichte zentraleuropäisher Städte in neuerer Zeit, . . . Basel, Frankfurt a. M., Hamburg, Hannover und München* (Göttingen, 1960), pp. 26–30.

2. Quoted in Edgar Bonjour, H. S. Offen, and G. R. Potter, *A Short History of Switzerland* (Oxford, 1960), p. 338.

3. On the work of this commission and its results, see Edgar Bonjour, *Die Universität Basel* (Basel, 1960), chaps. 22, 23.

4. Ibid., p. 353.

5. Franz Dorotheus Gerlach, ancient historian, quoted in ibid., p. 353.

6. Letter of Overbeck to Nietzsche, 13 March 1870, in Carl Albrecht Bernoulli, *Franz Overbeck und Friedrich Nietzsche, eine Freundschaft* (Jena, 1908), I, 30.

7. Curt Paul Janz, *Friedrich Nietzsche. Biographie,* 3 vols. (Munich, 1978–79), I, 351.

8. Bonjour, *Die Universität Basel,* pp. 549–50.

9. Quoted from Bachofen's autobiographical letter to F. C. von Savigny, legal historian, by Lionel Gossman, *Orpheus Philologus. Bachofen versus Mommsen on

the *Study of Antiquity: Transactions of the American Philosophical Society* (1983): 17.

10. Bachofen letter to Rudolf Müller, 7 November 1879, in *Johann Jakob Bachofens Gesammelte Werke,* ed. Karl Meuli (Basel and Stuttgart, 1967), X, letter 300.

11. For Bachofen's antagonism to Mommsen, see Gossman, *Orpheus Philologus,* pp. 21–41.

12. Quoted in ibid., p. 29.

13. For a condensed statement of the nature of matriarchal culture and its passage to patriarchy, see Bachofen's introduction to "The Myth of Tanaquil," in *Myths, Religion and Motherright: Selected Writings of J. J. Bachofen,* Bollingen Series LXXXIV (Princeton, N.J., paperback ed., 1973), pp. 211–46.

14. *Kuratel* to Dr. J. J. Burckhardt, 24 January 1858, quoted in Bonjour, *Die Universität Basel,* p. 686.

15. A number of these lectures are collected in Jakob Burckhardt, *Kulturgeschichtliche Vorträge,* ed. Rudolf Marx (Stuttgart, 1959). See, for the circumstances, educational aims, and style of the lectures, Marx's "Nachwort," pp. 419–45.

16. Jacob Burckhardt, *Letters,* sel., ed., trans. Alexander Dru (London, 1955), p. 32.

17. Quoted in Marx, "Nachwort," in Burckhardt, *Kulturgeschichtliche Vorträge,* pp. 442–43.

18. Jacob Burckhardt, *The Civilization of the Renaissance in Italy* (London, 1951), p. 2.

12

The University, the City, and the World: Chicago and the University of Chicago

Edward Shils

Universities, for the most part, transmit truths which they themselves have not discovered. Those which they discover are not for their own contemplation exclusively; they have to be diffused to wider, even worldwide, intellectual communities. What is essential in a university—knowledge—must be drawn from and offered to students, teachers, and investigators in other parts of the world. Intellectually, no university can be wholly self-contained.

Every institution exists in an ecological setting. No institution or any part of an institution is free from the necessity of interaction with its immediate locality. Its physical existence is located in a particular place; its members live in particular places; they often live near each other; their survival as physiological organisms depends on local institutions to supply food, maintain lines of transportation, and ensure public order—all of these occur within places of relatively narrow radius.

No modern university has ever lived entirely from the sale of its services. Universities have received subsidies from the church, the state, and private philanthropists as individuals and as foundations. The fees paid by their students for tuition have only in very few cases come close to covering the costs of conducting a university. The patrons might be mainly local or widely dispersed.

Universities might offer instruction primarily to local residents; they might offer instruction to local residents, outside regular academic courses of study. They might open their libraries and gymnaisums and playing fields to local residents; offer medical, legal, and social services to local residents; perform research for and give advice to local industries and local governmental bodies. Their teachers might be active in local political and civic affairs.

It would be very misleading to think about universities as local institutions in the way in which a municipal government or a civic association is a local institution. It is imperative that they attend to local affairs, but they would not amount to much as universities if they attended largely to them. Universities are intellectual institutions, and intellectual activities have their objects everywhere in the world and beyond the world of time and space. A university which taught only about local phenomena, which did research only on local phenomena, and which did not transcend the vague but real boundaries of locality would not be a respectable university.

Any single university is a local intellectual community—even if a very loosely articulated one—within a local community which is also a municipal community. A university is also a local intellectual community within an intellectual community made up of many universities, each of which is also a local institution and each of which is at some distance from the others. Within each university and among universities there are also subcommunities made up of scientists and scholars, each of whom "belongs," more or less wittingly, to one or several of those subcommunities of disciplines and intellectual interests. These are communities and subcommunities of common problems, common bodies of knowledge, common rules of observation, interpretation, and assessment and also a common collective consciousness of vague boundaries, both concentric and overlapping. These latter intellectual communities of substance and method are more far-flung than those of the local communities, both the local municipal community and the local intellectual community.

The truths of science and scholarship are put forward by their possessors and discoverers with aspirations to universal validity. Only a very small part of what is studied, taught, and investigated in a university refers to the locality, and when it does it refers to it "in the categories of eternity," as an instance of a more general class of phenomena which exist beyond the local community.

There are numerous lines of dependence between locality and university which are so important for both; these local connections do not belie or weaken the aspiration and the sense of obligation of a university to enunciate truths of universal validity and to illuminate phenomena which are far outside the boundaries of the local community. Locality and universality are not antithetical. The aspiration of a university toward universality and its partial attainment owes much to locality, and it does so in many ways. A local society can affect a university positively and negatively. It can affect not only the ecological conditions in which a university works but also its internal life for good and for ill. The University of Chicago is an interesting instance of how a local society has affected the growth of a university, the claim of which to respect in the world of learning and in the world at large rests in its fruitful participation in the world intellectual community. No less interesting but even more defiant to analysis is the contribution which the University of Chicago has made to the city of Chicago.

Put in other words, what has the University of Chicago got from its existence in Chicago, and what has Chicago got from having the university in its midst?

I will try to answer these questions very simply and preliminarily. From the society of Chicago the University of Chicago has received financial support. It has received not only financial support but moral support as well. It has received the deference of the lay public which has been proud to count the University of Chicago as belonging to it. It has received the stimulation of living in the midst of a harsh, animated, and demanding environment. What Chicago has received from the university is an even more difficult problem. More important than anything else, Chicago has benefited by the "possession" of a serious university. A city without an important university is an incomplete city. Chicago has benefited by the pride, intermittently felt by its inhabitants, in an institution which bears its name and is famous in the world. It has gained many particular services. It has had the collaboration of teachers of the university in activities which at least some parts of Chicago society have thought to be desirable.

"The University of Chicago" was originally the name given in the charter issued by the state of Illinois in 1857 to an institution founded on the initiative of local businessmen, Stephen A. Douglas, and a Baptist clergyman. It ceased its activities in 1886. There was also a Baptist Union Theological Seminary which had been chartered by the state of Illinois in 1865. Both had a wider than local patronage. Both also had severe financial difficulties, but the seminary, unlike the university, survived. There was a period of about half a decade in which there was no institution which was called the University of Chicago, although the charter which provided for the use of that name remained legally valid. There was, however, a desire on the part of leading Baptists, especially but not only in the Midwest, that the work of training Baptist ministers should be taken up again in the Midwest and that it should be done in the setting of a university of the highest intellectual standard. Frederick T. Gates, a former Baptist clergyman in Minneapolis, who later became adviser to John D. Rockefeller, Sr., on his philanthropic activities, was strongly of the opinion that such an institution should be established. It was probably in response to the growth of biblical studies, primarily in Germany in the nineteenth century, that American Baptists thought that a conventional training in a specialized traditional theological college was insufficient if the Baptist denomination was to hold its own in the modern world. Modern learning enjoyed among pious laymen such prestige that a denomination whose clergy was without it would be deemed to have forfeited its right to respect in the world.

The residual trustees of the old University of Chicago, who were legally the custodians of the charter, concurred to the establishment of the new University of Chicago. This happened only after long preparation by Thomas W. Goodspeed and Gates in discussions with local notables and especially in discussions with Rockefeller. From the very beginning of the history of the first University of Chicago, local businessmen and local clergymen had been very active. The businessmen were usually members of the Baptist denomination. (Stephen Douglas, who drafted the first charter, stipulated in it that all the trustees of the old university must be Baptists. This was carried over to the new University of Chicago, although it was emphasized that such restrictions must not apply to the appointment of teachers and the admission of students.) No governmental authority, encouragement, or financial support whatsoever was sought—neither federal, state, nor municipal—and no advisers from existing universities were appointed or consulted. Action was initiated and taken on the basis that there was a necessity for an outstanding university under Baptist sponsorship in the Midwest; it was to be a university which, among other things, would train Baptist clergymen in the setting of the entire cosmos of knowledge being explored by modern universities. (The Baptist Union Theological Seminary became the school of divinity of the University of Chicago in 1892.)

Why it had to be a university, teaching and investigating over the whole range of subjects appropriate to a university, is a question that is not easy to answer in any definitive manner. It is plausible to assert that these businessmen, lawyers, physicians, publishers, and clergymen believed that the local and the religious communities of which they were members would, in a fundamental, almost metaphysical sense, be incomplete if each did not have a modern university. For persons with civic spirit in modern societies a university appears to be indispensable for all sorts of practical and impractical reasons. Most of the practical reasons could be satisfied by technical colleges and professional schools. But a university is different from these. It can, of course, perform practical services and train the persons who can perform such services, but there is something in it which is regarded by those who seek to promote it as of intrinsic value. A city without a university is to some extent stunted or incomplete.

Once the decision was made to restart the University of Chicago, the next task was to find a person to become the head of the institution. The first choice from the very beginning was William Rainey Harper, who had been teaching Hebrew, Assyrian, Arabic, Aramaic, and Syriac at Yale since 1886 but had formerly taught at the Baptist Union Theological Seminary in Morgan Park and had been invited, unsuccessfully, to accept the presidency of the failing old University of Chicago. He was a biblical scholar; he was abreast of German scholarship; he was known for his high intellectual qualities, his limitless energy, his idealistic ambition, and his piety.

When Harper was invited to become the president of the new University of Chicago, he had before him the examples of Johns Hopkins University and Clark University, both of which had been inspired by the achievements of the German universities of the first three-quarters of the nineteenth century; later he also had his own observations of German universities of the last decade of the century. Once he was appointed to the presidency but before the university opened for its first classes, Harper went to Germany to gain a more intimate knowledge of German universities and to purchase books for the library.

Harper did not think only of divinity. He thought of the whole range of humanistic, social science, and natural scientific subjects which were required if an institution of higher education were to be a university in the sense that a German university was a university.

Despite his seven years as a professor at the Baptist Union Theological Seminary, Harper had little contact with the life of Chicago; he knew little of its businessmen. Born in Ohio and educated in Michigan, he was, however, free from eastern prejudice and snobbery about businessmen or about a city already renowned for its industrial and commercial enterprise and located at a nodal point in the national system of transportation.

Harper knew that a university, if it was to do serious work in scholarship, had to have a library. Except for the Newberry Library, which had been founded only a few years earlier, there was no scholarly library in Chicago on which the scholars of the university could draw. Harper was determined to establish such a library, being rightly convinced that he could not persuade serious scholars to join the University of Chicago if there were no library there. The Newberry library was the only fairly large scholarly collection in Chicago, but it was about ten miles from the university and could not be used regularly without great inconvenience. Harper therefore purchased the entire stock of Calvary, a great Berlin dealer in second-hand and antiquarian academic books. The number of books was variously estimated at from one hundred thousand to two hundred and fifty thousand. (In the end only sixty thousand books and forty thousand dissertations have been definitively confirmed as having come from Calvary.) Under Harper, within a few years the University of Chicago library contained a quarter of a million books.

The acquisition of this great collection, which immediately placed the University of Chicago library among the leading scholarly libraries of the country, was achieved against the obstacle that the meager funds available for the university—six hundred thousand dollars provided by Rockefeller and four hundred thousand dollars gathered from local businessmen—could not be used for such a purchase. Yet it was the businessmen of Chicago who banded together behind the intrepid Harper. The success of Harper's daring enterprise was made possible only through his desperate enlistment of the support of a group of businessmen of Chicago. As was to be the case over the rest of his career as president of the university, Harper had moved to the realization of his plans before there was money to pay for them. He did so with a justified confidence that his wealthy patrons would understand what he was trying to do. Practically none of his local patrons or Rockefeller had any experience of a university of the sort Harper wished to create, but they had a dim notion of it. Of course, they had faith in Harper's integrity, but they probably also knew that his ideal was a good one. Twice Rockefeller's generosity provided a million dollars beyond his original gift. Without those gifts, the University of Chicago could not have been established. Those gifts, however grand they were according to the wealth and standards of that time, were insufficient. Even the third gift of one million dollars from Rockefeller was not enough without the readiness of businessmen in Chicago to contribute substantially to the wealth and income of the university.

The generosity of Martin Ryerson, Helen Culver, Mrs. Emmons Blaine,

William B. Ogden, Charles Yerkes, Julius Rosenwald, Elizabeth Kelley, Marshall Field, Mrs. Charles Hitchcock, Mrs. Frederick Haskell, Leon Mandel, Charles Hutchinson, and many others made a very great difference to the University of Chicago:

> The benefactors of the University became in very many instances its fast friends and were always ready when the need arose to repeat their gifts, so that their names appear as contributors on the books twice ten times, and in some cases thirty times more.[1]

They were joined in subsequent generations by the Regenstein and the Pritzker families, the Goldblatts, Bernard Mitchell, and many others. That relationship between the University of Chicago and the wealthy businessmen of the city continued approximately on the same pattern until well after World War II when Chicago lost its industrial preeminence in the country to the Far West, the Southwest, and to some extent to New England. Nevertheless, the gifts by no means ceased even after the economic decline of Chicago became quite marked.

Chicago businessmen endowed many professorial chairs at the University of Chicago, in subjects which promised no pecuniary benefits to their patrons or even to the branches of industry and commerce in which they had made their fortunes. From the beginning they provided funds to erect buildings. Harper Memorial Library was built mainly from gifts by Rockefeller and local businessmen; the Regenstein Library was made possible by the gifts of the Regenstein family of Chicago; the university hospitals and the medical school were all built from funds contributed by Chicago businessmen and the private philanthropic foundations which were of increasing importance by the time the University of Chicago established it own medical school.

Private philanthropic foundations had begun to function before World War I. After that war they took a position in the very front line of the patrons of the institutions of higher education. The General Education Board—a product of Rockefeller's munificence—had already been very active before the war. The University of Chicago benefited particularly from the Rockefeller Foundation and the Laura Spelman Memorial. The Rosenwald Fund, which was very generous, was the only one of the great foundations located in Chicago. Its founder had been one of the greatest local patrons of the university before the fund was created. It was housed very near the university and had a "special relationship" with it.

The contributions of the private philanthropic foundations did not displace those of private businessmen and their families in Chicago. They continued the philanthropy individually practiced by Rockefeller, but they never acquired the magnitude of his philanthropy in the flow of money to the university. Large sums were contributed in the 1920s by individuals in Chicago. Thus, the Wieboldt family, who owned a department store in Chicago, gave funds to construct a building for the teaching and study of modern languages and literatures; the Swift family provided the funds for the divinity school.

It has been asserted that the wealthy patrons of higher learning in Chicago came more frequently from the second generation rather than the first generation of wealth.[2] This might well be so, but it does not belie the fact that many wealthy persons—whether of the first or second generation—made possible the successful existence of the University of Chicago in its first quarter of a century because they believed that there should be a university of high intellectual quality in their city.

Why did these individuals and families give some of their wealth to the University of Chicago? "Class interest," expected economic benefits, and the desire of "rising professional classes" to legitimate themselves have been adduced to explain this philanthropic activity. It has also been asserted that the aim was to maintain the existing social order and to prevent revolutionary action to subvert it. Such a desire might have been operative in a few cases, but most of the objects for which large sums of money were given to the University of Chicago had practically no connection with the subversion or the conservation of the social order.

Certainly those persons who supported research in the social sciences in the University of Chicago before World War I—they were not so many— were interested in holding conflict in check or in reducing it; they favored harmony in society. Insofar as they supported the social sciences in universities, they often asserted that the reduction of conflict, prejudice, and antagonism was among the objectives to whose attainment they thought the social sciences would contribute. There was only one major sociological investigation supported by private philanthropy in the first quarter-century of the university; this was the study of *The Polish Peasant in Europe and in America.* Its senior author, W. I. Thomas, justified his research as a contribution to the reduction of conflict within the Polish immigrant community and between the Polish immigrants and the surrounding society. Nevertheless, it is fairly clear that Thomas's main objective was to understand the relationships between processes of assimilation and conflict. More pertinent for our purpose is that the donors of the funds wished to give Thomas a free hand to study the subject as he wished and to follow his intellectual bent as the spirit moved him. Similar intellectual interests presided over most of the research done at the University of Chicago; the patrons of that research did not demand anything different.

A university which teaches at the higest level and does research of similar quality cannot concentrate mainly on matters of local and practical interest. A partial exception must be made of some parts of the social sciences and a few descriptive subjects such as geology or geography for which local phenomena are appropriate for study, even though only as instances of more general patterns. Nor can a university which seeks to attain the highest levels of knowledge, general and historical, be directed preponderantly toward the satisfaction of practical interests.

When the University of Chicago was founded, the practical advantage of discovery and study was not in view except in a very vague and remote way.

There was no provision for a school of engineering, no school of agriculture, no school of law; there was not even a school of medicine—it was only after thirty-five years that the university established a medical school. The school of social service administration was brought into the university a quarter of a century after the university itself; previously it had been an independent institution. Thus, it could not be reasonably assumed that the University of Chicago was helped along its way because the businessmen who gave it their patronage wished to gain practical benefits for themselves individually, for their "social class," for their business enterprises, or for the economic system as a whole. There was certainly little articulated expectation that great practical benefits would flow to Chicago from the existence there of the university. What was expected was that it would be a university of very high quality, training, among others, highly educated Baptist clergymen. By the time the University of Chicago held its first classes, the last task was given only a secondary place.

It seems to me that the Chicago businessmen who supported the University of Chicago did so because they wished generally to promote the growth of knowledge and, no less important, because they wished to help the University of Chicago to be the kind of university Harper wanted it to be and thereby to be the kind of university which would be appropriate to the greatness of Chicago. By supporting the University of Chicago, they were contributing to the fuller realization of the urban society to which they were attached.

The University of Chicago was established and formed when the higher educational institutions of the country were growing in number, in size, and in their intellectual aspirations and accomplishments. That period was also one in which there was much contention about social and economic policy and about the proper role of government. Many of the academics, particularly social scientists, had been educated in Germany, where social scientists regarded themselves as commentators on and guides of governmental action regarding social and economic conditions. That tradition was one of those brought to the United States.

The period when the University of Chicago was taking form was also a period during which businessmen in the United States were proud and even self-righteous about their calling. They expected to be obeyed in their business firms and to be regarded with great respect everywhere else. They regarded trusteeships of universities and colleges as evidence of their probity, reliability, and soundness in judgment and decision. They regarded trusteeships as a heavy responsibility. In many cases they had very little understanding of the idea of a university; they understood little of the nature and necessity of far-reaching autonomy in academic matters. They took their trusteeships so much to heart that they regarded themselves as responsible for everything that went on in the university under their care.

The language of public contention and partisanship in the United States has long been hyperbolic and accusatory and not least in the decades preceding World War I. Academics who spoke to or wrote for the larger non-academic public tended to be almost as inclined to use strong language as were the main protagonists to this contention, namely "capital" and "labor." Members of boards of trustees, many of them businessmen, were sometimes alarmed by the attitudes expressed by academics in their public declarations. These declarations were usually hostile toward businessmen and the market economy, and they often demanded governmental intervention on behalf of the industrial working classes and farmers. There were in consequence many situations in which there were real or threatened infringements of academic freedom; *academic freedom* is taken here to refer to the right of academics to espouse a political position in public outside the course of academic duties.

In the last decade of the nineteenth century and in the first half of the twentieth there were numerous instances of dismissals of college and university teachers for their expression of collectivistic liberal or radical opinions outside their academic institutions or for membership or participation in associations that proclaimed revolutionary intentions.

The trustees of the University of Chicago, many of whom were notable financial benefactors of the university as well as successful businessmen, were exceptional in their self-restraint in such situations. It is possible, of course, that they were so impressed by the forceful character of William Rainey Harper and so persuaded by his resounding eloquence that they became pliant to his desires. They also probably felt an elevating kinship with his ideal; as local patriots they saw Chicago as elevated by it. In any case the trustees of the University of Chicago, despite assertions by critics such as Thorstein Veblen and Upton Sinclair, have an impressive history of self-restraint, for which there is ample evidence.

There is another benefit from the city of Chicago which has been enjoyed by the teachers of the University of Chicago which has little direct connection with the benefits conferred by businessmen. This is the city itself. Chicago, until recently, was unique in the world for its workaday vigor, the variety of cultures within it, its extraordinary animation and disorder, and its reputation for dramatic wars between gangsters. It was much more than that. At the one extreme it was the city Max Weber saw when he spent a short time there in about 1904. His widow summarized and then reproduced his own account of his impressions:

> Chicago, that monstrous city. Here every contrast is accentuated: Ostentatious new wealth which exhibits itself in magnificent buildings of marble and gilded bronze, neglected poverty which stares out of dirty windows or dark and dirty doorways along endless, villainous streets, the restless agitation of a population, mixed from all the races and parts of the earth, a breathless pursuit of booty, the squandering of human lives which every day places the lives of thousands unthinkingly at risk, eternal building and tearing down, streets dug up, bottomless dirt, deafening sounds made louder by their competition with each other, and over all this a thick

smoke which throws a veil over every stone and every blade of grass and only rarely allows passage to the golden blue light of the sky or the silvery brilliance of the stars.[3]

Weber himself wrote:

Chicago is one of the most incredible cities. Alongside the lake, there are some comfortable and pretty residential areas, made up mainly of stone houses built in a very heavy and boring style; directly behind them are small old cottages exactly like what we have in Heligoland. Then we come to the workers' tenements; insanely filthy streets, unpaved, or outside the residential areas, atrociously paved. In the commercial and financial areas among the skyscrapers, the streets are in a hair-raising condition. Bituminous coal is burned there, when the hot dry winds blow through the streets from the deserts of the Southwest, the city makes a phantastic impression especially when the dark-yellow sun is setting. On a clear day one can see only about three blocks away—every thing—mist, smoke, the entire lake is covered by a mountainously high cloud of violet smoke, from which little steamers suddenly appear and into which the sails of the departing vessels disappear.

Throughout all this there is an infinite desert of human beings. One travels out of the commercial and financial district through Halsted Street—I think it is 20 English miles long—into infinite distance, past buildings with Greek signs *"xenodochien"* and the others with Chinese taverns, Polish advertisements, German beer saloons—until one reaches the stockyards. As far as one can see from the clock tower of the firm of Armour and Son—nothing but cattle lowing, bleating, endless filth—in all directions—for the town goes on for miles and miles until it loses itself in the vastness of the suburbs—churches and chapels, storage elevators, smoking chimneys (every large hotel has its own elevator run on a steam engine) and houses of every kind. Most of them are small—for only two families. This is why the town is so extraordinarily far-flung; the areas of the city are distinguished from each other in degrees of cleanliness in accordance with the nationality of the residents. The devil has broken loose in the stockyards: a lost strike with great numbers of Italians and Negroes brought in as strike-breakers; shootings daily with dozens dead at both sides; a trolley car was pitched over and a dozen women were crushed because a "non-union man" was sitting in it. There were threats of the use of dynamite against the "elevated-railway" on which a car was derailed and fell into the river. Close to our hotel, a cigar dealer was killed in broad daylight, a few streets away at dusk, three Negroes robbed a trolley car—all in all, a unique flowering of culture! There is a swarming interaction of all the peoples of the human race on every street. Greeks are polishing the shoes of Yankees for 5 cents, the Germans are their waiters, the Italians do the dirtiest heavy labor. The whole powerful city, more extensive than London—resembles, except for the better residential areas, a human being with his skin removed, and in which all the physiological process can be seen going on.[4]

There was much more to Chicago than the things described by Weber. Chicago was not only abhorrent; it also aroused a powerful moral reaction.

That moral reaction strengthened the bond between the strata from which the patrons of the university and a considerable fraction of the teachers of the university came.

No other American city had grown to the extent that Chicago had grown, and none had such a large fraction of its population made up of persons not native to the city. The immigrants in New York were disproportionately in the needle trades, which was a relatively genteel industrial occupation in comparison with the iron and steel industry and meatpacking which had become the major industries of Chicago. The laborers lived in conditions of squalor and discomfort. Many of the respectable immigrants from central, southern, and eastern Europe were organized around churches and associations comprising persons from particular villages or districts in the "old country." Many others, however, and particularly their children, fell outside these bodies. Thrust into self-dependence and isolation, they lost their way.

Against the corruption and many-sided disorder and the horrors described by Weber, citizens of the upper-middle classes tried to take action, partly by influencing public opinion so that in its turn it could precipitate changes in governmental practices and institutions. There was also much activity which was not aimed at bringing about changes in governmental practices but rather at creating private institutions for the benefit of the victims of the terrible conditions of urban life and also to stimulate the voluntary activities of the victims for their own benefit. There were also movements of governmental reform in Chicago.

The reformers were businessmen, lawyers, social workers, publishers, newspapermen, and clergymen, and the wives of all of these as well. Nearly a quarter of the teachers of the University of Chicago were very active in these movements of reform during their height. The civic interests of the reformers overlapped with the civic and intellectual interests of the university teachers. Some of the latter were social scientists who were interested primarily in learning about the situations which the reformers were attempting to change; some of these social scientists were also eager to contribute directly to the improvement of those situations.

The history of the reform movements in Chicago from the time of the founding of the university until the election of President Franklin Roosevelt is intricately intertwined with the history of the university. John Dewey, James H. Tufts, George Herbert Mead, Charles Judd, and Marion Talbot were active in efforts to improve the education offered in the public schools. They sought to influence the mode of governing the schools, the training and appointment of teachers, the provision of vocational education and guidance, and nearly every other problem of elementary and secondary education. They interested themselves in the revision of the city charter and the relations between the state of Illinois and the city of Chicago, the organization of the collection of taxes, and the distribution of the taxing power. They interested themselves in labor legislation and industrial health. They interested themselves in morals, in the control if not the elimination of prostitution, venereal disease, and alcoholism. They interested themselves in the care and protection of newly arrived immigrants. They interested themselves in Negro migrants. They were especially interested in establishing a rational system of probation and parole. They interested themselves in harbors and transportation.

To all these problems they brought what they regarded as the scientific approach. From the Hull House Papers to the surveys about the conditions of life and work in and around the stockyards, they continued the tradition which had reached a high point in Charles Booth's *Survey of London Life and Labour* and which was brought into the United States in the Springfield and Pittsburgh Surveys. In these activities Sophonisba Breckenridge and Edith Abbott, both professors of social service administration at the University of Chicago following the incorporation of the Chicago School of Civics and Philanthropy into the university, were dynamos who communicated their energy throughout the reform movement. Charles Merriam, professor of political science, served on the aldermanic council for some years and in one mayoral campaign came close to election. Even Robert Park and William I. Thomas, the sociologists who were distrustful of the unrealism of reformers, were drawn into the movement, Thomas as a member of the Vice Commission of Chicago and Park as the first president of the Chicago branch of the National Urban League as well as (informal) research director of the Commission on Race Relations.

None of these myriad activities was entirely in the hands of university teachers from the University of Chicago alone or from the University of Chicago and Northwestern University together. There was an intense and relatively harmonious collaboration with other reformers who lived in Chicago and cared about it—businessmen, lawyers, physicians, social workers, journalists and publishers, and clergymen.

These jointly conducted activities made for a sense of community among the participants, most of whom were also "civic patriots," very conscious of being Chicagoans and proud of their city's importance in the world, even though they found much in it that was in great need of improvement. The teachers at the University of Chicago shared these attitudes—at least some of them did—and their pride in their city and their university was sustained by their associations with these critical but loyal civic patriots.

There have been intermittent efforts ever since antiquity to describe contemporary societies. The formation of the large urban agglomerations rendered more visible and more horrifying the "state of the poor." Social reformers, statisticians, criminologists, and others became preoccupied with the poor in the large cities. The department of sociology of the University of Chicago was established to make of the systematic observation and analysis of modern society an academic subject. *Modern society* was interpreted to mean urban society.

It took some years for the program to be put into practice. From the beginning Professor Charles H. Henderson had inspired his students to write reports on their firsthand observations of some small bit of life in Chicago. Henderson himself was not a very sophisticated investigator, but his expectations of his students helped to set a pattern which became a tradition at the university. Albion Small, the head of the department of sociology and dean of the arts and sciences, also regarded this kind of fieldwork as most important, although as a professor he never did any such research himself. Under his teaching and encouragement this new kind of sociological research slowly got under way at the University of Chicago.

Beginning in about 1908, W. I. Thomas, then a teacher in the department of sociology, became interested in the Polish immigrants in Chicago, whom he wished to investigate against the background of their earlier lives in Poland. (Thomas himself was one of the first recipients of the doctoral degree from the department of sociology at the university.) This landmark of local and international sociological research was supported by a Chicago philanthropist, Helen Culver, a notable woman of strong intellectual and civic interests and heiress to a great fortune made in Chicago. She supplied the funds for Thomas to be free from the obligations of teaching for a certain period each year for a number of years.

In 1912 Thomas succeeded in persuading a selfless seeker after an understanding of society named Robert Park to join the department at the University of Chicago. Park was an exceptionally sensitive and imaginative person of vast experience of the world and a curiosity of universal scope. Once well settled in Chicago, Park, who had once been a newspaperman in Detroit, began a series of explorations of the city of Chicago, together with his graduate students. The result was a series of monographs based on unprecedentedly intensive participant-observation, historical study, and the examination of governmental and private archival records.

Boys' gangs, family life, residential mobility, ethnic and religious communities, juvenile delinquency, divorce, suicide, the life of the wealthy, vagrants, entertainers, and the professions were among the constituents of the life of Chicago studied under Park's inspiration. Some of these works when published became established as contributions of lasting value to the academic discipline of sociology. More important for our interest is their precipitation of a sense of intimacy among University of Chicago sociologists with the city and the awareness of various strata of Chicago society that the city was under study. These studies were contributions to a more differentiated and realistic collective self-consciousness.

It was not Park alone who was active in this kind of work. Ernest Burgess, Park's younger colleague and collaborator, continued this work after Park retired in the first half of the 1930s. Burgess deepened the intimate contact with the lower strata of Chicago society while continuing the close relationship with the reformers of the upper-middle class and social workers. Burgess was interested in the family, especially in familial stability and instability, and in juvenile crime which had been associated with familial instability in the eyes of the reformers of the years before World War I. Burgess's interests and views kept alive the alliance between the university and the urban reformers of those earlier years.

Burgess went farther than the earlier partners in the alliance but along the same lines; he was an active participant in the work of the Illinois Crime Commission. His pupil John Landesco, once a student in the department of sociology, published as part of the report of the commission a monograph on the "42 gang"; it was a pioneering study of organized crime which later became famous as a sociological monograph.

Civic-spirited members of the upper strata were kept in awareness of the University of Chicago by Burgess, and they were ready to turn to him whenever they desired detached, systematic knowledge and judgment. Burgess, at the request of the Crime Commission, investigated the factors affecting success and failure in the granting of parole. Here again, although the collaboration was relatively specialized and narrow, the tradition of close relations between leading citizens and the University of Chicago was kept alive.

Burgess extended his collaboration with citizen reformers in Chicago outside the university when he took a hand in the establishment and work of the Institute for Juvenile Research. This body was a section of a larger institution, the Illinois Institute of Mental Health. Burgess placed several of his best students in sociology in a program of research at the institute into juvenile delinquency. Clifford Shaw and Henry McKay were among them. They developed further the technique of documentation created by Thomas in *The Polish Peasant,* namely the life history. A number of important books, such as *The Jack Roller* and *The Natural History of a Delinquent Career,* as well as a solid piece of work on *Delinquency Areas,* came out of the institute's program. These books were illuminating to magistrates, social workers, penologists, and penal administrators.

In the 1930s Burgess undertook a new project which required an even closer collaboration between the university and the inhabitants of the city of Chicago. The Area Project was a practical application of the results of scholarly studies of the conditions which gave rise to juvenile delinquency. Proceeding on the basis of Thomas's ideas about "social organization and disorganization," Burgess persuaded some of his graduate students to take up residence in working-class districts with high rates of delinquency and criminality. Then, with the collaboration of leading figures of the neighborhood, they fostered the formation of informal institutions which could assimilate, guide, and discipline the conduct of adolescent boys and youths so that they would be law-abiding instead of becoming delinquents and then criminals. The collaboration went so far that after World War II two of Burgess's former student collaborators became, respectively, chief warden of the Cook County Prison and sheriff of Cook County.

These were the high points of one side of sociological study of the city of Chicago. Another side was the study of the human ecology of Chicago developed by Park and Burgess in a series of studies of the residential location and the social institutions of ethnic groups such as Italians, Poles, Jews, and Negroes, and of the location of industrial and commercial activities in specialized zones within the city and its suburbs. The study of *A Century of Urban Land Values,* by Homer Hoyt, particularly in the central business district, brought the University of Chicago into a connection with businessmen in a way quite different from the relationship between benefactor and beneficiary, or trustee and teacher, or civic reformer and university professor.

This relationship began to change as soon as the interests of the department of sociology changed from the study of local society toward the study of national institutions and situations. The interest in national technological trends, in the professions (without any particular local reference), in labor relations without reference to particular local industries, and in social stratification outside Chicago, and the development of the sample opinion survey as a technique of research for national surveys, meant that Chicago as an object of sociological attention receded from vision, and the once very close cognitive and social relationships between the department of sociology and the city diminished. The intimacy with the city which teachers of sociology possessed and which students acquired became greatly attenuated. It still exists, but the interest in the city is no longer the most actively pursued interest of the department.

Charles Merriam, professor of political science, had a similar intimacy with Chicago; his pupils and junior colleagues, like Park's, explored the political system in a way in which no other city had been studied. They studied the local political machines, the local civil service and public attitudes toward it, differences in the voting of the wards of Chicago, political bosses, Negro political leaders, the relations between municipal and suburban governments, and so on. The department of economics, at a time when economics was more descriptive or institutional than it has since become, studied, through the research of teachers and graduates, rates of remuneration and relations between employers and employees in particular industries in Chicago, standards of living of the poorer strata of the population of the city, the financial influence of Chicago in the Midwest, and fiscal problems of the city and the county. Such research gained the attention of employers, trade union leaders, politicians and municipal officials, social workers, and bankers. Sometimes economists were invited to serve as arbitrators in disputes about such matters as wages or conditions of work. As economics became more analytical and more interested in seeing its objects in a national and worldwide perspective, the study of economic institutions and economic activities in Chicago fell by the wayside.

The department of education of the University of Chicago has long had a very active interest in the public educational system of Chicago and has maintained cooperative relations with the authorities of the Chicago educational system not only through consultation and the instruction of teachers, prospective and currently active, but also through the performance of research. Historians at the University of Chicago have for a long time interested themselves in the history of Chicago in a wide variety of aspects. Forty years ago Bessie Pierce, a professor in the department of history, completed a history of Chicago in three large volumes, and since that time there have been numerous dissertations on the history of particular parts of Chicago society, ethnic groups, philanthropic activities of the higher strata, politicians, and political organizations.

The very productive investigation of Chicago society by the sociologists, political scientists, and to a lesser extent educationists, economists, and historians did two things for the university in its relation to the city. It gave the university an intimacy with the day-to-day life of the lower and lower-middle strata of the population which academics seldom acquire. And it extended and enriched the collective consciousness of at least a part of the university academic staff. These investigations contributed to a greater awareness of the more educated and better-off strata with the other parts of the population. It is certainly true that newspapers and fiction contributed to this enlarged, more comprehensive collective consciousness. In Chicago the process was greatly aided by the academic investigation of the city.

In the many-sided relationship between the University of Chicago and the life of the city of Chicago, there was one striking lacuna. This occurred in relation to Chicago as a literary center.

Chicago was one of the main centers of American literature in the period when the University of Chicago was ascending. While it had a very lively interchange with the upper-middle classes in the professions and in business, it had very little connection with the society of literary men and women. There is no indication of any relationship between Willa Cather or Sherwood Anderson or Theodore Dreiser and the University of Chicago or between Floyd Dell or Carl Sandburg or Maxwell Bodenheim or Ben Hecht or David Graham Philips or Edward Fuller and the University of Chicago. Nor is there any sign that *The Dial,* from 1916 onward, when it became the chief organ of "the new spirit" on life and letters, had any significant connection with the University of Chicago. Indeed, so negligible was the journal's relationship to the University of Chicago that two years after it took on its new role it left Chicago for New York. Previously, when *The Dial* was not yet an organ of the new literary and artistic culture but was a sober and seemly magazine which claimed to carry on the tradition of *The Dial* of the Cambridge transcendentalists, it had numerous contributors from the University of Chicago. These included Paul Shorey, Charles Henderson, Albion Small, and William Rainey Harper himself. In its rebirth its only connection with the university was Robert Morss Lovett, who was already connected with progressivistic thought in New York through his participation in the editorial work of *The New Republic.*

There was a sickly Bohemia at the eastern perimeter of the university quarter, but it had no connection with the University of Chicago. There was none at all with the bohemia of the near north side except for the occasional inquiries of a graduate student from the department of sociology.

The Little Review, which was a periodical no less important in modern literature than *The Dial* between the time of its founding in 1916 and its cessation in 1929, remained in Chicago only for the first two years of its life. It moved to New York at about the same time as *The Dial.* Its editor, Margaret Anderson, called herself an anarchist; she had no connections with the University of Chicago.

In contrast with this mutual indifference of the literary men and women who lived in Chicago and the University of Chicago is the sympathetic relationship of the latter with *Poetry: A Magazine of Verse*. This magazine, founded and edited by Harriet Monroe, who came from a wealthy Chicago family, was supported financially by the same section of Chicago society as contributed to the support of the University of Chicago and collaborated with the teachers of the university in various projects of social and political reform. *Poetry* was the chief organ of the greatest achievements of English and American poetry of the twentieth century. It published very early the work of T. S. Eliot, Ezra Pound, Wallace Stevens, Edgar Lee Masters, Robert Frost, and James Joyce. But it had only one contributor of note from the University of Chicago: William Vaughan Moody.

After Monroe ceased to be editor, two academics, Morton Dauwen Zabel and Henry Rago, served as editors of *Poetry*. Zabel was not a professor at the University of Chicago when he was editor; he came there only subsequently. Rago was a teacher at Chicago during his editorship. But these relationships developed rather late in the history of *Poetry*. Nevertheless, there was more sympathy between the department of English at the university and *Poetry* than there was with any of the manifestations of the new spirit in literature. This might have been more a consequence of Monroe's connection with "high society" in Chicago than of the kind of literary works she published.

The very weak ties of the University of Chicago to the literary life of Chicago help to define more precisely the relationship between the university and the city. A certain part of Chicago society and the university had in common a puritanical outlook on life. Both the society of the patrons of the university and the teachers and administrators of the university shared the belief that life was a serious matter. Despite the removal of the requirement of Baptist affiliation for the presidency and membership in the board of trustees, and regardless of church attendance or theological belief, there was more than a trace of Christian piety, both in the circles of patrons of the university and among the university teachers. Frivolity and sacrilegious attitudes were frowned upon in both circles. This strengthened the bond. But it also separated the university from the literary life of Chicago in its great period.

While the University of Chicago was being recast from a college, which it was intended to be by Rockefeller, to the university which Harper wanted it to be, the universities which would have been its two main rivals, Johns Hopkins and Clark, were in difficulties. Johns Hopkins was hamstrung financially by its obligation to keep its endowment in shares of the Baltimore and Ohio Railroad; Clark was breaking up in the conflict between its president, G. Stanley Hall, and its founder, Jonas Gilman Clark, over the issue of whether the university should concentrate on undergraduate education or on graduate training. Harvard, Yale, and Columbia were moving unsteadily and unevenly into the condition of being modern universities in the sense of assigning as much importance to research and the training of graduate students as to the education of undergraduates.

Harper went to great pains to attract the leading scholars and scientists of the country to the University of Chicago. He offered relatively large salaries to win them away from other universities; he also attempted to persuade young scholars and scientists of outstanding promise or achievement. Already by 1892 there were men who in a short time became known for originality of thought and productivity: Thomas Chamberlin, Charles O. Whitman, Albert Michelson, George E. Hale, Albion W. Small, Paul Shorey, James Tufts, Jacques Loeb, Carl D. Buck, William M. Wheeler, James Breasted, John Dewey, and Thorstein Veblen joined the university not long afterward.

Within two decades the University of Chicago established itself as one of the leading universities of the United States, and it was beginning to be appreciated as such by European universities. Albert Michelson, professor of physics at the university, was the first American to be awarded a Nobel prize in a scientific subject; this was fifteen years after the opening of the university. The second American to win the Nobel prize in physics, Robert K. Millikan, had spent his formative years as a teacher at the University of Chicago. (He was won away from Chicago by a former professor of the university, the astronomer George Hale, who had made a great name at Chicago and who became the president of the California Institute of Technology.) The third American to receive a Nobel prize in physics was also a teacher at the University of Chicago. This was Arthur H. Compton in 1927. Professors at the university soon became important in scientific organizations. Hale became very crucial in the National Academy of Sciences. Woods Hole Marine Biological Laboratory, which came to be of the greatest importance in the development of biological research in the United States, was stimulated and directed by C. O. Whitman, professor of zoology at the university. James Breasted, although not generously treated by Harper, became greatly esteemed in Egyptological circles everywhere. In the 1930s the Oriental Institute, which had been founded by Breasted and made famous by his work, was greatly strengthened by a number of very distinguished German refugees. It was one of the major centers in the world for the study of the ancient Middle East. By the 1920s and 1930s the University of Chicago was at the very forefront in the social sciences, especially in sociology, economics, and political science.

The University of Chicago has been in a paradoxical situation. No other university of worldwide eminence in intellectual and educational achievement has at the same time been so intimately linked with its local society in so many ways. It is certainly true that its financial support has not been predominantly local, but that support has probably come to a greater extent from locally resident and locally active benefactors than any other major university in the world. Columbia University has undoubtedly received a great deal of its support from local benefactors, but it is not as local a university as the University of Chicago in the sense that in New York the stratum of prospective benefactors is far larger than it is in Chicago, and the objects of their benefactions are also very much more numerous.

In Chicago the university was one of a small number of important objects of benefaction by a much smaller circle of benefactors. The University of Chicago has had for this reason a very special relationship to the city of Chicago and particularly to the plutocracy of Chicago. Each meant more to the other than was the case of Columbia in relation to New York. Harvard, Yale, Princeton, and Stanford, the other leading private universities of the United States, are again in a rather different situation from Chicago. They have depended far less on local benefaction; their local societies have been too small and not as generously respectful toward learning to become important to their respective universities.

For these reasons the University of Chicago is bound to be more sensitive to changes in the pattern of American society than other important universities which are less richly linked to their local settings. All universities in the United States as well as in Europe have become less local in the past half-century. They all depend much more on the central government of their respective countries for research funds. They have also become very dependent on the central government for the funds needed for teaching activities and the support of students. Large private philanthropic foundations, with national programs and without special relationships to the universities in the cities in which they are located, are also very important patrons of universities. The financial support provided by private individual benefactors, locally resident and locally active, has become less important in the life of American universities. But it has certainly not evaporated.

There are several reasons for this. For one thing, universities have become so much more costly that private patronage by individuals can now no longer meet the costs of the university, even to the extent that it once did. Furthermore, locally resident plutocracies are less interested in their localities than they were in earlier generations. Resident plutocracies do not have their wealth in local property and local business enterprises to the extent that they used to. They share less in the local collective consciousness since their wealth is not local.

The mode of acquisition of wealth and forms of wealth of the plutocracy are both less local. Takeovers disregard the moral claims of local institutions. Fortunes made by speculation in options trading have no particular local connection.

There have been other changes in American society which have changed the relationships between universities in large cities and the populations of those cities. The large cities of the United States are increasingly and predominantly black and Latin American in the composition of their population. These groups are recent immigrants to the cities; they are generally ill educated and live in more socially disorganized settlements than was true of the European immigrants who came to the United States between 1880 and 1912.

The European immigrants tended to be more deferential to the educated classes and were more reliant on themselves for their necessities. They were not clamorous in their demands for goods and services. They were more pervaded by the Protestant ethic—this was also true of the Roman Catholics. Their local political domination was generally not unsympathetic with universities except perhaps in Cambridge, Massachusetts, where the Irish Roman Catholics thought they were spurned and maltreated by Harvard University. In Chicago, despite the fact that some professors of the University of Chicago were very active in reform movements and were supported by the residents of the university area in their efforts to displace the incumbent local politicians and to hamstring their political organizations, the professional politicians had a respectful and at times benevolent attitude toward the university. This tradition seems to be in danger of dissipation. There is a prospect that after having lived in relative harmony for many years there will in the future be a greatly increased strain in the relations between the University of Chicago and the ruling politicians.

There is another, quite unrelated factor, which is weakening the tie between the University of Chicago and the city of Chicago. Social investigation has become more national and less local. Its mode of organization does not foster the growth of intimate knowledge in the investigation of the object studied. The University of Chicago grew up at a time when the mode of social investigation favored the growth of such intimate knowledge of the local society. This has now changed for reasons both of the method or technique of investigation and of the investigator's interest. Hence the unique cognitive bond between the social scientists of a particular university and their local society, which was especially strong in Chicago in the past, has become greatly attenuated.

These are all relatively minor matters as far as the quality of performance of a university is concerned. It is obvious that there have been great universities which have thrived without local private patronage and without extensive treatment in the local press. The important factors in the life of a university are the intellectual quality of its teachers and students, their moral concern for learning, and their respect for the tradition which they receive and their capacity to revise and enrich that tradition. Internal academic citizenship, internal arrangements, and the relationships with other universities are important. The intellectual morale of teachers and students makes a tangible difference, and there the appreciation of the laity is vital. It need not, however, be entirely a local laity; a national laity is perhaps more important nowadays in the United States, and it has long been so as far back as the ancient universities of England. Still, a laity which is near at hand and visible, generous and appreciative, is bound to remain of great value to a university.

Local philanthropy is valuable not only for the money it provides but also for the tangible confidence it shows in the university. A favorable state of opinion regarding universities in general and the particular university encourages university teachers. Local opinion is manfested not only in monetary patronage but also in friendliness and conviviality and political support. All these are necessary to strengthen and support a university against various groups and individuals who wish to hamper research or to restrict the intellectual freedom of university teachers.

The University of Chicago from the beginning has been exceptionally fortunate in its relations with the city of Chicago. The situation at present is less favorable than it was in earlier decades. Nevertheless, there is no likelihood that the society of the city of Chicago in its present form will do anything to break abruptly the ties between itself and the university which have flourished for many decades; nor is there any likelihood that the university would do so. What is much more of a danger is that the wealthy businessmen and powerful politicians will fail to nourish that image of the completeness of a city which required a great university in its midst. Aristotle said that willful negligence is one of the causes of revolution. Willful negligence can also be a cause of the ruin of cities and institutions.

NOTES

1. Thomas Wakefield Goodspeed, *A History of the University of Chicago: The First Quarter Century* (Chicago, 1916), p. 274.
2. Frederick Jaher, *The Urban Establishment* (Urbana, Ill., 1982), pp. 520–21.
3. Marianne Weber, *Max Weber: Ein Letensbild* (Tuebingen, 1926), p. 298.
4. Ibid., pp. 298–99.

13

Urban Flights: The Institute of Social Research Between Frankfurt and New York

Martin Jay

The theme of the city and the university provides a welcome opportunity to clarify an aspect of the Frankfurt School's history that has always troubled me. I refer to the vexed problem of its roots in the social and cultural conditions of its day, the link between its Critical Theory and the context which in some sense or another allowed it to emerge. As wary as I have always been of the sociology of knowledge in its more reductionist forms, I have also never felt comfortable with the school's reticence about exploring its own origins, an attitude best expressed in Theodor Adorno's remark that "a stroke of undeserved luck has kept the mental composition of some individuals not quite adjusted to the prevailing norms."[1] Even luck, deserved or not, seems to me worth trying to explain, and perhaps in the case of the Frankfurt School, looking at its relations to the cities and universities with which it was connected may provide some help. For, after all, it is not every group of intellectuals whose very name suggests both an urban and an academic link.

Even more understanding may ensue if we remember that the sobriquet "Frankfurt School" was only a late concoction of the 1960s and was never perfectly congruent with the Institute of Social Research out of which it came. The disparity between the research institute and the school of thought which emerged within its walls has, in fact, led some observers to call into question the coherence of the phenomenon as a whole. No less involved a figure than Jürgen Habermas has recently remarked that although the institute continues, "there is no longer any question of a school, and that is undoubtedly a good thing."[2]

Rather than abandoning the search for coherence because of the historical and nominal displacements of the institute and the school, it seems to me more fruitful to acknowledge the unsettled and protean nature of a cultural formation that nonetheless did retain a certain fluid identity over time. As

231

I have tried to argue in my study of Adorno, that identity may best be understood as the product of a force field of untotalized and sometimes contesting impulses that defy any harmonious integration.[3] In that work I identified several salient forces in Adorno's personal intellectual field: Hegelian Marxism, aesthetic modernism, cultural mandarinism, a certain Jewish self-awareness, and, from the point of view of the reception rather than the generation of his ideas, poststructuralism. If we add psychoanalysis and a nuanced appreciation of Max Weber's critique of rationalization, we can perhaps see the major forces operating to constitute the intellectual field of both the institute and the school, at least until the time of Habermas's introduction of several new elements from linguistics, cognitive psychology, hermeneutics, and anthropology.[4] Now, to do justice to all of the constellations of these elements during the various phases of the group's history is obviously beyond the scope of this essay. Instead, I would prefer to focus on only a few of them and explore the possibility that their interaction may in some way reflect the school's genesis in its specific urban and academic contexts.

To make these connections will perhaps be especially revealing because the members of the school themselves rarely, if ever, thought to make them themselves. In fact, with the salient exception of Walter Benjamin, himself only obliquely related to the institute, its members never directed their attention to the important role of the city in modern society.[5] Perhaps because they knew that the critique of urban life was the stock and trade of anti-modernist, protofascist ideologies—a point clearly made in Leo Lowenthal's celebrated 1937 essay on Knut Hamsun[6]—they aimed their own critique at other targets. Georg Simmel's explorations of metropolitan life or the urban sociology of the University of Chicago's Robert Park had little resonance in their work. In fact, it was not until the institute returned to Germany after the war that it participated in an empirical community study, that of the city of Darmstadt.[7] And even then its members warned against the dangers of isolating its results from a more theoretically informed analysis of society as a whole.[8] Frankfurt itself, the environment that nurtured their own work, was never an object of systematic analysis.

No less ignored during the school's earlier history was the role of the university. Perhaps because an emphasis on education was characteristic of the revisionist Marxism they scorned, it was not one of their central preoccupations. Only after their return to Frankfurt, when Horkheimer in particular was deeply involved in the reconstitution of the German higher educational system, did a Frankfurt School member seriously ponder the importance of academic issues.[9] Far more characteristic of their first Frankfurt period is the caustic remark of the young and still militant Horkheimer in his essay collection *Dämmerung* that the absorption of Marxism into the academy as a legitimate part of the curriculum was "a step toward breaking the will of the workers to fight capitalism."[10]

What makes such a charge so ironic, of course, is that the institute itself clearly did not emerge out of the working class but rather from a particular stratum of the urban educated bourgeoisie (the *Bildungsbürgertum*) in crisis. As such, it has been seen by some observers as the first instance of an elitist Western Marxism distanced from the real concerns of the masses.[11] Whether or not this is fair to the complexities of its members' development, it does correctly register the fact that the institute must be understood as much in the context of what Fritz Ringer has called "the decline of the German mandarins"[12] as in that of the working-class struggle for socialism. However, what made the institute's unique achievement possible was the specific urban and academic situation in which its particular response to that decline was enacted. To understand that situation we will have to pause and focus on certain features of the Frankfurt am Main of their youth.

The old imperial free city had been a center of international trade and finance since the Middle Ages, even if its hegemony had been challenged by the rise of Basel, Mannheim, and especially Leipzig in the eighteenth century.[13] Along with its economic prosperity went a certain political autonomy from the larger German states, which survived until its absorption into Prussia in 1866. The ill-fated parliament in the Paulskirche in 1848 reflected the city's symbolic role as a center of liberalism as well as its earlier function as the site of the Holy Roman Emperor's election and coronation. Not surprisingly, the greatest organ of German liberalism, the *Frankfurter Zeitung,* was founded in the city by Leopold Sonnemann in 1856.

Frankfurt was also distinguished by its large and relatively thriving Jewish community, which numbered some thirty thousand members during the Weimar years and was second only to Berlin's in importance. Originally protected by both the emperor and the city council, it weathered the enmity of gentile competitors and the political reverses of the post-Napoleonic era to emerge after 1848 as an integral part of the city's economic, social, and political life.[14] Although assimilation was probably as advanced as anywhere else in Germany, Frankfurt's Jews were noted for their innovative responses to the challenges of modernity. Reform, conservative, and orthodox branches of Judaism were creatively developed within its walls.[15] It was, of course, in the Frankfurt of the 1920s that the famous Freie Jüdische Lehrhaus was organized around the charismatic rabbi Nehemiah Nobel, bringing together such powerful intellectuals as Franz Rosenzweig, Martin Buber, and Ernst Simon.

Although lacking its own university until 1914,[16] Frankfurt had enjoyed a long tradition of private support for scholarly institutions, stretching back to the efforts of Dr. Johann Christian Senckenberg in the eighteenth century. When the university was founded as the amalgamation of several of these academies and institutes, it was as a so-called *Stiftungsuniversität,* funded by private contributors, often from the Jewish community, rather than by the state.[17] The philanthropist Wilhelm Merton, an assimilated Jewish director of a giant metallurgical concern, was the major benefactor. Independent of the anti-Semitic and increasingly statist university system that had long since left behind the liberal intentions of its founder Wilhelm von Humboldt,[18] the new Frankfurt University offered a radical departure in German academic life on the eve of the war. Its self-consciously modern outlook was demonstrated by its being the first German university not to have a separate theology faculty and by its express willingness to open its ranks to a broad range of students and faculty.

Before the war Merton had also funded a mercantile academy and an institute for public welfare, which have been seen as the prototype for the research institutes that were launched after 1918.[19] Included in their number was one founded in 1924 with the backing of millionaire grain merchant Hermann Weil, which chose the name Institut für Sozialforschung. This is not the place to retell the story of that founding, a task recently performed in detail by the German historian Ulrike Migdal,[20] but several points merit emphasis. First, the relative autonomy of the institute, guaranteed by Weil's largesse, was very much in the time-honored Frankfurt tradition of private, bourgeois underwriting of scholarly enterprises. Although after the war and the inflation the university itself had to call on state support to survive, Weil's continued generosity combined with his aloofness from the institute's actual work meant that it was remarkably free from political and bureaucratic pressures. Although an attenuated link with the Prussian state was forged through an arrangement that specified that the institute's director had to be a university professor, clearly something very different from a traditional academic institution was created.

The difference was manifested in several important ways. First, unlike the many seminars and institutes that proliferated during the Wilhelmian era,[21] the Institute of Social Research was not dedicated to the goal of scientific specialization and compartmentalization. Instead, it drew on the concept of totalized, integrated knowledge then recently emphasized by Georg Lukács in his influential study *History and Class Consciousness*.[22] Although the early leadership of the institute was by no means explicitly Hegelian Marxist, it nonetheless eschewed the fragmentation of knowledge characteristic of bourgeois *Wissenschaft*. Second, the institute was launched solely to foster research and without any explicit pedagogical responsibilities. This privilege meant, among other things, that the traditional mandarin function of training an educated elite designed to serve the state, a function which had become increasingly onerous during the Wilhelmian years,[23] was completely absent from the institute's agenda. That agenda, and this is the third obvious difference from normal academic institutions, included the critique and ultimate overthrow of the capitalist order.

The irony of a millionaire businessman like Hermann Weil supporting such a venture has not been lost on subsequent observers from Bertolt Brecht on.[24] Perhaps his son Felix, the disciple of Karl Korsch on whose urging the institute was created, had sugar-coated the pill by saying that it would be devoted only to the dispassionate study of the workers' movement and anti-Semitism. Perhaps, as Migdal has speculated, the senior Weil was cynically hoping for access to the Soviet grain market through the goodwill accumulated by linking his institute to the Marx-Engels Institute in Moscow. For whatever reason, the Institute of Social Research was the first unabashedly Marxist enterprise to be connected, however loosely, to a university in Germany and most likely anywhere else outside of the USSR. As such, it has led to the suspicion that the proper context in which to situate its founding is neither urban nor academic but political. One particularly wild and unsubstantiated version of this contention is Lewis Feuer's bizarre suggestion that it might well have been a Willi Münzenberg front organization that soon became a "recruiting ground . . . for the Soviet espionage service."[25]

Despite the absurdity of this particular charge, it is, of course, true that the institute was not founded in a political vacuum. Several of its earliest members did, in fact, have personal links to radical parties, most notably the KPD (German Communist Party).[26] And there was a friendly interchange with David Ryazanov's institute in Moscow, largely having to do with the preparation of the Marx-Engels Gesamtausgabe. The student nickname "Café Marx" was thus not unwarranted. And yet what is no less true and ultimately of more importance is that the institute was never institutionally linked with any faction, sect, or party on the left, nor did it hew to any single political or even theoretical line during its earliest years. In this sense the popular notion of a school, which was rarely applied to earlier groups of Marxist intellectuals,[27] along with that of a research institute, does capture an important truth about their status. Neither a traditional academic institution nor a party-oriented cadre of theoreticians, it presented something radically new in the history of leftist intellectuals.

The notion of a school implies not only detachment from practical concerns but also the presence of a guiding figure setting the program of inquiry. To the extent that such a master figure was able to emerge, and it was perhaps not until Horkheimer replaced Carl Grunberg as official director that one did,[28] the institute's constitution made it possible. For it gave the director explicitly "dictatorial" powers to organize research. According to the sociologist Helmut Dubiel, an elaborate interdisciplinary program was inaugurated by Horkheimer on the basis of Marx's model of dialectical *Forschung* and *Darstellung*, research and presentation, in which philosophy oriented and was in turn modified by social scientific investigation.[29] How closely the institute actually followed this model has been debated, but it is clear that for a long time the common approach known after Horkheimer's seminal 1937 essay as Critical Theory[30] did give the work of most institute members a shared perspective.

To understand its provenance, however, we cannot stay solely within the confines of academic or political life in the Weimar Republic. For the cultural milieu of Frankfurt itself also played a crucial role. Although not as stimulating an environment for nonacademic intellectual pursuits as prewar Munich or postwar Berlin,[31] Frankfurt could still boast a cultural atmosphere open to the most experimental currents of Weimar life. A rapid *tour d'horizon* reveals a variety of important innovations. Frankfurt, for example, was the locus for the great modernist workers' housing projects of Ernst May, the city's chief architect after 1925. Along with such contributions to interior design as Schütte-Lihotsky's famous "Frankfurt Kitchen," these monuments to socially conscious functionalism earned Frankfurt the honor of being called "the first twentieth-century city" by one recent observer.[32]

It was also in Frankfurt that the recent invention of the radio took on a new and powerful role as an experimental cultural medium.[33] The Süddeutsche Rundfunk was the third station in Germany to be established, after Berlin and Leipzig. Rather than pandering to the lowest common denominator of taste, Radio Frankfurt, as it was popularly known, often scheduled concerts of the most challenging modern music and broadcast innovative radio plays and serious lectures on a wide variety of subjects. The so-called wandering microphone of reporters such as Paul Lavan opened up perspectives on modern urban life that have been likened to the documentary films of William Ruttman, the director of the celebrated *Berlin: Symphony of a City*.[34]

It was in Frankfurt as well that the *Frankfurter Zeitung,* then under the direction of Sonnemann's grandson Heinrich Simon, allowed writers such as Siegfried Kracauer, Joseph Roth, Soma Morgenstern, and Benno Reifenberg to analyze a broad spectrum of cultural and social issues in its famous feuilleton section. The city was also home for one of the first German psychoanalytic institutes, established in 1929 under the direction of Heinrich Meng and Karl Landauer. No less characteristically innovative was the city's decision the following year to grant its highest honor, the Goethe Prize, to the still controversial Sigmund Freud.[35] If we add to this picture the Jewish renaissance sparked by the already mentioned Frankfurt Lehrhaus, we have a sense of how lively and progressive nonuniversity life could be in Weimar Frankfurt.

As a result, many members of the Institute of Social Research were able to leave their academic ghetto behind and enjoy intimate contact with an experimental and often modernist urban culture. At the Café Laumer on the corner of the Bockenheimer Landstrasse and the Brentanostrasse, they created an off-campus outpost which attracted many nonuniversity intellectuals. Years later the writer Ernst Erich Noth would remember the "Nachseminar" conducted there by the young Theodor Wiesengrund Adorno as far more stimulating than anything going on at the university itself.[36] Through friendships with Kracauer, closest in the cases of Lowenthal and Adorno, members of the institute had ties to the *Frankfurter Zeitung,* which also carried the work of a later colleague, Walter Benjamin. Also by way of personal ties, especially with Ernst Schoen, several institute figures were given access to Radio Frankfurt, where they held forth on cultural questions, including the modern music Adorno was so anxious to promote. In the early 1920s there were also important links between the Frankfurt Lehrhaus and future institute figures, most notably Lowenthal and Fromm.[37] Similar ties were forged with the Frankfurt psychoanalysts at the end of the decade. Not surprisingly, one institute member, Lowenthal, played an important role in initiating the city's decision to honor the founder of psychoanalysis in 1930.[38]

Even the institute's new building, a spare, fortresslike edifice built by Franz Röckle on the corner of the Bockenheimer Landstrasse and the Victoria Allee, bespoke a kinship with urban modernism. Posing a visual challenge to the ornately decorated villas in Frankfurt's fashionable West End, the Neue Sachlichkeit structure expressed the institute's defiance of the out-moded cultural ambiance of the Wilhelmian past. Although Horkheimer was later to criticize the spirit of the Neue Sachlichkeit in general as too techno-logically rationalist and thus complicitous with reification,[39] the institute's building was initially understood as an expression of the no-nonsense goals of a Marxist research institute dedicated to unmasking the illusory façades of bourgeois society.

If, however, the Frankfurt School's debt to the nonacademic modernist culture of their urban environment must be acknowledged, so too must its measured distance from it. As in the case of their relation to the university, most institute members maintained a certain aloofness from the urban cul-tural scene and the intellectual milieu it fostered. If one compares their status with that of friends such as Kracauer or Benjamin, who were entirely outside the academic hierarchy,[40] it is possible to see the effects of this distance. The latter were often dependent on the demands of the cultural marketplace in ways that influenced the form and substance of their work, which tended to be less systematic and more journalistic. Not surprisingly, Kracauer and Ben-jamin wrote more frequently on mass culture and urban life than institute members, and they generally did so with a more nuanced appreciation of their implications. Here the influence of Simmel's pioneering explorations of metropolitan life was clearly discernible.[41] Moreover, as demonstrated by Kracauer's 1931 essay on the economic pressure on all writers to become journalists and Benjamin's 1934 discussion of the author as producer,[42] they were far more vulnerable to the proletarianization of intellectual life than the more privileged members of the institute. The contrast is demonstrated by their differing responses to the worsening crisis of Weimar's political and cul-tural scene, which was already evident in ominous changes in the direction of the *Frankfurter Zeitung* and Radio Frankfurt in the last years of the re-public.[43] Whereas Kracauer and Benjamin had great personal and profes-sional difficulties in the 1930s, the institute was able to make provisions for an orderly escape from Germany in 1933 with virtually all of its resources, save its library, intact.

In short, the institute's relations with both the official university structure and the modernist urban subculture—and, one might add, the radical po-litical parties of the day as well—were always somewhat eccentric and mar-ginal. The phenomenon that later became known as the Frankfurt School was thus never merely a direct product of its urban or academic origins or of any organized political movement. Rather, it emerged as the dynamic nodal point of all three, suspended in the middle of a sociocultural force field without gravitating to any of its poles. Hostage to no particular defining con-text, it hovered in a kind of intellectual no-man's land. This ambiguous status, as might be expected, was even more strongly exacerbated after the flight from Frankfurt via Geneva to New York in 1934. For here the distance be-tween the institute and American university life, as well as the urban culture of its adopted city, grew more attenuated than it had been in relation to its members' preexilic German counterparts. And, of course, whatever links any of its original members may have had with political praxis in Weimar were now utterly shattered.

The institute's move to Columbia University in 1934 has recently been the occasion for a polemic launched by Lewis Feuer in the English journal *Survey*.[44] Having been a participant in the exchange that followed, I don't want to rehearse all of its unpleasantness now. I would only want to emphasize that Feuer's attempt to turn the institute members into fellow-traveling crypto-Communists who duped a naive Columbia administration into welcoming them to New York is incompatible with the complicated triangulated reality of their initial Frankfurt years. As we have seen, that story cannot be flattened out into an essentially political narrative of the kind which Feuer, with his penchant for conspiracy theories, imagines.

In New York the institute's financial self-sufficiency, maintained at least until the end of the 1930s, meant that it could enjoy the luxury of relative withdrawal from all of its originally defining contexts—academic, urban, and political. Unlike other less fortunate émigrés, its members could generally avoid the compromises forced by the exigencies of their situation. Continuing to write almost exclusively in German, confining their teaching to the occasional course in the Columbia extension program, only rarely opening the pages of their journal to American authors,[45] they managed to keep the local academic world at arm's distance. Although ties with the sociology department at Columbia were slowly developed, they were as likely to be through other refugees like Paul Lazarsfeld as through native scholars like Robert Lynd or Robert MacIver. Virtually no sympathetic connections appear to have been made with the philosophers in New York. Collaborative projects with Americans did not materialize until the 1940s and then often under nonuniversity auspices, such as the American Jewish Committee, the Jewish Labor Committee, or the Central European Section of the OSS. Although some younger American scholars, later to gain prominence, such as M. I. Finley, Alvin Gouldner, C. Wright Mills, and even Daniel Bell,[46] were influenced by their fleeting contacts with the institute, it would be impossible to call them legitimate students of a school. In short, relatively secure behind the walls of the building at 429 West 117th Street provided by Columbia, the institute remained a hidden enclave of Weimar culture in exile and not in any meaningful way a part of American academic life.

If one looks at the building itself and compares it with the one the institute left behind in Frankfurt another difference from its German days can be noted. Rather than a visual provocation to the surrounding environment, a symbol of its inhabitants' defiant modernism and innovative Marxism, the building on 117th Street was merely one of a row of similarly innocuous brownstones with pseudoclassical columns and balustrades flanking the entrance. As such, it unintentionally expressed the institute's wariness about standing out in a vulnerable way in their new surroundings. Understandably anxious about their status as exiles, often reluctant to address specifically American issues out of ignorance, unsure of their own political direction, and cautious about highlighting the radicalism of their past, they remained aloof from any oppositional intellectual movement in the 1930s and early 1940s.[47]

When Horkheimer and Adorno moved to southern California in 1941 they were absorbed almost entirely into the German exile community there. They seem to have had little to do with either the academic or urban intellectual culture of Los Angeles, such as it was in those days. In fact, as the wrenchingly painful aphorisms in Adorno's *Minima Moralia* demonstrate, their alienation from any nurturing context was never as great as during these years.[48] Only the collaboration with the Berkeley Public Opinion Study Group in the late 1940s, which led to the publication of *The Authoritarian Personality*, broke this pattern. As for those institute members who remained on the East Coast, such as Neumann, Marcuse, and Lowenthal, it was only in connection with governmental service during the war that they began sustained interactions with American intellectuals.[49]

Symptomatic of their general isolation from the nonacademic intellectual urban life of their host country is the fact that in the now rapidly proliferating histories of the most important group of American cultural figures of the 1930s and 1940s, the so-called New York intellectuals, their names are rarely to be found.[50] Although they shared many of the same leftist and modernist sympathies as writers around such journals as *The Partisan Review*, there seems to have been virtually no contact between them. Only in the incipient debate over mass culture did Americans such as Dwight MacDonald find any inspiration in Frankfurt School ideas before the war's end.[51] It was not until well after the institute's return to Germany that an American oppositional culture, and then an oppositional political movement, began to recover the work done by the institute during its exile.[52]

It was, of course, only during the second Frankfurt period of the institute, begun when Horkheimer, Pollock, and Adorno returned for good in the early 1950s, that its isolation from its academic, urban, and ultimately political contexts was undone. Now for really the first time, the Frankfurt School, as it soon became known, was no longer relatively marginalized. Lured back by some of the same officials who had blithely presided over the dissolution of the institute's unrescued property during the Nazi era,[53] its leaders were feted as honored links with the Weimar past. Horkheimer was elected rector of the University of Frankfurt in 1951 and reelected the following year. He wrote and lectured on matters of educational policy and gave frequent interviews to the press on a wide variety of timely subjects.[54] The columns of the Frankfurt newspapers and the airwaves of its radio station were open to him and Adorno, who overcame their animosity to the mass media in a self-conscious effort to influence public opinion. Even the new institute building, to return to an indicator we have examined previously, bespoke a certain fit with postwar Frankfurt. Although it was similar to the Neue Sachlichkeit structure of the 1920s, it was now perfectly in accord with the International Style architecture then rising on the ruins of the bombed-out inner city. Thus, while it would certainly be overstated to say that the institute leadership had made its peace with the modern world, it was palpably less estranged from it than during either its first Frankfurt era or its exile in America.

Ironically, however, in a short time the new public for the institute's work become increasingly curious about the ideas formulated during those earlier periods. And much to the discomfort of Horkheimer in particular, it insisted on applying them to contemporary problems. Although this is not the place to analyze the Frankfurt School's complicated relationship to the German New Left, it should be noted that it was largely the ideas generated before that reception began which earned the school its reputation. It is thus appropriate to return in conclusion to the question posed earlier, of the relationship between Critical Theory and the institute's academic and urban environments during its most creative and formative years, the years before it found its audience. Can we, in other words, make sense of the force field of its intellectual impulses by situating them in their generative contexts?

The most important of those forces, it bears repeating, were Hegelian Marxism, cultural mandarinism, aesthetic modernism, Jewish self-awareness, psychoanalysis, Weberian rationalization theory, and poststructuralism. The last of these, as mentioned earlier, makes sense only from the point of view of the school's reception rather than its genesis and so cannot be meaningfully linked to the contexts we have described, even if we want to emphasize, as some commentators have recently done, the links between Jewish hermeneutic traditions and poststructuralist thought.[55] What of the others? Although a renewed interest in Hegel can be discerned in the 1920s in certain university circles,[56] Hegelian Marxism was clearly a product of the politically generated reconceptualization of Marxist theory begun by Lukács and Korsch outside the academy. During the Grünberg years the institute itself was not really beholden to a Hegelian Marxist methodology, even if, as we have seen, its program was aimed at overcoming the fragmentation of bourgeois *Wissenschaft*. Moreover, insofar as one of the chief implications of the recovery of the Hegelian dimension in Marxism was the unity of theory and practice, to the extent that the institute was a nonpolitical research enterprise, its specific institutional framework was at odds with the lessons of Lukács and Korsch.

And yet in one sense we might find a link between the Hegelian Marxist component of Critical Theory, which was especially evident in the 1930s, and the institute's peculiar academic status. By stressing the difference between appearance and essence and splitting the empirical class consciousnss of the working class from its ascribed or objective class consciousness, Hegelian Marxism opened up the possibility of a vanguard speaking for the class it claimed to represent. In the case of Leninists such as Lukács and, at least for a while, Korsch, that role was played by the Communist party. For the institute members who were not able to accept that solution, it was perhaps possible to see small groups of intellectuals fulfilling a similar function. That is, without fooling themselves into thinking they were substitutes for the revolutionary meta-subject promised by Hegelian Marxism, they could at least consider themselves the temporary repositories of its totalistic epistemological vantage point. The insulated and protected quality of the institute, especially acute during its American exile, might therefore have helped sustain the assumption that the Frankfurt School, unsullied by the political and commercial compromises forced on most intellectuals, was the spokesman for the totality. Although this was a fragile hope, for reasons I want to explore shortly, it might at least be explicable in terms of the institute's peculiar academic status.

Similarly, the residues of cultural mandarinism in Critical Theory, its suspicion of technological, instrumental rationality, and its almost visceral distaste for mass culture might be explained in part by its exponents' attenuated links with the *Bildungsbürgertum* and the university system. The elitism, which Frankfurt School members often accepted as a valid description of their position, was thus not merely a function of the vanguardist implications of Hegelian Marxism; it also reflected their roots in a hierarchical academic structure. Acknowledging this possibility, however, must not blind us to the complicated relationship they had to that structure mentioned earlier. As a research institute in a privately initiated university, they were able to avoid the obligation of bureaucratic service to the state or the need to train its future leaders. Thus, they were never simply mandarins conservatively resisting challenges to the hegemony of their status group. Even though they adopted much of the pathos of Weber's theory of rationalization as an iron cage limiting the prospects of modernization, they never gave up the hope for an alternative future based on the realization of substantive reason denied by the more pessimistic mandarins.

Their refusal to follow the mandarin lesson of despair was motivated not only by their Marxist inclinations but also by their general sympathy for the creative impulses that we have seen were so prevalent in their urban environment. The messianic hopes evident in the Jewish renaissance stimulated by the Frankfurt Lehrhaus were expressed in various forms and with different degrees of intensity in the work of such institute figures as Fromm, Lowenthal, Benjamin, and Adorno.[57] So, too, the introduction of psychoanalytic themes in their work was facilitated by the hospitable climate Frankfurt provided for Freud's ideas. And finally the aesthetic modernism of Frankfurt, "the first twentieth-century city," found a ready echo in their defense of avant-garde art, even if more of the esoteric than exoteric kind represented by the Neue Sachlichkeit.[58]

Their preference for esoteric rather than exoteric modernism, the art of Schoenberg, Kafka, and Beckett rather than that of, say, the Surrealists, suggests one final observation about the institute's relation to its urban environment. As Carl Schorske has noted, the ideal of the burgher city as an ethical community had informed the neohumanism of German idealists such as Fichte.[59] Often serving as an antidote to the competing image of the modern industrial city as an inhuman locus of alienation and vice, this model emphasized the possibility of reconstituting the civic virtue of the ancient polis or Renaissance city-state. Now, although the Frankfurt of the early twentieth century may have approached this ideal in some modest respects, in the context of a national culture and polity as fragmented as that of Weimar Germany it was clear that no genuinely ethical community could arise on an urban level alone. The institute's members, with their penchant for totalistic explanations of social problems, never entertained the possibility that a renovated city life alone would make much difference. In addition, it might be speculated that the Hellenic ideal of the virtuous polis held little attraction for them because of their attenuated debt to a Hebraic tradition, whose nostalgia, as George Steiner has recently reminded us, was more for a garden than for a city.[60] Reconciliation with nature was, in fact, one of their most ardently held goals, even if they were suspicious of attempts by *völkisch* and, one might add, Zionist thinkers to realize it without radical social change. Still, reinforced by the traditional Marxist expectation that communism would mean the overcoming of the very distinction between urban and rural,[61] they never speculated on the renewal of civic virtue as an end in itself.

When the institute fled to New York this dream must have seemed even more remote from reality. Not only were they foreigners precariously situated in an alien environment, but that environment itself was even farther removed from the ethical community ideal than Frankfurt had been. For, as Thomas Bender has argued,[62] American cities like New York had long since ceased to support a vibrant metropolitan culture, and anything approaching a common intellectual life had been replaced by one-sided professional elites incapable of talking to each other about larger problems outside their fields of knowledge. An interdisciplinary school of thinkers, whose institute was founded precisely to combat the specialization of apparently incommensurable discourses, could therefore only withdraw into itself under these circumstances. As a result their holistic inclinations, already called into question by the failure of a universal class to appear, were further damaged by the lack of a true public during their years of exile. Not surprisingly, their very faith in the concept of totality itself was severely shaken by the time they returned to Germany after the war. As I have tried to demonstrate elsewhere,[63] their disillusionment was a central episode in the general loss of confidence in totality evident in the history of Western Marxism as a whole.

Even when they returned to a Frankfurt now anxious to listen to them, they were far too chastened by their American experience to hold out any hope for the dream of a city of virtue. Thus, as mentioned earlier, when they did engage in a community analysis it was always with the warning that the proper unit of analysis could not be merely urban, for the manipulation of popular consciousness by a national and even international culture industry precluded any purely urban renaissance of civic virtue. Although Jürgen Habermas later introduced the notion of a resurrected public sphere as a possible antidote to the totally manipulated consciousness of one-dimensional society, he did so with a definite awareness of the limits of the older model. "The question that is brought to mind," he recently argued in an essay on "Modern and Postmodern Architecture," is whether the actual *notion* of the city has not itself been superseded. As a comprehensible habitat, the city could at one time be architecturally designed and mentally represented. The social functions of urban life, political and economic, private and public, the assignments of cultural and religious representation, of work, habitation, recreation, and celebration could be *translated* into use-purposes, into functions of temporarily regulated use of designed spaces. However, by the nineteenth century at the latest, the city became the intersection point of a *different kind* of functional relationship. It was embedded in abstract systems, which could no longer be captured aesthetically in an intelligible presence. . . . The urban agglomerations have outgrown the old concept of the city that people so cherish.[64]

What lessons, if any, can be gleaned from this overview of the Frankfurt School's relations to the universities and cities with which it was associated during its history? First, it is evident that no straightforward, reductive contextual analysis can provide a satisfactory key to explain the content of the school's ideas. They were simply too many overlapping contexts—academic, urban, political, and we might have added personal and intellectual as well— to allow us to ground Critical Theory or the institute's work in any one master context. Dominick LaCapra's contention in his powerful critique of just such an attempt, Janik and Toulmin's *Wittgenstein's Vienna,* is thus borne out by our analysis: no single-minded contextual account can arrogate to itself the power to saturate texts or constellations of ideas with one essential meaning.[65] Indeed, if the point made earlier with reference to the importance of the poststructuralist reception of Critical Theory is taken seriously, no generative contextualism, however open to multiple dimensions, can exhaust the meaning of a cultural phenomenon for us. Its force field necessarily includes both generative and receptive moments, and it is an illusion to think we can completely bracket out the latter in the hope of merely recapturing the former.

But some limited explanatory power must nonetheless be granted to contextual analysis, if we remember the need to respect the untotalizability of multiple contexts. In the case of the Frankfurt School it is precisely the dynamic intersection and overlapping of discrete contexts that provided the stimulus to their work. Their constellation of tensely interrelated ideas, themselves never achieving a perfectly harmonious synthesis, was thus enabled by the irreducibly plural and often conflicting contexts of their lives. Without pretending that a perfect correspondence can be established between specific stars in their intellectual constellation and specific contexts out of which they emerged, I hope it has been demonstrated that some attention to their academic and urban situations helps demystify the claim of "a stroke of undeserved luck" as an explanation for their critical acumen.

One final observation is in order. It is a staple of intellectual history to credit social or cultural marginality with stimulating heterodox or innovative ideas. In the case we have been examining it would be more accurate to speak of multiple marginalities, most notably those we have identified in rela-

244 THE MODERN UNIVERSITY AND THE MODERN CITY

tion to their academic, urban, and political contexts, and conceptualize the school and the institute as nodal points (close but not precisely identical) of their intersection. Or rather in the manner of a Venn diagram we can see them occupying the overlapping area where three eccentric circles come together. The Frankfurt School's favorite phrase *nicht mitmachen,* not playing along, thus comes to mean more than just a defiance of conventionality and political camp–following; it defines instead the very conditions of their intellectual productivity, and perhaps not theirs alone.

NOTES

1. Theodor W. Adorno, *Negative Dialectics,* trans. E. B. Ashton (New York, 1973), p. 41.

2. Jürgen Habermas, *Autonomy and Solidarity: Interviews,* ed. Peter Dews (London, 1986), p. 49.

3. Martin Jay, *Adorno* (Cambridge, Mass., 1984).

4. Habermas's departures from classical Critical Theory have sometimes seemed sufficiently extensive to justify excluding him from the Frankfurt School in favor of his own "Starnberg School." See, for example, Gerhard Brandt, "Ansichten kritischer Sozialforschung 1930–1980," *Leviathan* 4 (1981): 25. For an overview of the continuities that nonetheless exist, see David Held, *Introduction to Critical Theory: Horkheimer to Habermas* (Berkeley, Calif., 1980).

5. Benjamin's work on the modern metropolis included studies of Berlin, Paris, Marseilles, Moscow, and Naples. See, in particular, *Charles Baudelaire: A Lyric Poet in the Era of High Capitalism,* trans. Harry Zohn (London, 1973); *Reflections: Essays, Aphorisms, Autobiographical Writings,* ed. Peter Demetz, trans. Edmund Jephcott (New York, 1978); and *One-Way Street and Other Writings,* trans. Edmund Jephcott and Kingsley Shorter (London, 1979). For a discussion of his work on the city, see Henning Günther, *Walter Benjamin: Zwischen Marxismus und Theologie* (Olten, 1973), p. 165f.

6. Leo Lowenthal, *Literature and the Image of Man: Studies of the European Drama and Novel, 1600–1900* (Boston, 1957), p. 212.

7. *Gemeindestudie des Instituts für sozialwissenschaftliche Forschung* (Darmstadt, 1952–54). The institute consulted on this project. See the discussion of it in *Aspects of Sociology* by the Frankfurt Institute of Social Research, preface by Max Horkheimer and Theodor W. Adorno, trans. John Viertel (Boston, 1972), p. 156.

8. *Aspects of Sociology,* p. 163.

9. Max Horkheimer, *Gesammelte Schriften, Band 8: Vorträge und Aufzeichnungen 1949–1973,* ed. Gunzelin Schmid-Noerr (Frankfurt, 1985), pp. 361–453. See also the draft of his 1944/45 memorandum for an international academy to be set up after the war, which is included in volume 12 of the *Gesammelte Schriften: Nachgelassene Schriften,* ed. Gunzelin Schmid-Noerr (Frankfurt, 1985). It was also Horkheimer who urged Paul Kluke to write his massive history of the University of Frankfurt; see Kluke, *Die Stiftungsuniversität Frankfurt am Main 1914–1932* (Frankfurt, 1972), p. 7.

10. Max Horkheimer, *Dawn and Decline: Notes 1926–1931 and 1950–1969,* trans. Michael Shaw (New York, 1978), p. 75.

11. Perry Anderson, *Considerations on Western Marxism* (London, 1976), p. 32.

12. Fritz Ringer, *The Decline of the German Mandarins: The German Academic Community 1890–1933* (Cambridge, Mass., 1969).

13. For a history of Frankfurt in the early modern period, see Gerald Lyman Soliday, *A Community in Conflict: Frankfurt Society in the Seventeenth and Early Eighteenth Centuries* (Hanover, N.H., 1974). For an account of Frankfurt in the 1920s, see Madlen Lorei and Richard Kirn, *Frankfurt und die goldenen Zwanziger Jahre* (Frankfurt, 1966).

14. The classic study of Frankfurt Jewry is Isidor Kracauer, *Geschichte der Juden in Frankfurt,* 2 vols. (Frankfurt, 1927). He was Siegfried Kracauer's uncle.

15. The assimilation of Frankfurt Jews is shown by the comparatively low attendance figures for high holy day services in the 1920s: Breslau, 58 percent; Berlin, 49 percent; Frankfurt, 41 percent. Cited in Donald L. Niewyk, *The Jews in Weimar Germany* (Baton Rouge, La., 1980), p. 102. For a discussion of the creative response of Frankfurt Jews to modernization, see Jakob J. Petuchowski, "Frankfurt Jewry—A Model of Transition to Modernity," *Leo Baeck Yearbook* 29 (1984): 405–17.

16. It was one of three new universities begun in this era, along with Hamburg and Cologne founded in 1919. In 1932 it was officially named the Johann-Wolfgang-Goethe Universität in honor of Frankfurt's most illustrious citizen. For a full account, see Kluke, *Die Stiftungsuniversität.*

17. Ibid., p. 53.

18. For a history of the decline of the German university from its Humboldtian origins, see Charles E. McClelland, *State, Society and University in Germany 1700–1914* (Cambridge, 1980); for a study of the growing nationalism of students, see Konrad Jarausch, *Students, Society, and Politics in Imperial Germany* (Princeton, N.J., 1982).

19. Wolfgang Schivelbusch, *Intellektuellendämmerung: Zur Lage der Frankfurter Intelligenz in den zwanziger Jahren* (Frankfurt, 1982), p. 18.

20. Ulrike Migdal, *Die Frühgeschichte des Frankfurter Instituts für Sozialforschung* (Frankfurt, 1981).

21. McClelland, *State, Society and University,* p. 280.

22. For a discussion of the institute's holistic inclinations, see Martin Jay, *Marxism and Totality: The Adventures of a Concept from Lukács to Habermas* (Berkeley, Calif., 1984); for a different account of Horkheimer's initial attitude toward totality, see Michiel Korthals, "Die kritische Gesellschaftstheorie des frühen Horkheimer: Misverständnisse über das Verhältnis von Horkheimer, Lukács und dem Positivismus," *Zeitschrift für Soziologie* 14 (August 1985).

23. McClelland, *State, Society and University,* chap. 8.

24. Brecht's scornful discussion of the relationship appeared in his account of "Tui-intellectuals" in his *Arbeitsjournal,* ed. Werner Hecht (Frankfurt, 1973), Vol. I.

25. Lewis S. Feuer, "The Frankfurt Marxists and the Columbia Liberals," *Survey* 25 (Summer 1980): 167. Richard Sorge was later unmasked as a Soviet spy, but there is no evidence that he recruited anyone else during his brief institute stay.

26. Among the acknowledged Communists were Karl August Wittfogel, Julien Gumperz, and Richard Sorge. There has also been some speculation about the possible allegiance of others in the early 1920s. See Migdal, *Die Früggeschichte*, p. 102.

27. One important precedent was the so-called Austro-Marxist School, which has been compared to the Frankfurt School in the introduction to *Austro-Marxism*, ed. Tom Bottomore and Patrick Goode (Oxford, 1978), p. 2. The link between the two was Carl Grünberg, who was known as the father of Austro-Marxism before he became the institute's director. Another possible model was the "Kathedersozialisten" (socialists of the lectern) around the Verein für Sozialpolitik during the Wilhelmian era, although they were very distant from Marxism per se.

28. Migdal claims that the institute during its Grünberg phase was more open, pluralistic, and undogmatic than later. She chides my account in *The Dialectical Imagination: The Frankfurt School and the Institute of Social Research, 1923–1950* (Boston, 1973), for failing to appreciate the virtues of Grünberg's lack of firm direction. She refers to a letter by Oscar Swede to Max Eastman (which she inadvertently attributes to "Oscar Eastman"), which I cite to make the case that Grünberg's leadership was dogmatic, but she doesn't really refute it. For a critique of her tendentious comparison between the two eras, see the review of her book by Hauke Brunkhorst in *Soziologische Revue* 3 (1982): 81.

29. Helmut Dubiel, *Theory and Politics: Studies in the Development of Critical Theory*, trans. Benjamin Gregg (Cambridge, Mass., 1985).

30. Max Horkheimer, "Traditional and Critical Theory," *Critical Theory: Selected Essays*, trans. Matthew J. O'Connell et al. (New York, 1972).

31. On prewar Munich, see Peter Jelavich, *Munich and Theatrical Modernism: Politics, Playwriting, and Performance, 1890–1914* (Cambridge, Mass., 1985). Berlin's preeminence during the Weimar Republic is discussed in such works as Peter Gay, *Weimar Culture: The Outsider as Insider* (New York, 1968); John Willett, *Art and Politics in the Weimar Period: The New Sobriety 1917–1933* (New York, 1978); and Henry Pachter, *Weimar Etudes* (New York, 1982).

32. Willett, *Art and Politics*, p. 124. For more on Frankfurt's role in modern architecture, see Kenneth Frampton, *Modern Architecture: A Critical History* (London, 1985), p. 136; and Barbara Miller Lane, "Architects in Power: Politics and Ideology in the Work of Ernst May and Albert Speer," *Journal of Interdisciplinary History* 17 (Summer 1986): 283–310.

33. For an account of Radio Frankfurt, see Schivelbusch, *Intellektuellendämmerung*, chap. 4.

34. Ibid., p. 68.

35. For an account of the decision to grant the prize, see ibid., chap. 5.

36. Ernst Erich Noth, *Errinerungen eines Deutschen* (Hamburg, 1971), p. 194.

37. For discussions of the Lehrhaus, see Schivelbusch, *Intellektuellendämmerung*, chap. 2; Nahum N. Glatzer, "The Frankfort [sic] Lehrhaus," *Leo Baeck Yearbook* I (1956); and Erich Ahrens, "Reminiscences of the Men of the Frankfurt Lehrhaus," *Leo Baeck Yearbook* 19 (1974).

38. Leo Lowenthal, *Mitmachen wollte ich nie: Ein autobiographisches Gespräch mit Helmut Dubiel* (Frankfurt, 1980), p. 61.

39. Max Horkheimer, *Dawn and Decline*, p. 96.

40. Benjamin's failure to earn his *Habilitation* in 1925 ended his hopes for an academic career. Kracauer, thwarted by a speech defect, never pursued a teaching career, moving instead from architecture to journalism.

41. For a comparison of Simmel with Kracauer and Benjamin, see David Frisby, *Fragments of Modernity: Theories of Modernity in the Work of Simmel, Kracauer and Benjamin* (Cambridge, Mass., 1986).

42. Siegfried Kracauer, "Uber den Schriftsteller," *Die Neue Rundschau* 42 (June 1931): 860–62; Walter Benjamin, "The Author as Producer," in *Reflections*. The proletarianization of intellectual life had been a preoccupation of German thinkers well before this period. See the discussion of it among the Naturalists of the 1890s in Peter Jelavich, "Popular Dimensions of Modernist Elite Culture: The Case of Theater in Fin-de-Siècle Munich," in Dominick LaCapra and Steven L. Kaplan, eds., *Modern European Intellectual History: Reappraisals and New Perspectives* (Ithaca, N.Y., 1982), p. 230.

43. Schivelbusch, *Intellektuellendämmerung,* chaps. 3, 4.

44. See n. 25. The debate continued in *Survey,* 26 (Spring 1982) with Martin Jay, "Misrepresentations of the Frankfurt School"; G. L. Ulmen, "Heresy? Yes! Conspiracy? No!"; and Lewis S. Feuer, "The Social Role of the Frankfurt Marxists."

45. During the seven years the *Zeitschrift für Sozialforschung* was published while the institute was in New York, only eight major articles were contributed by Americans; three of those were in the 1941 volume. As for the audience at the institute's extension course lectures, a letter of Karl Korsch written on 20 November 1938 may be indicative of its limits. Horkheimer's "circle of hearers," Korsch wrote, "was for the most part the people in the Institute and their wives, and a few confused students." See Douglas Kellner, ed., *Karl Korsch: Revolutionary Theory* (Austin, Texas, 1977), p. 284.

46. The connections between Finley, Gouldner, and Mills and the institute have been widely remarked in the literature on them and in their own writings. Bell's has been ignored. His essay, "The Grass Roots of American Jew Hatred," *Jewish Frontier* 11 (June 1944): 15–20, clearly displays the influence of the institute's work on anti-Semitism. Although Bell has become very critical of the Frankfurt School, he circulated this piece forty years later among his friends to warn against the neoconservative weakness for populist bedfellows.

47. See, for example, the account of an unsuccessful meeting with the editors of *The Marxist Quarterly* during the late 1930s by Sidney Hook, "The Institute for Social Research—Addendum," *Survey* 25 (1980): 177–78. Korsch's letter, cited in n. 45, also testifies to the institute's aloofness from political movements of any kind.

48. Theodor W. Adorno, *Minima Moralia: Reflections from Damaged Life,* trans. E. F. N. Jephcott (London, 1974). For an account of the general problems of life in southern California for refugees, see Anthony Heilbut, *Exiled in Paradise: German Refugee Artists and Intellectuals in America from the 1930s to the Present* (New York, 1983).

49. For an account of the institute's contribution to the war effort, see Alfons Söllner, ed., *Zur Archäologie der Demokratie in Deutschland,* 2 vols. (Frankfurt, 1986). Marcuse's role is discussed in Bary Kātz, *Herbert Marcuse and the Art of Liberation* (London, 1982), p. 109.

50. See, for example, Mark Krupnick, *Lionel Trilling and the Fate of Cultural Criticism* (Evanston, Ill., 1986), in which potential comparisons with Adorno are mentioned several times (e.g., p. 110). See also James Gilbert, *Writers and Partisans: A History of Literary Radicals in America* (New York, 1968); William Barrett, *The Truants: Adventures among the Intellectuals* (Garden City, N.Y.,

1982); Irving Howe, *A Margin of Hope: An Intellectual Autobiography* (San Diego, Calif., 1982). Only the last of these mentions a Frankfurt School figure, Marcuse, and then with contempt (p. 309).

51. Dwight MacDonald, "A Theory of Popular Culture," *Politics* 1 (February 1944).

52. On the reception of the Frankfurt School, see Martin Jay, "The Frankfurt School in Exile" and "Adorno and America," in *Permanent Exiles: Essays on the Intellectual Migration from Germany to America* (New York, 1985).

53. Schivelbusch, *Intellektuellendämmerung*, chap. 6.

54. Horkheimer's lectures, interviews, and articles of these years are available in the seventh and eighth volumes of his *Gesammelte Schriften*.

55. Susan Handelman, *The Slayers of Moses: The Emergence of Rabbinic Interpretation in Modern Literary Theory* (Albany, N.Y., 1982).

56. Heinrich Levy, *Die Hegel-Renaissance in der Deutschen Philosophie* (Charlottenburg, 1927).

57. In *Mitmachen wollte ich nie* (p. 156), Lowenthal has recently acknowledged the importance of his experience at the Lehrhaus for the development of Critical Theory.

58. For a good account of the Frankfurt School position on aesthetic modernism, see Eugene Lunn, *Marxism and Modernism: An Historical Study of Lukács, Brecht, Benjamin and Adorno* (Berkeley, Calif., 1982).

59. Carl E. Schorske, "The Idea of the City in European Thought: Voltaire to Spengler," in Oscar Handlin and John Burchard, eds., *The Historian and the City* (Cambridge, Mass., 1963), p. 60.

60. George Steiner, "The City under Attack," *Salmagundi* 24 (Fall 1973): 3–18.

61. The most important expression of this hope appeared in Friedrich Engels, "The Housing Question," in Karl Marx and Friedrich Engels, *Selected Works*, 2 vols. (Moscow, 1958), I, 546–635. See also Raymond Williams, *The Country and the City* (New York, 1973).

62. Thomas Bender, "The Cultures of Intellectual Life: The City and the Professions," in John Higham and Paul K. Conklin, eds., *New Directions in American Intellectual History* (Baltimore, Md., 1979), p. 63.

63. Martin Jay, *Marxism and Totality*.

64. Jürgen Habermas, "Modern and Postmodern Architecture," in John Forester, ed., *Critical Theory and Public Life* (Cambridge, Mass., 1985), pp. 326–27.

65. Dominick LaCapra, *Rethinking Intellectual History: Texts, Contexts, Language* (Ithaca, N.Y., 1983), chap. 3.

14

Two NYUs and "The Obligation of Universities to the Social Order" in the Great Depression

David A. Hollinger

The Great Depression happened along at a uniquely inconvenient time for the leaders of New York University. NYU was ready to celebrate its centennial, but what kind of celebration would be appropriate amid "the disorganized economic conditions" and the "widespread personal distress and social confusion" to which NYU leaders professed to be sensitive in 1932? Finding the right tone for a big party at the Waldorf-Astoria was far from the most serious challenge created for academic administrators by the Great Depression, but the problem was a delicate one. The solution, explained the editor of the published proceedings of the centennial event, was to select a theme suitably responsive to the times: "The Obligation of Universities to the Social Order." NYU would project no ivory-tower aloofness, no complacent self-absorption; it would instead confront society head-on. It would convene at the Waldorf an ambitious conference on the social responsibilities of higher education.[1]

Twentieth-century universities routinely produce symposiums, but this gathering of American intellectual leaders invites our attention for several reasons, only one of which is the opportunity to watch a private university struggle for a credible public identity amid the pressures of the Great Depression. The conference was a peculiar episode in the history of urban consciousness: NYU was, of course, an urban university, but it chose in 1932 to address its social obligations in terms that ignored this fact. In both the content and the style of its centennial celebrations NYU revealed a wish to escape altogether from its own city of New York and from urban life in general. This wish was not countered even by the dozens of guests who were invited to address the social obligations of the academy. That there might be a distinctly urban role for universities was not even suggested by these speakers and discussants, whose obliviousness toward this notion—such a

249

commonplace today—shows how easily NYU found contemporary support for its exercise in urban denial. NYU's invited guests also cooperated with the university's use of the conference to associate itself with a conservative, genteel culture increasingly on the defensive in metropolitan New York. The NYU centennial conference was a modest event but one at which the unique circumstances of a single university served to focus the commitments and uncertainties of a larger, depression-shocked community.

That larger community was represented at the conference by a number of individuals whose contemporary prominence lends historical significance to the event. These included the era's most influential political scientist (Charles E. Merriam of Chicago), economist (Wesley Clair Mitchell of Columbia), aend political commentator (Walter Lippmann of the *New York Herald Tribune*), as well as the presidents of Yale (James Rowland Angell), Columbia (Nicholas Murray Butler), Union Theological Seminary (Henry Sloane Coffin), and the University of California (Robert Gordon Sproul). The heads of the Brookings Institution (Harold G. Moulton) and the Carnegie Institution (John C. Merriam) also participated, as did George Soule of *The New Republic,* Harvard's eminent philosopher William Ernest Hocking, and the financial titan Thomas W. Lamont of J. P. Morgan and Company. The conferees also included a handful of European dignitaries, a few government officials, the then-famous poet Alfred Noyes, and several dozen garden-variety college presidents, deans, and senior professors.

The wish to escape the city was expressed not only through shared silence about cities. NYU Chancellor Elmer Ellsworth Brown revealed at the outset his own social ideal: he opened the conference by urging his guests to think of themselves as, in effect, farmers. Universities are like "pioneer institutions," Brown explained, ready to help one another perform tasks of construction. In "olden days" when "a barn was to be built, or a new roadway made through the forest" amid "widely scattered plantations," neighbors assembled to carry out the task cooperatively.[2] Brown's casual characterization of the conferees as rural barn raisers was perhaps a trivial aside, but it betrayed with unconscious eloquence an ambivalence about modernity that Chancellor Brown brought to the task of organizing the conference. This ambivalence served to structure the discourse in terms that make the event all the more revealing an indicator of the convictions and uncertainties of NYU's loquacious guests. Before scrutinizing Brown and his university any further, however, we must attend to the intellectual content of the conference itself.

The conference was dominated by two strong intellectual impulses. One was resoundingly technocratic and progressive: social engineering, it was said, must go forward immediately, casting aside anachronistic traditions. Our universities must more aggressively supply experts and trained statesmen to bring society's chaos under rational and, it is hoped, democratic control. The social sciences must be developed more extensively, following in the footsteps of the physical and biological sciences, in order to produce more and better knowledge, and this social-scientific knowledge must be put to concrete use by managers and officials at all levels of social organization.[3] This first, technocratic-progressive impulse was, of course, merely an intensification of the talk about social engineering that social scientists and many other liberal intellectuals had been promoting off and on throughout the 1920s and the progressive era.[4]

The second impulse was adamantly religious and conservative: "spiritual values," it was said, must be reaffirmed lest a godless materialism take over the world. Our universities must teach the insights of traditional religious faith in order that the new generation not lose sight of the "eternal verities" wrongly rejected by inexplicably popular "pseudo-intellectuals" and cynics claiming to speak on behalf of modern science and modern art. What we really need on our campuses are mechanisms that will somehow recreate the atmosphere that we once maintained with chapel services.[5] This second, religious-conservative impulse possessed an even longer ancestry than technocratic-progressivism, but it was by 1932 self-consciously reactionary, protesting against contemporary culture in the name of a timeless wisdom ostensibly institutionalized the most perfectly in the old-fashioned Christian college of nineteenth-century America.[6] Yet a sign of its strength was the praise the *New York Times* offered for the conference's emphasis on "spiritual values."[7]

The technocratic-progressive impulse was predictably the most evident in two symposiums addressed to the relation of universities to the political and economic changes then being experienced by industrial societies. Merriam, Soule, Mitchell, Moulton, Lamont, and their colleagues in both social science and business management sang the praises of scientific method, of intelligence, of knowledge, of expertise, of planning; indeed, these terms were virtually incanted amid expressions of the faith that social science would soon produce its Newtons and its Pasteurs. But the social obligation of the university in this connection was not simply to sustain research; universities were to train experts for government and industry and to educate citizens so that the electorate could respond appropriately to the initiatives of the experts. The Depression simply made these services of the university all the more imperative. A very large proportion of the conference was given over to the earnest articulation in persistently general terms of this familiar technocratic-progressive vision.

The elitist character of this vision was expressed by Sir Arthur Salter, a British delegate and longtime official of the League of Nations. What we need, Salter explained, is "a few central leaders, a great number of specialized and local leaders, and an informed and receptive public opinion."[8] What could be more "technocratic" than this notion of informed public opinion as ideally "receptive" rather than an as the proper, ultimate agent of political change? Many of the conferees understood that such ideas stood in tension with classical "democratic" ideology. None renounced democracy by name, but many referred guardedly to the "experiments" in centralized planning being carried out by Mussolini and Stalin. Even Charles E. Merriam, the most persistent and self-conscious of democracy's defenders at the conference, spoke in a realistic idiom about "propaganda" and "mass manipulation." But Merriam believed that such techniques as used by democratic leaders in conjunction with an aggressive program of "civic education" would consolidate a polity based on knowledge, not arbitrary will. "The heart of modern power," he insisted, "is not brutality but intelligence and organization for the purpose of putting that intelligence into effective operation."[9]

It was fitting that Merriam's address, the conference's most pointed and carefully formulated expression of faith in the political efficacy of knowledge and education, should end with an impassioned vindication of science as a broad, cultural ideal. "I have seen the red tide flowing down the streets of Moscow," he testified, and in Berlin "the 100,000 shouting 'Heil, Hitler' with shining faces." But here at home, "Who will supply the great idealisms that sweep men's souls from time to time and stir their hearts?" Merriam's answer was highly cognitive. He called his audience to look to "science," and he charged the university with the mission of spreading a sympathetic understanding of science as "not a cold figure of stone" but an agent of "life and light."[10]

Merriam's peroration was but one of a number of signs that the technocratic-progressives at the NYU conference were in possession of a rudimentary program for *culture*. Yet the conference provided an altogether separate symposium for cultural issues, and in it Merriam's secular-liberal ideas were not voiced. The cultural symposium, entitled "The University and Spiritual Values," was a religious-conservative monolith to which we will turn in a moment. Amid the political and economic talk and in Lippmann's address at the conference's final banquet there was heard a plea for a culture organized around the scientific enterprise. Education was to foster a critical attitude, a capacity for discerning judgment, a disposition to base one's beliefs on evidence, a willingness to consider new ideas, a commitment to look empirical realities in the face, and a suspicion of partisanship. If modern society was to be increasingly dependent on knowledge, then the citizens of that society needed themselves to be knowers, to be comfortable with what the conferees again and again called the spirit of science. When they spoke in this vein the conferees quite clearly hoped for the spreading throughout society of a distinctly cognitive ethic, a cluster of commitments to such classically "scientific" ideals as objectivity, rationality, disinterestedness, and veracity; and they saw the university as an agency of the spreading of such a cognitive, scientific ethic.[11] The type of mind an ideal university ought to produce, suggested NYU economist Walter E. Spahr, was the mind of Francis Bacon: discursive, discerning, searching, patient, experimental, skeptical, and independent.[12]

The explicit cultural program advanced in the "spiritual values" symposium was far indeed from Francis Bacon and the Enlightenment, far from John Dewey and the ethic of science, and far from the implicit, if not illicit, cultural program hinted at by the technocratic-progressives at other symposiums within the conference. The constant theme was not the potential of scientific culture but the inability of science to provide any culture at all and the imperative to make universities more like churches. "One of the most essential functions . . . of the university today," said Aurelia H. Reinhardt, the president of Mills College, is the opportunity it can provide "for group worship."[13]

Although Union's Coffin projected a nondefensive attitude toward the modern, scientific intellect and directed prophetic religion instead against the values of "main street," his colleagues were less troubled by commercial culture than by the encroachments of science on the sphere of old-time religion.[14] Speaker after speaker protested that the secular trend had gone too far, that the commendable idea of academic autonomy had been taken so far that our colleges and universities were losing their religious roots. Philosophy, one speaker suggested, ought to be taught only by positive believers, never by a skeptic.[15] The mode celebrated the most consistently was not knowledge but inspiration. The president of Lafayette College, Lewis, declared that more "than any other influences of the university," the one most beneficial "to the social order" was probably the inspiration provided by the paintings and statues past which a student walks while going to and from class.[16]

The antagonism toward science and secularism manifest in the religious-conservative impulse was most cogently expressed in the biblical phrase one speaker attributed to a sincere university student confronted with academic life: "They have taken away the Lord . . . and we know not where they have laid Him." The phrase was picked up and quoted by other speakers, just as Salter's words about "leaders" and a "receptive public" were quoted repeatedly. If Salter voiced the political consensus of the conference, this plaintive cry of the spiritually searching undergraduate voiced the consensus of the cultural symposium. The speaker who introduced this anxiety about the missing Jesus Christ was the poet Alfred Noyes, author of "The Highwayman" and other popular, neo-Romantic works of verse. Noyes was introduced as one who had wisely recognized the limitations of "scientific philosophy" and who saw to "those deeper things which we call religion."[17]

Noyes's speech was decidedly the most polemical and contentious in the entire conference. It condemned materialists in philosophy and science, agnostics in religion, and modernists in the arts. Although the failure to keep science in its place was annoying enough to Noyes, nothing was more anathema to him than modernist literature. The "pseudo-intellectuals" who wrote and celebrated such literature too often mocked and discredited the structure of religious belief which has so long energized, stabilized, and unified "the civilized world." These modernists, complained Noyes, have taken away "our dogmas, creeds, and traditions." The young, Noyes continued, are being "robbed of their birthright in Christendom by the jaded cynicism" of irresponsible men of letters, and their allies in philosophy who exalt mere knowledge over religious insight. As if to counter the demystifying tendencies of the age, Noyes quoted at some length from his own mystical verse about nature and nature's God:

> There's many a proud wizard in Araby and Egypt
> Can read the silver writings of the stars as they run;
> . . . But I know a Wizardry can take a buried acorn
> And whisper forests out of it, to tower against the sun.[18]

The frank mystifications of the religious-conservative impulse are all the more noticeable since historians remember the year 1932 for so many efforts at demystification made around that time, especially in New York City. About two weeks after the conference a young professor at Union Theological Seminary published *Moral Man and Immoral Society*. In that famous attack on protestant idealism Reinhold Niebuhr offered a largely materialist explanation of and a revolutionary solution for the problems of the Depression. Almost simultaneous with the conference there appeared another legendary work of 1932, by two young professors from Columbia, Adolph Berle and Gardner Means: *The Modern Corporation and Private Property*, the most influential deflation of capitalist ideology published in the United States during the 1930s. Six weeks before the conference there appeared the notorious manifesto *Culture and Crisis*, in which a host of intellectuals, mostly New Yorkers, announced that the established culture was serving to obfuscate a corrupt capitalist system. The signers of this manifesto, including Edmund Wilson, John Dos Passos, Malcolm Cowley, James Rorty, Lincoln Steffens, Sherwood Anderson, and Sidney Hook, declared their support for the communist candidates in the election of 1932.[19]

These enterprises of polemical demystification may help to place the "spiritual values" symposium in bold relief, but for this effect one need not look beyond the conference itself. The very titles assigned to the several symposiums by conference organizers carried the implication that politics and the economy are subject to change, but culture is not. "The University and Governmental Changes" and "The University and Economic Changes" were juxtaposed not to "The University and Cultural Changes" but to "The University and Spiritual Values."

The emphasis on timeless, "spiritual" values was fully consistent with the mission Chancellor Brown had been pursuing during his two decades as head of NYU. That mission, as described respectfully in the NYU Centennial History published in 1933 by NYU historian Theodore Francis Jones, was to "spiritualize the machine created by an earlier age."[20] Jones did not make any connection between Brown and George Santayana's concept of the "genteel tradition," but it is an apt coincidence for our purposes that exactly during the summer Brown had taken office as chancellor of NYU in 1911 Santayana was delivering at Berkeley his sardonic lecture on the idealistic academic culture of the United States. No doubt historians have made too much of Santayana's invidious contrast: a cloyingly wholesome, flaccid, narrowly Protestant idealism mocked by the vigor and authenticity of an aggressive, earthy, modern civilization. This contrast has long since become a cliché, but its terms do speak very directly to what was going on at NYU in 1932, especially to the obvious use of "spiritual values" to keep the polyglot, contingent cultural life of the metropolis at a distance. Santayana identified urban life as the concentration of everything with which the genteel tradition was not prepared to cope: "the American Will inhabits the sky-scraper," he said, while the American intellect continues to reside in a colonial mansion.[21]

NYU leaders sometimes celebrated the colonial mansion as the ideal setting for a university. The NYU campus in the Bronx, "University Heights," was praised by the dean of its principal unit, University College of Arts and Pure Science, as a form of country life: "a retired hill-top," "quiet" and "secluded." There was explicit talk of "walling in" this campus in order to "shut out the city." The history of "the Heights" throughout the 1910s and 1920s had been, according to historian Jones, largely an effort to protect this stately cloister "from the overwhelming forces of the new city."[22]

By far the most disturbing of these urban forces were, of course, immigrant Jews. As more and more Jewish students had sought and gained entry into the "retired hill-top" during the 1910s, NYU leaders worried that this institution would be overrun by "aliens."[23] Such worries were common to many universities of the northeastern United States during the 1920s.[24] The "problem," as it was termed at the time, was more acute for New York City institutions as a result of the high concentration of immigrant Jews in that city. Alumni and student groups at "the Heights" were sometimes stridently anti-Semitic. Jewish organizations were systematically discriminated against in campus life, especially during World War I and the subsequent Red Scare, when East European Jewish immigrants were linked in the popular mind with bolshevism. In 1919, shortly after undergraduate leaders had formally petitioned Chancellor Brown to limit Jewish enrollment to 20 percent, NYU introduced into its admission procedures "a personal and psychological examination." Although Brown denied publicly that this test was designed to enable NYU to more easily reject Jewish applicants, the nature of the examination itself and the private correspondence surrounding it leave no doubt whatsoever as to its purpose.[25] And it worked, at least for a few years: Jewish enrollment at the Bronx campus dropped during the early and mid-1920s from nearly 50 percent to less than 30 percent.

This infamous test was still in use in 1932, although Jones speculated that it might soon be dropped because the problem to which it was addressed had been dealt with at the source: immigration from eastern Europe had been restricted.[26] No one had more reason to feel triumphant about this restriction than Brown's chief aide in the matter of the conference and editor of the published proceedings, NYU sociologist Henry Pratt Fairchild. During the debates over immigration restriction in the 1920s Fairchild had proven to be one of the most intellectually able and influential nativists in the United States. His greatest claim to fame was his book of 1926, *The Melting Pot Mistake*. At the time of the centennial celebration itself, Fairchild had just finished his term as president of the American Eugenics Society.[27] Although Fairchild's own editorial comments in *The Obligation of Universities to the Social Order* did not address eugenicist issues, his prominent involvement in the centennial is a reminder of the nativist heritage brought to the centennial by NYU leadership.

Yet during the same thirteen years since NYU had formally institution-alized admissions discrimination against Jews on the Bronx campus, NYU had been developing an antithetical response to New York City and to immi-grant Jews which renders all the more striking the centennial conference's studied aloofness from urban life. Beginning in 1919 NYU developed its downtown Washington Square facilities to meet the educational needs of exactly those New York City young people who would not or could not attend college outside the city yet were prevented by cost or discrimination from attending Columbia or the Bronx campus of NYU. Only the City College of New York served this constituency on a large scale before the de-velopment of NYU's Washington Square College. While this venture in self-consciously urban education appealed to NYU leadership in part as a sur-vival measure—a way to pick up revenue from an expanding and imperfectly addressed educational market—it soon generated a certain pride in its own mission.[28] Nowhere was this pride more evident than in the person of its dean, Percy Buell Munn, during the four years immediately prior to the cen-tennial.

Dean Munn's frank enthusiasm for Washington Square's service to urban Jews is worth dwelling on because it prefigures NYU's subsequent forthright acceptance of an urban mission and because it helps to identify voices silenced, in effect, by Brown's design of the events of 1932. Munn exalted the city as a setting for education with the same intensity that other NYU deans held forth on the virtues of cloistered hilltops and regular chapel. While his colleagues treated the city as culturally unnatural, as a menace to true cul-ture, Munn steadfastly defended it as filled with "natural cultural opportuni-ties" and as a "laboratory." While Jewish students had no difficulty gauging the limits of their welcome at the Bronx campus, they were similarly quick to understand the eagerness of this wealthy Mayflower descendant—Munn traced his lineage to William Bradford himself—to see that they got a good education. Toward this end Munn devoted not only his pedagogic and admin-istrative energies but money from his private inheritance as well. The per-sonal correspondence between Washington Square students and the patrician Munn now fills twenty-eight substantial folders in the NYU archives.[29]

The friendly interaction between Munn and Jewish students is of some historical significance: it was an episode in the emergence of an ethnically diverse, cosmopolitan, largely urban intelligentsia in the United States.[30] Such episodes are easy to overlook amid today's proper eagerness to confront honestly the anti-Semitism and snobbish exclusivity we now find so striking when we scrutinize the era between about 1910 and World War II. Yet it was during these same years that there took place—especially in New York City—a historic transformation in the ethnic foundation of American intellectual life: intellectuals of East European Jewish origin did make their way into the academic and literary professions and, in so doing, altered the culture of these professions in secular, cosmopolitan directions. If this de-Christianization did not become fully visible until the 1950s, when so many of its leading agents became prominent writers and professors, the basic steps in the transformation were made earlier, when the careers of these Jewish writers and professors were begun. The beginnings of these careers, in turn, depended in part on measures of support—small from our perspective today but substantial in their context—offered by established intellectuals of Protestant Anglo-Saxon stock. Randolph Bourne and Justice Oliver Wendell Holmes, Jr., are among the most famous of these "old WASPs" who celebrated and helped to sponsor the enlivening of American intellectual life by immigrant Jews and their offspring.[31] In the company of these influential WASP Semitophiles belongs NYU's Dean Munn.

If Munn represents the coming of a "new" NYU—the institution that has now developed from Washington Square College into the proudly urban, ethnically diverse university that celebrates Munn's memory and finds it natural to convene a conference on "universities and cities"—the centennial celebrations of 1932 were a studied affirmation of an "old" NYU.[32] A few months before the centennial celebrations Munn left NYU to join the English department at Harvard University. His perspective on urban education was detailed in the chapter on Washington Square College that he wrote for Jones's centennial history,[33] but Brown's conference proceeded as though Munn and his Washington Square skyscraper never existed. The official culture of NYU as displayed at the centennial celebrations remained that of the colonial mansion in the Bronx.[34]

How different the conference would have looked had the cultural symposium been a forum for the articulation and defense of the liberal-secular program so obviously consistent with the technocratic-progressive impulse. Where was John Dewey? If the technocratic-progressive impulse had a philosopher, one ready to state what might be the cultural dimensions of technocratic-progressivism, such a philosopher was, of course, Dewey himself. And Dewey was close at hand, uptown at Columbia University. But Dewey was not involved in the NYU conference.[35] Other secular-liberal philosophers were easy to find in New York but seem not to have been invited. Prominent among these were Morris R. Cohen of CCNY, Horace Kallen of the New School for Social Research, and NYU's own Sidney Hook, who, although still very young, had already become a prominent controversialist in the intellectual life of New York City.[36]

Brown seems to have wanted something very different from Deweyite secular liberalism, whether emanating from Dewey himself—a lapsed Protestant—or from Dewey's Jewish as well as gentile followers in New York City academia. The first indication in the archival sources of Brown's intentions concerning the cultural segment of the conference is Brown's decision to turn this whole segment over to John C. Merriam, president of the Carnegie Institution of Washington and elder brother of the Chicago political scientist

Charles E. Merriam, one of the conference's leading technocratic-progressives. This sibling connection played little role in the conference, but Brown approached Charles Merriam only after obtaining John Merriam's commitment to participate.[37] John Merriam, then aged sixty-three, was a paleontologist of some note and a journeyman convocation speaker specializing in inspirational talks on vaguely scientific themes.[38] We are left to guess just how calculating was Brown's decision to involve John Merriam in the conference. In the earliest relevant written correspondence between the two men they refer to a prior agreement—first reached by telephone, or at a 15 January luncheon at the Century Club—that "spiritual values and the university" should be the topic of the symposium over which John Merriam was to preside.[39] Although Brown and his staff left copious records of the centennial, they left very little of what a historian would now most like to have: a record of the grounds on which they asked certain individuals and not others to participate in the conference.[40] One thing we do not have to guess about is the degree of enthusiasm Brown felt toward John Merriam's approach. Brown allowed Merriam to invite whomever he wished to hold forth on "spiritual values." Thus, Brown managed to keep his conference free of "scientific," classically "New York" philosophers such as Dewey and Cohen, who were always eager for an opportunity to criticize the genteel tradition.

That Brown himself bears major responsibility for the character of the conference is rendered more plausible by what may be the earliest surviving planning document for the centennial celebration. "Tentative Suggestions relating to the Centennial Celebration of New York University" was apparently written by Vice-President Harold O. Voorhis or a member of his staff. This memorandum offers, as its very first proposal, the theme of NYU as an "exponent of the City of New York." The "central features of the celebration should be three convocations" addressed to higher education: first as "a concern of the City," second as a concern of "the Nation," and third as a "world concern."[41] How the conference was transformed from this into what actually took place is now lost in Brown's private conversations with John Merriam and perhaps Yale's James Rowland Angell, whom Brown consulted frequently while planning the conference.

Whatever may have been Brown's designs, the religious-conservatives and the technocratic-progressives remained remarkably oblivious to one another throughout the conference. Fairchild hinted in his editorial afterword that he, at least, was troubled by the failure of the conference's two major intellectual directions to connect up with one another. "How," Fairchild asked, are "spiritual values" to be related to "specialized scientific expertise"? Fairchild did not pretend to have an answer to this question. He merely raised it as an afterthought, an example of an issue not resolved by the conference[42]—not even formulated, it would have been more accurate to say. Yet the conference did contain one setting in which one might expect to find this issue formulated and addressed: a fourth symposium, on the "Aims and Province of the University Today." Here technocratic-progressivism might actually confront religious-conservativism. But at this symposium, organized for Brown by Angell, very little was heard of the religious-conservative impulse.[43]

Technocratic progressivism was on the defensive at this fourth symposium, but against an antiutilitarian disposition whose spokesmen did not directly challenge the liberal-secular orientation of the technocratic progressives. Might applied social science and the training of experts and professionals diminish the university's commitment to basic research and to liberal arts education? Was the obligation of universities to the social order proudly nonutilitarian, simply to search for truth, and to share it with the world, especially with students, or was this obligation broader, requiring schools of engineering and business? Cardinal Newman figured prominently in these debates, but not as the champion of religion; he was quoted rather as a defender of a nonutilitarian ideal of higher education. Many of the symposiasts regarded themselves as bold iconoclasts for finding the educational ideals of Newman too narrow. President Angell, playing the role of liberal innovator, declared in a spirit of great magnanimity that engineering was not necessarily incompatible with intellectual excellence.[44]

The symposium on the aims and province of the university was the liveliest, frankest, most spontaneous within the entire conference, yet the upshot was easily predictable: universities ought to be pluralistic communities, striving for excellence in the three classic modes of the American university—research, teaching, and service. What cultural talk there was paralleled that of the political and economic symposiums. A life of discerning inquiry was said to be of great moral worth. Einstein was quoted to the effect that civilization depended on its moral forces, and Sir James Irvine of St. Andrews University, Scotland, offered the ethic of science as exactly such a force. Cosmopolitanism was endorsed against the claims of provincial traditions.[45]

The failure of Charles Merriam and other proponents of "scientific culture" to challenge the religious-conservatives on the floor is at first glance the most surprising feature of the discourse of the conference, but this lack of contentiousness has a certain logic. They were the guests, after all, of Chancellor Brown, whose center of cultural gravity was no secret. And in the absence of more argumentative champions of secular liberalism such as Dewey and Cohen, the obvious leader of that persuasion was Charles Merriam, younger brother of the man who presided over and dominated the conference's conservative-religious element. The Merriams, moreover, were on friendly terms with each other. Indeed, Charles Merriam had emulated his older sibling since childhood and continued to rely on John Merriam's influence in support of his various projects.[46]

The live-and-let-live attitude of the technocratic progressives toward the religious-conservatives was consistent, moreover, with the tone of most of the conference, which was an exceedingly circumspect affair. It avoided all mention of the presidential election of two weeks before, was guarded in its response to the crisis of the Depression, remained altogether aloof from New York City, proved to be conventional in the issues it framed, and was fastidious in its concern for propriety.[47] Brown's summary of the conference reduced it to a list of fifteen platitudes.[48] Fairchild was somewhat more bold. In his afterword to *The Obligation of Universities to the Social Order* Fairchild observed that the conference really did not provide much guidance for how universities should deal with the future.

Fairchild also offered his own piece of social analysis which, had it been prominent on the agenda of the conference itself, might have made the affair more exciting than it had been. "In the era that is dawning," he suggested, "in every department and interest of life, the producer's philosophy must be supplanted by a consumer's philosophy." In the realm of knowledge, for example, the point would be not so much to get more of it but to make more active and extensive application of the knowledge already in existence.[49] Here was the basis for a real argument within the technocratic-progressive tradition: should the priority be the finding of new truth or the more effective application and distribution of what we now know? Do our society's problems endure and worsen because we lack knowledge or because we have failed to reform our economic practices and political institutions in the light of truths we now possess? At ultimate issue, of course, was the extent to which society's health could be achieved and maintained through purely cognitive as opposed to overtly political measures. A number of speakers and discussants did express what can be fairly characterized as conflicting dispositions on this issue. Soule, Salter, Charles Merriam, and University of Minnesota president Lotus Delta Coffman placed more emphasis on "application," while Irvine and University of Pennsylvania economist Thomas Gates came down more strongly on the side of "pure" science.[50] Yet none formulated Fairchild's issue as sharply as Fairchild did, and none made an argument as sustained as his for one side or the other. A *New York Times* article claimed the conferees had significantly differed over the question of seeking new truths as opposed to applying existing truths, but the *Times*—prompted, one wonders, by Fairchild himself?—made the conflict seem more vivid than it had been.[51]

It would be a mistake, however, to exaggerate Fairchild's departure from the circumspect tone of the NYU centennial conference. He concluded *The Obligation of Universities to the Social Order* very generally: "there must be," on the part of universities, "an immediate and practical translation" of the ideal of social obligation "into terms of direct social guidance and participation."[52] Fairchild was perhaps the most confident and forthright of the conference's technocratic progressives, but even he did not claim to know just how the university ought to involve itself in what he took to be a new consumer's world.

The intellectual perimeter within which the technocratic progressives operated at the NYU conference was no doubt determined more by the genuine uncertainties of the conferees than by an excess of deference for their religious-conservative host. These uncertainties were felt, moreover, by people who had been accustomed to living with religious conservativism in American universities throughout the 1920s and the Progressive Era. As late as 1932 virtually all American universities continued to display in their official culture a strong religious-conservative aspect. This was true even of the great secular, state universities: Robert Gordon Sproul of the University of California explicitly identified himself with Noyes, Hocking, and John Merriam, and concluded his own contribution to the "spiritual values" symposium by quoting his Victorian predecessor, Benjamin Ide Wheeler. Wheeler's call to "nobler living" might have been grist for Santayana's irreverence, but according to Sproul, Wheeler had said it all. There was no need to revise or even to reformulate inherited ideas about universities and values.[53] Hence Chancellor Brown's technocratic-progressive guests were not thrown so sharply on the defensive as one might suppose. They were accustomed to such talk. From the magnates of higher education it was to be expected.

Such expectations were soon to change. By the time of the "Harvard Red Book" in 1945 the secular-liberal program for culture voiced intermittently at NYU in 1932 had supplanted the religious-conservative program in more and more of the academic space of the United States.[54] This program drew its share of critics, but Robert Hutchins, Mortimer Adler, and their allies developed educational models more classical than Christian and less given to the justification of ethnocentric policies and practices than were the preachments of Noyes, Hocking, and John Merriam.[55] But 1932 was very distant from 1945 in the history of American higher education's public ideologies. Speeches that could be hooted at as anachronistic if delivered in the 1940s or 1950s were still, in 1932, blandly conventional.

The genteel tradition in the culture of American universities declined at different speeds and in response to different pressures from one institution to another. Nothing threatened that tradition more directly than did polyglot cities, especially the city of New York. The challenge presented by New York City was uniquely acute at NYU, moreover, as a result of NYU's peculiar position as a private university forced to find its student market in what Columbia counted as its leftovers.[56] NYU tried for years to be a junior Columbia but found itself increasingly dependent on a student clientele drawn from the city. The nativist Fairchild did not see the irony, but his "consumerist" vision of the modern political economy was being vindicated all around him in the transformation of NYU by Jewish consumer-students. The university was forced to allow its Jewish enrollment to climb again. Even before the added financial pressures of the Depression, Jewish enrollment at "the Heights" had returned in 1929 to the 1919 levels of more than 50 percent. Yet in that same year of 1929 an effort was made to build a chapel there and to endow a department of religion "to counteract," as Dean Archibald L. Boulton phrased it, "the manifold influences of the city." No donor could be found.[57] Three years later, at the Centennial Conference, the genteel tradition made what was, in effect, its last stand at NYU. That institution's future social obligations were defined not by Dean Boulton and Chancellor Brown but by the recently departed Dean Munn, and by the city of New York.

NOTES

For critical reactions to a draft of this essay, I wish to thank Thomas Bender and Paul Mattingly. For many favors concerning archival materials, I am indebted to Thomas J. Frusciano and his staff.

1. Henry Pratt Fairchild, ed., *The Obligation of Universities to the Social Order: Addresses and Discussion at a Conference of Universities under the Auspices of New York University at the Waldorf-Astoria in New York, November 15–17, 1932* (New York, 1933), p. xiii. Hereafter this volume will be cited as *OUSO*.

2. Brown, in *OUSO*, p. 203.

3. For examples of the sentiment that social science must now produce the triumphs eariler wrought by physical and biological sciences, see *OUSO*, pp. 188–89, 194–95 (Thomas S. Gates), 200 (Osward W. Knauth), 207 (Walter E. Spahr), 234 (Harold G. Moulton), and 310 (C. E. A. Winslow).

4. The tradition of technocratic-progressivism is the subject of an extensive secondary literature, much of which has been influenced by Morton G. White, *Social Thought in America: The Revolt against Formalism*, 2nd ed. (New York, 1957); and Robert Wiebe, *The Search for Order, 1877–1920* (New York, 1967). The aspects of this tradition most manifest at the NYU Centennial Conference are helpfully addressed in two more narrowly focused studies: James A. Nuechterlein, "The Dream of Scientific Liberalism: *The New Republic* and American Progressive Thought, 1914–1920," *Review of Politics* 42 (1980): 167–90; and Donald T. Critchlow, *The Brookings Institution, 1916–1952: Expertise and the Public Interest in a Democratic Society* (Dekalb, Ill., 1985).

5. For an unironic plea for attention to "eternal verities," see *OUSO*, p. 397 (William Mather Lewis); for an attack on the "Pseudo-intelligentsia of modern literature," see p. 358 (Alfred Noyes); for celebrations of chapel, see pp. 349–50 (William Ernest Hocking), 405 (Frederick C. Ferry), and 414–16 (James L. McConaughy).

6. For this religious-conservative tradition in American universities between the Civil War and 1910, see the section on "Discipline and Piety" in Laurence R. Veysey, *The Emergence of the American University* (Chicago, 1965), pp. 21–56.

7. The *Times* gave extensive coverage to the conference but editorialized the most enthusiastically about defenses of "spiritual values" against the pretentions of science; see the issue of 20 November 1932, II, 1.

8. Sir Arthur Salter, in *OUSO*, p. 161. This phrase was quoted by others as the essence of the matter; see, e.g., pp. 197 (John T. Madden) and 446 (Chancellor Brown).

9. Charles E. Merriam, in *OUSO*, pp. 240, 248. Soule's contribution to the proceedings was strongly supportive of Merriam's; see George Soule, in *OUSO*, pp. 288–95.

10. Merriam, in *OUSO*, pp. 255–57. On Merriam's career, see Barry Karl, *Charles E. Merriam and the Study of Politics* (Chicago, 1975).

11. This faith in the cultural capabilities of men and women in their capacities as scientific "knowers" is a major presence in modern American and European intellectual history, yet we do not have an accepted term for addressing it. I have

proposed that we call it cognitivism; see David A. Hollinger, "The Knower and the Artificer," *American Quarterly* 39 (1987): 37–55, esp. 42–43.

12. Walter E. Spahr, in *OUSO,* p. 209.

13. Aurelia H. Reinhardt, in *OUSO,* p. 421. For the explicit complaint that the modern technical mind "lacks culture," see Angel Guido, in *OUSO,* p. 437.

14. Henry Sloane Coffin, in *OUSO,* pp. 457–65.

15. Philip M. Brown, in *OUSO,* p. 425.

16. *OUSO,* p. 403 (Lewis).

17. Noyes, in *OUSO,* p. 363; see also *OUSO,* p. 350 (John C. Merriam).

18. Noyes, in *OUSO,* pp. 355–56, 361–63.

19. Reinhold Niebuhr, *Moral Man and Immoral Society* (New York, 1932); Adolph Berle and Gardner Means, *The Modern Corporation and Private Property* (New York, 1932); *Culture and Crisis: An Open Letter to the Writers, Artists, Teachers, Physicians, Engineers, Scientists and Other Professional Workers of America* (New York, 1932). See also three other works of polemical demystification receiving widespread attention at the same moment: Jerome Frank, *Law and the Modern Mind* (New York, 1930); Lincoln Steffens, *The Autobiography of Lincoln Steffens* (New York, 1931); and John Chamberlin, *Farewell to Reform: The Rise, Life and Decay of the Progressive Mind in America* (New York, 1932). The spate of recent studies of "the New York Intellectuals" can serve to remind us how much of the intellectual life of New York City in the 1930s remained outside academic institutions. See, e.g., Terry A. Cooney, *The Rise of the New York Intellectuals: Partisan Review and Its Circle, 1934–1945* (Madison, Wisc., 1986); and Alan M. Wald, *The New York Intellectuals: The Rise and Decline of the Anti-Stalinist Left from the 1930s to the 1980s* (Chapel Hill, N.C., 1987).

20. Theodore Francis Jones, *New York University 1832–1932* (New York, 1933), p. 193.

21. George Santayana, "The Genteel Tradition in American Philosophy," in *Winds of Doctrine* (New York, 1913), pp. 186–215, esp. 188.

22. Jones, *New York University,* pp. 220–21.

23. For a guarded account of this concern on the part of NYU administrators of the period, see ibid., pp. 234–35.

24. The controversy over "quotas" for Jewish students at Harvard is perhaps the most famous of these episodes. For a recent study of the leading Ivy League universities in this connection, see Marcia Graham Synott, *The Half-Open Door: Discrimination and Admissions at Harvard, Yale, and Princeton, 1900–1970* (Westport, Conn., 1979). NYU's case was addressed briefly and critically in a popular book published shortly before the conference, Heywood Broun and George Britt, *Christians Only: A Study in Prejudice* (New York, 1931), pp. 106–11.

25. A detailed and well-documented account of these develoments is in Robert Shaffer, "Jews, Reds, and Violets: Anti-Semitism and Anti-Radicalism at New York University, 1916–1933," Master's essay, New York University, 1985; copy in NYU Archives. Of special interest are the letters of 1922, quoted by Shaffer, between President Emeritus Charles W. Eliot of Harvard and Chancellor Brown. In this correspondence Eliot deftly destroys Brown's claim that the admissions tests were for purposes other than the exclusion of Jews from NYU. These letters can be found in the Chancellor Elmer E. Brown Papers, Box 52, Folder 4, NYU Archives.

26. Jones, *New York University,* p. 235. Jones's reference was to the congressional legislation in 1924.

27. Fairchild's view on the "melting pot" fit comfortably with the general outlook of the NYU leadership, but his politics were decidedly to the left. While Brown was supporting Herbert Hoover for reelection in 1932, the socialist Fairchild published a sweeping attack on the "profit motive" in the pages of *Harper's.* The following year he visited the Soviet Union. When he died in 1956 he was the subject of a warm memorial essay by two of the nation's leading socialist intellectuals: Leo Huberman and Paul Sweezy, "In Affectionate Memory of Henry Pratt Fairchild, 1880–1956," *Monthly Review* 8 (1956): 242–43. For Fairchild's political analysis in 1932, see "The Fallacy of Profits," reprinted as "Profits vs. Prosperity" in Henry Pratt Fairchild, *Versus: Reflections of a Sociologist* (New York, 1950), pp. 21–44. The relevant holdings in the NYU Archives do not indicate how and why Brown entrusted Fairchild with the responsibility of editing the proceedings of the conference; see Records of the Centennial Conference, Box 2, Folder 13, "Henry P. Fairchild." For information on Fairchild's career, I am indebted to Robert C. Bannister.

28. For a very helpful account of the relationships between Columbia, NYU, and CCNY in the demographic and cultural context of metropolitan New York during the early decades of the twentieth century, see Thomas Bender, *New York Intellect: A History of Intellectual Life in New York City, from 1750 to the Beginning of Our Own Time* (New York, 1987), pp. 266–93, esp. 286–92.

29. James B. Munn, "The Washington Square College," in Jones, *New York University,* pp. 386–87. For a sketch of Munn's career, see the pamphlet by Bayrd Still, *James Buell Munn, 1890–1967* (New York, 1979). Munn's correspondence with Washington Square students, during and after the years these students spent in college, are in the James Buell Munn Estate Collection, Series II, subseries C, Folders 8 through 36, NYU Archives. I have not studied these letters, but it is clear that they constitute an important source for clarifying the dynamics of interaction between Jews and Anglo-Saxon Protestant patricians during Munn's generation.

30. I have addressed this historic transition in "Ethnic Diversity, Cosmopolitanism, and the Emergence of the American Liberal Intelligentsia," in David A. Hollinger, *In the American Province: Studies in the History and Historiography of Ideas* (Bloomington, Ind., 1985), pp. 56–73. For a more detailed study on the basis of a single but pivotal career, see David A. Hollinger, *Morris R. Cohen and the Scientific Ideal* (Cambridge, Mass., 1975).

31. The locus classicus in the literary record of this celebration is Randolph Bourne, "Trans-National America," *Atlantic* 118 (1916): 86–97. Holmes's intense engagement with young Jewish intellectuals is addressed in David A. Hollinger, "The 'Tough-Minded' Justice Holmes, Jewish Intellectuals, and the Making of an American Icon," in Robert W. Gordon, ed., untitled collection of essays on Holmes (Stanford, forthcoming).

32. The notion of two NYUs was sometimes suggested even at the time; for example, Broun and Britt, *Christians Only,* p. 107.

33. Munn, "The Washington Square College," pp. 379–90.

34. There is some irony in the fact that this "Heights campus," once a symbolic bastion of genteel WASP exclusivity, has become in our time a campus of the City University of New York devoted especially to the education of black and Hispanic citizens of the city.

35. As far as I have been able to determine, the records of the conference contain no evidence that Dewey was invited or that his appropriateness as a speaker was ever discussed.

36. For Hook's troubles with NYU administrators at this time (he was a candidate for promotion in 1932), see his recently published memoirs, *Out of Step: An Unquiet Life in the Twentieth Century* (New York, 1987), pp. 529–32. In his account of NYU in 1932 Hook is explicit in distinguishing Munn's style from other faculty and administrative personnel with whom Hook had to deal. For the development elsewhere in New York of an academic culture at variance with prevailing norms, see Peter M. Rutkoff and William B. Scott, *The New School: A History of the New School for Social Research* (New York, 1986), esp. pp. 19–64.

37. John Merriam was authorized by Brown to approach his brother Charles for ideas about the political symposium. See Elmer E. Brown to John C. Merriam, 20 February and 2 March 1932, in NYU Archives, Centennial Conference Records, Box 6, Folder 1.

38. John C. Merriam's relevant work is reprinted in *Published Papers and Addresses of John Campbell Merriam*, 4 vols. (Washington, 1938), Vol. IV.

39. John C. Merriam to Elmer E. Brown, 4 January and 27 February 1932, NYU Archives, Centennial Conference Records, Box 6, Folder 1.

40. My search for information of this sort has been greatly assisted by Thomas J. Frusciano, university archivist at NYU.

41. "Tentative Suggestions relating to the Centennial Celebration of New York University," Records of the Office of Vice-President and Secretary (Harold R. Voorhis), Box 4, Folder 6, NYU Archives.

42. Fairchild, in *OUSO*, p. 491.

43. For hints of religious-conservatism in this symposium, see *OUSO*, pp. 87 (Daniel L. Marsh), 92 (Philip M. Brown), and 97 (Edgar Dawson).

44. James Rowland Angell, in *OUSO*, p. 21.

45. *OUSO*, pp. 25, 28 (Lotus Delta Coffman), 56 (Irvine), and 58–59 (Samuel P. Capen).

46. Karl, Charles E. *Merriam*, pp. 13, 207, 263.

47. *OUSO* is ostentatious in its ceremonial display, squandering twenty-one pages of large type on a listing of the universities who sent representatives, even though some of these were simply the New York consul-general for this or that foreign nation. Pains were taken to impress the reader with how exclusive was the list of men and women invited to the conference. A "high society" tone was suggested; Fairchild thought it worth mentioning (p. xvii) that "the wives of those invited were included in the invitation."

48. Brown, in *OUSO*, pp. 443–50.

49. Fairchild, in *OUSO*, pp. 484–86. The notion that early-twentieth-century America experienced a basic transition from an economy and culture of production to an economy and culture of consumption has recently become very popular among historians; see, for example, Warren I. Susman, *Culture as History: The Transformation of American Society in the Twentieth Century* (New York, 1984), esp. pp. xix–xxx.

50. *OUSO*, pp. 24–38 (Coffman), 40–56 (Irvine), 150–68 (Salter), 184–95 (Gates), 239–57 (C. Merriam), 288–95 (Soule).

51. *New York Times,* 20 November 1932, VIII, 1.

52. Fairchild, in *OUSO*, p. 492.

53. Robert Gordon Sproul, in *OUSO*, pp. 376–86, esp. 386.

54. Paul H. Buck et al., *General Education in a Free Society: Report of the Harvard Committee* (Cambridge, Mass., 1945), popularly known as the "Red Book" on account of its crimson dust jacket, became a prominent referent point in the consolidation during the 1940s and 1950s of a more secular and liberal ideal for the cultural functions of American universities.

55. The Hutchins-Adler attack on technocratic progressivism and "the cult of science" began to alter the discourse about higher education as early as 1936, with the publication of Hutchins's *The Higher Learning in America* (New Haven, Conn., 1936). For a cogent account of the controversy in the late 1930s and early 1940s, see Edward A. Purcell, Jr., *The Crisis of Democratic Theory* (Lexington, Ky., 1973), pp. 147–52.

56. Columbia's President Butler (who served from 1901 to 1945) envisioned a hierarchical division of educational labor, Thomas Bender has explained, according to which Columbia "educated Wall Street lawyers and city and state school administrators," while "NYU and CCNY could supply neighborhood lawyers and public school teachers." Butler used the prestige of the Columbia presidency to support the growth of CCNY and the creation of Brooklyn College in 1932, "hoping to divert immigrant students" from Columbia. See Bender, *New York Intellect*, p. 288.

57. Evidence of the financial calculations behind the relaxation of anti-Jewish admissions practices is presented in Shaffer, "Jews, Reds, and Violets," pp. 43–47. Dean Boulton's remarks in a letter of 4 April 1929 are cited by Shaffer on p. 43.

15

Facing Three Ways: City and University in New York Since World War II

Nathan Glazer

I am a graduate of the City College of New York, then a free-standing, and free, and public undergraduate institution, now part of the City University of New York, one of those huge complexes that American higher education seems to breed in its public sector. Its seal, which until recently could be seen in somewhat battered purple ceramic tile on the walls of the 137th Street Broadway subway line station (all of City College's students arrive by subway or other forms of public transportation, since it had and has no dormitories, and very few of its students live within walking distance) shows a three-faced Roman goddess looking backwards, toward us into the present, and into the future, and bears the Latin inscription, "Respice, Adspice, Prospice." When I went to City College in the early 1940s most of its students could probably understand the meaning of that inscription from their Latin; Latin was required for the B.A. degree.

It is a good motto for a college and provides a good theme for a treatment of the relationship between city and university in New York since World War II. Clearly, there are three primary candidates for such a study of university and city in New York. There is first, of course, New York's great private university and the first institution of higher education founded in New York City, Columbia, which began life as King's College in 1754. Then there is New York University, founded as the University of the City of New York in 1832. And there is the third institution of higher education in the city, City College, the oldest college of the City University of New York, founded in 1847 as the Free Academy.

There are reasons to concentrate on these three institutions in considering university and city in New York, ranging from the trivial to the most substantial. All three, perhaps uniquely, bear the name of the city in their formal appellations and their seals (Columbia University is officially "Columbia University in the City of New York" since 1912). More important, they exemplify further three kinds of institutions that make up higher education in New York: an institution aspiring to national and international standing as a great university, working in all fields, and a peer to the major private universities of the United States; an institution addressed to the broad middle classes of the city, and beyond, practically oriented, as was intended by its founders, with the model of the University of London in their minds; and an institution directed to the more humble and indeed the poor of the city, also with practical orientation.

"Facing three ways" may be taken, then, as referring to three broad constituencies: national and international; the great middle classes of the city; and the lower-middle, working, and lower classes of the city. This difference in orientation is reflected in the three institutions' tuitions, ranging from the stratospheric to the minimal, in the institutions they compete with, and in the kinds of programs they launch and maintain. Of course, one should not exaggerate these differences: all three institutions fulfill functions and take on roles that are quite similar and which put them in some respect in competition with each other as well as with institutions of their own type. Facing three ways may be taken further to describe broadly three major ways in which university connects with city: by providing education for the people of the city, by providing research and advice for the city, and by interacting concretely and physically with some part of the fabric of the city, with all its problems and opportunities. Finally, facing three ways may be taken, drawing directly from the City College seal—and this is the principal significance—to refer to the striking difference between past, present, and future in this most rapidly changing of cities.

Obviously, to select only three institutions, even if the first three in date of founding (not the first three anymore in size) is to ignore very many other institutions that play important roles in New York. They range from the academically elite Rockefeller University through such varied institutions as Cooper Union, Yeshiva University, the New School, the Pratt Institute, Juilliard, Long Island University, and the Catholic institutions (Fordham, St. John's, and many others), to more limited institutions oriented to art or fashion or business and commercial or technical training, but much of what we say in considering how three institutions have fared in the city since World War II will in various degrees bear on these others, too.

Three great changes have transformed New York City since World War II. They are linked, though we will not examine just how. The first is a change in population composition. In 1940 New York City had seven and a half million people. After a rise to almost eight million in 1950 and a 10 percent decline in the 1970s, it again may have as much as seven and a half million. But the composition of that seven and a half million is strikingly different. In 1940 New York was a white and largely working-class city. In terms of religion it was a city of Catholics and Jews, with a smaller Protestant element. In terms of ethnicity it was a city of the Irish, the Italians, and the

Jews. A mere 6 percent of its population in 1940 was black. Twenty-eight percent of its population was still foreign-born (this had dropped from 37 percent at the peak in 1900). The Hispanic population (in that varied city there were, of course, many different Hispanic American groups) was minimal. In 1980, by contrast, one-quarter of the population was black, 20 percent were of Hispanic origin, there was an additional and rapidly rising number of Asians (about 4 percent), and these changes had reduced the "others," the white non-Hispanic population, to at best a bare majority.

Within the white population other major transformations had occurred. The Jewish community, which for decades had been estimated at two million, by far the largest Jewish concentration in the world, had shrunk in the 1960s and 1970s to perhaps three-fifths of that number. Germans and Irish, the dominant white population elements of the late nineteenth and early twentieth centuries, were less visible as major ethnic groups as they assimilated and moved off to the suburbs. The dominant white ethnic groups demographically were the Italians and the Jews, and their dominance was made evident in their hold on the major state and city offices.

This enormous change affected the city more than the metropolitan area. There the "others" were still in a comfortable majority. The institutions of higher education, even those trying to attract students from across the United States, draw their students primarily from the city and metropolitan area: a change in ethnic and local composition had to affect their potential pool of students.

A second major change: New York in the 1940s was a great port city, a great manufacturing city. It was, of course, a great commercial city and a great center of finance. But the port and the manufacturing industries—clothing, printing, furs, and many others—dominated the occupational opportunities offered by the city. There has been in thirty years a radical shrinkage in manufacturing jobs and in the importance of the port. The manufacturing lofts of lower Manhattan, areas that have in recent decades acquired the new names of Soho and Tribeca, have been taken over as living spaces, often first by artists and then by the more prosperous (not that the two terms are now necessarily exclusive). The greatest development on New York's City's shoreline is Battery Park City, where huge buildings are rising on the Hudson River to house financial companies and the upper-middle class, neither of whom has any relationship to its river location. The river now serves as a view rather than a transportation artery (though, of course, it serves that function, too). The great piers of the Hudson River along which transatlantic liners once tied up are derelict. Even as New York recovered in the later 1970s and early 1980s from the economic disaster that accompanied its near bankruptcy in 1975, the new jobs that were being added were in services, finances, government—not in manufacturing. The new fortunes of New York—not unimportant to the fate of its private universities—are in finance and real estate, which serves largely the expansion of the financial industry, and they quite eclipse the old money of any source or ethnic group.

A third change, perhaps another facet of the first and second: New York has developed a huge underclass and a permanent crime problem of massive dimensions. This is the kind of assertion that is more challengeable than the first two, for there is no good definition of an underclass. But I believe that as New York City emerged from the Depression and war in the late 1940s and 1950s there was no great sense that New York was a particularly dangerous city or that it maintained a huge dependent population. The numbers on welfare, while disturbing, were less than 5 percent of the population until the early 1960s, exploded in the late 1960s, and were only with difficulty maintained through the 1970s and 1980s at about 14 or 15 percent of the population. New York, the statistics show, is no more dangerous than other large American cities, but it certainly became more dangerous than it was, and it was perceived by its residents and by outsiders as a city in which special precautions had to be taken. In the early 1970s the graffiti plague struck the New York City subway system—a system on which its universities, as well as its economic life, depend—symbolizing a growing loss of control of the social environment. These social changes had enormous consequences for specific parts of the city and for the immediate environments of its universities.

Within this changing environment each of the three institutions—Columbia, New York University, and City College—faced different tasks and different problems.[1] Ideally, Columbia should have been least affected by the changes in the urban environment. It is a national institution, in aspiration and reality. But it is also physically fixed in a neighborhood in which a substantial part of its students—undergraduate, graduate, and professional— must live and in which its faculty should desirably live. One of its great tasks in the 1950s, 1960s, and 1970s and still in the 1980s is controlling and shaping its environment.

It is striking to contrast the self-satisfied discussion of Columbia's relationship to New York in the 1957 *Report of the President's Committee on the Future of the University,* at a time when Columbia's preeminence was not yet challenged, with the tone of alarm, of near desperation, of a report twenty years later, after Columbia had undergone, in its own eyes and in that of the raters of university standing, a considerable decline. The President's Committee tells us, in 1957,

> The potent influences of location and setting . . . leave room for choice. It is not enough to say that Columbia is metropolitan, nor even that it is in the unique metropolitan setting of New York City. . . . For more than seven decades, Columbia University has been prominently identified with the national and international features of the locality that is the country's largest city and a world center. The University can serve New York City most truly by seeking to improve itself as an institution.

The city is seen as a major opportunity, not a burden:

> The location of the University in metropolitan New York helps its role as a national institution by providing unique resources in many fields of instruction and research. . . . Columbia's most important service to the

City of New York and its people is to maintain its availability as a university of wide repute, marked by high standards of admission and instruction, and contributing through a distinguished faculty to the City's prestige as a cultural center.

We look with interest to any hint of shadows and urban problems. The committee proposes an office of community affairs: a few years later the central function of such a committee would have had to be to keep the barbarians from the gates, but in 1957 its major proposed function is to advertise lectures and cultural events to the community.

In the ratings of universities made by polling leading academics Columbia had maintained its high position for thirty years: third in 1925, third in 1957. Of course, the committee points to warning signs—loss of some eminent faculty members, growing competition from state institutions, some refusals to accept offers to join the faculty, the leaving of some good younger faculty, upcoming retirements of eminent scholars, an urgent need for new physical facilities—but these are "hardly grounds for dismay."[2]

Celebrating its two hundredth anniversary in 1954 with a remarkable array of studies and histories, Columbia saw few grounds for alarm. And certainly there was little ground for it in the immediate neighborhood of Morningside Heights, divided from Harlem by a park in which one could (possibly) still walk, surrounded by other eminent institutions of higher education—Union Theological Seminary, Jewish Theological Seminary, Juilliard—and by great European-style apartment houses lining the Hudson River and the streets leading to it for faculty.

There is not a hint in this report that Columbia should adapt to the changing demographic realities of New York. Indeed, Columbia had hardly found it necessary to adapt much to a considerably earlier demographic change, the great increase in the number of Jews in New York City and their rising role in the city. Columbia's relationship to the Jewish community was an uneasy one. Its college had tried hard to keep the number of Jewish students down by various means, only one of which could be publicly discussed, and that was to become national in its recruitment efforts. The 1957 report tells us that "as a result of an admissions and recruitment policy instituted about 1930, Columbia College made a deliberate effort to recruit a nationally representative student body . . . one-third from New York City, one-third from a fifty mile radius around New York City, and one-third from the rest of the country."[3] This was not fully realized: while the country outside metropolitan New York provided one-third of the students, the metropolitan ring provided only about 20 percent. There were many eminent Jews on the faculty, and the undergraduate student body had a very large Jewish component despite determined efforts that had been maintained in the 1920s, 1930s, and 1940s to reduce their number. Postwar antidiscrimination legislation in New York State, passed because of Jewish demands, had made it impossible to maintain the quotas in the undergraduate college, the medical school, and the law school, that had kept the Jewish percentage down, even if this had continued to be the policy of the administration.[4]

The delicacy with which even Jewish faculty referred to this situation in the celebratory volumes of 1954 is fascinating. Irwin Edman, the philosopher, writing "Prologue" and "Epilogue" to *A History of Columbia College on Morningside,* is nostalgic and graceful. Lionel Trilling, covering the first years of the history of the college after the university moved to Morningside Heights, tells us the undergraduate student body had increased substantially in diversity, "and a very considerable number came from ethnic and social groups not formerly represented. . . . [Dean] Frederick Keppel speaks in praise of the 'picturesqueness' of a student body which included men of Italian, Spanish, Czech, Turkish, Syrian, Hindu and Chinese origin, and this is perhaps a little specious of him."[5] One wonders at the significance of the word *specious.* Is it because Keppel does not mention Jews? From Harold Wechsler's account we know that much of his effort, and that of his successors, was devoted to devising means of admission that would reduce the Jewish percentage at Columbia. But Trilling does not mention Jews either. The matter is left in a delicate darkness.

Columbia, of course, was not alone in these efforts to hold down the number of Jewish students; the record of many institutions in this rather unsavory business has now been explored at length.[6] Nor was it as simple a matter as anti-Semitism, though that was almost always involved. There was a more legitimate concern about large numbers of Jews making the college less attractive to potential non-Jewish students and about the loss of alumni children as students and prospective alumni donors.

This history did not play any substantial role in the crises that beset Columbia and City College in the late 1960s. But the background of Jewish exclusion was crucial in shaping the response of the Jewish community to proposed quotas at City College. And at Columbia, as it began to confront difficulties in the later 1950s and 1960s, the Jewish connection—or, more specifically, the lack of sufficient Jewish connection—may well have played a role in reducing Columbia's fundraising ability and its capacity to compete with the rising state institutions with their access to state funds and to deal with the problems of decline around its immediate neighborhood.[7] Jews were numerous in the 1960s on the faculty and in the student body, and discrimination was a thing of the past, but as for connections with potential donors, one senses that Columbia's past exclusiveness in regard to New York Jews did not help.

In any case, decline there was. In those national ratings that administrators of leading research universities take so seriously, Columbia began to drop from an overall third position which it had maintained from 1925 to 1957, to twelfth and eleventh positions in rating surveys in 1970, 1979, and 1982. In salaries for faculty Columbia fell from number five to seventeenth from 1963–64 to 1967–68.[8] Simultaneously, the neighborhood began to be seen as an ever more serious problem. In 1967 Jacques Barzun, then provost, described the Columbia neighborhood as "uninviting, abnormal, sinister and dangerous."[9] Only Chicago, among major American research universities, faced a more difficult neighborhood situation.

Some of the great apartment buildings around Columbia were turning into welfare hotels and SROs (single-room occupancy buildings, also primarily for welfare clients). Using urban-renewal powers through an organization of institutions on the Heights of which it was the principal member, Columbia tried to shape its neighborhood, buying up deteriorated buildings, removing the tenants, and remodeling for faculty and students. But Columbia to its misfortune was also located in reform Democratic country. Few of the residents it wanted to remove voted or had political influence: not so the middle-class residents of the West Side, whose liberal inclinations fought with their self-interest and made great difficulties for the university's efforts to shape the social composition of the area. Of course, in many cases their own self-interest was also involved, as university purchase and rehabilitation impinged on middle-class families who benefited from New York City's strong laws protecting tenants and keeping rents low. These families were perhaps willing to trade off the advantages they had in reduced rents even in deteriorated buildings and neighborhoods against neighborhood improvement in which they could be replaced by faculty and employees. Or they were sophisticated enough—having perhaps read Jane Jacobs's *The Life and Death of Great American Cities*—to suspect that the university and its planners didn't really know how to improve the neighborhood, whatever governmental powers they disposed of for urban renewal and whatever they spent on the declining properties around them. The university in any case earned a good deal of hostility from the surrounding community for heartlessness and certainly gained no sympathy from Harlem below Morningside Heights, for it was driving out blacks and Puerto Ricans as well as welfare families and mentally unstable residents of SROs—in New York every class identification carries with it a simultaneous ethnic-racial identification.

How did the complex of declining prestige ratings, lower salaries, and declining neighborhood interrelate? To some extent independent, these factors were connected. Thus, Columbia could not compete, in salaries and facilities, with other universities, in part because it had to invest so much in neighborhood defense. (In any case, hemmed in by dense residential areas, it found it difficult to expand, which made it particularly difficult to compete in science with other universities.) But there were other factors in its perceived decline. Throughout the 1950s and 1960s there was a strong feeling that Columbia had unimaginative leadership. Christopher Jencks and David Riesman wrote of Columbia in the 1960s, "Its leadership is bankrupt, its location dysfunctional, and its faculty deteriorating."[10] A presidential Commission on Academic Priorities in the Arts and Sciences, chaired by Stephen Marcus and reporting in December 1979, is as harsh on previous administrations: "In the decades that preceded 1971, Columbia suffered from a general lack of administrative leadership at the highest level and from a concomitant diffusion of academic/administrative authority." One may accept this statement as expressing the dominant view on the Columbia faculty. Yet it is put in third place in explaining Columbia's decline; first is "The phenomenal expansion of higher education following World War II, [which] has entailed . . .

the dispersal of research and higher-degree granting programs throughout the national society," and in second place is "circumstances relating to Columbia's location in New York City and its specific location on Morningside Heights. . . . Columbia seems to have suffered from the disadvantages of its urban environment, and has not been notably successful in taking advantage of opportunities offered by that same environment." The fervor with which the neighborhood is decried is not often found in committee reports: "Shopping is terrible, decent restaurants few; astonishingly, there isn't a major bookstore, a quality movie house or an art gallery." From a plus in 1957, locacation in New York and on the Heights had become a minus in 1979.[11] The report believes Columbia can do a better job of shaping its neighborhood to make it more desirable, but that is just what Columbia had tried to do in the 1960s, and it earned the ire of its neighbors and an explosion of student riot and associated race conflict that further contributed to its troubles.

The Columbia student explosion of 1968 had many causes, and we do not mean to add to the literature of student revolt here. But one cannot escape noticing that the ostensible initiating cause was Columbia's effort to build a gymnasium for its students, one that rose in the dangerous stretch of Morningside Park, which covers the steep slope between Morningside Heights and Harlem. This would provide facilities for Columbia on the upper portions, entered from the Heights, and facilities for Harlem on the power portion, entered from Harlem. The symbolism (made inevitable by the physical contours of the land) was devastating: the university above, the minority community in the basement. It was the period of summer ghetto riots and black anger. White radical students of the Students for a Democratic Society initiated the confrontation, but black students joined in. Just as at Berkeley and Harvard, the issues of war, civil rights, and university response and "relevance" were inextricably mixed. One cannot ascribe Columbia's long-range troubles to its student revolt; Berkeley and Harvard seemed to have recovered quite nicely from student disorders as severe. But Columbia had other ailments to deal with. And these—its inability to tap into the new money of New York sufficiently (and in any case New York was entering its own period of crisis, which peaked in 1975) and its location—hobbled it in its efforts to recover. The reports of William J. McGill (president 1970–80) are dominated by the struggle with the deficit.

In the 1980s things looked up, for the city as well as for Columbia. By the end of McGill's tenure the deficit had been conquered. The appointment of Columbia's first Jewish president, in 1980, was a clear indication that its relations with the Jewish community were fully healed, and its neighborhood will be the beneficiary of a gentrification moving rapidly north along the Upper West Side. The gentrification of large parts of Manhattan is spurred by the disastrous social circumstances of much of the Bronx and Brooklyn, which have driven the middle classes to the suburbs or to the relative protection of Manhattan. This serves to raise rents in Manhattan to the point where, despite the restraints of rent control, the poor are slowly driven out. The real estate boom in Manhattan raises rents to forbidding levels, affecting

Columbia's ability to provide decent housing for its faculty; at the same time, however, the boom has enabled Columbia to sell the land on which Rockefeller Center stands for the enormous sum of four hundred million dollars— the equivalent of the return from a major fund drive—and this should help in its competition with other universities.

Columbia was not the kind of institution that was expected to play a major role in providing education for the new minorities that make up half the population of New York City; its undergraduate college is small, it is a national and international institution, and it is expected to serve the city more through research and eminence than as a major provider of higher education for the city's minorities. Columbia in the 1960s made a considerable effort to provide innovative social and educational services for Harlem on the basis of a substantial Ford Foundation grant (ten million dollars in 1966, the equivalent of three times that today), but this had as little effect in improving Harlem as the hundreds of millions of city, state, and federal funds. The money was used up in the community conflicts of that period of militancy and confrontation, and Columbia withdrew. While its minority enrollment is not large,[12] like other private universities it provides scholarship funds and services and presumably some preference on the basis of race which help to increase the enrollment beyond what it might otherwise be.

The situation of City College, located twenty blocks farther north, on another height overlooking a now dangerous and unused park built along a slope in Harlem, is quite different. It was established without tuition to serve the public school students of New York City. It is an institution exclusively for the residents of the city. For years it prided itself on providing a means of upward social mobility for the city's poor. And it achieved surprising results in this endeavor. In 1971 a study showed that it was second only to Berkeley in the number of its graduates who went on to receive Ph.D.'s. This record was even more remarkable in that City College was smaller than Berkeley, had nowhere near as eminent a faculty, had nothing like Berkeley's resources in libraries and scientific equipment, and, in the period covered, had no connection to a major research university. City College and its sister schools in New York's free higher education system—Hunter, Brooklyn, and Queens—achieved their distinction for a simple reason that it would be folly to ignore: they drew their students, overwhelmingly in the case of City, Hunter, and Brooklyn and to no small degree in the case of Queens, from the children of eastern European Jewish immigrants, a group that, wherever it has settled, has shown a remarkable aptitude for academic work.

It was given its distinctive character primarily by the specific composition of the poor of New York in the decades of and following the mass East European immigration. City College's enrollment was not representative of the poor of New York generally; the poor of New York in the 1920s, 1930s, and 1940s included Italians as prominently as Jews, but though present they were not particularly evident in City and its sister colleges. It is true that the Italians had the Catholic colleges to go to, but it is also true that many fewer of them than Jews went to college. City College was a test-based institution: admission was based on high school average scores and the taking of a requisite number of courses in various fields such as mathematics, sciences, and foreign languages. There were no interviews, no exceptions for alumni, race, religion, or distinctive achievement. The City Colleges operated on a pure meritocratic basis of admission through test scores and nothing else. City College was almost completely a creation of its unique student body, not of its faculty, its administration, its free tuition, its facilities, or anything else.

And that was the problem that became increasingly evident during the 1960s as the number of blacks and Puerto Ricans in the city increased, and their representation in the City Colleges did not. Black demands rose in intensity during the civil rights revolution, and each summer cities wondered which would be hit by riot and arson. A city university had been created in 1961 to group together the senior four-year colleges and community colleges which had been established throughout the city. In 1963 Albert H. Bowker of Stanford University became chancellor of the City University and saw trouble in the highly selective character of the student body of the senior colleges, in which there were so few blacks and Puerto Ricans. He had many allies in pushing for various programs to increase their representation, including the minority communities themselves and the liberal forces of the city, which in 1965 elected the reform Republican, John Lindsay, as mayor. New programs, under which students who could not enter the senior colleges under the no-nonsense test score requirement were admitted, brought additional black and Puerto Rican students into the City University (though generally they were in segregated programs, taking remedial classes, and in the community colleges).

Bowker's allies in pushing for a broader measure of representation of black and Puerto Rican students were matched by opponents. The opponents were to be found in the working-class and lower-middle-class sections of the city, where it was widely believed by 1969 that "too much" was being done for the blacks; in Jewish civil rights organizations, which responded antagonistically, because of the past use of quotas against Jews, to any suggestion of quota (and it would have to be some kind of quota, or some approach to such, that would be necessary to increase black and Puerto Rican enrollment since relatively few qualified for entry under prevailing admission standards); among the faculty, who were used to teaching bright students; and among alumni of the college, who had become New York's accountants, lawyers, dentists, businessmen, schoolteachers, and engineers. The schoolteachers had just come through a bruising struggle with black community activists on the question of control of the schools in black neighborhoods.

The crisis erupted when black and Puerto Rican students occupied the south campus (on which the liberal arts were located), closed it to students, and demanded, in addition to a separate school of black and Puerto Rican studies and greater power generally for black and Puerto Rican students, that future entering classes of the City College reflect the black and Puerto Rican population of the high schools of the city. Thus the dread quota issue was raised.

New York was in the middle of a mayoral campaign, in which Mayor Lindsay, having alienated many of his supporters by policies seen as too favorable to minorities in his first term, hoped to forge an alliance of the liberal upper and upper-middle classes (mostly Jewish) and the minorities against the outraged lower-middle classes and working classes, Jewish and Catholic. All his opponents in the campaign, except Norman Mailer, the writer, who was also running, denounced any approach to quotas. Lindsay was forced to go along. One may point out that Mailer had gone to Harvard, and few Jews who had gone to Harvard and similar schools could understand why the poorer Jews fought so fiercely against either quotas or the later proposal of open enrollment (that is, admission offered to every high school graduate regardless of grades or program, the policy which was finally adopted by the City University as a solution to the crisis).

The fact was that many of New York's Jews no longer needed City College; they had enough resources to go elsewhere and were sufficiently interested in schools that provided fellow students of good middle-class background for their children to spurn the free City College, even if they had the grades to get in.

But this was not the situation of lower-middle-class and working-class Jews, for whom City College was still the only alternative and, more than that, a valuable alternative, because its selectivity gave value to its degrees (and also to the education provided). They feared that when selectivity went the quality of education and the value of the degrees would decline. City College played a less significant role for the lower-middle-class and working-class Catholics, dominantly Italian, but they, too, and their representatives, were opposed to quotas. They were confused by rather than opposed to the alternative proposal of open enrollment—that meant that their less academically adept children would now have an opportunity to enter City College and its sister schools rather than being required to pay tuition at Catholic colleges and other colleges of lesser distinction. City College alumni, violently opposed to quotas, grumbled at open enrollment, which they believed would reduce the quality of the college and its reputation and by backward reflection diminish their own achievement and prestige. But open enrollment was a way of placating the minority communities and avoiding the dread mechanism of quotas: the main costs would be borne by a faculty facing a huge increase in enrollment of students of a quality they had never taught before, requiring much remedial work; and by a city and state that in the heady days of 1969 believed the public coffers could provide for a huge increase in enrollment.

In September 1970 forty-five thousand to fifty thousand freshmen entered the colleges of the City University of New York, more than double the number that had enrolled in 1969. The senior colleges were somewhat protected: requirements to enter them were higher under open enrollment than for the community colleges. City College nevertheless admitted 2742 freshmen, compared to 1752 the year before. The entering class was transformed. From 8.5 percent black and 5 percent Puerto Rican in 1969, it went to 24 percent black and 8 percent Puerto Rican in 1970. Whites, 81.5 percent in 1969, were reduced to 62 percent in 1970, and that proportion steadily went down with the passing years. The absolute numbers of black freshmen increased from 149 to 655, of Puerto Ricans from 86 to 225. The Jewish percentage at City College, still 50 percent in 1969, dropped precipitously to 26 percent in 1971. The Jewish predominance in the student body at City College, maintained over a period of sixty years, had come to an end, ironically just at the time when City College's first Jewish president, Robert Marshak, a distinguished theoretical physicist, took office.[13]

Marshak was a remarkable president; one can only admire his heroic efforts over ten years to deal with this radical transformation. He was committed to adapting City College to a changed city and to maintaining its intellectual preeminence. He himself had been a student at City College for a year before going on to Columbia under a Pulitzer scholarship (these scholarships were one means for the poor of New York to attend Columbia; despite the Jewish origins of the endowment, the number of poor Jews who gained admission through Pulitzers in the 1930s was suspiciously low). He performed wonders in raising money for a public institution for new and imaginative programs that would bring attention to the City College, would signal to bright students that this was still a place for them, and simultaneously served the large new numbers of black and Puerto Rican students. But it was City College's misfortune, from the point of view of maintaining its attractiveness to the nonminority population, that it was located just where it was most accessible to black and Puerto Rican students: it was at the edge of Harlem. Its sister senior colleges were more fortunate. Hunter was located in Bloomingdale country; Brooklyn and Queens and Lehman were in areas which still had large college-going nonminority populations.

Nor could Marshak escape from endless racial-ethnic struggles over access to the desirable programs he created. The saddest part of his memoir describes his efforts to create (he succeeded) an imaginative biomedical program in which the college would link up with a number of medical schools, the college providing the basic science courses, the medical schools the necessary medical training, and which would permit students to complete college and medical school in six years instead of eight. How could Marshak hope that this would help minority students, who typically need more time to complete a program? Would not the program be dominated by white students, Jewish and Italian, who are eager to become doctors and who often don't have the grades or the money to get into medical schools? Marshak believed he had an answer to this problem because the program would admit students on the basis of interest in and capacity for primary health care in underserved communities.

Marshak underestimated the passion for the study of medicine, and for litigation, in New York City. While there was no quota for black and Puerto Rican students, it was the case that on the basis of interviews to determine suitability for primary health care in underserved areas white applicants were disproportionately weeded out. Jewish and Italian organizations decided to sue, and President Marshak lost in federal court, though he bravely defends himself in his memoir against the charge that quotas for admissions had been set.

There was simply no way of escaping the ethnic and racial struggles for place in the city. Consider the questions posed to Marshak by a major Jewish organization: "How many students with averages below 85 were admitted to the biomedical program and how many of them were from minority groups—broken down into black, Puerto Rican, Asian, etc. If there was a waiting list, were those on that list given a numerical ranking, or, if someone selected did not accept admission, did they take someone from the same ethnic group from the waiting list to replace the position of the person originally selected?" Nor could one expect a white united front, despite the joint Jewish-Italian suit. An Italian parent wrote: "A perusal of names of selected students reveals a pattern of excessive admittance of Jewish applicants and a gross rejection of Italians. . . . Further, as many Asians as Italians were admitted, and as I have no quarrel with them, based on population ratios, how is that justified? My main quarrel is with a system that is geared to accept a disproportionate number of Jews, allowing them to hog and dominate the student body of this desirable program, while only allowing tokenism where the Italians are concerned." Nor were the blacks happy. A black community leader argued that "the cards are stacked against minority group members who apply to the city's medical schools—schools that use the traditionally narrow criteria of grades and test scores for selecting their students. . . . For example, here are two questions from last year's Medical College Admissions Test: 'Who composed the Jupiter Symphony?' 'What is a stem christi?' If those questions do not imply a cultural bias, what does?"[14]

Marshak failed to maintain the white proportion at City College. A 1981 survey showed less than a quarter white, but to call all the rest minority, as the official figures do, is to miss the social reality. When one used the term *minority* in 1969, one meant deprived groups, groups that did poorly on academic tests and for whom some special effort or concession was required if they were to enter academic programs in substantial numbers. At the time of the City College crisis in 1969, this term denoted almost entirely blacks and Puerto Ricans, though one notes even then in the statistics a substantial bulge of Asians (5 percent in 1969). By 1987 the picture had entirely changed. The minorities are now very different. As a result of the change in the immigration laws in 1965, which came into effect in 1968, new large streams of immigrants have entered and continue to enter the city, at a rate of eighty thousand to ninety thousand a year. The new immigrants are primarily Caribbean blacks, Dominicans, Latin Americans (Colombians, Ecuadorians, and others), and Asians from China, the Philippines, Korea, India, and other countries. A new city is being shaped, as a new city was shaped by the last great European immigration, cut off in 1924, and as a new city was shaped by the huge immigration of blacks from the South and Puerto Ricans in the 1940s and 1950s. The minorities of 1988 are thus no longer the minorities of 1969. The blacks among them include large numbers of foreign-born Caribbean blacks from Jamaica and elsewhere; the Hispanics among them are increasingly non–Puerto Rican Latin American; and there is a rapidly rising number of Asians. These new immigrants, with their strong drive for education, may well permit City College to maintain its necessary role in providing higher education for the poor and to recapture to some degree the intellectual eminence it once possessed. One notes in the 1981 ethnic-racial breakdown for City College that Asians made up a surprising 17 percent of its enrollment, which was then four times their percentage in the city. Among the Hispanics and blacks are very large numbers of new foreign-born immigrants. No less than an astonishing 40 percent of students are foreign-born (when I attended City College in the early 1940s there were very few foreign-born students). One reason why the Asian enrollment is so high at City College is because the engineering school of the City University is located there, because its science programs are strong, and because the architectural school is there.

One may read a portent for the future in the *City College Alumnus* for October 1986. It reports on a group of high school students who participated in the college's High School Science Apprenticeship program and who were finalists or semifinalists in the Westinghouse Science Talent Search. They are Mark Huan-Fu Kuo, John Bumsuk Ba, Jeffrey Lee, Michelle Ng, and Paul Lee. This is a summer program in which students carry out research in the biomedical sciences. But one wonders whether these students will go to City College, in view of the enormous broadening in opportunities for the talented that has occurred in the last twenty or thirty years. There were few alternatives to City College for the bright and low-income student in the 1920s, 1930s, and 1940s, compared to the situation today, and City College will have to live with that reality, as Columbia must live with the reality of many new research universities crowding into the field with substantial resources to compete for faculty and students.

As in the case of Columbia, New York University in the postwar period looked on New York City as one of its greatest resources. Its massive self-study of the 1950s began with what can well be described as a paean to New York City:

> A dweller in New York City should say with pride, "I am a citizen of no mean city," for he stands at the center of today's world. Founded on this site primarily because it controlled the greatest harbor on the Eastern coast, New York is still a major distribution center. New York leads in the food-processing, garment, fur and printing industries, and controls more financial operations than . . . any other city in the world. This great city, the largest metropolitan network the world has ever seen, has come of age. Its inhabitants have been described as restless, energetic, and curious. They deserve university opportunities commensurate with the metropolis itself.[15]

In subsequent pages, looking for the distinctive opportunities that the social changes of the future may offer the university, the self-study concentrates on the great amount of leisure that the America of the future will dispose of, offering an opportunity to a university many of whose programs appeal to adults. There is not a hint of the possible trials of ethnic and racial change and economic decline and social crisis that were to come.

NYU was to be spared the worst of this. This is not to suggest that NYU's course was placid, but its crisis was primarily a financial one, typical of a large and diverse metropolitan university without a strong claim to public money or the money of city philanthropists, dependent on tuition, and of modest endowment. And yet while Columbia and City College underwent crisis and by some measures decline, NYU has moved ahead. It seized, as it had to, targets of opportunity, provided by its location in New York City and its specific location around Washington Square.

New York University is an institution of the middle—neither the eminent research university that Columbia is nor the college of the poor and new minorities that City College was, and is, and will have to be. Geographical location has meant much for Columbia and City College. It has also meant much for New York University. NYU was able to avoid the racial traumas of the late 1960s. It neither had to bear the brunt, as the preeminent research university of the city did, of strong public demands that it involve itself in the urban and minority crisis, nor was it expected, as a private fee-charging institution, to play a key role in providing education for the new minorities. NYU's postwar story is more complex than either Columbia's or City College's and cannot be shaped, as their stories have been, by the drama of a fall from great heights, with the melodramatic addition of fears of Harlem marching on the university. Harlem was far away from Washington Square. The SDS did not make the kind of inroads on NYU students, with a middle-class student body of middling-level achievement, that it made at Columbia.

As targets of opportunity were seized by a series of able administrators, NYU edged up. If one looks at the various ratings of research universities, one finds NYU invisible in 1925, nineteen to twenty-three between 1932 and 1982 in national ratings, but these amalgams conceal substantial areas of distinction. In 1957 NYU is second in fine arts, sixth in music, eighth in mathematics. When Columbia's faculty was fretting over weak leadership, NYU had strong or, at any rate, risk-taking leadership. But this also risked financial disaster. In 1975–76 an informant in the president's office at NYU commented to Harold Orlans that James Hester, president from 1962 to 1975, "took big risks over and over again, and time after time he pulled them off— during one three-year period, Hester raised one million dollars a week. Even today, it is not obvious that the difficulties of NYU cannot be overcome. Sawhill is a 'good manager.' A great entrepreneur followed by a good manager. How else do great institutions get built?"[16]

The financial difficulties of the mid-1970s were awesome—as they were at Columbia. Struggling with its financial crisis, NYU sold its beautiful McKim, Mead, and White–designed campus on University Heights in the Bronx overlooking the Harlem River to the state for a new campus for the City University. The sixty-one million dollars was, of course, a boon; even more of a boon was the fact that it would have been impossible to maintain the Heights campus as a fee-paying private college as the Bronx burned around it in that terrible urban disaster in which vast stretches of that borough, built up with solid middle-class housing, became uninhabitable. Here was one case in which strategic retreat paid off. A doomed outpost was abandoned, and resources could be concentrated on the Washington Square buildings, the main seat of NYU.

Here NYU benefited from what was happening in the social geography of the city in the 1970s and 1980s. New York was imploding. Large sections of the Bronx and Brooklyn lost population as the urban fabric was destroyed, socially and physically, by drugs, crime, and arson. New York fell in upon its center, Manhattan below 96th Street, and a hectic and feverish prosperity prevailed in Manhattan after the financial crisis of the mid-1970s. There, it was believed, some modicum of safety could be found, and one might avoid using the declining and increasingly dangerous subways. New York began to present a double face of prosperity and activity—commercial, cultural, social—in the center, contrasted with large stretches of urban near-desert in formerly prosperous working-class and middle-class sections beyond. NYU benefited because it was in the right place. Undergraduates—not all, of course, but enough—were willing and eager to live and study in Greenwich Village. (NYU's chief competition is the somewhat similarly located and also improving Boston University.) Graduate students also found the area attractive. NYU invested, as Columbia did, in buying buildings for faculty and student housing and building new ones. But whereas Columbia during most of the postwar period was fighting against a downward neighborhood trend, against which its resources could only effect a delaying holding action, NYU was going along with a generally upward trend, as its surrounding area moved from shabby industry and commerce to attractive artists' lofts and galleries, new condominiums, and remodeled offices, boutiques, and restaurants.

Because of where it was located, NYU could, and did, develop programs in the arts, theater, and film. Some of the professional schools were also fortunate. The law school was the beneficiary of a very large gift from Mueller's, the manufacturer of noodles and pasta. The business school benefited from its location in the heart of Wall Street, accessible to adjunct faculty and part-time students.

NYU's alumni also became an important support as New York City's economy revived after 1980. They had attended a nonresidential college, were reputed to be neither as bright as City College students nor as prosperous as Columbia students, and this did not make them a likely resource for support. But the 1980s were the epoch of new and expanded fortunes in real estate and finance, and some of the NYU graduates who were making these fortunes showed surprising loyalty. As one account puts it, "Lawrence A. Tisch, Leonard M. Stern and Lewis Rudin [all major benefactors of NYU] never had much desire to see their Alma Mater again after they graduated from New York University in the 1940's and 1950's. They certainly never expected to come back to campus the way they have, as benefactors and members of the board of trustees.

"Until 1970, N.Y.U. was a commuter college for New Yorkers whose parents wanted them to stay at home while they received a practical education, usually in business."[17] And commuter colleges are not known for developing loyalty. But the skill of NYU's administrators, the success of the businesses—primarily real estate—these alumni had entered, perhaps the desire to reap prestige retroactively by raising the status of the institution they had attended, has made NYU a formidable fundraiser.

Like all private universities NYU faces enormous difficulties in raising the huge funds an aspiring research university needs to maintain its programs, but reflecting on our theme one can only conclude that NYU benefited from the accident of where it was, as Columbia and City College suffered from the accidents of where they were, in a city that changes too fast for any placidity and stability, with a social geography in which sinister urban threat and delightful urban pleasures are divided from each other by the thinnest of membranes. While to the visitor from Middle America and suburbia the NYU neighborhood will still appear shabby and rundown, and Washington Square Park, until recently infested with drug dealers, may appear menacing, the New Yorker bred or born, or those aspiring to urban sophistication, will see behind the façades bookstores and record stores, the Pottery Barn and the raffish boutiques, the fashionable, oversized, architect-designed restaurants, and all the other signs that tell a reader of *The Village Voice* or *New York* magazine that the action is here and it's a good place to be.

Since NYU does not perform the public function of City College and the City University or the symbolic function of Columbia, no one expected it to save the city by educating blacks and Puerto Ricans and incorporating them productively into the life of the city. Since it is a private university without very large endowment and grand buildings, it is neither exhorted to spend its resources on fulfilling major public needs nor frowned upon if it does not. It is not subject to great expectations on the basis of an illustrious past; as a result, its real achievements and the improvement of its programs in many areas come as a pleasant surprise.

Despite this, of course, NYU does fulfill a public role. It is a large employer and landlord and developer in its area, working together with the city and other employers and landlords of the area to improve it. The upwardly aspiring new immigrants of the 1970s and 1980s are drawn to it because it provides many programs that cannot be found in the City University, and, like so many private institutions in and around the city that are not the beneficiaries of large endowments or public funds, it tries harder to find niches that are of interest to paying customers.

NYU, along with other private universities, has also benefited from the fact that in 1976, because of the city financial crisis, the City University had to give up its no-tuition policy. Because they were required to pay tuition, the more prosperous City University students began to consider other fee-charging institutions. The City University tuition was low, and the low-income students should have been able to make it all up from federal and state grants and loans. But the effect of the tuition was drastic. President Marshak, fighting to maintain the attractiveness of City College to students from non-minority families somewhat higher on the occupational and income ladder than the average black and Puerto Rican student, describes what the effect of tuition charges could be expected to be:

> The imposition of tuition would . . . have a deleterious effect on the enrollment of students from lower-middle and middle-class families because the pegging of tuition—as proposed—to the SUNY level [State University of New York, with undergraduate colleges near New York City at Purchase in Westchester, Old Westbury on Long Island, and a University Center at Stony Brook on Long Island] would make CUNY much less attractive for a college education. With small additional financial support—either from families or part-time work—many of the students could enroll in the SUNY system and enjoy the vastly superior facilities and amenities to those of CUNY. [President Marshak could have added that with somewhat more they could attend NYU or Long Island University; St. John's, Adelphi, or Hofstra; or many other private universities enterprisingly engaged in creating programs to compete with the public institutions.] The loss of thousands of these lower-middle and middle-class students from the CUNY system would dilute the social mission of the public sector of higher education in New York City, which is to maintain a balanced academic, ethnic and class mix in its student body.[18]

Tuition was imposed in 1976, along with some tightening of the standards for admission to the senior colleges, with substantial effects on numbers and ethnic composition at City College. The tuition encouraged whites (as well as undoubtedly blacks, Puerto Ricans, and Asians, too) to explore private tuition-paying alternatives as well as SUNY campuses at Purchase, Old Westbury, and Stony Brook. Thus, in the complex ecology of college and university relationships in New York City, tuition charges in the City Colleges helped the private sector and, one would hazard, NYU, and contributed to ethnic and racial change at the City Colleges.

We have discussed two of three possible relationships between the university and the city. One is the relationship imposed by physical location and nearby neighborhoods. The second is restraints and opportunities offered by the changing racial and ethnic demography of New York. A third relationship, referred to at the beginning, connects the university to the city somewhat as a physician is connected to a patient. The hope was widely expressed in the 1960s, and given much support by the Ford Foundation, that universities would, through research and service, contribute to amelioration of conditions in the cities, which meant for the most part the conditions of the black and Puerto Rican minorities. *Urban* in the 1960s and 1970s was often used as a euphemism for "black." There is no suggestion in this formulation as to which way causation runs—whether it was the fact that cities were unwelcome or discriminatory, their educational systems inadequate, their economies incapable of absorbing blacks and minorities, that was the cause of the difficulties of minority groups, or whether conditions within the groups, as a result of history and culture, made them in some way unsuitable for a relatively smooth assimilation to urban life. But Columbia with its Ford grant, City College with its urban commitment by President Marshak, and City University with its urban program all hoped in some way to contribute to the amelioration or solution of urban and minority problems. One cannot record any marked success in these endeavors, or indeed any success at all. NYU was also involved, particularly through its Graduate School of Public Administration under Dick Netzer. Research there is—and it is important and useful research. One may particularly note the important series of volumes, *Setting Muncipal Priorities,* edited by Charles Brecher of the Graduate School of Public Administration at NYU and Raymond D. Horton of the Graduate School of Business of Columbia.

But the early promise of urban studies, urban research, urban observatories, as they were once called, of action programs under university sponsorship to deal with urban problems, has not been fulfilled. The outpouring of proposals on how the university could and should respond to the urban crisis of the later 1960s and 1970s now reads curiously. There seems to have been an unwarranted optimism about what on the one hand could be *known* about causes and solutions, and on the other hand about what could be *done* on the basis of what was known. This optimism, undoubtedly to be attributed to two decades of almost uninterrupted growth in our economy, reflected in the even more rapid growth of universities and colleges, was general: we were optimistic not only about our ability to understand and deal with urban problems but also about our ability to guide and encourage the economic growth of underdeveloped countries, to keep our own economy growing on an even keel, to create or help create the conditions that would prevent revolution and support democracy in the newly independent ex-colonies and in nations of Latin America that had been prone to military rule for a century and a half, and so on. It was an age of general hubris.

The hope that the application of research and thought to our urban problems—and who better than the universities could do this?—would help with the problems of depressed minorities, crime, racial integration, changing and declining neighborhoods, inadequate housing, and the like were sadly disappointed. We did not know enough to propose sound policies for most of these problems, and even if we (or some of us) thought we knew enough, the political conditions did not permit these solutions. By the late 1960s and early 1970s the universities and colleges, overwhelmed by their own problems of student revolt (which they understood as little as the causes of the urban crisis) were too busy dealing with their own internal crises to worry much about urban crises. The 1970s added the additional burden of financial crisis, for private and public institutions. The universities had to worry more about saving themselves than saving the cities.

The universities did not do much to help New York City in its travails. One might well add that the federal, state, and local governments, with their enormously greater resources and their far more legitimate mandate, did not seem able to do much either. New York's surprising recovery, as well as that of the entire Northeast, seems to have little to do with government policy, even less with the insights of research and urban theory. The revival was entirely unexpected. One can find little in public policy, aside from some modest tax cutting to encourage business, in this most highly taxed of states and cities, to which we can attribute this revival. Nor has the economic revival as yet made much impact on the severe urban problems that initially led to university involvement in urban issues; indeed, this revival coexists with unparalled and crippling problems in housing, education, and crime.

Perhaps in the end the only effective role the universities can play in ameliorating urban crisis is to continue doing that for which they are best qualified: education and research. New York's prosperity in the past owed a great deal to the outpouring of educated and talented people from the City Colleges and from other institutions, who became New York's businessmen, accountants, lawyers, doctors, and civil servants. It owed a great deal to a school system that turnd out competent secretaries, clerks, salespeople, craftsmen, and so on. The colleges and universities depended in good part on an elementary and high school system that brought qualified students to them. The New York City school system has been struggling with the problems of maintaining such a flow for the last two or three decades, and it is perhaps here that the universities and colleges can make a contribution.

As I have suggested, the colleges and universities also contribute to dealing with the city's problems through research. But the colleges and universities of New York City have never been as closely identified with study and action in the city as has been, for example, at various times the University of Chicago. Perhaps the city was simply too daunting, as a field of study too overwhelming. The Bureau of Applied Social Research of Columbia University, with its important role in shaping American empirical and problem-oriented social sciences under the leadership of Paul Lazarsfeld and Robert Merton, did not take the city, New York, as a subject for research, to the same extent that the sociologists of the University of Chicago took their city as a subject for research. The major sociologists who worked in New York City—Merton, Lazarsfeld, Robert Lynd, C. Wright Mills, S. M. Lipset, Daniel Bell—were not, at least in their writings, students of New York, and thus there were no New York City equivalents to Robert E. Park, Ernest Burgess, Louis Wirth, or Franklin Frazier.

I have said very little about what is most distinctive of the university, its intellectual life and its contribution to knowledge and thought. Did it matter for their intellectual life that Columbia, NYU, and City College were in New York City rather than somewhere else? Or was every discipline part of a national or international system, such that a scientific discovery in Copenhagen, or a new approach in literary criticism in Paris, was more influential in the universities of New York City than anything happening in the city itself? Did the city give a twist to disciplines and ways of thought and research that made some of the work done in the universities of New York distinctively of the city, shaped in some ways by its characteristics? This is an intriguing question, but one very difficult to say much about. In some fields one senses New York City placed a distinctive stamp on work and attitudes. There was clearly something distinctive about philosophy in New York: Morris Raphael Cohen at City College, John Dewey at Columbia, Sidney Hook at NYU, and some of their colleagues and students were involved in the public life to an extent that was not matched, I believe, at other centers of American philosophy. They were through the experience of the city and its intellectual and political life somewhat deacademicized, as Thomas Bender puts it.[19] The possibility of this deacademicization is still something that characterizes at least parts of university life in New York, and that makes it somewhat different from university life elsewhere. The city, because of its size, the size of its intellectual and artistic groupings, and its major non-university institutions, can create alternative contenders for loyalty and involvement, in ways which Boston, Chicago, or Philadelphia cannot. It permits and encourages careers—an Irving Howe, or Dennis Wrong, or Richard Sennett—that strike one as distinctively of New York, and that one would not expect elsewhere in the United States. Paris would be an equivalent, in which the intellectual life of the city easily matches the intellectual life of the universities.

There are fascinating questions here for consideration. I have taken a more mundane approach, exploring the connections between the universities and the city's rapidly changing population, its successive elites of money and power, its difficulties in sustaining the kind of ambience and amenities that universities—or indeed any institutions—would like to have around them. New York's colleges and universities, despite the enormous changes that have overtaken the city in the last forty years, have shown a gritty capacity to endure, survive, grow, and adapt, which is very typical of the city itself. They have known periods of overarching ambition and of severe internal conflict and financial stress. The three institutions I have discussed have emerged to some degree from periods of eclipse and find themselves in the buoyant atmosphere of a city reviving from the financial crisis of the mid-1970s and once again a magnet for immigrants. But it is hardly likely that New York's universities and colleges will again be tempted to play a significant role in dealing with the problems of an enormous world city. Conservative institutions inherently, they will continue to do what they have done in the past, educating and training those who come to them, contributing in research to the understanding of the city's problems, and adapting to change rather than guiding it.

NOTES

1. This view—that different institutions of higher education have different functions and roles in a metropolitan area—is scarcely unique. As Thomas Bender writes:

> By 1920 Columbia had clearly established itself at the top of a newly defined hierarchy of institutions in the city. Much as urban geographers

speak of a rank-ordered distribution of functions among cities in an urban system, so higher learning had (and has) its ranked differentiation of function. What makes this metropolitan process of hierarchical sorting so interesting and important is its relationship to the distinctive class structure and ethnic composition of New York City. To the extent that segments of the population identified by class and ethnicity were channeled to different levels in the local system of higher learning, the promise of cultural democracy in the city was seriously compromised. The reorganization of higher learning in New York promoted by [Nicolas Murray] Butler in the first two decades of the twentieth century made the always strained association of democracy and higher learning even more tenuous.

Thomas Bender, *New York Intellect* (New York, 1987), p. 287. Of course, one could say the same, with variations, for the ecology of institutions of higher (or, as some now say, postsecondary) education for Chicago, Philadelphia, and other cities.

2. *The Report of the President's Committee on the Future of the University* (1957), pp. 1, 17–18, 49–50, 13, 14.

3. Ibid., p. 72.

4. For these efforts, see the invaluable book by Harold Wechsler, *The Qualified Student* (New York, 1977).

5. Lionell Trilling, in *A History of Columbia College on Morningside* (New York, 1954), p. 35.

6. In addition to Wechsler's *The Qualified Student*, see Marcia Synnott, *The Half-Opened Door: Discrimination and Admissions at Harvard, Yale, and Princeton, 1900–1970* (Westport, Conn., 1979); David O. Levine, *The American College and the Culture of Aspiration, 1915–1940* (Ithaca, N.Y., 1986), chap. 7.

7. Wechsler details the efforts of prominent and wealthy Jews, beginning with Jacob Schiff even before the twentieth century, to get Columbia to recognize the position of the Jewish community. Only in 1928 did Columbia appoint its first Jewish trustee—first, that is, since Gershom Seixas in the eighteenth century, who was a trustee by virtue of his position as a minister in New York City—the distinguished jurist Benjamin Cardozo. The second was Arthur H. Sulzberger, the publisher of the *New York Times,* in 1944, after another "long and commented upon hiatus" (*The Qualified Student,* pp. 136–40). Even that did not, I would think, end the story: Sulzberger was not only a German Jew, but the *Times* was then strongly anti-Zionist and was not viewed warmly by the dominant East European element in the Jewish community of New York.

8. Robert Price, in George Nash, ed., *The University and the City* (New York, 1973), p. 102.

9. Ibid., p. 97.

10. Christopher Jencks and David Riesman, *The Academic Revolution* (Garden City, N.Y., 1967), p. 403.

11. *Commission on Academic Priorities in the Arts and Sciences* (1979), pp. 1–2, 17–18.

12. The Columbia College class admitted in the spring of 1987 was 9.2 percent black and 7.3 percent Hispanic, the highest minority percentage ever admitted. These are the highest percentages of blacks and Hispanics in the Ivy League, but not by much. See Meg Dooley, "Bridging the Access Gap," *Columbia* (June 1987):

27. Harvard's entering class in 1987 was 8.7 percent black and 5.5 percent Hispanic (*Harvard Gazette,* 29 May 1987).

13. For the above account, see Nathan Glazer, "City College," in David Riesman and Verne A. Stadtman, eds., *Academic Transformations* (New York, 1973); Jerome Karabel, "The Politics of Structural Change in American Higher Education: The Case of Open Admission at the City University of New York," in Harry Hermanns et al., eds., *The Complete University* (Cambridge, 1983); David E. Lavin, Richard D. Alba, and Richard A. Silberstein, *Right versus Privilege: The Open Admissions Experiment at the City University of New York* (New York, 1981); Robert E. Marshak, *Academic Renewal in the 1970s: Memoirs of a City College President* (Washington, D.C., 1982). There are many other reports, accounts, and studies, for this is one of the best-researched episodes in American higher education.

14. Marshak, *Academic Renewal in the 1970s,* p. 197.

15. *New York University Self-Study* (1956), p. 16.

16. Harold Orlans to author, 4 November 1986.

17. Albert Scardino, "A Boom in Benefactors for N.Y.U.," *New York Times,* 23 November 1986.

18. Marshak, *Academic Renewal in the 1970s,* pp. 66–67.

19. Bender, *New York Intellect,* esp. pp. 311–12.

16

Afterword

Thomas Bender

A moment's reflection about the city and the university—and their interrelations—prompts a startling recognition. Considering several conventional and formal sociological characteristics—secularity, tolerance, specialization, concentration, diversity—one is tempted to assume that a homology exists between the university and the city. Such thinking is apparent in several of these essays, and it is explicitly and effectively deployed in J. K. Hyde's essay on medieval Italian cities and universities. By making this point, even in the most general terms, Hyde is able to elucidate with great effect the difference between the monastery and the university as alternative sponsors of higher learning.

Yet one must be cautious in making such an argument. Without denying the heuristic value of proposing a homological relationship between the city and the university, I want to urge considerable restraint in the development of this notion, for it can lead, I think, to a significant distortion. While they seem to share a number of formal sociological similarities, cities and universities are very different social constructs. Certainly, we know the experiential difference between arriving in a great city and stepping onto the campus of a great university.

The difference separating the university and the city extends beyond the obvious contrast between their principal functions in society: economic exchange for one, the nurturance of learning in the other. I would put the difference rather abstractly. I propose that we understand the urban university as *semicloistered heterogeneity* in the midst of uncloistered heterogeneity (that is to say, the city, especially after the walls come down). Because of this difference, relations between the two are necessarily tense, and they cannot be assimilated into one another. To do so, either practically or conceptually, is to empty each of its distinctive cultural meaning and to falsify the sociology of each.[1]

What the city and the university share—heterogenity—ought to warn us of another danger, that of thinking of either the city or the university in organic terms, as unified wholes. In fact, both are incompletely bounded fields of contention, comprising various traditions, interests, and ideals. Too often the essays here evoke *the* city rather than giving specificity to the social and cultural and political processes that constitute and reconstitute the city.

It is no mean feat to conceptualize the city as a social phenomenon in terms that can guide research. Although there is no shortage of notable essayistic attempts to characterize the "culture" of the city, historians and social scientists have yet to develop a theoretical understanding at an order of magnitude between the essayistic brilliance of, say, Georg Simmel, Oswald Spengler, Robert Park, Lewis Wirth, Milton Singer and Robert Redfield, Lewis Mumford, Jane Jacobs, and Richard Sennett, and the rather limited, in fact trivial, theory and empirical work that mostly passes as urban sociology.[2] It may well be, however, that the demands of the comparative and interactive study implied by the topic at hand, the university and the city, may prompt the piecemeal development of such theory. At the least, it offers a mode of proceeding to detailed accounts of the way city culture is made and remade.

If one of the assumptions of this volume is that the city—a place—provides a focus for the actual enactment of the relationship between university and society, it remains only an assumption, and it will remain so until more social and cultural detail (description) is provided. To achieve a working knowledge of this interaction, we will need fuller and more precise analysis of the city as a place within a larger geographical system and of the internal relations of the elements of the city itself.[3] Of the essays in this volume, only the one on Berlin by Charles McClelland seriously addresses such geographical issues, and his thesis is much clarified and strengthened by his simple indication of the precise location of the university. In other cities we may have to ponder the cultural meaning of other locations for the university—in the central business district, in an elite neighborhood, near other cultural institutions and parks, in a suburb. Urban culture, of course, is not merely the geographical configuration of cultural institutions. Yet one would err seriously in underplaying the practical and symbolic meaning of location. That, too, constitutes university and city culture.

But simply locating the university, rare as such an act is among educational historians, is only a beginning. If the city and the university are both highly differentiated entities, we must ask whether particular parts of the university have distinctive relations to different parts of the city—and by parts here, I mean to combine social and geographical distinctions. University medical schools, for example, are rarely located with the arts and science core of a university. In New York most of the great medical schools (Columbia, which is isolated, being the notable exception) are concentrated in an awesome medical research and health delivery complex on the East River—adjoining the Midtown business district and the elite Upper East Side residential district. How would an alternative geographical arrangement affect the constitution of the universtiy, the research and therapeutic missions of the medical schools, and the shape of the city's self-understanding of its own culture? Again, universities often provide a variety of "services" (educational, welfare, recreational) to their neighbors. Here, then, physical proximity is important, but other services to society seem to be less place-specific (liberal education of the elite, scientific product development).

Although the city has been the focus of scholarly inquiry since the emergence of academic disciplines as we know them (to say nothing of Aristotle's brilliant analysis of the polis), we still seem to lack the analytical tools to distinguish city life and city culture from broader social and cultural processes. Yet several of the contributors to this volume come rather close to identifying the specifically urban content of cultural production, including the place-specific social circumstances that nourished those urban qualities. I refer particularly to Grafton's account of Lipsius in Leiden, Schorske's interpretation of Burckhardt and Bachofen in Basel, and Ferruolo's concluding observations, drawing on the work of John Baldwin, in respect to the Doctors of Paris, and Heyd on the emergence of cosmopolitanism at Geneva. In each instance, it seems to me, the city provides a locus of mediation between tradition and new circumstance. If the university represents tradition in this case, the city mediates, indeed defines, the transaction between tradition and present social and cultural circumstances.

More broadly illuminating is Jay's account of the Institute for Social Research. He opens the question more widely, something that must be done in such inquiry as this volume proposes, to assess the *relative* weight of several contexts for cultural innovation. Here the city gets its due, but it is presented in relation to other claimants. In order to avoid what J. H. Hexter once dubbed "tunnel" history, we must be attentive to the surrounding of the university in the city and beyond the city.[4] One must reconstruct the place of the university within the city and among the city's alternative institutions for consciously transmitting advanced culture. That is a good deal to ask, but even more is required. All of this must be done with a keen attention to translocal mechanisms of cultural transmission and innovation.

The university, as Hyde emphasized, began by adopting a corporate form not unlike that of merchants, shoemakers, and other artisans. As late as 1831, when NYU was founded, it was possible for artisans and merchants to collaborate in creating a specifically urban and modern university.[5] Carl Schorske makes a point of the strength of the artisanal base of Basel's economy, particularly in the intellectual trade of printing. One wonders, at least I do, about the changing relation of university culture to the artisanal culture of cities. How does the advent of industrialism, a process distinct from urbanization, change the terms of this relationship? Although I'm not sure how hard I would push the point, there is a good deal of historical evidence to support an argument that mercantile/artisan-based urban economies are more likely to nourish specifically city culture, while such civic culture is threatened by the industrial production of goods and knowledge. The organizational imperative of corporate industrialism, driven by the abstraction of the market, seems to undermine the economic and cultural significance of place.[6]

The nexus that connects the twentieth-century university to society may well be the industrial system, including the knowledge and service industries, rather than the city. Similarly, the industrialization of research, if the metaphor be allowed, not only emphasizes productivity but also an abstracted universalism that subtracts those qualities that might identify scholarship with a specific place and culture. It was on precisely this point, as I understand Schorske's essay, that Burckhardt rejected the German academic model.

Though neither the modern university nor the industrial corporation is enclosed by the city as the guild might have been, both are still deeply involved with the living communities that surround them, whether they identify with these communities or not. The urban university as a significant employer, customer, and actor in the real estate market are all long-played and rather constant roles. Today, however, this historical pattern of issues, opportunities, and tensions has become more problematical insofar as the university (or corporation) is perceived as an outsider institution. Even more recently, public concern about the extraordinary power of scientific technique, whether developed under university or corporate auspices, has made for uncomfortable relations between them and their neighbors. Fearful of pollution and of mutant genes run rampant, local living communities have increasingly insisted upon a role in defining the intellectual work of universities—as well as the organizational imperatives, including job policies, of businesses. While we today interpret such aspirations by civilians as not only hostile to the university but also reactionary, it is interesting to recall that at Geneva and Edinburgh in paricular such intervention was "liberal" and "modern."

Just as one cannot begin to specify the degree, if any, of the city's autonomy over time—and thus its status as an independent variable—without addressing the economy, so one must inquire into the relation of the city and the university to modern state building. How did the dissolution of the city-state and its replacement by the strong nation-state affect the city and the university's relation to it? The university seems to have been quite vulnerable at the moment when modern states were beginning to be formed, and these states, moreover, invested first in royal academies, not universities. How did universities successfully associate themselves with national improvement? There is, at least to my view, considerable evidence in these essays that associates nationalism, modernization, urban growth, and university revitalization. While Nicholas Phillipson comes closest to addressing this thicket of potential questions, the whole area begs for systematic inquiry, including attention to the rather different ways in which the university and the city were incorporated into this process in the early modern period and in the modern one (particularly 1860 to 1930).[7]

There is a collateral cluster of questions that concern themselves with the relation of the university to the urban system. How can one isolate the relative advantages or disadvantages of a university's location in the primate city or a secondary city of a nation-state? To put the matter more precisely with an example, one wonders how it was possible for Oxford and Cambridge—one in a small city, at best a tertiary city, the other a purely academical village—to be national forces? Does it challenge the idea of primate cities? Or does it derive from England's historic antiurbanism?[8] Or metropolitan London's suburbanism? Such a circumstance is unimaginable, I think, in France. What characteristics of the organization of the education system, the hierarchy of cities, and the structure of the nation-state might account for these differences? A similar set of questions is invited by the multinodal or decentralized pattern of competing cities and universities that developed in Germany and the United States.

The university has always claimed the world, not its host city, as its domain. Whatever its local roots, the university historically has striven for learning that at least reaches toward universal significance. Clearly, however, the relation between provincialism and locality on the one hand and universalism and translocality on the other has not always been direct. The local in some cities—one thinks of Paris in the nineteenth century and New York in the twentieth—is at least cosmopolitan, if not universal. Contrast Geneva and its Protestant academy. Before the localistic, urban-inspired reforms that Michael Heyd describes in his essay, its culture was a profoundly parochial translocal Protestant movement. Acknowledging such complexities, one still wants to understand how a university, deeply rooted in a place, speaks beyond that place with legitimacy, as Paris did in the thirteenth century and Chicago did for a good part of the twentieth.

What makes this question peculiarly interesting is that it forces the inquirer to ask whether one is to find the answer entirely within the intellectual realm (the sheer brilliance of the ideas produced) or by inquiring into the ways in which certain cities, for reasons that can be specified, better situate their institutions of higher learning to make such claims. What are the elements of cultural power that may be at work? How much are they cultural, how much political and economic? How much are they grounded in the facts of specifically urban dominance, how much deriving from national power?[9]

The great bulk of these essays address, whether directly or indirectly, the role of the university and (always implicitly) the city in the making of public culture. Herein lies one of the principal services of the university in preparing young men (only recently women), as Louise Stevenson and Nicholas Phillipson point out, for public life. So stated, it sounds as if the history of universities and cities brings us only to the banal pronouncements of university presidents. But, in fact, the essays in this volume point toward much more. Just what is this public culture that the university proposes to serve? Although we often examine the admissions policies of our universities to determine how responsibly they are serving society, the first question we must ask is how inclusive the public sphere is conceived to be. Universities, not often innovators in social relations, are unlikely to deviate far from such external definitions.

The notion of the public sphere as we understand it derives from the early-eighteenth-century writings of Joseph Addison.[10] What he called politeness was urbanity, and it was enacted in the public sphere. The notion of a public sphere, in other words, is inextricably associated with the actual experience of urban life. Its social basis is the milieu of the city, the newly created (in the eighteenth century) urban public spaces, including London's famous coffee houses.[11] The polite or urban public culture defined by Addison marked the emergence of a bourgeois cultural and political interest, and it left out many other interests we would today recognize. (Indeed, the creation of the public sphere is deeply bound up with the sexual division of social life. The notion of women's domestic sphere was understood by Addison as the counterpart of men's new public sphere.) [12]

To make the concept analytically useful, then, we must transcend the limits of its origins. When we recognize that the notion of a public culture hides patterns of inclusion and exclusion—whether in respect to social practice or symbolic representation—we begin to understand how far from banal the concept is. It thus becomes a critical position from which to understand the process of culture making and legitimation in the city. [13] The place to begin one's inquiry into the university's relation to the public is the configuration of public culture itself. How inclusive does a given society want (allow?) its public life to be? What forces are trying to expand that definition? What is the role of the university in that contest? Is it an innovator or a point of resistance? Such contests are peculiarly energetic in cities, and extensions of the boundaries of the public have generally been pressed upon society from cities. Not surprisingly, urban universities have generally responded to these changes more quickly and more fully than isolated campuses.

But more needs to be specified here. The question is whether such responses that enlarge the public culture should be understood as "social work" or whether they enhance the work of intellect. Too often, I think, such extensions of university "responsibility" have been praised as social service. (Most conferences on the university and the city are really about what universities should do for the poor.) But there is a cultural approach to this matter. In fact, there are at least two cultural approaches. One derives from Matthew Arnold's injunction to the cultivated to extend their own culture, always increasing the boundaries of the public but doing it in a way that assimilates difference. The other, articulated most powerfully in New York at the beginning of this century by Randolph Bourne, proposed a more dynamic understanding of culture. He insisted that culture was not simply an inheritance from the past but something constantly enriched by new participants, including the poor, immigrants, women, and others excluded from the original bourgeois vision of the public. [14] With such an expanded notion of the public, it is possible to historicize both the making of urban public culture and the university's role in that process.

The history of the university and the city—in their mutual relations—is, then, a subject of considerable richness that we only begin to explore in this volume. Here we have a topic that at once extends and gives specificity to the practice of cultural history. And I would argue, as the approaches taken by the authors in this volume reveal, that what is being proposed is cultural history, not urban history, not the history of education. Too much scholarship has already been enclosed within one or the other of those specialisms. The virtue of this theme and the approaches offered here is to open up, to ventilate, the study of both the city and the university.

While most historical writing does not embrace the international range and the chronological sweep of this collection, students pursuing more limited problems will surely profit from the large architecture suggested, if not fully elaborated, by this collection. Should these essays in fact prompt the particular researches that they seem to invite, a subsequent collection will have the historiographical means to tell us much more—to go beyond, if we may return to the architectural metaphor, this initial sketch to actual working drawings and, perhaps, even begin construction on the building.

NOTES

1. For an egregious example, see Paul Venable Turner, *Campus: An American Planning Tradition* (Cambridge, Mass., 1984).
2. There are selections from the work of Simmel, Spengler, Park, Wirth, Singer, and Redfield in Richard Sennett, ed., *Classic Essays on the Culture of Cities* (New York, 1970). See, in addition, Lewis Mumford, *The City in History* (New York, 1961); Jane Jacobs, *The Death and Life of Great American Cities* (New York, 1961); and Richard Sennett, *The Fall of Public Man* (New York, 1977).
3. For some recent and illuminating work in geography (or in the social sciences generally but incorporating geographical perspectives), see David Harvey, *Consciousness and the Urban Experience* (Baltimore, Md., 1985), and *The Urbanization of Capital* (Baltimore, Md., 1985); Manuel Castels, *The City and the Grassroots* (Berkeley, Calif., 1983); M. Gottdiener, *The Social Production of Space* (Austin, Tex., 1985); Ira Katznelson, *City Trenches* (New York, 1981); Alan Pred, *Urban Growth and the Circulation of Information* (Cambridge, Mass., 1973), and *Urban Growth and City-Systems in the United States, 1840–1860* (Cambridge, 1980); David Rosner, *A Once Charitable Enterprise: Hospitals and Health Care in Brooklyn and New York 1885–1915* (New York, 1982).
4. J. H. Hexter, *Reappraisals in History* (Evanston, Ill., 1961), p. 195.
5. Thomas Bender, *New York Intellect: A History of Intellectual Life in New York City from 1750 to the Beginnings of Our Own Time* (New York, 1987), chap. 3.
6. Alfred D. Chandler, *The Visible Hand* (Cambridge, 1977); Thomas Bender, "The Erosion of Public Culture: Cities, Discourses, and Professional Disciplines," in Thomas L. Haskell, ed., *The Authority of Experts* (Bloomington, Ind., 1984), pp. 84–106; Magali Sarfatti Larson, *The Rise of Professionalism* (Berkeley, Calif., 1977); Thomas L. Haskell, *The Emergence of Professional Social Science* (Urbana, Ill., 1977).
7. For the later period, see two studies, both too sociologically mechanical but useful, that begin to explore the subject: Konrad Jarausch, ed., *The Transformation of Higher Learning, 1860–1930* (Chicago, 1983); Roger L. Geiger, *To Advance Knowledge: The Growth of American Research Universities, 1900–1940* (New York, 1986).
8. On English antiurbanism, see Andrew Lees, *Cities Perceived: Urban Society in European and American Thought, 1820–1940* (New York, 1985).
9. On the distinction between urban dominance and national power, see the

very interesting argument in Jane Jacobs, *Cities and the Wealth of Nations* (New York, 1984). For an earlier and more particularized version of her analysis, see Jane Jacobs, *The Question of Separatism: Quebec and the Struggle over Sovereignty* (New York, 1980).

10. For a seminal discussion, see Jürgen Habermas, "The Public Sphere: An Encyclopedia Article," *New German Critique* 3 (Fall 1974): 49–55. It was originally published in 1964. For a recent and interesting gloss that begins with Addison and tracks the theme through British literature, see Terry Eagleton, *The Function of Criticism* (London, 1984).

11. See Dorothy Marshall, *Dr. Johnson's London* (New York, 1968); Lewis Coser, *Men of Ideas* (New York, 1965), chap. 3; Peter Borsay, "The English Urban Renaissance: The Development of Provincial Urban Culture, c 1650–1750," *Social History* 5 (1977): 581–603.

12. Margaret Hunt, "English Urban Families in Trade, 1660–1800: The Culture of Early Modern Capitalism," Ph.D. diss., New York University, 1986, pp. 245–46, 305–6; and Katherine M. Rogers, *Feminism in Eighteenth Century England* (Brighton, Eng., 1982), pp. 30, 122–23.

13. See Thomas Bender, "Making History Whole Again," *New York Times Book Review* (6 October 1985), pp. 1, 42–43; idem, "Wholes and Parts: The Need for Synthesis in American History," *Journal of American History* 73 (1986): 120–36; idem, "Wholes and Parts: Continuing the Conversation," *Journal of American History* 74 (1987): 123–30; idem, "Metropolitan Life and Public Culture," in John Mollenkopf, ed., *Power, Culture, and Place: Essays on New York City* (New York, forthcoming).

14. Matthew Arnold, *Culture and Anarchy,* in A. D. Culler, ed., *The Poetry and Criticism of Matthew Arnold* (Boston, 1961), pp. 407–75; Randolph Bourne, "Trans-National America," in Carl Resek, ed., *War and the Intellectuals: Collected Essays of Randolph Bourne, 1915–1919* (New York, 1964), pp. 107–23. See also Bender, *New York Intellect,* pp. 209–15, 228–49.

Contributors

Thomas Bender, University Professor of the Humanities at New York University, is a cultural historian with a particular interest in cities. His books include *Toward an Urban Vision* (1975); *Community and Social Change in America* (1978); with Edwin Rozwenc, *The Making of American Society* (1978); and *New York Intellect: A History of Intellectual Life in New York City, from 1750 to the Beginnings of Our Own Time* (1987).

J. K. Hyde was Professor of Medieval History at the University of Manchester until his death in 1986. His publications include *Padua in the Age of Dante* (1966).

Stephen C. Ferruolo, who has taught at Princeton, Bennington, and Stanford, is the author of *The Origins of the University: The Schools of Paris and Their Critics, 1100–1215* (1985). He is currently studying law at Stanford and working on a general history of European universities to 1300.

Gene Brucker is Shepard Professor of History at the University of California, Berkeley. A specialist in the history of Renaissance Italy, especially Florence, his publications include *Florentine Politics and Society, 1343–1378* (1962); *The Civic World of Renaissance Florence* (1977); *Renaissance Florence* (1983); and *Giovanni and Lusanna: Love and Marriage in Renaissance Florence* (1986).

Anthony Grafton is Professor of History at Princeton University. He is interested in the history of humanistic scholarship, ancient and early modern science, and education. He has written *Joseph Scaliger,* Vol. I (1983); translated (with G. Most and J. Zetzel) F. A. Wolf's *Prolegomena to Homer;* and collaborated with Lisa Jardine in writing *From Humanism to the Humanities* (1987).

Michael Heyd is Associate Professor in the Department of History, the Hebrew University in Jerusalem. His principal research interests are in intellectual, social, and religious history of the early modern period, particularly the history of the universities and the relationship between science and religion. He is the author of *Between Orthodoxy and the Enlightenment: Jean-Robert Chouet and the Introduction of Cartesian Science in the Academy of Geneva* (1982).

299

Nicholas Phillipson, Senior Lecturer in History, Edinburgh University, has held visiting appointments at Princeton, Yale, Tulsa, and the Folger Institute. He has edited (with Rosalind Mitchison) *Scotland in the Age of Improvement* (1970); and *Universities, Society, and the Future* (1983). He is currently completing a book on David Hume as historian and working on a study of the Scottish Enlightenment to be called *The Pursuit of Virtue.*

Sheldon Rothblatt, Professor of History at the University of California, Berkeley, is interested in the history of higher education in relation to society and culture, with a special emphasis on modern Britain. He is the author of *The Revolution of the Dons: Cambridge and Society in Victorian England* (1968); and *Tradition and Change in English Liberal Education: An Essay in History and Culture* (1976).

Louise L. Stevenson is a member of the History Department and American Studies Program at Franklin and Marshall College, with particular interests in nineteenth-century cultural and intellectual history and women's history. She has authored *Scholarly Means to Evangelical Ends: The New Haven Scholars and the Transformation of Higher Learning in America, 1830–1890* (1986).

Charles E. McLelland is Professor of History at the University of New Mexico. His special interests include the intellectual, social, and educational history of modern Central Europe. He has published *German Historians and England* (1971), with S. P. Scher; *Postwar German Culture* (1974); *State, Society and University in Germany, 1700–1914* (1980); and *The Rise of Modern Professions in Germany, 1840–1940* (forthcoming).

Carl E. Schorske has been concerned with the relationship between the development of high culture and social and political change in modern Europe. Emeritus Professor of History at Princeton University, he is the author of *German Social Democracy, 1905–1917* (1955); and *Fin-de-Siecle Vienna: Politics and Culture* (1980).

Edward Shils is Distinguished Service Professor of Social Thought and Sociology at the University of Chicago and Honorary Fellow of Peterhouse, Cambridge. His writings include *The Intellectual between Tradition and Modernity* (1961); *The Intellectuals and the Powers* (1972); *Center and Periphery: Essays in Macrosociology* (1975); *The Calling of Sociology* (1980); *The Constitution of Society* (1982); *Tradition* (1981); with Hans Daalder, *Universities, Politicians and Bureaucrats* (1982); and *The Academic Ethic* (1983).

Martin Jay is Professor of History at the University of California, Berkeley, where he teaches European Intellectual History. His books include *The Dialectical Imagination* (1973); *Marxism and Totality* (1984); *Adorno* (1984); *Permanent Exiles* (1985); and *Fin-de-Siecle Socialism and Other Essays* (1988). He is currently writing on the problematic of vision in twentieth-century French thought.

David Hollinger is Professor of History at the University of Michigan. He works primarily on the intellectual history of the United States since the middle of the nineteenth century. He is the author of *Morris R. Cohen and the Scientific Ideal* (1975); and *In the American Province: Studies in the History and Historiography of Ideas* (1985). He is coeditor, with Charles Capper, of *The American Intellectual Tradition* (1988).

Nathan Glazer is Professor of Education and Sociology at Harvard University. He is the author of *American Judaism* (1957); *The Social Basis of American Communism* (1961); *Affirmative Discrimination* (1975); *Ethnic Dilemmas, 1964–1982* (1983); *The Limits of Social Policy* (1988); and, with Daniel P. Moynihan, *Beyond the Melting Pot* (1963).

Index